XML: Content and Data

XML: Content and Data

Kelly Carey and Stanko Blatnik

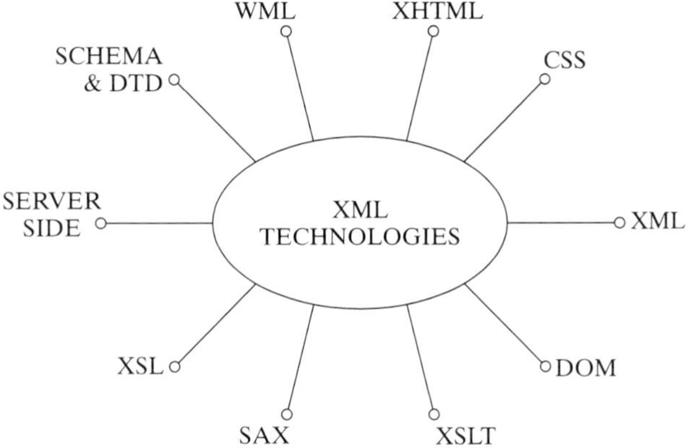

Pearson Education Inc.
Upper Saddle River, NJ 07458

Library of Congress Cataloging-in-Publication Data

CIP data on file

Vice President and Editorial Director, ECS: *Marcia J. Horton*
Acquisitions Editor: *Petra J. Recter*
Assistant Editor: *Sarah Burrows*
Vice President and Director of Production and Manufacturing, ESM: *David W. Riccardi*
Executive Managing Editor: *Vince O'Brien*
Assistant Managing Editor: *Camille Trentacoste*
Production Editor: *Joan Wolk*
Director of Creative Services: *Paul Belfanti*
Creative Director: *Carole Anson*
Art Director: *Jayne Conte*
Cover Designer: *Bruce Kenselaar*
Art Editor: *Greg Dulles*
Manufacturing Manager: *Trudy Pisciotti*
Manufacturing Buyer: *Lynda Castillo*

Printed in the United States of America

10 9 8 7 6 5 4 3 2 1

ISBN 0-13-028229-4

Pearson Education Ltd., *London*
Pearson Education Australia Pty. Ltd., *Sydney*
Pearson Education Singapore, Pte. Ltd.
Pearson Education North Asia Ltd., *Hong Kong*
Pearson Education Canada, Inc., *Toronto*
Pearson Educacíon de Mexico, S.A. de C.V.
Pearson Education—Japan, *Tokyo*
Pearson Education Malaysia, Pte. Ltd.
Pearson Education, *Upper Saddle River, New Jersey*

Contents

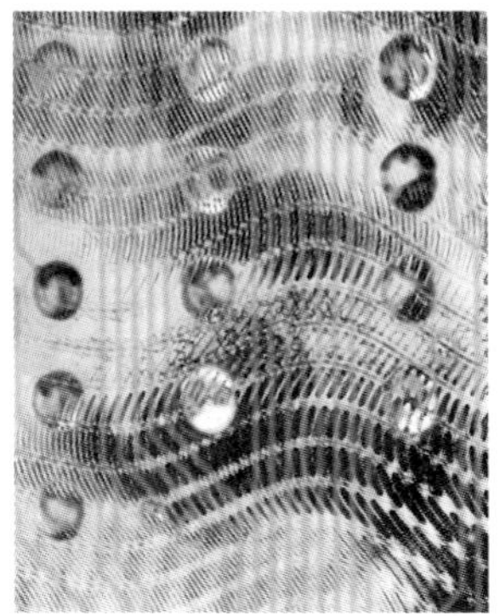

Preface

<preface>

<objective>

XML: Content and Data explores XML and XML-related technologies. Developed for students new to code and students with development experience, *XML: Content and Data* offers clear explanations and skill-building exercises.

XML is changing and growing. *XML: Content and Data* combines the text with an up-to-date web site addressing XML technologies beyond the materials at the time of publication.

We teach XML technologies at West Valley College in Saratoga, California, and online for the University of Sarajevo. Additionally, we teach XML to students in Slovenia, Bosnia, and Austria. As such, the text's teaching approach reflects a wide range of users' educational backgrounds, languages, and skills. *XML: Content and Data* transcends the typical text and acts as a set of learning components for students and a set of support components for faculty.

</objective>

<examplesAndExercises>

The goal of *XML: Content and Data* is to transition students from creating simple XML documents to creating components of or complete commercial XML applications. As such, examples are relevant to the workplace and exercises move from simple to more complex. There are many exercises for students eager to move forward and clear explanations for students struggling with a concept.

Commercial projects in Chapter 13 of the text and on the web site offer client-based problems for student planning, developing, and testing. Additional materials supporting the commercial materials, such as a tools resource center, are included on the companion web site at www.prenhall.com/carey or www.praxis.ws.

</examplesAndExercises>

<facultyResources>

The instructor CD-Rom offers PowerPoint, PowerPoint saved as .html presentations, and a test bank for each topic of the book. Solution sets for demonstrating every example and exercise allow professors to present code and results on a computer screen.

The instructor portion of the companion web site offers solution examples for commercial projects, additional commercial projects, a discussion board for Q&A, and additional resources. The authors know the workload of keeping current in the classroom and offering enough code for students to develop. The focus of this project was to assist in teaching students and to support faculty in order to maximize creative development time for the professor.

</facultyResources>

<studentResources>

Throughout the text, we ask students to question, "Do I understand it? Can I do it?" Support materials on the companion web site at www.prenhall.com/carey or www.praxis.ws are available to assist in the debugging process, tools selection and implementation, and odd-numbered solution sets. As teachers, we realize how many things there are to learn when it comes to Information Technology. We hope this text will support student learning and help to transition students away from short pseudocode examples, and into more worklike projects.

</studentResources>

<textOutline>

<chapter1> Extensible Markup Language (XHTML)

This chapter defines and explores the basic concepts of XHTML. Understanding semantic, structure, style, the W3C XHTML recommendations, and XHTML syntax is the focus of the chapter. Additional concepts include attributes, tree structure, namespace, well-formed, and valid documents. XHTML tables and forms are developed along with a review of basic XHTML elements.

</chapter1>

<chapter2> Cascading Style Sheets (CSS)

This chapter describes and illustrates CSS as a style sheet language for use with XHTML and XML (XSL is not currently fully implemented). CSS syntax, cascading, and the levels of CSS are explained. Applying CSS attributes, pseudo-elements, and pseudo-classes and utilizing inheritance, attribute selectors, and substring matching selectors are demonstrated toward efficient CSS development. Designing and developing using absolute, relative, and fixed positioning is explored in the text and on the companion web site.

`</chapter2>`

`<chapter3>` Extensible Markup Language (XML)

This chapter describes in detail XML syntax and the hierarchical structure of XML. Validating and nonvalidating parsers are defined and illustrated. The modeling process and developing efficient XML application are practiced using several examples and exercises. Creating XML applications utilizing the correct syntax for attributes, subelements, PCDATA, CDATA, processing instructions, and entities is explored and applied.

`</chapter3>`

`<chapter4>` Document Object Model (DOM)

This chapter defines, explains, and applies DOM, an API for XHTML, HTML, and XML. The concept of DOM nodes, the DOM tree, and DOM node properties and methods are described and illustrated. The process of parsing and loading using ActiveX technology and the process of developing simple applications for modifying and navigating small XML documents are demonstrated and practiced.

`</chapter4>`

`<chapter5>` DOM with Larger Documents

This chapter explains and applies navigating and manipulating larger documents using node list objects. More complex applications using `getElementsByTagname` methods and child nodes properties are explained and demonstrated. Treatment of attributes in XML documents using DOM is shown. Using the JavaScript language, several DOM applications are developed and modifications are practiced.

`</chapter5>`

`<chapter6>` Extensible Style Sheet Langage Transformation (XSLT)

This chapter defines and explains the difference between XSLT, DOM, and SAX and when to use each approach in navigating and modifying XML documents. XSLT's syntax and main elements are defined and demonstrated. XPath is used to address and locate sections of an XML document is illustrated. XML documents are transformed to HTML for browser presentation. Tools are explored and demonstrated in the text and on the companion web site.

`</chapter6>`

<chapter7> XSLT -Toward More Complex Application

This chapter explores working with additional and more sophisticated elements and functions. Writing medium complexity XSLT applications and transforming existing XML documents to HTML or XML documents is practiced. Executing some arithmetic operations and using `xsl:variable` in XSLT applications is demonstrated along with formatting numerical results using `format-number`. Tools are explored and demonstrated in the text and on the companion web site.

</chapter7>

<chapter8> Simple API for XML (SAX)

This chapter defines and explains the differences between DOM, as a document tree-based and SAX, as an event-based application programming interface. The most frequent SAX interfaces are described and illustrated to create Java-based applications. Tools are explored and demonstrated in the text and on the companion web site.

</chapter8>

<chapter9> Extensible Style Sheet Language (XSL)

This chapter explores and applies the main concept and elements of XSL as a language for expressing style sheets. The most frequently used formatting objects are defined and demonstrated. Transforming original XML documents into pdf files using fop is illustrated and practiced.

</chapter9>

<chapter10> Server Side XML

This chapter defines and explores XML technologies used to develop server side applications. In addition to working with ASP in the text and JSP on the companion web site, XML processing using DOM and XSLT on the server side is demonstrated and practiced. The Active Data Object (ADO) technology for connection to databases is used to illustrate XML strengths in the exchange of data.

</chapter10>

<chapter11> Schema and DTD

This chapter describes and demonstrates the role and use of schemas and DTDs in checking validity of the structure of the document. The concept of schema complex and simple data types is explained and illustrated in several examples. The structure and elements of DTDs are described and illustrated using several examples. Creating and editing schemas and DTDs is planned and practiced.

</chapter11>

<chapter12> Wireless Markup Language (WML)

This chapter describes and illustrates WAP technology and the WML language. The difference between classical Internet applications and wireless applications is explained and demonstrated. The syntax of WML and its main elements is explored and wireless applications are developed.

</chapter12>

<chapter13> Commercial Projects

This chapter illustrates client-based projects as a critical component of transitioning from simple pseudo-code examples to commercial code. Practicing projects and more complex processes build experience in developing in more of a work-life environment with its trouble-shooting and debugging needs. Five potential commercial applications of XML technologies are presented for individual and group building and testing.

</chapter13>

</textOutline>

<acknowledgments>

<prenticeHall>
Brian Goldenberg, Senior Account Representative
Petra Recter, Acquisitions Editor
Sarah Burrows, Assistant Editor
Mary Aguilar, Assistant CD-Rom and web site
Camille Trentacoste, Assistant Managing Editor
Manufacturing Buyer, Lynda Castillo
</prenticeHall>

<reviewers>
Simon North, Synopsis
Rick Shepherd, Independent Consultant
Devan Shepherd, XMaLpha Technologies LLC
</reviewers>

<students>
<westValleyCollege>
Steve Contreras, Rory Condon, Gita Hazemi, Noushin Tehrani
</westValleyCollege>
<ipak>
Jana Pahovnik, Bojana Hrzenjak, Mateja Hribar, artes="Jure Londrant"
</ipak>
<universityOfSarajevo>
Online XML Students, Diana Protic, Elma Mujagic
</universityOfSarajevo>
<students>

<friendsFamily>
<coFaculty>
Fred George, Jeff Rascov, Jean McIntosh
</coFaculty>
<family>
Manuel Jimenez, baseball star. John Focht, basketball star.
Mrs. Olga Blatnik, for providing space, power, and fantastic food.
Dave McMorrine, for encouragement and support.
</family>
</friendsFamily>

</acknowledgments>

<authors>
Kelly Carey's email address is: kelly@praxis.ws
Stanko Blatnik's email address is: stanko@praxis.ws
The companion web site is located at www.prenhall.com/carey and at www.praxis.ws
</authors>

</preface>

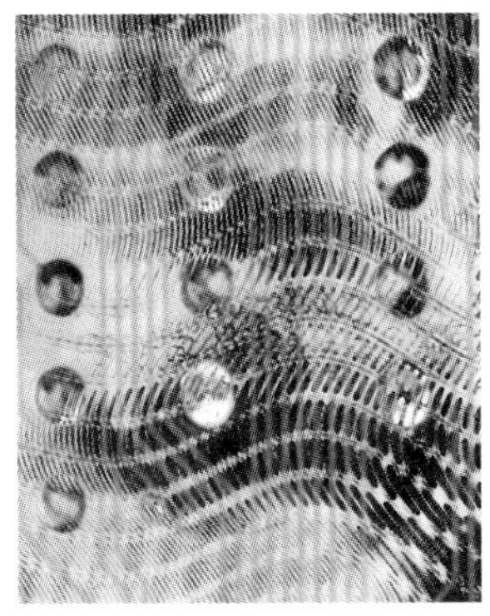

1 Extensible Hypertext Markup Language

CHAPTER OBJECTIVES

By reading the information and practicing the code in this chapter, you will understand and be able to:

1. Differentiate between semantic, structure, and style.
2. Determine and utilize extensible hypertext markup language (XHTML) 1.0, XHTML Modularization 1.1, and/or XHTML Basic 1.0 based on user needs and output devices.
3. Develop well-formed and valid XHTML documents.
4. Utilize document type declarations (DTDs), namespace, attributes, and subelements toward efficient application development.
5. Create XHTML tables and forms.

1.1 SEMANTIC, STRUCTURE, AND STYLE

With the three languages HTML, XHTML, and XML, individually or in combination, the focus on your thought process as a developer is on semantic, structure, and style. **Semantic** refers to content meaning and to the possible ways information may be interpreted, accessed, and manipulated. Semantic meaning exists outside of the document. Rather than simply presenting content, a semantic web will create an environment where tasks can be carried out for users. **Structure** expresses the form of a document, how it is organized logically, regardless of meaning. Structure divides documents into a hierarchical tree of elements. **Style** refers to presentation, to how the document is rendered, whether visually or with a Braille-based or auditory user agent.

Thinking of semantic, structure, and style allows you to design and develop web-based applications, maximizing file performance, data manipulation capabilities, and screen design while minimizing editing obstacles.

XHTML consists of three sets of recommendations, as developed by the World Wide Web Consortium (W3C).

1. XHTML 1.0 is the W3C's recommendation for the latest version of HTML 4.0. XHTML 1.0 reformulates HTML 4.01 in XML for the purpose of bridging HTML's strengths (such as browser compatibility and support) to the power of XML (such as well-formedness, validation, and data manipulation).
2. XHTML 1.1 Modularization. The modularization of HTML provides a way to subset and to extend XHTML, bridging XHTML to XML and allowing for better transition to emerging platforms. XHTML 1.1 modules serve as a basis for clean, forward-focused documents separated from the deprecated functionality of HTML 4.0 tags still supported by XHTML 1.0. Modules include images, simple tables, simple forms, object support, and additional features.

   The extensibility of XML is supported by allowing the creation of hybrid documents. XHTML 1.1 may incorporate XML and XHTML elements, may be validated with XML DTD language or, in the future, XML schemas. Modules can be combined to create XHTML subsets and extend document types to meet the needs of emerging platforms. Modularization also allows developers to specify which elements will be supported by certain devices such as monitors and kiosks.
3. XHTML Basic is a minimal set of modules used for output devices such as mobile phones, personal digital assistants (PDAs), televisions, pagers, car navigation systems, and portable game machines in which a simple XHTML can also be shared across multiple output devices.

   XHTML Basic is comparable yet different from compact HTML (CHTML) and wireless markup language (WML).

1.2 XHTML DOCUMENTS

The first important XHTML idea one must understand is the **element**.

When you work with XHTML and XML, you will refer to code at the element level. Elements consist of the start tag, the element's contents, and the end tag. Four examples of elements are:

```
<title>Films</title>
<h1>Classic Films</h1>
<h2>American Classics</h2>
<p>A few examples of classic American films include City Lights, The
Apartment,
Vertigo, and The 39 Steps</p>
```

The start tags (sometimes called opening tags) of these four elements are `<title>`, `<h1>`, `<h2>`, and `<p>`. The end tags (sometimes called closing tags) of these four elements are `</title>`, `</h1>`, `</h2>`, and `</p>`.

XHTML tags are **case-sensitive** and should be keyed in lower case. All end tags must close an element in one of two ways:

1. `<p>Paragraph contents</p>`
   or
2. `<hr />`

In the first example, elements containing content include a start tag and an end tag. If you have been using HTML, you will want to be careful as single tag elements, such as list elements, will result in an error message with XHTML.

Generally, option 1. `<p>...</p>` should be used for elements containing content and option 2. `<hr />` for empty elements. Either option will run in a browser.

Empty elements contain no text content and often represent future content such as images and line breaks. The syntax for this empty element incorporates a space **before** the slash and final angle bracket.

1.3 CREATING AN XHTML FILE

The step-by-step process for keying XHTML on a PC, using Notepad, is in *Example 1-1*.

Example 1-1

Authors' Note: See the companion web site for Mac and Unix platform keying process (www.prenhall.com/carey).

1. Click on Start, Programs, Accessories, Notepad
2. Key the XHTML code. XML is case-sensitive. The W3C recommendation advises XHTML documents must use lowercase for element and attribute names. **Note that the third line of code reads "`DTD/xhtml1-strict.dtd`". There is `xhtm` followed by the letter `l` (from `xhtml`) and then the number 1. This isn't easy to see with some fonts, so make sure you don't enter two letter "`l`"s. For this step-by-step introduction, please key:

```
<?xml version ="1.0"?>
<!DOCTYPE html PUBLIC "-//W3C//DTD XHTML 1.0 Strict//EN"
"http://www.w3.org/TR/xhtml1/DTD/xhtml1-strict.dtd">
<html xmlns="http://www.w3.org/1999/xhtml" xml:lang="en" lang="en">
<head>
<title>Practicing XHTML</title>
</head>
<body>
<h1>Semantic, Structure, Style</h1>
```

```
<h2>XHTML provides structure, CSS provides style</h2>
<h3>XML provides structure, XSL provides style</h3>
</body>
</html>
```

3. Click on File, Save As. Click on the icon to create a new folder. Name the folder `Intro`
4. Make sure the folder is created on your zip, floppy, desktop, or in the correct location on your hard drive. Save the file within the folder by keying `intro.html` or `intro.htm` in the box next to File name: and by selecting All Files in the box next to Save as type: (not Text Documents). This way you will not inadvertently add a .txt extension onto your file name, which would result in `intro.html.txt`. Should you have a problem with a file ending with .txt extension rather than .html or .htm, do not try to resave without .txt. Copy the file content (drag to select text, key Ctrl C), open a new file in Notepad (File, New), and paste XHTML code onto the file (key Ctrl V). Go through the save process again, this time selecting All Files at the Save as type: .html
5. After your file(s) is saved in Notepad, open up your browser. Select your `intro.html` file and open your XHTML document into your browser window.

Authors' Note: As a professional web developer, you should test all sites thoroughly on PC, Mac, and Unix (when included in user analysis) platforms and in potential user versions of Netscape, Internet Explorer, America Online, and Opera. You will design for clients who must communicate to all of their potential customers. Personal preference for one browser or platform over the other holds no relevance. In the United States, don't ignore AOL and its massive consumer audience.

1.4 XHTML SYNTAX OVERVIEW

In this section you will work with introductory XHTML syntax. After introductory examples of XHTML, you will work with tables and forms.

There are three basic levels to the structure of an XHTML document. In the first level, the document structure, are the **major sections**, depending on their purpose, such as head, body, and script components.

In the second level, are the **divisions within these major sections.** This level refers primarily to the groups of content, such as title, paragraph, and headings.

In the third level, typically within `body`, is the **substructure of elements and their children**, such as lists and list items and tables with table rows and data cells.

The `head` element includes information for the browser, including a title for the document, keywords, link information, and information not necessary for the user to view directly. The only required element of `head` is `<title>`. The content of the title tag does not show in the content presentation of the site; it appears in the browser's title bar.

Content within <body> is what the end user sees when the document is rendered in the browser or another user agent. This content includes text and objects, such as images, along with markup tags to define their structure and relationship.

1.4.1 The XML Declaration

The `intro.html` document you keyed is a good place to begin understanding XHTML syntax. XHTML documents must conform to XML syntax, and they must meet rules set by the DOCTYPE declaration and the declaration of the root element.

XML documents begin with the XML declaration:

```
<?xml version="1.0"?>
```

The XML declaration is not mandatory for XHTML files, although it is required if you plan to use Unicode character sets other than the default UTF-8 or UTF-16. The Unicode Consortium's Universal Character Set (UCA), includes special characters, punctuation, mathematical symbols, and foreign language characters and alphabets (explained in Chapter 3, Extensible Markup Language [XML]).

The XML declaration tells parsers, "this is an XML document." You will use the XML declaration in your examples because your purpose is to learn to develop commercial code with data manipulation capabilities. A simple web site with presentation requirements includes the DOCTYPE declaration and the declaration of the root element but not the XML declaration.

1.4.2 The Document Type Declaration: XHTML 1.0

The second line of code in your `intro.html` XHTML 1.0 document is the DOCTYPE declaration. The DOCTYPE declaration must declare the document type and refer to one of three XHTML 1.0 DTDs at the W3C or another stored on your computer.

1. Strict XHTML 1.0: `Strict` refers to a strict version of XHTML 1.0 in which elements and attributes that have been **deprecated** (identified elements and attributes that will not appear in future versions) are not included. The XHTML 1.0 `Strict` DTD supports clean, structured code free of layout-associated tags (the document will link to a cascading style sheet document for style presentation).

   ```
   <!DOCTYPE html PUBLIC "-//W3C//DTD XHTML 1.0 Strict//EN"
   "http://www.w3.org/TR/xhtml1/DTD/xhtml1-strict.dtd">
   ```

2. Transitional XHTML 1.0: `Transitional` includes all elements and attributes, including those that have been deprecated. Although Transitional DTDs seem to give you more flexibility with browser issues, deprecated code creates major

future editing problems. The Transitional DTD allows internal style sheets and small style adjustment to markup supported in older browsers.

```
<!DOCTYPE html PUBLIC "-//W3C//DTD XHTML 1.0 Transitional//EN"
"http://www.w3.org/TR/xhtml1/DTD/xhtml1-transitional.dtd">
```

3. Frameset XHTML: `Frameset` is devoted to framed documents (partitioned browser window into two or more frames). Frames are not supported in XHTML Basic and will not be supported in future versions of XHTML.

```
<!DOCTYPE html PUBLIC "-//W3C//DTD XHTML 1.0 Frameset//EN"
"http://www.w3.org/TR/xhtml1/DTD/xhtml1-frameset.dtd">
```

1.4.3 The Document Type Declaration: XHTML 1.1 Modularization

```
<!DOCTYPE html PUBLIC "-//W3C//DTD XHTML 1.1//EN" "http://www.w3.org/
TR/xhtml11/DTD/xhtml11.dtd">
```

1.4.4 The Document Type Declaration: XHTML Basic 1.0

```
<!DOCTYPE html PUBLIC "-//W3C//DTD XHTML Basic 1.0//EN"
"http://www.w3.org/TR/xhtml-basic/xhtml-basic10.dtd">
```

The statements of the document type declaration reads as:

1. Each document type declaration begins with the < delimiter, a statement declaring the document type (`DOCTYPE`) is HTML.
2. ! indicates a keyword follows.
3. `PUBLIC` tells the processor to look for a public DTD at the following location. `SYSTEM` tells the processor to look for the private DTD at the following location.
4. `W3C` represents the World Wide Web Consortium, the standards group working on XHTML, XML, and several other languages (www.w3c.org).
5. `DTD` is the file type, XHTML 1.0 is the current version of XHTML at the time of this writing. `Strict`, `Transitional`, `Frameset`, `XHTML 1.1`, and `XHTML Basic 1.0` identify the type of DTD.
6. `EN` represents the English language.
7. The URL after `SYSTEM` or `PUBLIC` is the name of the DTD file. All DTDs end with the extension .dtd as in: `"http://www.w3.org/TR/xhtml-basic/xhtml-basic10.dtd"` refers to the actual DTD.

1.4.5 The Root Element and Namespace

The root element is the parent of all other elements, the element within which other elements are nested. The root element begins the **document tree**, the structure that will determine the structure and data manipulation capabilities of your document(s). In HTML, the root element was `<HTML>` and the last line of the document was `</HTML>`. In XHTML, the root element is also `html`, although a namespace is added. The last line of the XHTML document remains `</html>`. The syntax for a root element with namespace (in this case for a document in English) is:

```
<root xmlns="namespace" xml:lang="en" lang="en">
```

The `html` start tag must include the `xmlns` keyword attribute, state the uniform resource indicator (URI) of the XHTML namespace, and refer to the default language.

Namespace solves the potential problems of ambiguity and name collision with XHTML and XML documents on the web. Think of how many XHTML and XML files have been and will be developed around the world. In addition to elements defined in HTML, XHTML and XML element names will be developed for millions of web sites. Imagine how many XHTML and XML documents will include elements such as `<partnumber>`, `<stockitem>`, `<time>`, `<date>`, `<name>`, `<email>`, `<address>`, or `<sales>`.

One way for these duplicated element names for multiple sites to be separated would be to add a prefix to the element. These prefixes could be `<dock5partnumber>`, `<holidaystockitem>`, `<starttime>`, `<enrolldate>`, `<custname>`, `<newemail>`, `<mailaddress>` or `<q2sales>`. However, there is no guarantee that someone will not select the same prefix and element name for some other purpose.

Namespace is the mechanism that uniquely determines prefixes. A namespace is a collection of names that can be used in XHTML and XML documents as elements or attributes that identify the names with a particular domain. In other words, identifying `<partnumber>`, `<stockitem>`, `<time>`, `<date>`, `<name>`, `<email>`, `<address>`, or `<sales>` with the purpose you determined when you created your initial XHTML or XML document is accomplished by declaring a namespace. The syntax for the XHTML namespace is:

```
<html xmlns="http://www.w3.org/1999/xhtml" xml:lang="en" lang="en">
```

1. Each namespace expression begins with the mandatory `<html>` root element.
2. `xmlns` is the keyword to declare a namespace (all words or abbreviations beginning with `xml` are reserved as W3C for current and future keywords; do not create elements beginning with `xml`).
3. `"http://www.w3.org/1999/xhtml"` is the uniform resource indicator (URI). URI is used to define the namespace because it allows for its associated documents to be identified as unique. URI and URL (uniform resource locator) are slightly

different in their definition. Both are short strings that identify resources in the web, including documents, images, downloadable files, and other resources. URI is the generic set of all names and addresses that are short strings referring to web resources. URL is the set of URI schemes with explicit instructions on how to access the resource. The most common form of URI is the URL. URI typically describes the resource (its mechanism, computer, or name), while the URL contains the name of the protocol required to access the resource. In the namespace file above, the filename indicates the URI, the resource for the information. Keying a URI into your browser will not result in your accessing a page of rules. URI does not mean the user accesses information; it provides the browser with the resource for reference. The namespace in this examples refers to a URI located on the W3C site. The namespace you refer to may be located at the W3C or on your own computer. The purpose is to tell the parser that the element names referred to in your document will be interpreted as defined in the namespace listed, not to be confused with other web sites defining matching elements and attributes differently.

4. `xml:lang="en" lang="en"` specifies the language, `en`, for English. The use of both `xml:lang` and the `lang` attribute is the only valid way to specify a language code. The value of the `xml:lang` attribute takes precedence.

More than one namespace is allowed per XML document. `html` is shown above because it is the name of the root element for the XHTML namespace developed by the W3C. More than one namespace is possible, although only one root element is allowed per XML document. The W3C is currently working to determine how to best develop with multiple namespaces.

1.4.6 Well-Formed Documents

Well-formedness is a new concept introduced by XML. Well-formedness means all elements must be closed and all elements may be nested. XHTML and XML documents are considered well-formed if they meet the following set of W3C recommendation criteria:

1. Elements must be correctly nested (shown later in this chapter).
2. Element and attribute names must be in lowercase.
3. For non-empty elements, end tags are required.
4. Attribute values must always be quoted (shown later in this chapter).
5. Attribute-value pairs must be written in full (shown later in this chapter).
6. Empty elements must either have an end tag or the start tag must end with `/>`.
7. Whitespace handling in attribute values. User agents will strip whitespace from attribute values and map sequences of one or more whitespace characters to a single interwoven space.

8. script and style elements are declared as having #PCDATA (text). < and & will be treated as the start of markup. CDATA sections are defined in Chapter 3, XML.
9. SGML exclusions (the ability to exclude specific elements from being contained within an element in the DTD) are not allowed.
10. In XHTML, the id attribute is defined to be of type ID. id attribute must be used when defining fragment identifiers (in other words, use id attribute and not the name attribute, from HTML 4, which is now deprecated in XHTML with the exception of with forms). The value of id (the name given to id) may be used only once per document.

1.5 VALID DOCUMENTS

An XHTML or XML document is considered valid if it meets all of the W3C well-formedness criteria and if it validates against the referenced DTD. The XHTML DTDs approximate the HTML DTDs.

XHTML is extensible; elements and entities may be created in addition to those provided by the HTML W3C specifications. A second DTD, in addition to the W3C DTD, would be internal. The W3C DTDs cannot be modified. Instructions for writing this additional DTD are covered in Chapter 11.

EXERCISE

Beginning with the major sections, key the following document.

1.1 Please create a new folder, named Begin, on your desktop, hard drive, zip, or diskette. Open a new file in Notepad and key the following:

```
<?xml version ="1.0"?>
<!DOCTYPE html PUBLIC "-//W3C//DTD XHTML 1.0 Strict//EN"
"http://www.w3.org/TR/xhtml1/DTD/xhtml1-strict.dtd">
<html xmlns="http://www.w3.org/1999/xhtml" xml:lang="en" lang="en">
<!-- begin.html by Your Name -->
<head>
<title>Begin</title>
</head>
<body>
</body>
</html>
```

Please save the file as begin.html within your Begin folder. You can use this begin.html file to begin future XHTML documents. To do so, create and name a folder for each XHTML document you will create and open begin.html in Notepad. In each folder, save the document as newfilename.html, adjusting the comment lines as needed and adding your additional code. Comments begin with the special start tag <!-- and end with -->. Comments will not be included in the browser display of your document; they offer information for anyone viewing your source code. This empty, formatted document is referred to as an XHTML shell. Whitespace between lines is added for the purpose of readability. It is important, as a developer, to create clean, readable code.

Authors' Note: Over-commenting isn't necessary, but not adding comments can cause issues for developers editing code after you create it or for you coming back to code you worked on months before. Our vote is to add the identifying comments at the beginning of the file and to comment anywhere in the code where you think need to make a note to yourself so you can remember what you were doing or what you intended. If you want to reach for paper to remind yourself what's happening in the code for later reference, add a comment instead.

1.6 ADDITIONAL ELEMENTS

At this point you are ready to add additional items at the division level and the third level, the balance of elements within the body. Rather than demonstrate each possible addition, one sample will be shown, followed by a listing of available elements, and exercises for practicing keying and viewing .html files. Before you begin, it is important to note that within XHTML and XML, elements must be nested correctly.

Most XHTML and XML documents are made up of several generations of elements. Later, you will learn to access, sort, modify, add, and delete by the hierarchical relationship of elements and attributes. The first step to building clean documents for this data manipulation is to correctly nest elements. In this example **nesting** is correct. <partnumber> has a child element, <partname>. The start tag and end tag for that child element fall within the start tag and end tag for their parent, <partnumber>:

```
<partnumber>..<partname>..</partname>..</partnumber>
```

or

```
<ol>..<li>..</li>..</ol>
```

Incorrect nesting occurs when tags are out of order in this parent-child relationship. Incorrectly nested tags will not parse and might look like:

```
<partnumber>..<partname>..</partnumber>..</partname>
```

or

```
<ol>..<li>..</ol>..</li>
```

XHTML and XML do not allow the flexibility of HTML when it comes to nesting. The power of XHTML and XML comes with what you can do in addition to presentation. In order for data manipulation to take place, the parent and child elements must be clearly defined.

1.6.1 Headers, Paragraphs, and Lists

1. Headers allow you to define sections of your text by giving them titles. Header tags are placed within the `body` section of your XHTML shell. Header tags run from level 1, the largest `<h1>..</h1>` to level 6, the smallest `<h6>..</h6>`
2. Paragraphs of text are introduced with the element `<p>`. Using `<p>..</p>`, the paragraph tag, your text will drop down one line of space before the next element appears. `<p>` also helps to validate `<br />`.
3. Three types of lists, unordered lists (also called bulleted lists), ordered lists (also called numbered lists), and definition lists (a list of terms paired with associated definitions, such as in a glossary) are available.
4. For unordered lists, the `<ul>` element tells the document that each individual list item, `<li>` receives a bullet beside it. The order of the tags must be `<ul> <li>..<li> <li>..</li> <li>..</li> <li>..</li> </ul>`. You can create an unordered list as long as you like, but the list items must nest within the start `<ul>` tag and the end `</ul>` tag.
5. The ordered list displays numbers to distinguish list items. For ordered lists, the `<ol>` element tells the document that each individual list item receives a number beside it. You don't place the numbers; the browser automatically orders the list for you. Correctly nesting tags is again mandatory; the `<li>..</li>` tags must be between the start tag `<ol>` and `</ol>`.
6. For definition lists, the `<dl>` element tells the document that each individual definition term `<dt>` and its associated definition (meaning) `<dd>` will be formatted so that the definition term is left-aligned and the definition meaning follows, indented, on the subsequent line. Definition lists should not be used to force XHTML code to indent; you will use style sheets for all style functions.

EXERCISES

1.2 Below is a sample of an HTML document incorporating an HTML shell and the elements defined above. Please key this document, save it as `food.html`, and open it in your browser. Keying simple documents such as this one will help you to get comfortable with the XHTML shell, which, in turn, allows you to focus on moving forward rather than whether you are keying the basics correctly.

```
<?xml version ="1.0"?>
<!DOCTYPE html PUBLIC "-//W3C//DTD XHTML 1.0 Strict//EN"
"http://www.w3.org/TR/xhtml1/DTD/xhtml1-strict.dtd">
<html xmlns="http://www.w3.org/1999/xhtml" xml:lang="en" lang="en">
<!-- food.html by Your Name -->
<!-- contact: yourname@yourEmail.com -->
<head>
  <title>Tech Cafe Menu</title>
</head>
  <body>
    <h1>Great Lunches at the Tech Cafe</h1>
    <h2>Eat In or Order To Go</h2>
    <p>Online Orders Accepted. techcafe.com</p>
      <ul>
        <li>Sarma</li>
        <li>Chicken Curry</li>
        <li>Mongolian Beef with Steamed Rice</li>
        <li>Spicy Chicken with Rice Noodles</li>
        <li>Teriyaki Chicken and Tempura Vegetables</li>
        <li>Homemade Soup and a Fresh Salad</li>
      </ul>
    <h3>Accepted Payment Methods</h3>
      <ol>
        <li>Tech Cafe Smart Card</li>
        <li>Major Credit Card</li>
        <li>Cash</li>
        <li>Code</li>
      </ol>
      <dl>
        <dt>Sarma</dt>
         <dd>A fantastic lunch in Slovenia made better by Mrs. Blatnik.
Cabbage rolls with meat and rice inside, juice and sour cream on top.
</dd>
        <dt>Chicken Curry</dt>
          <dd>Yellow, Green, or Red available</dd>
      </dl>
  </body>
</html>
```

1.3 Use headers and a definition list to organize the following information. The primary header is Downloadable Music. It has two list items: jazz and its definition, 40s-style jazz club sound, and folk and its definition 60s-style acoustic sound. The secondary header is Downloadable Sound. It has two list items: street and its definition, cars in urban setting; restaurant and its definition, coffeehouse, dishes, and guitar in background. Name file `dmusic.html`.

1.4 A bookstore web site needs information posted on its site regarding its return policy. Use header and list elements to present the information to the store's clientele. Name the file `bookshop.html`.

IT Technical Bookshop
Returns are accepted within 30 days of purchase
Receipt required for cash or credit card return
Exchange of books for missing receipt
Books must be in new condition for return
Special order books may have a 20% send back fee, depending on distributor
Book returns and exchanges must take place in store, rather than on web site
We will purchase used computer books with publication date of no more than 2 years from current year. Purchase price is 1/4 of retail, for resale at 1/2 of retail, or you may trade the book for a new book and receive a credit toward your new purchase at 40% of retail.
Thanks for your business...etc.

1.5 The card game canasta has many versions. Create a web page with the basic canasta rules (feel free to add additional rules of your own). Name the file `canasta.html`.

2-player. Minimum 2 decks. Each person gets 15 cards. Each play draws 2 cards and discards 1 card. Each red 3 drawn lays on the table and an additional card is drawn. Black 3s are for discard purposes only. Jokers and 2s are wild. Discard pile may be picked up if player has two cards in hand matching top card on discard pile. Player must also have a minimum of 50 points in hand to lay down. Jokers count as 50 points, 2s and aces as 20 points, K–8 as 10 points, 7–black 3 as 5 points. Red 3s count as 100 points for 1 per player, 300 points for 2 per player, 500 points for 3 per player, and 1000 points for all four red 3s per player. Two books are needed to go out. Books may be naturals or unnaturals. Natural is 7 of a kind, stacked as a book (worth 500 points plus face value of cards). Unnatural is 7, although 4 must be in suit and balance may be wildcards (worth 300 points plus face value of cards). Player going out may discard or not (going out worth 100 points).

1.6 A small company wants you to create a simple page for its intranet announcing available job openings. Name the file `developer.html`.

Title: XHTML Developer
Skills: XHTML
Location: Cupertino
Pay: Market
Length: 6 Months

Position Number: HTML445
Responsibilities: XHTML developer for WWW interactive marketing projects. Responsibilities include design, implementation, and support of interactive solutions using XHTML and other tools/technologies in NT, Windows, Linux, and Unix setting.
Requirements: Minimum of 1 year professional web development experience. Expertise with XHTML to include tables and forms. URLs to demonstrate proficiency. Demonstrated ability to manually create XHTML code without reliance on editor applications. Strong verbal and written communication skills.
Title: XHTML Developer
Skills: XHTML
Location: Sunnyvale
Term: Full-time
Pay: $35–$50 per hour
Length: Permanent
Position Number: XHTML 446
Responsibilities: Health-services department looking for XHTML developer who demonstrates detail orientation, a team player with graphical user interface (GUI) experience. Responsible for the creation of prototype page layouts, hands-on graphic design, and XHTML scratch coding.
Requirements: Proven XHTML experience, URLs

1.7 XHTML CORE ATTRIBUTES

Attributes allow specific identification of elements for the purposes of data manipulation and style formats. XHTML attributes are placed in the start tag. Attributes must have a quoted value. Avoid line breaks or multiple whitespace characters within attribute values as they are handled inconsistently by user agents. The following attributes and elements are available to develop XHTML documents:

1.7.1 Universal/Core Attributes

The purpose of universal/core attributes is to distinguish elements for future reference. XHTML universal attributes include `id`, `class`, `style`, and `title`.

The purpose of the `id` attribute is to identify a unique name for a tag in a document. Its value must be unique in the document or the parser will throw an error. As an example:

```
<p id="IntroParagraph">Introduction: New Product Presentation</p>
```

1. < begins the start tag
2. `p` is the element name

3. id is the attribute name
4. "IntroParagraph" is value of the attribute that gives the unique identity
5. > closes the start tag
6. Introduction: New Product Presentation is the content of the element
7. </p> is the end tag

The value of an id attribute must begin with a letter or an underscore, and contain alphanumeric characters. The name you select should reflect the content of the element in order to easily identify the element at a later date. The HTML name attribute is deprecated and should not be used. Use the id attribute as you may have used name in the past.

The purpose of the class attribute is to identify a class or classes that a tag may belong to. A class, in this context, is similar to what you may think of as a category or group. As such, more than one element may have the same class name. If style is applied to that particular class, all elements (regardless of type) will receive the same style attribute. As an example:

```
<p id="IntroParagraph" class="LargeGroup">Introduction: New Product
Presentation</p>
<p id="OverviewProduct" class="LargeGroup">Development and Marketing
Strategy for New Product</p>
<p id="DevelopmentPlan" class="DevTeam">Market Expectations</p>
<p id="PromotionPlan" class="LargeGroup">Billboard, Radio, and
Television Campaign</p>
```

In this example, the id attribute allows each <p> element to be identified and later selected for potential changes in style. The class attribute allows three of the four <p> elements to be selected, thereby allowing for individual and group style changes to the text of the paragraphs.

8. The purpose of the style attribute is to add style sheet information directly to a tag. The style attribute will not be developed further in this text; you will link style, as recommended by W3C. The separation of style from within a document to be linked to another document better allows for browser adaptability of new technologies. An example of the style attribute is:

```
<p style= "font-size: 24pt">New Product Trade Show Schedule</p>
```

9. The purpose of the title attribute is to provide descriptive information about a tag or its contents. The title attribute works in IE 4.0 and above to display advisory text in the form of a tool tip, providing additional information to the user. An example of the title attribute is:

```
<p title="Order Now for Free Shipping">New Product is Available Now</p>
```

Using the anchor element allows for a tool tip to pop up when the cursor passes over the link. This can improve understanding of your links without taking away from the flow of your content. An example of the title attribute with the anchor element is:

```
<p>New Technologies is happy to announce the addition of the
<a href="NewProduct.html" title="Free Shipping This Month">New
Product</a> to its top performing product line.</p>
```

1.7.2 Element Attributes

Non-empty and empty elements may add attributes, although attributes and values related to style are, for the most part, deprecated, and you will use cascading style sheets (CSS) to format your documents. The syntax for non-empty elements is:

```
<elementname option1="value1"></elementname>
```

or

```
<elementname option1="value1" option2="value2"></elementname>
```

The syntax for empty elements is:

```
<elementname option1="value1" option2="value2" />
```

In XHTML, every attribute value must be surrounded by quotation marks or single quotes of the same type. A value beginning with a quotation mark must end with a quotation mark, and a value beginning with a single quote must end with a single quote.

XHTML does not allow any kind of abbreviation of an attribute and its value. The full attribute name and the full value, in quotation marks, must be available for the parser. If your browser returns a warning message or missing attribute value, look for absent or mismatched quotes.

EXERCISES

Although you will not apply style to core attributes until the next chapter, CSS, it is important to plan how you would plan attributes, such as id and class, for future use.

1.7 Create a web page with the following information, adding id and class attributes so that later you will be able to differentiate airlines, and apply style to their programs. Name the file flyer.html.

Pacific Airways. Receive triple miles when you travel:
Memphis via Houston, Newark, or Cleveland. Bonus ends July 31
Receive double miles when you travel:
Anchorage via Houston. Bonus ends August 14

Dallas (Love Field) via Cleveland. Bonus ends August 1
Oakland, CA via Houston. Bonus ends August 14
Sacramento via Houston. Bonus ends July 2
To receive the bonus miles, you must register the offer prior to travel. You will be asked to show your frequent flyer card at the check-in counter.

US Express. All full fare economy and first class tickets connecting through Detroit, Salt Lake, or Minneapolis are available at significant savings. Ticketing must be completed by August 31 and all travel completed by September 30. Fares include all classes. Certain restrictions apply.

Airborne. Get 500 bonus miles from Airborne (in addition to 500 miles from North American Air) when you book a shuttle flight:
Boston to New York City (LGA)
New York City (LGA) to Washington, DC (National-DCA)
Washington, DC (DCA) to Boston
Travel must be completed by December 31. You must be a member of both airline flyer programs.

1.8 Create a web page with the following information, adding `id` and `class` attributes so that later you will be able to differentiate category, product, quantity, and price and to apply style to the page. Name the file `teas.html`

Product, Size, Price
Green Teas
  Chinese Green Tea, Plain Tea Bags, 30 ea., $4.49
  Green Organic Whole-Leaf Tea Bags,15 ea., $3.99
  Green and Mild Citrus Tea Bags, 20 ea., $1.99
  Green Decaf & Cherry Jubilee Tea Bags, 20 ea., $2.59
Black Teas and Whole-Leaf Teas
  Caribbean Tea Bags, 18 ea., $3.59
  Indian Tea Bags, 18 ea., $3.59
  Mediterranean Tea Bags, 18 ea., $3.49
  Scottish Tea Bags, 18 ea., $3.59
  Black Forest Berry Whole-Leaf Tea Bags, 15 ea., $3.99
  Decaf Ceylon Whole-Leaf Tea Bags, 15 ea., $3.99
Herbal and Therapeutic Teas
  Caffeine-Free Chamomile Tea Bags, 30 ea., $3.77
  Caffeine Free Echinacea & Goldenseal Tea Bags, 24 ea., $7.59
  Caffeine-Free Ginger Root Tea Bags, 24 ea., $3.29
  Caffeine-Free Ginger-Peppermint Tea Bags, 24 ea., $3.57

1.8 ADDING ANCHORS AND IMAGES

1.8.1 <a>

The anchor element is the most common way to specify a hyperlink. Anchor content may include text, images, or both. By enclosing some text or other content within the <a> and </a> tags, you make the item into a link that, when selected, requests a new object to be accessed. The anchor element is located within the document body. Any formatting changes take place using style sheets. The link element will be used in the next chapter, CSS. The syntax of <a> is:

```
<a href=" "> Text here you determine</a>
```

1. To link, using the anchor element, within your site, use **relative URLs**. A relative URL describes the file location to be accessed with reference to the location of the file that contains the URL itself. The relative URL for a file in the same directory is the file name and extension:

   ```
   "file.html"
   ```

   As such, an example element is:

   ```
   <a href="sales.html">Total Sales Figures</a>
   ```

2. To reference a file in a directory at a higher level of the file hierarchy, use two periods and a forward slash:

   ```
   "../projects/file.html"
   ```

   As such, an example element is:

   ```
   <a href="../q1/sales.html">Quarterly Report</a>
   ```

3. To link to web pages on other sites, use **absolute URLs**. An absolute URL shows the entire path to the file including the scheme, server name, and the file name itself:

   ```
   "http://www.learningcentre.org/projects/file.html"
   ```

   As such, an example element is:

   ```
   <a href="http://www.learningcentre.org/projects/file.html">Learning
   Centre Projects</a>
   ```

4. An example of <a> used to link an HTML document to a specific page with a basic HTTP URL is:

```
<a href="http://www.website.com/SaleItems/">Today's Sale</a>
```

5. To link to a named location inside an HTML document, the user will click on a link to jump to a specific section of the web page. Linking moves to a specific anchor. To create an anchor, **place the cursor in the part of the web page that you wish the user to jump to**. As an example:

```
<a id="anchorname">Word or Image</a>
```

can appear as:

```
<a id="greenTeas">greenTea.gif</a>
```

The named anchor tag allows you to create an anchor for each section of a long document and link it to the corresponding item. After creating the anchor, define the link. As an example:

```
<a href="#anchorname">Word or Image</a>
```

can appear as:

```
<a href="#greenTeas">Green Tea Selection</a>
```

6. An example of <a> used to link to a named email location is:

```
<a href="mailto:name@website.com">Contact Us</a>
```

Additional uses of the anchor element can be found on the companion web site and other areas of the text.

1.8.2 <img>

1. To insert an image into a web page, use the <img> element and set the src attribute of the element equal to the URL of the image. An example of <img> with a relative URL is:

```
<img src="newProduct.gif" />
```

2. An absolute URL may be used to reference an image on another server. An example is:

```
<img src="http://www.NewTechnologies.com/images/logo.gif" />
```

It is important to organize graphics so they reside on a web site or in a directory with your code, not on an external URL where they may be moved. Loading your images will be slowed if the browser is searching for their location among a collection of a hundred files in your MyDocuments folder.

Authors' Note: To pick up an image off of the internet, right click on the image and save the file to your directory. All placement of images will take place within style sheets.

1.8.3 `<a>` and `<img>`

Images are valid content as the target for <a>. An image URL substitutes for the text portion of the link. An example is:

```
<a href="mailto:name@website.com"><img src="mailbox.gif"></a>
```

You can also have text and an image in the same link, as in:

```
<a href="http://www.dynamiclearning.org/index.html"><img
src="dynamic.gif" />Dynamic Learning Resource Site</a>
```

EXERCISES

You will practice using anchors and graphics throughout the text, the purpose here is to familiarize yourself with selecting and using anchors and images, separately and together.

1.9 Open up your XHTML shell, `begin.html`. Add the following into the body of your file, and name the file `practice.html`

```
<a href="http://www.yahoo.com">Yahoo! Home Page</a>
```

Open up your file in a browser and test the link.
After you link to Yahoo!, grab the logo graphic (right click, save as, save to folder). Add the following into the body of your `practice.html` file.

```
<img src="nameofgraphic.gif" />
```

Go back to your browser and refresh or reload your page. The Yahoo! graphic will be on your document.
In your original `practice.html` file, add the following link:

```
<a href="http://www.mail.yahoo.com">Yahoo! mail</a>
```

What happens if you do not include the end tag </a>?
What happens if you do not include `http`?

1.10 Reopen your file on the Intranet advertisement for an XHTML developer (developer.html). Add two email links to the page. One for emailing in an application, the other to email the advertisement to a friend. Use your own and a friend's email address in the code.

1.11 Reopen your file on frequent flyer miles (flyer.html). Find three travel agencies on the web. Link your file to two outside URLs for travel agencies.

1.12 Reopen your file on selling teas (teas.html). Find three graphical images on the web that represent the three tea categories. Link your file to move from the category title to a graphic representing the start of the tea information. Links will be within the same .html file.

1.13 As the file is not large, the tea anchors may seem awkward. Create a separate XHTML file, a simple splash page for the teas. The page will have a short announcement at the top and the three tea categories set up as a link that will refer to the information and graphic images on the page with the tea data.

1.9 A FEW MORE ELEMENTS

1.9.1

To insert returns or blank lines in a document, use the break element.
 contains no content and has no end tag.

 would result in three returns, creating two blank lines of space. Most commonly used for determining when text should end on one line and begin on another, <br /> shouldn't be used to manipulate space; you will use style sheets for placement purposes. An example of common <br /> use is:

```
<body>
<p>New Technologies, Inc.<br /></p>
<p>14000 Industrial Way<br /></p>
<p>Saratoga, Ca 95070<br /></p>
</body>
```

The br element is not always reliable with backward compatability. You may need to try <br>..</br> to run or <p>
</p> to validate.

1.9.2 <div>

To structure XHTML documents into unique sections or divisions. <div> has been used in the past to identify sections of text for alignment. You will use <div> for identifying sections of text for formatting or positioning with style sheets. The <div> tag is a block element that acts much like <p>, except it marks a section rather than an individual paragraph. Examples of <div> are:

```
<div>
<p>A section of text is keyed in for later manipulation.</p>
</div>
```

or

```
<div class="Planning">
<p>User Analysis</p>
<p>Prototype</p>
<p>Testing</p>
<p>Build</p>
<p>Test</p>
</div>
```

1.9.3 <span>

The span tag is similar to <div>, except it identifies content inline. As an inline element, span doesn't make use of the alignment attribute. An example of <span> is:

```
<p>The <span>New Product Line</span> will be available nationwide
within the quarter.</p>
```

or

```
<p>The <span class="Q2AD">New Product Line</span> will be available
nationwide within the quarter.</p>
```

Attributes, div and span serve the purpose of identifying content that will be selected for various style presentations. They are presented in this introductory XHTML chapter so that you will have as much flexibility as possible for presentation options in large-scale web sites.

EXERCISES

1.14 Create a small classified ad page with the following categories:

Airline Tickets, Antiques, Pets, Tickets for Events/Sale or Wanted. Name the file classified.html. Use <br /> to have one category per line in a linked table of contents on the top of the page.
Link each category to its appropriate ad section. Use span for keywords, you determine, in six ads. Use div to group the antique ads together.
Discount Airfare. Short Notice OK. Air Awards Wanted. 800-123-4567.
Discount Tickets. Top $$paid for miles. 408-456-7894
Most US Cities $349 RT LEAVE NOW! 800-456-7534

Din Set 1920s Cherry Wood Beaut 9-pc set inc. detailed din tbl w/ 2 lvs, 1 capt's chr, & 5 guest chrs. $1500/bo. email rrulker@mail.com

Authentic Vict. Shadow Box (3'×1 1/2') walnut w/ gold gilding. $1625. 2' stand-up jewelry box w/ drawers $40. 510-112-4564

German Shep Pups. AKS. OFA, imported lines. Training Avail. $500. 510-790-0023

Golden Ret AKC, 9 wks. Toy midget. dewclaw, 2 shots, vet check, 6 generation pedigree. Have parents. Male $150. 916-456-9996

Kittens Rescued. Various Breeds. fixed, shots, tested. Lots of colors. 650-433-4563

Olympic 18 day tour, inclds housing, 2 tix for T&F events, shuttle, sight seeing, pd $11,520. B/O. 925-845-6585

Giants 4 1st Base Row 2 Lwr Box + Prkg. $119–199 per ticket per game each. 650-345-6342

1.15 Reopen your `food.html` file from the beginning of the chapter. Use `<br />` to add an address to the page: Tech Cafe. 98000 Wolf Road at Hwy 280 Cupertino, CA, USA. Use `<div>` to group food items together.

Use `<span>` to later emphasize the cafe URL and anywhere on the page where the name Tech Cafe is used.

1.9.4 Differences between XHTML 1.1/XHTML Basic 1.0 and HTML 4/XHTML 1.0

You may decide to change the DTD in some of the examples above from XHTML 1.0 Strict to XHTML 1.1 Modularization or XHTML Basic 1.0. In this case, there would be little or no difference because many of the elements that change from among the three have to do with presentation. However, if you were asked to design the above exercises with the platforms of kiosk, PDA, mobile telephone, and monitor in mind, you would probably determine different content to include according to user needs. As an example, the classified ads might be further abbreviated or the food data would be simplified to the basic items available on the menu and a phone number.

To summarize the differences between XHTML 1.1 (including its subset XHTML Basic 1.0) and HTML 4 and XHTML 1.0:

1. Removal of the deprecated tags results in an increase in structural functionality, but relies on style sheets for presentation. HTML 4 tags such as `<center>` are deprecated.
2. On every element, the `lang` attribute has been replaced in favor of `xml: lang`
3. On `<a>` and `<map>` the `name` attribute has been removed and replaced with the `id` attribute

4. The "ruby" collection of elements has been added

ruby (in XHTML: `ruby`) specifies that an element defines a ruby structure
ruby-base (in XHTML: `rb`) specifies that an element defines a ruby base
ruby-text (in XHTML: `rt`) specifies that an element defines a ruby text
ruby-base-container (in XHTML: `rbc`) specifies that an element contains one or more ruby base
ruby-text-container (in XHTML: `rtc`) specifies that an element contains one or more ruby text

Ruby elements relate to text that runs together but is different in height and/or width. This text may be east Asian; it may be a combination of languages with different character height and width, including nearby translation. At the time of this writing, the "ruby" collection and the ruby box model is at the W3C working draft stage. The elements are included in the W3C XHTML 1.1 recommendation. The associated ruby properties and values may be a subset of CSS3.

XHTML is designed for multiple languages and multiple output devices. The table on the following pages will give you an overview of which elements are supported by which sections of the XHTML specification. The table is organized by XHTML 1.1 module sections. Due to space limitations, not all listed elements were described in the chapter.

Experimenting with all XHTML elements will give you more development potential, rather than limiting yourself to the more popular elements you may have used with HTML.

Table 1-1 XHTML Modules and Elements

Element	XHTML 1.0 Strict	XHTML 1.1 Modularization Module Name	XHTML Basic 1.0
`<body>` document body	yes	yes-structure module	yes-structure module
`<head>` document head	yes	yes-structure module	yes-structure module
`<html>` XHTML document	yes	yes-structure module	yes-structure module
`<title>` document title	yes	yes-structure module	yes-structure module
`<abbr>` abbreviation	yes	yes-text module	yes-text module
`<acronym>` acronym	yes	yes-text module	yes-text module
`<address>` address information	yes	yes-text module	yes-text module
`<blockquote>` block quotation	yes	yes-text module	yes-text module
`  forced line break`	yes	yes-text module	yes-text module
`<cite>` citation	yes	yes-text module	yes-text module
`<code>` typed code	yes	yes-text module	yes-text module

Table 1-1 XHTML Modules and Elements (continued)

Element	XHTML 1.0 Strict	XHTML 1.1 Modularization Module Name	XHTML Basic 1.0
<dfn> definition	yes	yes-text module	yes-text module
<div> block division of a document	yes	yes-text module	yes-text module
<em> emphasized	yes	yes-text module	yes-text module
<h1>-<h6> headings	yes	yes-text module	yes-text module
<kbd> keyboard input	yes	yes-text module	yes-text module
<p> paragraph	yes	yes-text module	yes-text module
<pre> preformatted text	yes	yes-text module	yes-text module
<q> inline quotation	yes	yes-text module	yes-text module
<samp> sample text	yes	yes-text module	yes-text module
<span> defines span of text for style or class attribute	yes	yes-text module	yes-text module
<strong> strongly emphasized	yes	yes-text module	yes-text module
<var> a variable	yes	yes-text module	yes-text module
<a> hypertext anchor	yes	yes-hypertext module	yes-hypertext module
<dl> glossary or description list	yes	yes-list module	yes-list module
<dt> term	yes	yes-list module	yes-list module
<dd> term description	yes	yes-list module	yes-list module
<ol> ordered list	yes	yes-list module	yes-list module
<ul> unordered list	yes	yes-list module	yes-list module
<li> list item	yes	yes-list module	yes-list module
<object> embed data and/or data handling program	yes	yes-object module	yes-object module
<param> applet parameter	yes	yes-object module	yes-object module
<applet> inline applet program	yes	no	no
<b> bold face	yes	yes-presentation module	no
<big> bigger	yes	yes-presentation module	no
<hr> horizontal rule	yes	yes-presentation module	no
<i> italics	yes	yes-presentation module	no
<small> smaller	yes	yes-presentation module	no
<sub> subscript	yes	yes-presentation module	no
<sup> superscript	yes	yes-presentation module	no
<tt> fixed-width/monospace	yes	yes-presentation module	no

Table 1-1 XHTML Modules and Elements (continued)

Element	XHTML 1.0 Strict	XHTML 1.1 Modularization Module Name	XHTML Basic 1.0
<basefont> set base font properties	yes	no	no
<del> deleted content	yes	yes-edit module	no
<ins> inserted content	yes	yes-edit module	no
<bdo> bidirectional override	yes	yes-bidirectional text module	no
<img> inline image	yes	yes-image module	yes-image module
<area> region of map	yes	yes-client-side image map module	no
<map> client-side image map	yes	yes-client-side image map module	no
attribute `ismap` on `img`	yes	yes-server-side image map module	no
Events attributes (described under events in this chapter)	yes	yes-intrinsic events module	no
<meta> document meta-information	yes	yes-meta-information module	yes-meta-information module
<noscript> markup alternative to script	yes	yes-scripting module	no
<script> inline script program	yes	yes-scripting module	no
<style> style sheet rules	yes	yes-style sheet module	no
<link> relationship to another document	yes	yes-link module	yes-link module
<base> base URL	yes	yes-base module	yes-base module
<ruby> ruby element	no	yes-Ruby annotation module	no
<rbc> ruby base collection	no	yes-Ruby annotation module	no
<rtc> ruby text collection	no	yes-Ruby annotation module	no
<rb> ruby base box	no	yes-Ruby annotation module	no
<rt> ruby text box	no	yes-Ruby annotation module	no
<rp> ruby position property	no	yes-Ruby annotation module	no

Additional tables and forms modules are incorporated into the following tables and forms portions of the chapter.

1.10 XHTML TABLES

Tables represent the relationship of data. XHTML tables are constructed row by row.

1. <table> defines the entire table and is the root table element. The remaining elements are child elements of table.
2. <caption> specifies the title of a table and is presented above, below, to the left, or to the right of the table. caption is an optional element, although it must be the first element after the <table> start tag. A table may only contain one caption element.
3. <tr> (table row) defines a single row in the table.
4. <th> (table heading) defines a single heading cell within a defined row. <th> is a child of <tr> and by default is formatted in boldface. A table-heading cell may appear anywhere in a table.
5. <td> (table data) the non-heading child element of <tr> defines a single data cell nested within a table row. Except for the boldface, <td> is identical to <th>.

The W3C does not recommend tables for the purpose of page layout.

A caption element provides a short description of the purpose of the table. A summary attribute provides a longer description of the table's purpose and structure. Although neither are necessary for the table to run, both provide information needed for the next generation of products. The summary information is useful for non-visual output such as Braille-based agents and audio output. Alternative output devices include web systems in automobiles, PDAs, small screens on digital telephones, pagers, wireless products, and other new technologies.

```
<table summary="This table charts the number of web site hits on our
beta site, for week #1, week #2, week #3, week #4, and the total hits
for month #1. These hit counts are listed over five columns.
Additionally, the chart tracks the source of the hits by country. Our
partner country categories are listed by rows to include: US, England,
Denmark, Austria, and Slovenia.">
<caption>Beta site hits Month #1 by partner countries  </caption>
</table>
```

Table rows are grouped into head <thead>, foot <tfoot>, and body <tbody> sections. The division of head, body, and foot sections of the table allow scrolling of the table body independently of the head and foot sections. This allows for an unlimited number of rows to be in a table, while the head and foot information remains fixed for better readability of the table.

The <thead> and <tfoot> should contain information describing the table's columns. <tfoot> must appear before <tbody> because <tfoot> is rendered before receiving all of the rows of data.

<thead> contains the rows <tr>, headings <th>, and cells <td> that make up the head of the table. <tfoot> contains the rows <tr>, headings <th>, and cells <td> that make up the foot of the table.

<tbody> contains rows of table data. <thead>, <tfoot>, and <tbody> sections must contain the same number of columns. Each <thead>, <tfoot>, and <tbody> contains a row group. Each row group begins with a <tr> element. <tr> marks the beginning of a row of cell definitions. Key *Example 1-2* and name the file `tablePractice.html`.

Example 1-2

```
<?xml version ="1.0"?>
<!DOCTYPE html PUBLIC "-//W3C//DTD XHTML 1.0 Strict//EN"
"http://www.w3.org/TR/xhtml1/DTD/xhtml1-strict.dtd">
<html xmlns="http://www.w3.org/1999/xhtml" xml:lang="en" lang="en">
<!-- tablePractice.html by Your Name -->
<head>
<title>Element Order for Tables</title>
</head>
<body>
<table>
<caption>Placement of thead, tfoot, tr</caption>
<thead>
  <tr><th>The data for the table head goes here such as Tech Cafe
</th></tr>
  <tr><td>td does not automatically bold, th does bold. tr is needed to
begin a new row</td></tr> </thead>
<tfoot>
  <tr><th>The data for the table foot is keyed before the table body
and renders after the table body</th></tr> </tfoot>
<tbody>
  <tr><td>This is where the table data goes, there can be an unlimited
number of table rows</td></tr>
  <tr><td>There can also be more than one table body in a table,
although only one thead or tfoot</td></tr> </tbody>
</table>
</body>
</html>
```

1.10.1 Table Cells

The beginning of each row is marked with <tr>. Two types of cell tags are used in a table, <th> a header cell and <td> a data cell. Cells may span more than one row and column. Individual cells may be labeled so non-visual user agents may communicate heading information about the cell to the user.

The <th> element defines a cell containing header information. The <td> element defines a cell that contains data.

Example 1-3 is a simple table (key and name as betaHit.html).

Example 1-3

```
<?xml version ="1.0"?>
<!DOCTYPE html PUBLIC "-//W3C//DTD XHTML 1.0 Strict//EN"
"http://www.w3.org/TR/xhtml1/DTD/xhtml1-strict.dtd">
<html xmlns="http://www.w3.org/1999/xhtml" xml:lang="en" lang="en">
<!-- betaHit.html by Your Name -->
<head>
<title>Beta Site Hit Count, Month #1</title>
</head>
<body>
<table summary="This table charts the number of web site hits on our
beta site,for week #1, week #2, week #3, week #4, and the total hits
for month #1. These hit counts are listed over five columns.
Additionally, the chart tracks the source of the hits by country. Our
partner country categories are listed by rows to include: US, England,
Denmark, Austria, and Slovenia.">
<caption>Beta site hits Month #1 by partner countries  </caption>
<tr>
  <th>Country</th>
  <th>week #1</th>
  <th>week #2</th>
  <th>week #3</th>
  <th>week #4</th>
  <th>month #1</th></tr>
<tr>
  <td>US</td><td>50</td><td>120</td><td>260</td><td>500</td>
  <td>930</td></tr>
<tr>
  <td>England</td><td>40</td><td>80</td><td>112</td><td>293</td>
  <td>525</td></tr>
<tr>
  <td>Denmark</td><td>30</td><td>90</td><td>132</td><td>245</td>
  <td>497</td></tr>
<tr>
  <td>Austria</td><td>30</td><td>49</td><td>93</td>
  <td>176</td><td>348</td></tr>
<tr>
  <td>Slovenia</td><td>20</td><td>71</td><td>144</td><td>269</td>
   <td>504</td></tr>
```

```
</table>
</body>
</html>
```

1.10.2 Table Cell Attributes

The `rowspan` and `colspan` attributes appear to combine adjacent cells into larger cells. In other words, you have the ability to make one cell appear to span more than one row or column. Adjacent cells aren't deleted, they are hidden for the purpose of flexibility in the table's presentation. Additional attributes, primarily for use by alternate user agents can be found on the companion web site. The syntax for `rowspan` and `colspan` is as follows:

```
rowspan="numberRows"
```

Example: `<td rowspan="2">`

specifies the number of rows spanned by the current cell. The default value is "1." The value "0" allows the cell to span all rows from the current to the last row of the table section in which the cell is defined.

```
colspan="numberColumns"
```

Example: `<td colspan="2">`

specifies the number of columns spanned by the current cell. The default value is "1." The value "0" allows the cell to span all columns from the current to the last column of the column group in which the cell is defined.

`colspan` and `rowspan` may be combined as in:

```
<td rowspan="numberRows" colspan="numberColumns">
```

EXERCISES

1.16 Create a table resembling a checkbook. Include summary and caption information. Name the file `checkbook.html`. There should be a header and footer. Additionally, columns should read: Check Number, Date, Description of Transaction, Tax Item, Amount of Debit or Payment, Amount of Credit or Deposit, and Balance Forward. Key in six sample rows of data.

1.17 Create a table showing the Domain Names your company owns. Include summary and caption information. Name the file `dns.html`. Columns include DNS, Purchased From, Purchase Amount, Purchase Date, Renewal Date, Owner, and Tech/Billing Contact. Key in four sample rows of data.

1.18 Create the following table (there will be no lines/borders yet, you will add them in CSS). Include summary and caption information. Name the file `jobs.html`. Use `rowspan` and `colspan` to simulate space needed.

Table 1-2 Data for Exercise 1-18. Position: Manager, Web Development:

Skills:	Management, XML, Web Servers		
Location:	Sunnyvale		
State:	CA	Pay Rate:	$85,000 – $110,000
Area:	408	Length:	Permanent

1.19 Create a table (without lines/borders) showing parts for a Minivan Parking Brake System. Include summary and caption information. Name the file `brakeSystem.html`.

Parking Brake System, Parts Breakdown

Item	Description
PBS201	Parking Brake Release Handle and Cable
PBS250	Parking Brake Release Lever Screws (2 Req'd)
PBS300	Cable Hold-Down Bracket Bolts
PBS350	Cable Hold-Down Bracket
PBS450	Parking Brake Rear Cable and Conduit

1.20 The following information on description and treatment of coughs needs to be set up into a table and links added where `See*` is listed. The client expects to set up a site where information can be accessed by description of a health problem or by its possible cause. Create a prototype table for possible site use. Name the file `proto_med.html`.

Table 1-3 Data for Excercise 1-20. Description and Treatment of Coughs

Type of Cough	Possible Causes
Loud, barking cough	`See` Croup
Dry cough in the morning, gets better as the day goes on	Dry air. Humidify the room
Hacking, dry, nonproductive cough	Postnasal drip. Increase fluids, try decongestang
Productive cough following a cold or flu	`See` Sinusitis, Bronchitis, Pneumonia
Dry, sudden cough after a choking episode	Foreign object in the throat. `See` choking

1.11 FORMS

Forms are in transition. This chapter approach forms from the perspective of commercial web site application and changing forms technologies. As an overview:

The XHTML Strict DTD supports a core group of form elements that will transition toward X-Forms.

The XHTML Transitional DTD supports the form elements of HTML 4.0, although some of these elements have been deprecated.

XHTML Modularization supports a Forms Module of form elements broader than the XHTML Strict DTD. XHTML Modularization also acts as a parent set for XHTML Basic Forms, a short, simple set of forms elements to be used for wireless, hand-held, and other portable devices supported by XHTML Basic.

X-Forms is the hope of the commercial form future because of its in-depth capabilities, although it is currently in the working draft stages at the W3C and may be too complex for developers looking for a simple approach to XML and forms generation. X-Forms will act as a parent set for X-Forms Simple, a simple interface approach to X-Forms. At the time of this writing, X-Forms is not implemented in any browser, see the companion web site for additional information.

This chapter will define and demonstrate XHTML 1.0-Strict DTD, XHTML 1.1 Forms Module and define the XHTML Basic 1.0 Forms Module.

Form creation, from an XHTML 1.0 Strict DTD perspective, looks like *Example 1-4.*

Example 1-4

```
<?xml version="1.0"?>
<!DOCTYPE html PUBLIC "-//W3C//DTD XHTML 1.0 Strict//EN"
"http://www.w3.org/TR/xhtml1/DTD/xhtml1-strict.dtd">
<html xmlns="http://www.w3.org/1999/xhtml" xml:lang="en" lang="en">
<head>
<title>Form with XHTML Strict DTD</title>
</head>
 <body>
  <h4>Please enter your account number:</h4>
   <form action="yourEmail@dns.com"
    method="post">
<p><input type="text" name="accountnumber" id="accountnumber" />
  <input type="submit" /></p>
  </form>
 </body>
</html>
```

All XHTML forms begin with the form element that defines the form. Most forms elements are named, for the purpose of identification in transmitting data, and all have several possible attributes for layout customization. In this example:

```
<form action="yourEmail@dns.com"
    method="post">
```

The form element starts the form and connects it to the resource at the indicated URL.

A form collects data, it does not process data. The form sends the gathered data to a program on a server or interacts with a server using a script program. The forms action attribute tells the browser where to send the data, in this case it asks the data to be emailed.

The form defines how the data will be packaged for delivery to the server, but the program on the server must understand the details in order to unpackage the information and use it. The form and the program to process the form must be designed together.

The form element also contains a `method` attribute. `method` tells the browser what method to employ to send the information to the server. Data can be sent in several ways, two examples include an action URL or data sent as a message. As an example:

```
<input type="text" name="accountnumber" id="accountnumber" />
```

In this example, a textbox is created to allow text to be keyed in. The text box is named account number (you must name `<input>` to transmit to a server).

```
<input type="submit" />
```

The second `input` element creates a button that will submit the information in the form back to the server. The submit button is a special control that makes a browser submit a form when it is activated. The submit button has a default caption "Submit Query" that can be modified.

EXERCISE

1.21 Using the code on the previous pages, create and view a form with a textbox and a submit button. The purpose of the textbox will be to enter your zip code to search for the nearest home appliance center in your neighborhood.

1.12 FORM CONTROLS

XHTML forms are composed of controls that are components supported by elements and their attributes. Within the `form` element (and occasionally outside of `<form>` for the purpose of a user interface) form controls can be created such as:

1. textboxes, password boxes, and text-area boxes
2. command buttons, radio buttons, checkboxes, and buttons with images
3. list boxes
4. dropdown boxes

As an example, to create a checkbox, use the control type:

```
<input type="checkbox" name="prefix" />
```

In this chapter you will make simple forms using the form controls textbox, checkbox, dropdown box, and command button.

If you would like to learn more about forms, please see the companion web site. The focus on these few pages is to create simple forms you will later use with active server pages (ASP).

The following table of supported forms elements defines which elements you will use to begin forms creation.

Table 1-4 Forms Elements

Element	XHTML Strict DTD	XHTML Forms Module	XHTMLBasic Forms Module
`<fieldset>`	yes	yes-form	no
`<form>`	yes	yes-form	yes-form
`<input>`	yes	yes-content set	yes-content set
`<label>`	yes	yes-content set	yes-content set
`<select>`	no	yes	yes-content set
`<option>`	no	yes	yes-content set
`<textarea>`	no	yes-content set	yes-content set
`<button>`	no	yes-content set	no
`<legend>`	no	yes	no
`<optgroup>`	no	yes	no

As mentioned earlier, each of the forms elements supports several attribute types. To complicate matters, in addition to differences in elements supported in the above XHTML technologies, attributes are supported differently as well.

Table 1-5 lists each element and its supported attributes.

Table 1-5 Forms Elements and Attributes

<fieldset> Groups form fields

XHTML Strict DTD Attributes: id, class, style, title, lang, xml:lang, dir

XHTML Forms Module Attributes: common

XHTML Basic Forms Module: does not support <fieldset>

<form> Generates an interactive form

XHTML Strict DTD Attributes: id, class, style, title, lang, xml:lang, dir, action(required), method, enctype, onsubmit, onreset, accept, accept-charset

XHTML Forms Module Attributes: common, accept(ContentTypes), accept-charset(Charsets), action*(URI), method("get"*|"post"), enctype(ContentType)

XHTML Basic Forms Module: common, action*(URI), method("get*|"post"), enctype.

<input> Specifies a form's input control

XHTML Strict DTD Attributes: id, class, style, title, lang, xml:lang, dir, type, name, value, checked, disabled, readonly, size, maxlength, src, alt, usemap, tabindex, accesskey, onfocus, onblur, onselect, onchange

XHTML Forms Module Attributes: common, accept(ContentTypes), accesskey(Character), alt(CDATA), checked("checked"), disabled("disabled"), maxlength(Number), name(CDATA), readonly("readonly"), size(Number), src(URI), tabindex(Number), type("text"*|"password"|"checkbox"|"button"|"radio" |"submit"|"reset"|"file"|"hidden"|"image"), value(CDATA)

XHTML Basic Forms Module: common, accesskey, checked("checked"), maxlength(Number), name(CDATA), size(Number), src(URI), type("text"* |"password"|"checkbox"|"radio"|"submit"|"reset"|"hidden"), value(CDATA)

<label> Labels a form field

XHTML Strict DTD Attributes: id, class, style, title, lang, xml:lang, dir, for, accesskey, onfocus, onblur

XHTML Forms Module Attributes: common, accesskey(Character), for(IDREF)

XHTML Basic Forms Module: common, accesskey(Character), for(IDREF), size(Number)

The four elements, fieldset, form, input, and label are supported by all three technologies, XHTML with the Strict DTD, the XHTML Forms Module, and the XHTML Basic Forms Module.

The common four elements listed will allow you to create many types of forms, when they are used in combination with their supported attributes, as in:

```
<input type="text" name="deadline" size="20">
```

As XHTML forms transition and X-Forms are implemented, you will most likely use the XHTML Strict DTD, XHTML Modularization, X-Forms Simple, or X-Forms, depending on your application needs. For the next few pages, you will be introduced to forms supported by XHTML 1.0 Strict DTD.

Developing forms is, for the most part, a three-step process.

1. The first and most important step is to plan the information to be gathered, prioritize the information in the design of the form, and edit out any information that is not important. You have a short user attention span with forms, make the most of getting the data you need.
2. The second step is to determine which elements and their attributes best allow you to request information from a user.
3. The third step is to plan and code the forms interface and the data transfer to the server and the end client.

The elements for your forms are defined below.

1.12.1 `<fieldset>`

`fieldset` groups together a set of related form input mechanisms, enabling them to be formatted and labeled as a group. `fieldset` content includes input elements and labels, the markup that organizes those elements, and a legend element to provide a label for `fieldset`. The legend should appear just after the fieldset start tag. Supported `fieldset` attributes include: `id, class, style, title, lang, xml:lang, dir.`

`dir` specifies the direction in which the controls text is displayed, left-to-right or right-to-left.

If you want to divide your form into sections, the fieldset element, followed directly by the legend element, followed by the elements and attributes for the form section allows for sectioning and labeling a form.

1.12.2 `<form>`

`form` holds the content of the fill-in form, as defined by the input elements that can appear inside of a form. Forms do not nest; there can be no form within a form. Supported `forms` attributes include: `id, class, style, title, lang, xml:lang, dir, action(required), method, enctype, onsubmit, onreset, accept, accept-charset.`

1. `action,` a required attribute, specifies a URL, server-side program or HTTP script that processes the filled-in information.
2. `method` specifies the HTTP method used to send the form to the server (W3C recommends `POST`).
3. `enctype` specifies the MIME-type encoding for data sent via the POST method.

4. onsubmit names a script to run when the user clicks the form's Submit button.
5. onreset names a script to run when the user sets the form's Reset button.
6. accept is a list of one or more MIME-types that this part of the form and the form-processing server will accept.
7. accept-charset lists character sets supported by the server processing the submitted forms.

1.12.3 <input>

input specifies editable fields and is only allowed inside a form. input takes a type attribute to define the type of input mechanism desired, a name attribute, to define the variable name associated with the input data, and other attributes to set size and alignment. Supported input attributes include: id, class, style, title, lang, xml:lang, dir, type, name, value, checked, disabled, readonly, size, maxlength, src, alt, usemap, tabindex, accesskey, onfocus, onblur, onselect, onchange

1. name labels the input control (for the most part all input elements are named for easier identification by scripting languages moving data)
2. value sets the input control initial value
3. checked sets the initial value to on
4. disabled, in the future, will disable input
5. readonly disallows user changes to input
6. size sets maximum size of textbox
7. maxlength sets maximum number of characters in a textbox
8. src specifies image for button
9. alt text only browser image description
10. usemap specifies client-side image map displayed in a form
11. tabindex defines position of input control for user to "tab" through form
12. accesskey assigns shortcut to element for focus
13. onfocus names script to run when user moves mouse to point to current element
14. onblur names script to run when user moves mouse away from current element
15. onselect names script to run when user moves mouse to select text
16. onchange names script to run when user moves mouse to element, off element, to another element

Form controls you will use for the exercises in this chapter include:

<input type="radio" plus additional attributes for a radio button
<input type="text" plus additional attributes for a textbox
<input type="checkbox" plus additional attributes for a checkbox

1.12.4 <label>

label defines a label for a specified input element. The for attribute of the label defines the relationship between a label and an input. The for attribute takes as its value the id value of the input element. Supported label attributes include: id, class, style, title, lang, xml:lang, dir, for, accesskey, onfocus, onblur.

A simple form incorporating the aforementioned four elements is *Example 1-5*:

Example 1-5

```
<?xml version="1.0"?>
<!DOCTYPE html PUBLIC "-//W3C//DTD XHTML 1.0 Strict//EN"
    "http://www.w3.org/TR/xhtml1/DTD/xhtml1-strict.dtd">
<html xmlns="http://www.w3.org/1999/xhtml" lang="en">
  <head>
    <title>Fieldset and Legend</title>
  </head>
  <body>
    <form action="yourEmail@dns.com" method="post">
      <fieldset>
        <legend>Wholesale Purchase Orders</legend>
               <p>
                <br />
                </p>
         <label>Dealers: Please key your order number to obtain current
order status
                 <input type="text" name="wOrderStatus"
id="wOrderStatus" size="30">
                 </label>
                 <input type="submit" />
      </fieldset>
   <p>
     <br />
   </p>
     <fieldset>
       <legend>Retail Purchase Orders</legend>
               <p><br /></p>
        <label>Retail Customers: Please key your account name to obtain
current order status
               <input type="text" name="rOrderStatus" id="rOrder
Status" size="30" />
               </label>
               <input type="submit" />
      </fieldset>
     </form>
```

```
  </body>
</html>
```

EXERCISES

Create the following forms. Do not use formatting tags, you will add style to the forms in Chapter 2, Cascading Style Sheets.

1.22 The manufacturing division of a start-up recently expanded into a hard-to-find materials facility. Create a fill-in form for their site that will later link to an online map service. For now, the client needs only the format of the form to see if the information will be complete. The form has two parts.

Part 1 includes:

Enter your starting location
Street Address or Intersection
City, State Zip
Country
(the first three will use textbox, country should be a pulldown menu)

Part 2 includes:

Choose one of our destination locations
(a pulldown menu will allow the choices, Corporate Headquarters or Manufacturing facility)
There should also be two buttons, one for get directions, another for clear

1.23 A reseller site needs a form with the following information:

Purch date
Item name
Buyer
Seller
Seller's comments
Condition
Item price
Shipping and handling
Total
Pay by
Shipping address
Received date

This form will be accessed by buyers and sellers; as such, it needs to be simple, clear, and easy to read and maintain.

1.24 A Domain Name Service offers several domain extensions for sale and needs a redesign of their current fill-in form. Use a textbox for checking availability of a domain, but use checkboxes for checking availability of domain extensions.

www.______________________________(textbox)

Table 1-6 Data for Exercise 1-24

`.co.uk`	`.org.uk`	`.ro`	`.com.ro`
`.co.il`	`.org.il`	`.co.nz`	`.org.nz`
`.net.nz`	`.to`	`.as`	`.ly`
`.ms`	`.kz`	`.ac`	`.tc`
`.ug`	`.dk`	`.fm`	`.gs`

(checkboxes)

1.25 An Internet Conference needs an online registration form—please incorporate the following information into the form.

Mr. Ms. Dr.
First Name, Last Name, Title, Company, Street, Division, City
State/Province, Zip/Postal Code, Country, Phone, Fax, Email
Select Conference. Package 1 day @525, 2 day @895, 3 day @ 1195, 4 day @1395
Payment Method. Check or Money Order, MasterCard, Visa, American Express
What is your organization's primary business activity at your location?
Web/Online Business(E-Business Sites/Portals/Content/Other)
Web/Software Development
Web Hosting Service/Data Center
Computer Communication/Network Equipment Manufacturer
Internet Service Provider
What is your primary job function?
Corporate Management
IT/Internet Management
Networking/Communications Management
Application Development Management
Marketing/Sales/Product Management
Operations/Financial Management
Web Site Technical Management
Web Content/Design Management

CHAPTER SUMMARY

1. Semantic refers to content meaning and to the possible ways information may be interpreted, accessed, and manipulated. Structure expresses the form of a document, how it is organized logically, regardless of meaning. Style refers to presentation, to how the document is rendered, whether visually or with a Braille-based or auditory user agent.
2. XHTML consists of three sets if recommendations, as developed by the W3C. XHTML 1.0 is the W3C's recommendation for the latest version of HTML 4.0. XHTML 1.1 Modularization provides modules of additionally available elements to extend XHTML, bridging XHTML to XML and allowing for better transition to emerging platforms. XHTML Basic is a minimal set of modules to be used for output devices such as mobile phones, PDAs, televisions, pagers, car navigation systems, portable game machines, and other devices where a simple XHTML can also be shared across multiple output devices.
3. When you work with XHTML and XML you will refer to code at the element level. Elements consist of the start tag, the element's contents, and the end tag. All elements must be closed, as in `<p>..</p>`
4. Empty element syntax is `<elementname />` Empty elements contain no text content and often represent future content such as images and line breaks. The syntax for this empty element incorporates a space before the slash and final angle bracket.
5. There are three basic levels to the structure of an XHTML document. In the first level, the document structure, are the major sections, depending on their purpose, such as head, body, and script components.
6. In the second level, are the divisions within these major sections. This level refers primarily to the groups of content, such as title, paragraph, and headings.
7. In the third level, typically within `body`, is the substructure of elements and their children, such as lists and list items, and tables with table rows and data cells.
8. The XHTML document begins with: (a) the XML prolog, (b) a document type definition, (c) a namespace declaration.
9. XML documents begin with the XML declaration:
   `<?xml version="1.0"?>`
10. The DOCTYPE declaration must declare the document type and refer to one of three DTDs at the W3C, or another stored on your computer.

    Strict XHTML 1.0: `Strict` refers to a strict version of XHTML 1.0 in which elements and attributes that have been **deprecated** (identified elements and attributes that will not appear in future versions) are not included.

    Transitional XHTML 1.0: `Transitional` includes all elements and attributes, including those that have been deprecated. Although Transitional DTDs seem to give you more flexibility with browser issues, deprecated code creates major future editing problems.

Frameset XHTML: `Frameset` is devoted to framed documents (partitioned browser window into two or more frames). Frames are not supported in XHTML Basic and will not be supported in future versions of XHTML.

Separate DTDs support XHTML 1.1 Modularization and XHTML Basic 1.0.

11. The root element is the parent of all other elements, the element within which other elements are nested. The root element begins the document tree. Only one root element is allowed per document.
12. In HTML, the root element was `<HTML>` and the last line of the document was `</HTML>`. In XHTML the root element is also `<html>` although a namespace is added. The last line of the XHTML document remains `</html>`.
13. The purpose of these attributes is to distinguish elements for future reference. XHTML universal attributes include `id`, `class`, `style`, and `title`. Attributes allow specific identification to elements for the purpose of data manipulation and style formats. Attributes must have a quoted value.
14. Well-formedness and validity are new concepts introduced by the W3C with XML. Documents that are well-formed or valid follow a set of criteria recommended by the W3C.
15. Tables represent the relationship of data. XHTML tables are constructed row by row.
16. The XHTML Strict DTD supports a core group of form elements that will transition toward X-Forms. The XHTML Transitional DTD supports the form elements of HTML 4.0, although some of these elements have been deprecated. XHTML Modularization supports a Forms Module of form elements broader than the XHTML Strict DTD. XHTML Modularization also acts as a parent set for XHTML Basic Forms, a short, simple set of forms elements to be used for wireless, handheld, and other portable devices supported by XHTML Basic.
17. A form collects data, it does not process data. The form sends the gathered data to a program on a server or interacts with a server using a script program. The forms `action` attribute tells the browser where to send the data, in this case it asks the data to be emailed. The form defines how the data will packaged for delivery to the server, but the program on the server must understand the details in order to unpackage the information and use it. The form and the program to process the form must be designed together.
18. XHTML forms are composed of controls that are components supported by elements and their attributes.
19. Developing forms is, for the most part, a three-step process. The first, and most important step, is to plan the information to be gathered, prioritize the information in the design of the form, and edit out any information that isn't important.

You have a short user attention span with forms; make the most of getting the data you need. The second step is to determine which elements and their attributes best allow you to request information from a user. The third step is to plan and code the forms interface and the data transfer to the server and the end client.

SELF-ASSESSMENT

To move on to the next chapter, you should feel comfortable that you understand and can do the following:

1. Create a simple XHTML document and open it on a browser.
2. Read and write a document type declaration and namespace declaration.
3. Add `id` and `class` attributes to an XHTML document, selecting names for later additions of style.
4. Identify the root element in an XHTML document.
5. Create lists, add anchors and images, to a simple XHTML document.
6. Plan and create XHTML documents using `div` and `span` attributes.
7. Plan and create XHTML documents using table elements.
8. Plan and create XHTML forms using the XHTML Strict DTD.

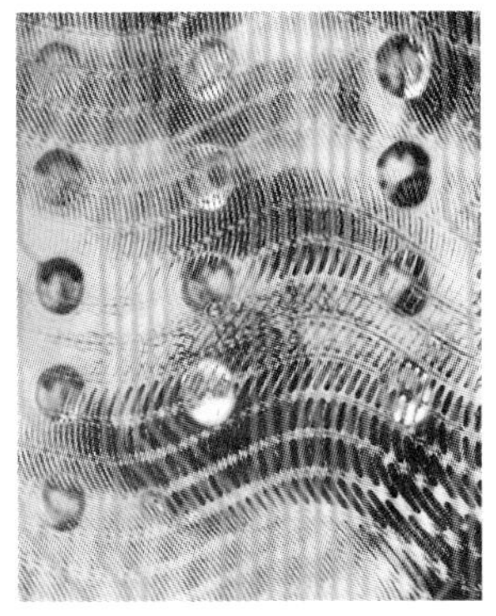

2 Cascading Style Sheets

CHAPTER OBJECTIVES

By reading the information and practicing the code in this chapter, you will understand and be able to:

1. Separate and apply style using cascading style sheets (CSS) rules.
2. Develop CSS declaration blocks, properties, values, and determine cascading order.
3. Apply CSS attributes, pseudo-elements, and pseudo-classes.
4. Utilize inheritance, attribute selectors, descendant selectors, and substring matching selectors to create efficient CSS.
5. Incorporate CSS into web applications, including tables.
6. Design and develop with CSS using absolute, relative, and fixed positioning. Incorporate space properties for multiple output devices.

2.1 STYLE SEPARATION

CSS allows developers to separate style from the semantic and structure of XHTML and XML. CSS is the style language used with XHTML. XML is compatible with CSS, and you will create documents linking both XHTML and XML with CSS. The preferred style language for XML will be extensible style language (XSL), when it is supported by the major browsers. Until that time, CSS works well and is supported, for the most part, by current browsers.

This chapter is divided into two sections:

1. Style code. Style code defines syntax used to apply rule-based style declarations.
2. Visual effects applying CSS style. Visual effects, introduced in the text and further explored on the web site section of this chapter, are better learned visually than with text. As such, the companion web site demonstrates CSS features beyond the text.

CSS emphasis on style separation allows more design freedom in site presentation and significantly decreases time spent on site editing and maintenance. As an example, commercial sites often have five or fewer page styles, regardless of the number of total pages on the site. There may be a splash or home page and three styles of additional pages. These styles are combined with large amounts of content and are presented back to the user as a web site.

With CSS, rules are created that communicate how a browser should present the site content. As such, two files are created, `fileName.html` and `fileName.css`. With XML, two files are created, `fileName.xml` and `fileName.css`. It is possible to add CSS rules within an XHTML file; however, the World Wide Web Consortium (W3C) recommends separation. Since XHTML and XML are CSS compatible, an XHTML document can link to the same .css file as an XML document. The purpose of the XHTML file is to recognize structure and to present the content. The purpose of the .css file is to inform the browser how and where to present the content (such as color or placement). If you worked previously with HTML, this separation will look a little odd at first, the XHTML file will have no formatting elements such as `BOLD` or `CENTER`.

All CSS style sheets are case-insensitive except for parts not under the control of CSS. However, XML is case sensitive and, as such, CSS is written in lower case, following XML syntax rules. In CSS, **identifiers** (element names, classes, ids, selectors) cannot begin with a hyphen or digit. Typically, identifiers begin with an alpha character, followed by digits or additional alpha characters.

CSS style sheets contain rules. These rules consist of a **selector** (XHTML, or XML) followed by a **declaration block**, as in:

```
h1 {color: red;}
```

A declaration block (referred to as a block) opens with a left curly brace and closes with a matching right curly brace. In between the braces, any characters are allowed including parentheses ( ), brackets [ ], and additional braces { }. Additional braces must occur in matching pairs and are said to nest inside of the block's opening and closing brace.

In between the block's opening and closing braces there must be zero or more declarations, each separated by semicolons. A CSS style sheet consists of a list of statements, as shown in the following exercise:

Starting with a simple example, you will create a CSS file, linked to an XHTML file, and then explore its syntax and capabilities.

Example 2-1

1. Create a folder, either on a diskette, your desktop, or hard drive, and name the folder `Example`.
2. Using Notepad, key the following code:

```
<?xml version ="1.0"?>
<!DOCTYPE html PUBLIC "-//W3C//DTD XHTML 1.0 Strict//EN" "http://
www.w3.org/TR/xhtml1/DTD/xhtml1-strict.dtd">
<html xmlns="http://www.w3.org/1999/xhtml" xml:lang="en" lang="en">
<head>
<title>CSS Example</title>
<link    rel="stylesheet"
         type="text/css"
         href="example.css">
</head>
<body>
<h1>CSS Separates Style from Content</h1>
</body>
</html>
```

3. Save this file as `example.html`
4. Make sure you do not keep the .txt extension.
5. Open a new file in Notepad and key the following code:

```
body  {background-color: yellow;}
h1    {color: blue; font-family: sans-serif;}
```

6. Save this file as `example.css`
7. Make sure you do not keep the .txt extension.
8. Open your browser. Locate and open your `example.html` file.
9. You should have your content displayed with the colors and fonts of the .css file. If you don't, there is a typo. Go back and look at the code. Check that you have used the appropriate { and }, not `[ ]` or `( )`. Also, make sure the file is saved correctly. If you see you do have the .txt extension, copy and paste the contents of your file into a new file and save. You cannot resave a .txt file to get rid of the .txt extension.

2.2 LINKING CSS

The link element used in the previous example,

```
<link   rel="stylesheet"
        type="text/css"
        href="example.css">
```

is typically placed within the head element. The XML equivalent would be

```
<?xml-stylesheet type="text/css" href="example.css"?>
```

or for a different CSS filename

```
<?xml-stylesheet type="text/css" href="wine.css"?>
```

placed after the XML declaration and before the root element.

2.3 CSS SYNTAX

The file you saved as .css is simply a collection of CSS rules. The XHTML document was able to read the CSS rules by referencing to the XHTML **selector**, the element name. As in

```
h1  {color: green;}
```

h1 is the selector. CSS supports applying the same rule to multiple selectors, by separating them with a comma, as in

```
h1, h2, h3  {color: green;}
```

Within the opening curly brace and the closing curly brace is the CSS **declaration**. The declaration block consists of the **property** and its **value**, as in

```
selector {property: value;}
```

Around each part of the declaration, there may be whitespace. A selector always goes together with a declaration block. If the selector cannot be parsed, the declaration block will be ignored. Multiple declarations may be applied to one or more selectors, as in

```
h1, h2, h3 {color: green; font-family: Arial, Helvetica; font-style:
italic;}
```

Properties and their values are always separated by a colon (:). Sets of properties and values are always separated by a semicolon (;).

2.4 COMMENTS

CSS comments begin with /* and end with */

```
/**********************************************
* may be used to create the appearance        *
* of a block note at the beginning of a file. *
***********************************************/
```

A comment block at the start of a file is often used to notify authorship and use privileges of code. Comments may not be nested, although any amount of text may occur between /* and */. CSS allows the SGML comment `<! comment -->` for CSS comments in an XHTML file using CSS inline style rules. The single or multiline comment /* and */ must be used in the linked CSS file.

2.5 CASCADING AND LEVELS OF CSS

Cascading means that style sheets may have three different points of origin for the same XHTML or XML document and, thus, cascade as they often overlap. The three points of origin include:

1. Author—typically the developer

   Authors link an XHTML or XML file to a CSS style sheet to specify style information, or they link to an interface that generates or behaves as if it generates a style sheet. As an example, a developer creates a web-based application to track frequent flyer miles. A user may use the airline web site to access frequent flyer mile status or a mobile device. Although the style will be significantly different on the two devices (screen and cellphone or PDA), the same XHTML or XML file is used.

2. User

   Users may be able to specify style information for a document. As an example, a user may need to hear information about mile status or see information in a larger font.

3. User Agents

   A conforming user agent must apply a default style sheet or a style sheet that behaves as a default prior to other style sheets for a document to satisfy the device output expectations. As an example, a palm device may be able to produce color in one model and not in another. The basic presentation will format as the author intended, but the behavior will be device dependent by the user agent to present within the confines of the device.

Style sheets from these different points of origin may overlap in scope. The CSS cascade assigns a weight to each style to determine priorities for how content will be presented. This order is determined as follows:

When several styles apply, the one with the greatest weight takes precedence.

1. Author style carries more weight.
2. This is reversed for `!important` rules.
3. `@import` style sheets also cascade. Their weight depends on their import order.

`!important` declarations (the keywords `!` and `important` follow the declaration) take precedence over a normal declaration. Author and user style sheets may contain `!important` declarations. User `!important` rules override author `!important` rules. This feature allows users who need audio output, larger fonts, different colors, to determine presentation as the balance of the author style is presented.

```
p {color: black !important; font-size: 18pt !important;}
```

results in all text with the `p` selector as black and `18 pt` for users who do not want to read text in colors and need a larger sized font.

`@import`, an alternative to linking to an external style sheet, allows users to import style rules from other style sheets. Any `@import` rules must precede all rule sets in a style sheet and are followed by the uniform resource indicator (URI) of the style sheet. As an example,

```
@import "food.css"
```

or

```
@import url ("food.css")
```

may be used and placed within a style tag such as

```
<style type="text/css">
  @import "food.css";
</style>
```

Multiple `@import` declarations may be used. The first takes precedence over the balance. You will use the `link` element for the bulk of the text exercises; however, `@import` works well when referring to multiple style sheets with one XHTML or XML document.

User agents must apply the following sorting order to find the value for an element/property combination:

1. Find all declarations that apply to the element and property for the target media type. Apply declarations if associated with selectors that match the element.
2. The primary sort of declarations is by weight and origin. Author declarations override users except in the case of `!important` where users override authors. An imported style sheet has the same origin as the style sheet that imported it.
3. More specific selectors override more general selectors at the secondary sort level. Pseudo-elements and pseudo-classes (explained later in this chapter) count as normal elements and classes.
4. Sort by order specified, if two rules have the same weight, origin, and specificity; specificity overrides. Rules in imported style sheets are considered before rules in the style sheet.

The W3C recommendation for dealing with all of these areas of precedence is to consider the user, what the needs may be, and design accordingly. This user-centered design approach eliminates much of the need for overriding and presents the user with a site that performs, for the most part, as expected.

2.6 VALUES

The next section, CSS Rules, contains information related to the values of properties as recommended by the W3C. To better interpret the values and select which to use, the following terms are first defined:

Specified values may be absolute or relative

1. **Absolute values** do not need computation to determine the computed value. As an example, `blue` is an absolute value. No computation needs to take place for the color blue to be presented. Absolute length units are only useful when the physical properties of the output medium are known.

   CSS Level 2, the current browser supported CSS, supports the following absolute units:

   `in`: inches
   `cm`: centimeters
   `mm`: millimeters
   `pt`: points (in CSS2=1/72 of an inch)
   `pc`: picas (1 pica=12 pts)

   If absolute length cannot be supported, user agents will approximate actual value.
2. **Relative values** are specified relative to another value. As an example, the value 12% must be transformed into a computed value. It must be multiplied by a reference value; 12% of something = the computed value. The keyword smaller or

bolder requires transformation into a computed value to be presented. Computed values can be used as long as the user agent is able to present the value in the specific environment. Relative units include:

em: the "font size" of the relevant font
ex: the "x height" of the relevant font
px: pixels, relative to the viewing device

As an example:

If em occurs in the value of the font-size property, it refers to the font size of the parent element.

```
li {line-height: 1.25cm;}
```

will result in the list line height to be 25% greater than the font size of the list elements. Note: Pixel units are relative to the resolution of the viewing device.

3. **Inheritance** for a document is defined in the document tree. Computed values are inherited, specified percentage values are not. Style applied, as an example, to body, results (in XHTML) in that style applied to all children in the body element. However, elements such as h1 may have additional or different applied style. In this case, inheritance can be used to apply one style to body and to apply another to h1, without affecting other elements.

```
body {color:green;}
h1 {color: navy;}
```

results in all text within the body element appearing as green (because body represents all content, in this case all text on the site unless otherwise specified) and all text within h1, which is within body, appearing as navy blue.

4. **Integers and real numbers**. Integer values, <integer>, consist of one or more digits '0' to '9.' Real number values, <number>, can either be an <integer>, or zero or more digits followed by a dot (.), followed by one or more digits. <integer> and <number> values may be preceded by a '+' or '-' to indicate sign, although some properties restrict value to positive values or a range of negative or positive values.
5. **Lengths** refer to horizontal (x-axis) or vertical (y-axis) measurements. The format of a <length> value is an optional sign character ('+' or '–', with '+' as the default) immediately followed by a <number> immediately followed by a unit identifier (i.e., 5 px). A unit identifier is optional with a 0 length. Some properties allow negative length values although this may complicate a formatting model.
6. **Percentages**, <percentage>, are formatted with an optional sign character ('+' or '–', with '+' as the default) immediately followed by a <number>. Percentage

values are relative to another value. Properties that allow percentages define the value to which the percentages refer. Specifying percentage incorrectly, applying to a non-allowed property, or misinterpreting inheritance will result in the user agent ignoring the percentage value.

2.7 CSS RULES

The following nine commonly used CSS `type` selectors are related to text and simple backgrounds. Understanding these nine rules in various combinations will help you to envision the what, how, and why of CSS. The additional, numerous options of CSS are defined, explained, and explored on the companion web site. More important than listing multiple properties, is helping to build your understanding of CSS syntax, enabling you to easily reference additional properties as you build a site. CSS rules, as with XHTML elements, can be learned by understanding the basic premise and referring to rules and elements as needed to best deliver a clients' products.

The W3C determines the following information for each font property:

1. Value: defines the values available for each property
2. Initial: defines the default value for each property
3. Applies to: defines which HTML elements the property and value are accepted by CSS
4. Inherited: defines whether parent-child relationships apply
5. Percentages: defines whether percentage values are accepted by CSS
6. Media: defines which media accepts the property

2.8 FONT PROPERTIES

2.8.1 `font-family`

Value: `family-name|generic-family|inherit`
Initial: depends on user agent
Applies to: all elements
Inherited: yes
Percentages: N/A
Media: visual

```
h1 {font-family: value, "second choice value", "third choice value";}
```

specifies a prioritized list of font family names and/or generic family names. In the above example, a list of fonts of the same size and style (called a font set) are specified. Font family names containing whitespace should be quoted. Generic font family names are keywords and must not be quoted. As an example,

```
h1  {font-family: Times, "Times New Roman", serif;}
```

Times needs no quotes; there is no whitespace. Times New Roman needs quotes due to whitespace. Serif is a generic font keyword and must not be quoted. In this example, the generic font, serif, will be used if Times or Times New Roman is unavailable. W3C encourages offering a generic font family as a last alternative for improved robustness.

2.8.2 `font-style`

Value: `normal|italic|oblique|inherit`
Initial: `normal`
Applies to: all elements
Inherited: yes
Percentages: N/A
Media: visual

specifies normal, italic, or oblique font style. The initial (default) style is normal. Font-style applies to all elements, accepts inheritance, and applies toward visual media. As an example:

```
li    {font-style: italic;}
li p  {font-style: normal;}
```

results in a list in italic font style, except `p` text inherited from `li` reverts to normal.

2.8.3 `font-weight`

Value: `normal|bold|bolder|lighter|100|200|300|400|500|600|700|800|900|inherit`
Initial: `normal`
Applies to: all elements
Inherited: yes
Percentages: N/A
Media: visual

specifies the weight, or darkness, of the font. Values for the property range from 100 to 900 in increments of 100. Typically the value bold is 700 while the normal font value is 400. Keywords are also supported such as bold, bolder, and lighter, which assign weight by inheritance, in other words, bolder or lighter than the parent element. As an example:

```
h1  {font-weight:  700;}
p   {font-weight: lighter;}
```

2.8.4 font-size

Value: absolute-size|relative-size|bolder| length|percentage|inherit
Initial: medium
Applies to: all elements
Inherited: yes
Percentages: N/A
Media: visual

The **absolute-size** keywords include:

```
xx-small|x-small|small|medium|large|x-large|xx-large
```

The **relative-size** keyword is interpreted relative to the table of font sizes and the font size of the parent element. Keywords include:

```
larger|smaller
```

The **length** keyword specifies an absolute font size. Negative lengths are not accepted.

The **percentage** keyword specifies an absolute font size relative to the parent element's font size.

As an example,

```
li  {font-size: 24pt;}
p class="Q1Sales"  {font-size: smaller;}
p class="Q2Sales"  {font-size:90%;}
```

2.8.5 font

Font specifies all of the font properties with one style rule. There is no separation by semicolon because all are values of the property font. One additional attribute included within font is line height, which specifies the distance between two lines of text, measured from baseline to baseline. Each font attribute can be indicated, separated by spaces, except for line height, which is used with font size and is separated by a slash. You may use as few or as many font rules in this shorthand notation as you want. Any property not given a value will appear as its initial value as specified in the CSS specification.

```
p {font: italic small-caps 600 18pt/24pt Arial, sans-serif;}
```

2.9 TEXT PROPERTY

2.9.1 text-align

Value: left|right|center|justify|string
Initial: depends on user agent and writing direction (left to right or right to left depending on language)
Applies to: block level elements
Inherited: yes
Percentages: N/A
Media: visual

Text-align specifies how inline content of a block is aligned. Left, right, and center justify are identical as defined in word processing applications. String applies to aligning table cells. The alignment of text is relative to the width of the element, not screen size of your output device. The text-align property is inherited, setting alignment in the body, sets alignment for the entire document.

```
h1 {text-align: center;}
```

2.10 COLOR PROPERTIES

2.10.1 color

Value: color
Initial: depends on user agent
Applies to: all elements
Inherited: yes
Percentages: N/A
Media: visual

Color takes one value, a color, and applies that value to text or a text decoration.

```
h1 {color: blue;}
h1 {color: rgb(51, 51, 153);}
h1 {color: #333399;}
h1 {color: 3333FF;}
```

2.10.2 `background-color`

Value: `color|transparent`
Initial: `transparent`
Applies to: all elements
Inherited: no
Percentages: N/A
Media: visual

Background-color has two values, a color and the keyword transparent. The color will be visible behind the element text. **`background-color` does not work in Netscape 4.

```
body  {background-color: white;}
body  {background-color: rgb(255, 255, 255);}
body  {background: #FFFFFF;}
```

2.10.3 `background-image`

Value: `url|none`
Initial: `none`
Applies to: all elements
Inherited: no
Percentages: N/A
Media: visual

`background-image` has two values, a URL and the keyword `none`. To specify an image as background, enter the URL of the image as the value. Typically background image and background color are used together. The color will fill transparent areas of the image, fill in the screen while the image is loading, and will be available if, for some reason, the image does not load.

```
body  {background-image: url (logo.gif);
       background-color: rgb(255, 255, 255);}
```

EXERCISES

2.1 In this exercise you will open the `food.html` document you created in Chapter 1, XHTML. Please add the CSS link to the XHTML document

```
<link   rel="stylesheet"
        type="text/css"
        href="example.css">
```

Add a comment line after the CSS link

```
<!-- food.html with CSS font and color by Your Name -->
```

Using the CSS properties referred to in the previous pages, create and save `food.css` in the same folder where you saved `food.html`. Create a CSS file with the following rules:

1. The color of the text in `h1` and `h2` elements will be `navy`
2. The color of the text `li` in elements will be `black`
3. The color of the text in the `h3` element will be `navy`
4. The color of the `dt` and `dd` elements will be `#6699FF`
5. The `body` background color will be rgb `255:255:255`
6. The `body` font family will be `Arial` or `sans-serif`

2.2 In Chapter 1, XHTML, you created a list called `dmusic.html`. Open this file, add the CSS link and a comment, and resave. Create and save `dmusic.css` in the folder with `dmusic.html`. Using the CSS properties described on the previous pages, change the text to a combination of `#666600`, `#999933`, and the background color to `#FFFFCC` or to a background image of your choice. Use `text-align` to organize the information for better readability.

2.3 In Chapter 1 you created a simple page, `canasta.html`. Open this file, add the CSS link and a comment, and resave. Create and save `canasta.css` in the folder with `canasta.html`. Using CSS rules described on the previous pages, change the background color to `black`, the text color to `white`, and use font-weight and text-align to create fun, yet readable page. In addition to `black` and `white`, you may also choose to use a third, accent color, `#FF3333` or `#CC0066`.

2.4 In exercise 2-3 you selected colors and font weight for a casual site. For this exercise, open the file `developer.html` you created in Chapter 1. Add the CSS link, a comment, and resave. Create and save `developer.css` in the folder with `developer.html`. Using the CSS rules described on the previous pages, add formatting to `developer.html` that is clean, businesslike, and simple for a fast download designed for quick access to information.

2.11 CLASS AND ID ATTRIBUTES

`class` and `id` attributes allow you to single out one instance of an XHTML element or an identified grouping of XHTML elements for the purpose of applying style. As an example, you may have a site with a large amount of text and, as such, several `p` elements. How can you select only one or two of those paragraphs to apply style toward? If you key;

```
p   {color: maroon;}
```

All p tags are selected. To select one element, use the XHTML id attribute. The id attribute, introduced in Chapter 1, is common to nearly all XHTML elements. id allows you to apply style to one particular occurrence of an attribute or to a few particular occurrences. The XHTML elements would look something like this:

```
<p id="q1sfmp">Quarter 1 Sales Forecast Narrative and Marketing Plan</p>
<p id="q2sfmp">Quarter 2 Sales Forecast Narrative and Marketing Plan</p>
<p id="q3sfmp">Quarter 3 Sales Forecast Narrative and Marketing Plan</p>
<p id="q4sfmp">Quarter 4 Sales Forecast Narrative and Marketing Plan</p>
```

To write a style rule for an id value, include the name of the id preceded by a pound symbol # as the selector for the rule. As an example,

```
#q4sfmp     {color: maroon;}
```

results in maroon element text for those elements matching the id name q4sfmp.

In the XHTML element, the id name is enclosed in " " or ' ' because it is a string. One thing you need to keep track of is every id name must be unique in the same XHTML file. As in all naming conventions, names should be selected with a meaning connected to the purpose of the label.

There are times when you may want to apply style not to a single element but to a group of elements. Class values don't have to be unique, many elements can be members of the same class. Elements don't have to be of the same type to be in a common class. As an example:

```
<h1 class="ytd">Year-to-Date Sales Forecast Narrative and Marketing
Plan Results</h1>
<p class="ytd">Year-to-Date Existing Markets</p>
<p class="ytd">Year-to-Date New Markets</p>
<p class="ytd">Year-to-Date Potential Markets</p>
<p class="future">Next Year Forecasts-Domestic</p>
<p class="future">Next Year Forecasts-International</p>
```

Class values allow you to group elements rather than to single out one id attribute.

To write a style rule for a class value, include the name of the class preceded by a dot (.), as the selector for the rule. As an example,

```
.ytd  {color: teal;}
```

results in teal element text for those elements matching the class name ytd.

EXERCISE

2.5 In Chapter 1 you created a simple XHTML document, `flyer.html`. You added `class` and `id` attributes to later apply style to the site. Open this file, add the CSS link and a comment, and resave. Create and save `flyer.css` in the folder with `flyer.html`. Using the CSS properties described earlier in the chapter, change the background color and the color of text to incorporate the following web-safe colors. `#FFFFFF`, `#FF0033`, `#3333CC`, and `#000000`. Use your `class` and `id` attributes to apply style.

2.12 DISPLAY PROPERTIES

The display property specifies each XHTML or XML element be displayed as

1. a block of text (typically `<p>` and `<h1-6>`)
2. part of a line of text (typically inline `<em>` and `<span>`)
3. a list item (typically `<li>`)
4. a cell or row in a table (typically `<tr>`)
5. a "run-in" header starting a new block of text without a `<br />`
6. a compact label in the margin such as `<dt>` in a list

A complete exercise set working with display is on the web site portion of the chapter. The transition to organizing space using CSS display and positioning takes some practice, but the transition is more of fitting puzzle pieces together and presenting on multiple browsers and platforms than it is of difficult coding. Browser issues still need to be tested, but most of CSS Level 2 has been implemented in current browsers. The W3C forecasts CSS and extensible style language (XSL) will eliminate the need to design with frames and tables. In fact, the W3C does not recommend the use of frames or tables for any sort of positioning or layout.

Thinking of elements as **block elements** (beginning on a new line and ending on a new line) or **inline elements** (occurring within a line, nested within block elements) allows for better control of display.

Additional properties related to space, such as padding, borders, and margins allow for spacial control around and between elements. This space allows for the arrangement of blocks on the page, screen, etc. without redundant code forcing elements into position. The next generation of CSS, Level 3, when implemented by browsers allows for yet more sophisticated positioning with additional pseudo-classes and output options. Continued use of frames, tables, and elements such as `<center>` take away from your ability to transition content to voice-, television-, and wireless-based output modes.

2.12.1 `display`

Value: `inline|block|list-item|run-in|compact|market|table|inline-table|table-row-group|table-header-group|table-footer-group|table-row|table-column-group|table-column|table-cell|table-caption|none`
Initial: `inline`
Applies to: all elements
Inherited: no
Percentages: N/A

The most common properties for display are `block` and `inline`. As mentioned earlier, block-value elements start and end on a new line while inline values start and end within a line. A typical inline value is to add color, emphasis, or weight to one word in a line of text, or to apply a link to a name, allowing the user to link to a new window or a new location within the document. As an example, XHTML would be

```
<p>Blocks of text <em>start and end</em> on a new line. Inline text is
nested within a line.</p>
```

The linked CSS would be

```
p {color:navy;}
em {display:inline;}
```

Examples and graphics of additional display values and properties, on platforms and in browsers, are on the web site portion of the chapter.

EXERCISE

2.6 Create a simple XHTML `freeEmail.html` document with the following text.

Set up a free email account, something like @yahoo, @hotmail, or a newer, smaller site. As you learn XML you will sign up at several sites for miscellaneous tools, products, and join lists. A separate email account for learning purposes allows you to access this information as you like but keeps these materials separate from your personal email correspondence.

Set up inline anchors so the user can go directly to the Yahoo! mail setup page or the Hotmail setup page, add any additional options for free email you might suggest. Use display block and inline properties to set the font at sans serif and to turn on the link.

2.13 ADDITIONAL SELECTOR SYNTAX

Selector options allow you to determine specific elements to target for style attributes. **All selector options must be browser tested.**

In addition to the type, id, and class selectors discussed above, CSS offers the following selectors to allow more exact style placement:

2.13.1 Universal Selector

1. The universal selector, written *, matches the name of any element type. As an example, with the type selector:

```
 h1  {color:blue;}
*h1  {color:blue;}
```

In both cases, all of the h1 elements will be selected. With id attributes and class attributes, the same holds true.

```
#q4sfmp  {color: olive;}
.ytd     {color: olive;}
```

and does the same job as

```
*#q4sfmp  {color: olive;}
*.ytd     {color: olive;}
```

One example where an "any" match could be helpful is in applying style to any instance within a specific hierarchy in the document tree. As an example,

```
ul * p {color: red;}
```

results in matching p elements that are descendants of any element that is a descendant of ul. This does not apply the color red to ul but rather to any descendants of ul.

2.13.2 Descendant Selector

2. The descendant selector matches an element that is the descendant of another element in the document tree. A descendant selector is made of two or more selectors separated by whitespace. A descendant selector match is made when the second element is a descendant of the first. As in the example,

```
dt      {color: black;}
dd      {color: gray;}
dd p    {font-family: Arial, sans-serif;}
```

results in Arial or sans-serif fonts for p elements within dd.

2.13.3 Child Selector

3. A child selector matches when an element is the child of another element and when the elements are separated by ">". As an example,

```
ol > li  {color: purple; font-family: sans-serif;}
```

matches all `li` items found within `ol`.

```
ol > li p  {color: purple; font-family: sans-serif;}
```

matches all `p` items, not from the entire `body` element but descending from `li`, as child to `ol`.

4. An adjacent sibling selector is keyed as `e1 + e2` (element1 + element2) when the elements share the same parents in the document tree and `element1` immediately precedes `element2`. As an example,

```
h3 + h4  {color: red;}
```

where `h1`, `h2` and `h5` or `h6` do not receive the color `red`. You cannot say `h3 + h4 + h5`. The siblings are adjacent but not selected by group.

EXERCISE

2.7 In Chapter 1 you created a simple XHTML document, `teas.html`. You added `class` and `id` attributes to later apply style to the site. Open this file, add the CSS link, a comment, and resave. Create and save `teas.css` in the folder with `teas.html`. Using the CSS properties described earlier in the chapter, change the font family to sans serif, the font weight on the headers (Green Teas, Herbal and Therapeutic Teas), and use the background and color combinations of: `#33CC99`, `#99FFCC`, `#FFFFFF`, `#FFFF99`, `#FF9933`. Use display properties to separate the elements with spacing. There are four options listed on the previous pages under Additional Selector Syntax. Select at least two for this exercise and study all four carefully.

Authors' Note: Sometimes, while developing, you will be focused on color or layout and it will seem simpler to create one rule for each element and not worry about learning hierarchical or grouping selector syntax. Remember, though, your focus is on using these simple, short exercises to transition into developing commercial sites. If this tea site offered 250 teas and 300 coffees, imagine changing each font, color, weight at the element level only. With CSS selector combinations you will have the opportunity to move closer and closer to applying style on a more detailed basis, allowing you to identify small portions or detailed areas for style, thus eliminating the frustration of having to use deprecated HTML tags to get the site to present as you would like.

2.14 PSEUDO-ELEMENTS AND PSEUDO-CLASSES

Pseudo-classes permit selection based on information outside of the document tree or that cannot be expressed using simple selectors. A pseudo-class always contains a colon (`:`) followed by the name of the pseudo-class and, optionally, by a value. Pseudo-classes should be browser tested.

```
a:visited {color:blue;}
```

All a links in a document with an `href` attribute are automatically classified as `visited` or `link` (unvisited). If the link has been visited recently, the browser puts in pseudo-class visited.

```
a:link {color:green;}
a:visited {color: blue;}
```

results in the link changing from green to blue when the user accesses the link, the length of time until the link returns to blue is up to the browser.

The `:active pseudo-class` applies while an element is activated by the user, such as pressing and releasing a mouse button.

The `:hover pseudo-class` applies when the user designates an element (typically by moving a mouse over a link or graphic link) but does not activate it.

The `:focus pseudo-class` applies when an element has the focus, it applies style when it is the active element.

An element may match more than one pseudo-class.

The `:lang pseudo-class` is demonstrated on the web site, along with the above listed properties, and proposed additional CSS Level 3 pseudo-classes allow for more flexibility and complexity but are not implemented at this time.

Pseudo-elements, supported by CSS Level 2, such as first-line and drop-cap, before, and after, are also demonstrated on the web site. The purpose of this text is to introduce pseudo-classes, which will become more important as CSS Level 3 is implemented, because of their ability to select elements from the document tree (resulting in more workability with XML and commercial level XHTML).

EXERCISES

2.8 Using the `freeEmail.html` document you created earlier in the chapter, apply pseudo-classes link, visited, and active, changing the font from `660033` (link), to `990033` (visited), and `CC0033` (active).

2.9 Using the `teas.html` document you created earlier in the chapter, add the hover and focus pseudo-classes, test hover and focus, add and test link, visited, and active.

2.15 ATTRIBUTE SELECTORS

Attribute selectors allow rules to match attributes defined in the source document (at this point your XHTML document). There will be times when you create and/or edit a style document but are not in a position to add or edit attributes to the original XHTML document (hopefully the original document will have consistent attributes). There may also be issues with a DTD that, again, limits your editing options with the XHTML file. In such cases, attribute selectors allow you to create a CSS file where you may apply style to existing element attributes by matching identifiers or strings of attribute values. Attribute selectors must be browser tested.

The case-sensitivity of attribute names and values matches the case of the XHTML or XML document. Attribute selectors match in four ways, the two most common uses are listed below, the remainder are in the web site portion of the chapter:

2.15.1 Matching Attribute Selector

1. A selector that matches attributes based on whether they have a certain attribute.
   syntax:

   ```
   selector [attribute]  {property: value;}
   ```

   example:

   ```
   p [q4sfmp]  {font-family: sans-serif;}
   ```

This selector option works well when there is an attribute in an existing XHTML or XML file, and you want to select it and add style.

2.15.2 Matching Attribute Value Selector

2. A selector that matches the value of an attribute.
   syntax:

   ```
   selector [att=val]  {property: value;}
   ```

   example:

   ```
   p [class="ytd"]  {color: teal;}
   ```

   or

   ```
   p [font-weight="bold"]  {color: teal;}
   ```

represents elements with a matching attribute name, its value being exactly `val`. This attribute selector matches well with `span`, `div`, `class`, as well as properties connected to specific elements. Multiple attribute selectors can be used to represent several attributes of an element, or several instances of the same attribute, as an example, with

```
<h1 class="ytd">Year-to-Date Sales Forecast Narrative and Marketing
Plan Results</h1>
<p class="ytd">Year-to-Date Existing Markets</p>
<p class="ytd">Year-to-Date New Markets</p>
<p class="ytd">Year-to-Date Potential Markets</p>
<p class="future">Next Year Forecasts-Domestic</p>
<p class="future">Next Year Forecasts-International</p>
```

Multiple attribute selectors may look like

```
p [class="ytd"][class="future"]  {color: teal;}
```

2.15.3 Substring Matching Attribute Selectors

A substring selector matches a portion of the string value of an attribute (need to be tested in your browser). If there were, as an example, similarly named attributes, substring matching attribute selectors would match as follows:

3. The first substring matches the beginning value of a string exactly.
   syntax:

```
selector [att^="val"] {property: value;}
```

An example of linking to this XHTML code is

```
<h1 class="YTDsales">Year-to-Date Sales Forecast Narrative and
Marketing Plan Results</h1>
<p class="Q1Sales">First Quarter Gross Sales</p>
<p class="Q2Sales">Second Quarter Gross Sales</p>
<p class="Q3Sales">Third Quarter Gross Sales</p>
<p class="Q4Sales">Fourth Quarter Gross Sales</p>
<p class="Q1ROI">First Quarter Return on Investment</p>
<p class="Q2ROI">Second Quarter Return on Investment</p>
<p class="Q3ROI">Third Quarter Return on Investment</p>
<p class="Q4ROI">Fourth Quarter Return on Investment</p>
```

A CSS example is

```
p [class^="Q"] {color: #3300FF;}
```

which results in a match where the string values beginning exactly with the value "Q," in this case the Quarterly Gross Sales and Quarterly Return on Investment, will format in a navy blue font.

4. The second substring selector matches the ending value of a string exactly.
   syntax:

```
selector [att$="val"] {property: value;}
```

An example linking to the XHTML code in the previous example is

```
p [class$="ROI"] {font-weight: bold;}
```

which results in a match where the string values ending exactly with the value "ROI," in this case Quarterly Return on Investment, will format in bold.

5. The third substring selector matches anywhere in the value with a portion of the substring "val".
   syntax:

```
selector [att$="val"] {property: value;}
```

As an example, linking to the XHTML code in the first substring selector,

```
selector [class$="Q2"] {font-style: italic;}
```

results in a match where the partial string values containing exactly the value "Q2," in this case Second Quarter Gross Sales and Second Quarter Return on Investment, will format in italic.

EXERCISE

2.10 In Chapter 1 you created a simple XHTML classified ad page, `classified.html`. You added `span` and `div` to later apply style to the page. Open this file, add the CSS link and a comment, and resave. Create and save `classified.css` in the folder with `classified.html`. Using the CSS properties described earlier in the chapter and the selector attributes described in the previous pages, format this page so that it resembles a Sunday newspaper classified ad section.

2.16 SPACE PROPERTIES

Properties related to space around block-level elements include `margin`, `padding`, and `border`. These properties are briefly defined in the text, and demonstrated on the companion web site. A table example is used for demonstration, and the properties work well with non-table elements as well.

The main idea with space is that `margin`, `padding`, and `border` are used to create space around block and inline elements. This space serves to separate blocks, each forming something like a piece of a mosaic, to be placed, positioned, and distanced, resulting in screen output. The difference with this type of approach to space and using frames or tables to force spacing, is that ideally all design and positioning elements are separated from all content. Using frames not only creates printing problems, it keeps style and content within one file, resulting in future problems related to searching, editing, and output mode.

A site with the purpose of offering networking parts, as an example, that is developed in frames limits searching capabilities and nearly necessitates a computer monitor as output mode. Whereas, style and content separation allows for the same content to be output on screen, accessed in the field by a handheld device, and manipulated in databases for a procurement system. Frames helped for awhile, but they are too limiting for the way you will want to work with web applications in the future. Remember, screen design for a 17-inch monitor is only one development option in commercial site development.

2.16.1 `margin`

Margin is the space between an element bounding box and the bounding box of an adjacent element. A bounding box is the combination of the block of text, the padding surrounding the text, and the border outlining the padding.

The margin property is commonly used to specify spacing in a document.

```
margin, margin-top, margin-right, margin-bottom, or margin-left
```

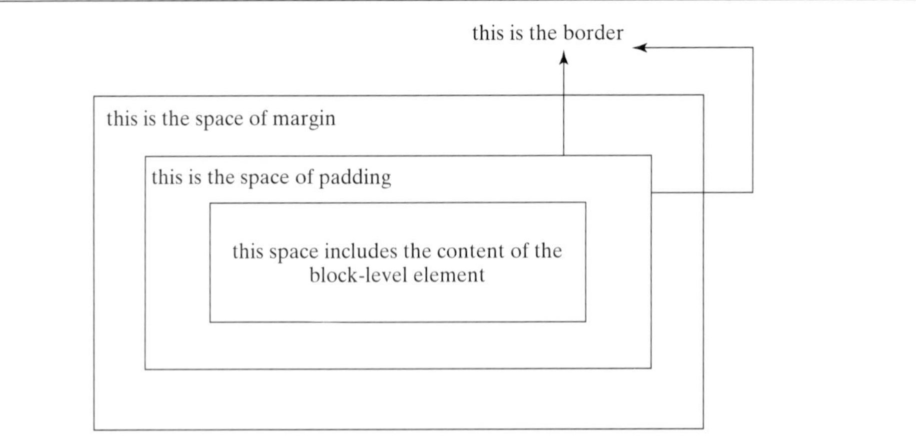

Figure 2-1 CSS Bounding Box

Value: `length|percentage|auto`
Initial: 0
Applies to: all elements
Inherited: no
Percentages: refers to width of containing block

specifies the margin around all content of an element. Lengths must be absolute or relative values, and auto is defined and demonstrated on the web site. As an example of using margin,

```
li p  {margin 2px}
```

gives `p` text within `li` a 2 pixel margin.

Margin, as with several CSS properties, sets the styles of all four sides at once. These values are listed within the rule, whether there are one, two, three, or four of them. As an example,

```
li p {margin: 2em 3em;}
```

The order of these values and their interpretation by a browser is as follows:

1. When one value is set, the value applies to all four sides.
2. When two values are set, the top and bottom borders are set to the first value, the right and left borders are set to the second.
3. When three values are set, the top border is set to the first value, the right and left borders are set to the second, and the bottom border is set to the third.
4. When four values are set, the values apply in top/right/bottom/left order.

EXERCISE

2.11 Open your `developer.html` file. Using the margin properties, position the elements of the job posting for clear reading. An additional property, text indent, can be used to indent the first line of text.

2.16.2 `padding`

The CSS padding properties describe how much space to insert between an element and its margin or between an element and its border.

Value: `length|percentage {1-4}`
Initial: 0
Applies to: all elements
Inherited: no

Percentages: refer to width of containing block
Media: visual

Percentage equals the width of the block-level element in which this element is contained. As an example, 25% adds padding that equals 25% of the width of the parent element.

Padding automatically takes on the appearance of the elements background, if the `background-color` has been set. The order of the values is identical to the `margin` property

```
tr {padding: 3px 2px;}
```

1. When one value is set, the value applies to all four sides.
2. When two values are set, the top and bottom borders are set to the first value, the right and left borders are set to the second.
3. When three values are set, the top border is set to the first value, the right and left borders are set to the second, and the bottom border is set to the third.
4. When four values are set, the values apply in top/right/bottom/left order.

2.16.3 `border`

Value: `length|percentage {1-4}`
Initial: `0`
Applies to: all elements
Inherited: no
Percentages: refer to width of containing block
Media: visual
syntax:

```
<table border="value">
```

example:

```
<table border="5">
```

The `border` attribute is located in the table element. The values are stated, by width, in pixels.

CSS properties set the styles of all four sides at once. These values are listed within the rule, whether there are one, two, three, or four of them. As an example,

```
table {border-width: medium thin;}
```

The order of these values and their interpretation by a browser is as follows:

1. When one value is set, the value applies to all four sides.
2. When two values are set, the top and bottom borders are set to the first value, the right and left borders are set to the second.
3. When three values are set, the top border is set to the first value, the right and left borders are set to the second, and the bottom border is set to the third.
4. When four values are set, the values apply in top/right/bottom/left order.

CSS border properties that may be used (although they need to be tested) for tables, or with all other XHTML elements, include

2.16.4 `border-width`

Value: `border-width{1,4}|inherit`
Initial: `medium`
Applies to: all elements
Inherited: no
Percentages: N/A
Media: visual

Border-width accepts four types of values:

`thin`
`medium`
`thick`
a `length` value (absolute or relative unit such as pt, px, em)

2.16.5 `border-style`

Value: `border-style{1,4}|inherit`
Initial: `none`
Applies to: all elements
Inherited: no
Percentages: N/A
Media: visual

Border-style accepts one of 10 keywords and needs browser testing.

1. `none`-no border is drawn. Default
2. `hidden`-the border is transparent, there is space but no color
3. `dotted`-a dotted line
4. `dashed`-a dashed line
5. `solid`-a solid line

6. `double`-a double line. The two lines and the space between equals the border-width value
7. `groove`-a 3D groove
8. `ridge`-a 3D ridge
9. `inset`-a 3D inset
10. `outset`-a 3D outset

2.16.6 `border-color`

Value: `color{1,4}|transparent|inherit`
Initial: taken from the `color` property of the element
Applies to: all elements
Inherited: no
Percentages: N/A
Media: visual

Colors may be specified using CSS predefined named colors, hexidecimal or RGB colors.

2.16.7 `border`

Border acts as a shortcut for the three properties listed previously. Its syntax is as follows:

```
{border: [border-width_value] [border-style_value]
[border-color_value];}
```

As an example,

```
table {border: medium solid red;}
```

EXERCISE

2.12 The entry page of a web site should act as a kind of newspaper front page, similar to the cover of the *Wall Street Journal*. Each of the following article introductions, within the site, links to the actual article. Key each using <p> and include an inline anchor element. After keying the XHTML document, use margins, padding, and borders to arrange the blocks so they are clearly separated and can be easily read.

Premiere Online Issue

Application Service Providers. We rate setup, service, and reliability for 10 top ASPs.

B2B. We introduce and interview players in the large-scale online procurement business.
Voice on the Web. We update sites, vendors, and forecast browser support trends.
Venture Capital Funds. Who's funding now? What criteria are they looking for?
Privacy. Are wireless transactions safe? How to build trust with your users.
Managed Service Providers. Who are they and what can they do for you?
Software. Check out the latest upgrades and new players.
Hardware. When to upgrade, ratings, and more. Printers and Monitors.
Economy. Your role in the networked economy. How alliances and partnerships profit the community as well as your company.
Third Sector. Social Trust, a critical element in sustainable economic growth and development.

2.16.8 `cellspacing` and `cellpadding`

Cell spacing is the space between adjacent cells, in a table. The attribute is set on the `table` element, the value (integer, a whole number of pixels) applies to every cell in the table. A common use of cell spacing is making the cell and table borders wider than the default. The number of pixels represents the distance between both the adjacent cells and the frame of the table.

XHTML syntax:

```
<table cellspacing="value">
```

example:

```
<table cellspacing="2">
```

Cell padding is the distance between the content of the cell and the border of the cell. The attribute is set on the `table` element, the value (integer, a whole number of pixels) applies to every cell in the table. A common use of `cellpadding` is to surround cell contents with additional whitespace.

XHTML syntax:

```
<table cellpadding="value">
```

example:

```
<table cellpadding="3">
```

or

```
<table border="5" cellspacing="2" cellpadding "3">
```

2.16.9 XHTML Height and Width

XHTML syntax:

```
<table height="height_px|height_%"  >
```

example:

```
<tr height="10px">
```

The `width` attribute can be used to set the width of both the table and its cells. Its value can be relative or absolute (in pixels) or a percentage. Width should be set in the columns on the first row of cells, resulting in all rows following at the same width, because the user agent reads from top to bottom. Setting cell spacing and cell padding before table width will save time in fine-tuning spacing within the table.

```
<table width="300px">
<th width="20px">
```

Authors' Note: The W3C specification excludes table columns and column groups from the `height` property along with rows and row groups from the `width` property. Use margin and padding properties to format the height and width of a table.

EXERCISES

2.13 Key the following table. Next, use the margin, padding, and border properties from the previous pages to create an effective layout for the table.

```
<?xml version ="1.0"?>
<!DOCTYPE html PUBLIC "-//W3C//DTD XHTML 1.0 Strict//EN"
"http://www.w3.org/TR/xhtml1/DTD/xhtml1-strict.dtd">
<html xmlns="http://www.w3.org/1999/xhtml" xml:lang="en" lang="en">
<!-- brightColor.html by your Name -->
<head>
   <title>Bright Color</title>
<link   rel="stylesheet"
        type="text/css"
        href="brightColor_2-13.css"/>
</head>
<body>
<h1> Bright! Colors</h1>
<table width="100%" summary="This table presents a short selection of
web-safe colors for reference purposes. The first column indicates a
word to indicate the approximate hue of the color, the second column
```

```
lists the equivalent hexidecimal number for the color, the third column
lists the equivalent rgb code for the color.">
   <tr id="row1">
       <th>Approximate Color Name</th>
       <th>Hexidecimal Number</th>
       <th>RGB Code</th>
   </tr>
   <tr id="row2">
       <td>Bright Pink</td>
       <td>#FF0066</td>
       <td>255:0:102</td>
   </tr>
   <tr id="row3">
       <td>Bright Purple</td>
       <td>#990099</td>
       <td>153:0:153</td>
   </tr>
   <tr id="row4">
       <td>Bright Green</td>
       <td>#00CC00</td>
       <td>0:204:0</td>
   </tr>
   <tr id="row5">
       <td>Bright Aqua</td>
       <td>#00CCFF</td>
       <td>0:204:255</td>
   </tr>
   <tr id="row6">
       <td>Bright Yellow</td>
       <td>#FFFF00</td>
       <td>255:255:0</td>
   </tr>
</table>
</body>
</html>
```

2.14 In Chapter 1 you created an XHTML table, `checkbook.html`. Open this file, add the CSS link and a comment, and resave. Create and save `checkbook.css` in the folder with `checkbook.html`. Using the CSS properties described earlier in the chapter, change the layout to look like a check register in a wallet-type checkbook.

2.15 In Chapter 1 you created an XHTML table, `dns.html`. Open this file, add the CSS link and a comment, and resave. Create and save `dns.css` in the folder with `dns.html`. Using the CSS properties described earlier in the chapter, change the format to a simple table to be displayed on a web site.

2.16 In Chapter 1 you created an XHTML table, `jobs.html`. Open this file, add the CSS link and a comment, and resave. Create and save `jobs.css` in the folder with `jobs.html`. Using the CSS properties described earlier in the chapter, change the font, color, and spacing to reflect a bright, playful style for a high school/college recruitment program.

2.17 POSITIONING

Relative positioning allows corrections to the positions of individual boxes, without altering the position of other boxes. **Absolute positioning** takes an element out of sequence and moves it to another position, regardless of additional block placement. Where relative positioning allows for position adjustments, absolute positioning would be used to place a box, regardless of user scrolling or screen size manipulations. **Fixed positioning** places an element in one position, never to move, regardless of scrolling or content change. The position property determines whether elements are static or subject to relative, absolute, or fixed positioning.

As an example, a graphic element, when viewed onscreen, would work better if moved 10 pixels down and 5 pixels to the left. This can be accomplished with relative positioning, without interrupting other block elements onscreen.

Typically, margin, padding, and border properties are used rather than relative positioning. Margin, padding, and border spacing allow for positioning in the placement of space around each element. As such, relative positioning is not used as often, although it can be effective in fine-tuning placement and with placement for simple output devices.

Absolute positioning, although also not used as often as margin, padding, and border properties, has a role in replacing framesets. If the reason you might want to continue to develop with frames is because of placement of links, tabs, icons, that would remain in place regardless of scrolling or linking to subpages, absolute positioning will act, onscreen, in much the same visual manner as constant placement with a top or side frame.

Fixed positioning places an element, such as a logo graphic, in the same place on the screen or on every page if the site is printed, regardless of scrolling and additional content. Fixed positioning is also useful in dividing a screen's contents, resulting in the appearance of a table. The differences in results between absolute and fixed positioning are demonstrated on the chapter web site.

Static elements (also called normal elements) are placed in relationship to their parent elements and other elements that precede them. In other words, using margin, padding, and border properties, what you really have is a hierarchy of elements, all nested within the root element, together making up the document tree. Within these elements (inline) and between these elements (block) space can be manipulated.

Positioned elements, on the other hand, are placed in relationship to containing blocks, which may be their parents or other elements higher up the document tree. The **containing block** for fixed position elements is the viewport, for browsers and other scrolling media, or the page box, for paged media. Relatively positioned elements, like static elements, do not have a containing block, although they may serve as a containing block for a positioned element. The containing block for an absolute positioned element is usually the root element, although if the element is inside of another positioned element, that element will be its containing block.

When an absolutely positioned element is inside of another absolutely positioned element, or inside a fixed positioned element, it is easy to establish the edges of the containing block. If the absolute positioned element is inside of a relative positioned element, the top and left edges of the become the top and left edges of the relative positioned containing block and the bottom, and right edges of the relative positioned element becomes the bottom and right edges of the containing block.

2.17.1 `position`

Value: `static|relative|absolute|fixed`
Initial: `static`
Applies to: all elements
Inherited: no
Percentages: N/A

Normal elements that do not use positioning methods are `static`, the initial value. The values absolute and fixed imply the element must be a block. The value of the display property is ignored in this case.

Non-static elements use four positioning properties:

`top, right, bottom, left`

Value: `length|percentage|auto`
Initial: `static`
Applies to: non-static elements
Inherited: no
Percentages: width or height of containing block

Understanding static, relative, and positioned elements and how they are manipulated for visual presentation is explored and demonstrated, in detail, in the web site portion of the chapter.

2.18 CSS AND PARSING ERRORS

Illegal style sheets and style sheets with errors will parse by the user agent to determine the beginning and end of the declaration although incorrect portions of the style sheet will typically be ignored by the browser. For the developer, this ignoring of a declaration may be viewed as an error or browser problem, although many times there may simply be a typographical error in the file.

To ensure new properties and new values for existing properties may be added in the future, user agents are required to follow rules when encountering the following scenarios:

1. Unknown properties are ignored by the user agent. For example,

   ```
   li {white-space: normal; sort: alpha;}
   ```

   will parse with normal whitespace only. `Sort` is not a CSS property.
2. Illegal values are ignored by the user agent. For example,

   ```
   li {white-space: 4 px;}
   ```

   will be ignored. `4 px` is not an allowed value of the white-space property.
3. Invalid `@` keywords are ignored by the user agent including everything following it though the next semicolon (`;`) or block `{ }`, whichever comes first.

   ```
   @sort
     @ columnone {
       color: red;
       font-family: sans-serif;}
     li {text-decoration: underline;}
   ```

   The only accepted property above is

   ```
   li {text-decoration: underline;}
   ```

It should be noted that the most common error for students is typographical errors in case, semicolon/colon transformation, parentheses in place of braces, and errors in the CSS link. Printing your code and proofreading your syntax will resolve many problems. Browser conflicts are listed on the companion web site.

EXERCISES

2.17 Create the following information page. Use CSS for page layout and add active and visited links.

If You're a Victim of ID Theft
Credit Cards
Review recent charges and close accounts if necessary.
Bank Accounts
Review transactions, stop payment on fraudulent checks. Close accounts and open new ones if necessary. Ask the bank to issue a secret password that must be used for every transaction.
Report the Incident
Credit reporting companies. Notify all three agencies: Equifax, (800) 525-6285; Experian (formerly TRW), (888) 397-3742; and Trans Union, (800) 680-7289.
Police. Call your local Police Department Fraud Detail.
Federal Trade Commission. File complaint online at www.consumer.gov/idtheft/ or call (877) 438-4338.
U.S. Postal Inspection Service. If information is stolen from your mailbox, or if the thief uses the mail in the crime, file online at www.usps.gov/postalinspectors/, call (415) 779-5900, or stop by any post office. Postal inpsectors expect to spend 100,000 hours investigating ID theft nationwide this year.
Department of Motor Vehicles. If your driver's license number is stolen, DMV can put a fraud alert on your license.
Social Security Administration. If you think your Social Security number is being misused, call (800) 269-0271 or report online at www.ssa.gov/oig/Hotline.htm
Be Vigilant
Get regular credit reports to watch for fraudulent activity, or subscribe to a paid service that notifies you of any new applications for credit. Some such services are Intersections, www.intersectins.com and ID Guard, www.privista.com
Source: Identity Theft Resource Center. *San Francisco Chronicle*, February 11, 2001.

2.18 Create the following table using XHTML and format with CSS properties.

Table 2-1 International Electricity Consumption Comparison in 1998

Country	Population (millions)	Electrical Consumption (Kwh/per cap)
Norway	4.42	25,304
Canada	30.30	16,349
Sweden	8.85	15,492
U.S.	269.09	13,388
Japan	126.49	8,008

Table 2-1 International Electricity Consumption Comparison in 1998 (continued)

Country	Population (millions)	Electrical Consumption (Kwh/per cap)
France	58.85	7,175
U.K.	59.24	5,800
Saudi Arabia	20.74	5,153.04
Russia	146.91	4,873.11
S. Africa	41.40	4,509.03
Brazil	165.87	1,850.78
Mexico	95.68	1,644
Turkey	64.75	1,439
Egypt	61.67	900.67
China	1,238.60	871.91
India	979.67	415.75
Sudan	28.35	47.80

Source: International Energy Agency. *San Francisco Chronicle*, February 11, 2001.

2.19 Create a page showing the following data, without using a table. Use CSS to position the elements for clear readability.

Best and Worst States

Total energy consumption per capita, 1997

Source: Combined State Energy Data Systems 1997 and *San Francisco Chronicle* February 1, 2001

Best 10 Consumers

State — Million Btu

Maryland — 266.8

New Hampshire — 259.0

Arizona — 252.9

Massachusetts — 250.6

Florida — 246.6

Connecticut — 243.3

California — 240.0

Rhode Island — 237.9

New York — 225.3

Hawaii — 201.0

Worst 10 Consumers
Alaska — 1,143.5
Louisiana — 940.0
Wyoming — 891.2
Texas — 587.8
North Dakota — 554.9
Kentucky — 462.6
Indiana — 457.5
Alabama — 457.3
West Virginia — 445.6
Maine — 445.3

CHAPTER SUMMARY

1. CSS allows developers to separate style from the semantic and structure of XHTML and XML. CSS is the style language used with XHTML. XML is compatible with CSS, and you will create documents both in XHTML and XML with CSS. However, the preferred style language for XML will be XSL, when it is supported by the major browsers.
2. CSS emphasis on style separation allows more design freedom in site presentation and significantly decreases time spent on site editing and maintenance.
3. With CSS, rules are created that communicate how a browser should present the site content in the XHTML or XML file. As such, two files are created, `fileName.html` and `fileName.css`, or in the case of XML, two files are created, `fileName.xml` and `fileName.css`.
4. All CSS style sheets are case-insensitive, except for parts not under the control of CSS. However, XML is case sensitive, and, as such, CSS is written in lower case, following XML syntax rules.
5. In CSS, identifiers (element names, classes, ids, selectors) cannot begin with a hyphen or digit. Typically, identifiers begin with an alpha character, followed by digits or additional alpha characters.
6. CSS style sheets contain rules. These rules consist of a selector (XHTML or XML) followed by a declaration block, as in

```
h1 {color: red;}
```

7. A declaration block (referred to as a block) opens with a left curly brace and closes with a matching right curly brace. In between the braces, any characters are allowed including parentheses `( )`, brackets `[ ]`, and additional braces `{ }`. Additional braces must occur in matching pairs and are said to nest inside of the block's opening and closing brace.

8. In between the block's opening and closing braces there must be zero or more declarations, each separated by semicolons.
9. Within the opening curly brace and the closing curly brace is the CSS declaration. The declaration block consists of the property and its value, as in

```
selector {property: value;}
```

10. Around each part of the declaration, there may be whitespace. A selector always goes together with a declaration block. If the selector cannot be parsed, the declaration block will be ignored. In the same way that multiple selectors may be applied by to one rule, multiple declarations may be applied to one or more selectors, as in

```
h1, h2, h3 {color: green; font-family; Arial, Helvetica; font-style:
italic;}
```

11. Properties and their values are always separated by a colon (`:`). Sets of properties and values are always separated by a semicolon (`;`).
12. Again, although it is possible to apply CSS within an XHTML file, the W3C recommendation and your focus on XML determines using the `link` element from the XHTML file to the CSS file as your best option.
13. CSS comments begin with /* and end with */
14. `class` and `id` attributes allow you to single out one instance of an XHTML element or an identified grouping of XHTML elements for the purpose of applying style.
15. Selector options allow you to determine specific elements to target for style attributes.
16. Pseudo-classes permit selection based on information outside of the document tree or that cannot be expressed using simple selectors. A pseudo-class always contains a colon (`:`) followed by the name of the pseudo-class and, optionally, by a value

```
a:visited {color:blue;}
```

17. Attribute selectors allow you to create a CSS file in which you may apply style to existing element attributes by matching identifiers or strings of attribute values.
18. A substring selector matches a portion of the string value of an attribute.
19. Properties related to space around block-level elements include `margin`, `padding`, and `border`.
20. Margin is the space between an element bounding box and the bounding box of an adjacent element. A bounding box is the combination of the block of text, the padding surrounding the text, and the border outlining the padding.

21. Relative positioning allows corrections to the positions of individual boxes, without altering the position of other boxes. Absolute positioning takes an element out of sequence and moves it to another position, regardless of additional block placement. Where relative positioning allows for position adjustments, absolute positioning would be used to place a box, regardless of user scrolling or screen size manipulations. Fixed positioning places an element in one position, never to move, regardless of scrolling or content change. The position property determines whether elements are static or subject to relative, absolute, or fixed positioning.
22. Illegal style sheets and style sheets with errors will parse by the user agent to determine the beginning and end of the declaration although incorrect portions of the style sheet will typically be ignored by the browser.

SELF-ASSESSMENT

1. Adding style to your XHTML and XML documents will improve more and more as you work with documents and determine how you want the user to interact with the content. For now, to move on to the XML chapter you should have a solid understanding of how CSS works and be able to build CSS files utilizing font, color, background, and additional properties defined on the web site.
2. Additionally, you will need an understanding of accessing elements using syntax for selection, rather than creating long lists of each element and matching that element with a rule. These syntax combinations shouldn't be memorized, rather, you will want to access them for use in applying style.
3. The use of margin, padding, and borders to lay out your elements is an important component of CSS. At this point you should feel, with a little experimentation, you can lay out block and inline elements to match a sketch prototype of how you plan the page to look.
4. Absolute, relative, and fixed positioning will be used less than margin, padding, and borders, although at this point you should understand the differences between and use of each.
5. Creating an XHTML document, planning how style should be applied, and implementing style are important skills to move on. Style should not be implemented based on rules you know, rather a sketch for a site, designed for the user should be created first, and the rules should be used as a tool to deliver that predesigned user interface.

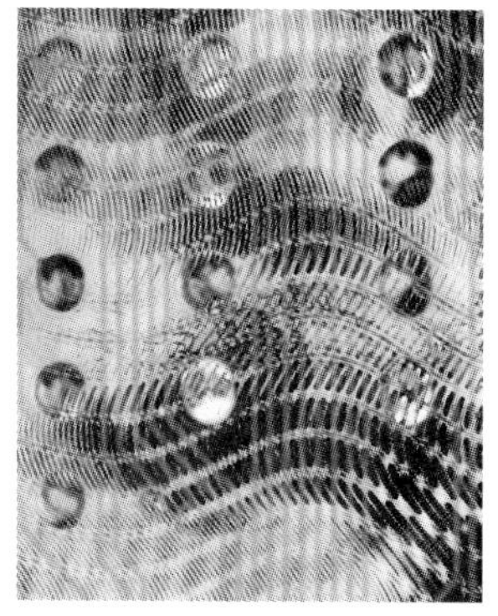

3 Extensible Markup Language

CHAPTER OBJECTIVES

By reading the information and practicing the code in this chapter, you will understand and be able to:

1. Develop well-formed extensible markup language (XML) documents as recommended by the World Wide Web Consortium (W3C).
2. Create XML applications utilizing correct syntax for attributes, subelements, PCDATA, CDATA, processing instructions, and entities.
3. Determine and incorporate namespace.
4. Read, key, and edit an XML hierarchical structure and document tree.
5. Model XML applications and work with an XML parser toward user-centered design and efficient application development.

3.1 PLANNING, DEVELOPING, PRESENTING, AND MANIPULATING DATA

Your thought process with XML is on creating a data bank, where information may be presented in numerous formats, where data may be combined in various combinations, and where a web-based product may range from a complex application running on a browser to content and images presented on a web site. This XML thought process is important because experience has taught us all that the best databases and spreadsheets were created based on how the data would be accessed and used, rather than how the code would run.

You will begin, in this chapter, by learning the basic ideas of XML as developed by the W3C. As you progress, the chapters will focus on planning, developing, and testing XML for commercial applications. The purpose of this first XML chapter is to familiarize you with XML basics and for you to practice, practice, practice.

XML is a meta-language, which means you create and format your own document markups (tags).

Three files are typically processed by an XML compliant application.

1. The .xml document contains the document data; XML elements, attributes, and data content. This document data is the semantic portion of the application.
2. The style sheet determines how the documents should be formatted and presented. Presentation is not always made via a browser; new technologies, audio output, and Braille-based output must be considered in presentation decisions. Additionally, one .xml document may be output through multiple style sheets. As an example, in a utility company, average monthly usage and current month usage data is typically output to: (a) a handheld device for entering current month usage by utility company meter reader, (b) an accounting department for billing purposes, (c) regulatory reports, and (d) internal reports analyzing expected power needs for subsequent months. The XML document is, as mentioned earlier, a data bank allowing multiple use output and manipulation.
3. The document type definition (DTD) or schemas specifies rules for how XML elements, attributes, and data are defined structurally and how they are logically related in an XML-compliant document. With HTML, the structural portion of the document is predetermined by a W3C DTD. With XML, you make this determination by developing a DTD or schema or by utilizing a third-party DTD or schema. Expected changes, including broader use of schemas, are discussed in a later chapter. For now, understand there is a third file, which you may create or reuse, that determines the structural hierarchy of your XML elements. Schemas or DTDs are not mandatory and, in fact, are left out in simple XML applications that need to be well formed but not valid. The decision to incorporate a schema or DTD is explored throughout the text.

XML elements consist of a start tag, content, and an end tag. As with extensible hypertext markup language (XHTML):

1. An XML element name must start with a letter or an underscore. Numbers, hyphens, periods, or additional underscores can follow, and there is no limit to characters per element.
2. Colons are permitted only for specifying namespaces.
3. Whitespace and symbols are illegal in an element name.
4. Non-empty elements must have a start and end tag. Elements such as `<p>` contain text and should be coded as `<p>.....</p>`

```
<sales>..</sales>
```

5. XML supports empty elements, typically used to add non-text content to a document. XML empty elements must still contain a forward slash.

```
<logo src="company.gif" />
```

6. XML tags must be nested correctly.

```
<partNumber>..<partName>..</partName>..</partNumber>
```

If these basic syntax rules are met in your XML document, the document is said to be well formed. In this chapter you will create well-formed documents. Valid documents (introduced in the XHTML chapter) are optional for XML developers, they can provide more reliability and are often used for commercial applications. Validation checks the document structure and some basic data types, and can provide assurance that a document is syntactically complete.

3.2 CREATING AN XML DOCUMENT

Starting with a simple example (Example 3-1), create an .xml file, linked to a .css file, and then explore its syntax and capabilities.

Example 3-1

1. Create a folder, either on a diskette, your desktop, or hard drive, and name the folder `journey`.
2. Using Notepad, key the following code:

```
<?xml version="1.0"?>
<?xml-stylesheet type="text/css" href="journey.css"?>
<proverb>
<first>A journey of a thousand miles begins with a single step.</first>
</proverb>
```

3. Save the file as `journey.xml`.
4. Make sure you do not add a .txt extension.

   XML documents begin with the XML declaration that specifies the XML version used. The XML declaration, while not mandatory for XHTML, is mandatory in an XML document. The initial portion of a document, preceding the first element, is the prolog. The prolog contains only declarations, whitespace, comments, and processing instructions.
5. Open a new file in Notepad and key the following code:

```
first {color:blue; display: block; font-size: 15pt; font-weight: bold;}
```

6. Save this file as `journey.css` in the same folder or directory as `journey.xml`.
7. Open an XML compatible browser. Locate and open your `journey.xml` file.

3.2.1 Case-Sensitive and the Use of "XML"

XML is case-sensitive. All declarations and markup must match in case. This applies throughout XML processing. Additionally, the name XML is reserved. You may not create an element, attribute, or name a file beginning with xml or XML. The W3C reserves "xml" for future specifications.

Key the following document (Example 3-2) to practice working with XML and case.

Example 3-2

1. Following the keying instructions in the previous section, create the following XML document. Name the directory "wine," the XML file `wine.xml`, and the style sheet `wine.css`.

```
<?xml version="1.0"?>
<?xml-stylesheet type="text/css" href="wine.css"?>
<wine>
<name>Kraski Teran</name>
<country>Slovenia</country>
<location>Sepulje</location>
<history>Some oenologists believe that Kraski Teran goes back to Roman
times.
</history>
<color>dark ruby-red wine - traditionally, it is called, <span> "black
as rabbit's blood"</span></color>
<perfect>Kraski Teran and prsut (prosciutto or air-dried ham) are the
legendary pair of Kras cuisine, but the wine is also perfect with other
pork dishes, sausages, or boiled ham with horseradish</perfect>
<served>Kraski Teran should be served at 15 - 16 C (59 - 60.8 F)
</served>
</wine>
```

2. Create a .css document using the CSS properties `color`, `font-weight`, and `font-family`.
3. Open the file in an XML compatible browser. Adjust the .css file as needed to present the wine information as it might be on a wine information web site.

3.3 ATTRIBUTES AND SUBELEMENTS

As with XHTML, attributes describe additional information about an element. Attributes consist of a name and a value and must appear in the start tag or the empty-element tag. The attribute name, paired with its quoted value, is an attribute specification.

```
<anthology proverb="journey">
```

The attribute value may use " " or ' ', but must always be quoted and follow the same character restrictions as element names. Some developers recommend and others do not recommend the use of attributes, you will work on projects using both methods throughout the text. One consideration is that there will be times when pairing an element with an attribute specification is less effective than creating subelements (nested elements). As an example,

```
<wine location="Primorska Slovenia" winemaker="Kraski Teran"></wine>
<wine location="Monterey California" winemaker="Morgan Pinot Noir
Monterey"></wine>
<wine location="Paso Robles California" winemaker="Seven Peaks
Shiraz"></wine>
```

uses attributes to identify while Example 3-3

Example 3-3

```
<wine>
<location>Primorska Slovenia</location>
<winemaker>Kraski Teran</winemaker>
</wine>
<wine>
<location>Monterey California</location>
<winemaker>Morgan Pinot Noir Monterey</winemaker>
</wine>
<wine>
<location>Paso Robles California</location>
<winemaker>Seven Peaks Shiraz</winemaker>
</wine>
```

uses nesting for the same purpose.

The decision to use attributes or subelements typically falls with intended use. Applying style to attributes has its advantages, although subelements allow for more data manipulation options later and attributes cannot be nested. No one has come up with a formula for determining which approach is better where. You will work with both in the introductory chapters and will later determine which to use depending on client needs in the commercial project chapters.

3.4 COMMENTS

Comments in XML match comments in XHTML. Comments cannot nest inside of a markup and cannot come before the XML declaration (Example 3-4).

Example 3-4

```
<?xml version="1.0"?>
<!-- Comment. -->
```

An illegal comment is shown in Example 3-5.

Example 3-5

```
<!--flight schedule application -->
<?xml version="1.0"?>
```

The purpose of comments is to guide you and other developers through the thought process of your code. This does not mean every page contains several comments, but it does mean that key points, problems, changes in direction, future options, and other important considerations need to be noted to enable reasonable future development and editing. Your role as a developer is not to baffle others with the complexities of your code but to be clear, informative, and play a part in minimizing of the high amount of recording companies and developers regularly face.

3.5 PCDATA AND CDATA

All XML documents consist of characters. There are two types of character data in XML documents.

1. PCDATA, which has to be parsed
2. CDATA, which is not parsed

Elements consist of PCDATA and attributes of CDATA.

With PCDATA (parsed element data) there are problems with characters such as <, >, ", ', and & , which are used as markup characters. You can not key these character data, on their own, because the parser will become confused as to whether they are data, characters, or markup that needs to be parsed. The solution to the problem is to insert them, by number or a special, predeclared name.

A sample of PCDATA predeclared names is listed in Table 3-1.

Table 3-1 PCDATA Predeclared Names

Character	Name	Number
<	lt	60
>	gt	62
"	quot	34
'	apos	39
&	amp	38

To use the characters in Table 3-1 with a name or number, you will begin with the & delimiter for characters or &# for numbers and end with the ; delimiter for either characters or numbers. As an example, > is presented as `>` or as; `>.`

If you want to write the XML code for Example 3–6:

Example 3-6

```
<condition>a>b & c<b</condition>
```

You will need to key

```
<condition>a &gt; b &amp; c &lt; b</condition>
```

for the parser to read the code and display on the browser as correct.

Using numbers from Table 3-1 above, `<condition>` can be written as Example 3-7.

Example 3-7

```
<condition>a &#62; b &#38; c &#60; b></condition>
```

If there are a lot of characters that need to be escaped, as described above, your document can become difficult to read. In this case you can use a CDATA section that will not be parsed. If you have a small JavaScript program, as an example, with several escaping characters to be inserted, as content of `<jscript>`, your code might read as Example 3-8.

Example 3-8

```
StrA="new"
if (a>b && d=="old")
{
 document.write("<br />"+StrA+"<br />")
}
```

The CDATA section will have the following form:

```
<![CDATA["<....>"]]>
```

The code, in this case, could be

```
<jscript><![CDATA[

StrA="new"
if (a>b && d=="old")
{
 document.write("<br />"+StrA+"<br />")
}
]]></jscript>
```

An example of an XML document incorporating CDATA is Example 3-9.

Example 3-9

```
<?xml version="1.0"?>
<famousPerson>
```

```
 <scientist>
  <name>Albert Einstein</name>
   <image><![CDATA["<img src='Einstein.gif'>"]]>
   </image>
 </scientist>
 <composer>
   <name> J.S. Bach</name>
   <image><![CDATA["<img src='Bach.jpeg'>"]]>
   </image>
 </composer>
</famousPerson>
```

3.6 PROCESSING INSTRUCTIONS

Using processing instructions, it is possible to incorporate applications not performed by the XML processor. Processing instructions take the following form:

```
<?NameTargetApplication ApplicationInstructions ?>
```

The `NameTargetApplication` is the name of the application that is to perform as specified in the `ApplicationInstructions`. Processing instructions are rarely used in XML documents. When a processing instruction is included, it is typically used to add a style sheet, as in

```
<?xml-stylesheet type="text/css" href="example.css"?>
```

The prolog of XML document has the form of processing instruction, although it is not considered to be processing instruction.

```
<?xml version="1.0"?>
```

An example of an XML document with a processing instruction is the style sheet declaration on the second line of Example 3-10.

Example 3-10

```
<?xml version="1.0"?>
<?xml-stylesheet type="text/xsl" href:="FinData.xsl"?>
<finDatSV>
 <company>
    <name>Aztek</name>
    <last>39.63</last>
    <high>55.38</high>
    <low>20.00</low>
 </company>
</finDatSV>
```

3.7 ENTITIES

When creating XML documents, it is common to have text or a graphic (for example, a company logo) appearing several times. In this case, you can create and use entities by associating repeating text with a name. As an example, you may have a long statement used repeatedly on all sales materials, such as:

We're #1 in Florida. South Florida's newest & largest authorized pre-owned facility. Worldwide shipping available. Financing & leasing. Please call for our most current availability as our inventory changes daily. Located close to Miami and F. Lauderdale International Airports. 444 Northwest 199th Street Miami, FL 33170 (305) 909-8000 Fax (305) 909-8001. Log on to our Internet web site www.miamimercedes.com

Whenever you have to insert that text into a document you can create an entity called `adInfo` and any time you key `adInfo` into your document, the output will be the complete paragraph as described. During the processing of the XML document, the entity name `adInfo` is replaced by the complete text. Entities have two parts, the declaration (in the DTD) and the entity reference (in the XML document).

There are two type of entities, general and parameter. General entities are included in XML documents and parameter entities are included in DTDs. Entities must be declared in both the XML document (general) and the DTD (parameter). This chapter shows you how to declare general entities. The schemas and DTD chapter explains how to declare parameter entities.

General entities can be declared as in Example 3-11.

Example 3-11

```
<!ENTITY NameOfEntity "This is an example of internal entity">
```

for internal entities, and

```
<!ENTITY NameOfEntity SYSTEM "http://www.learningcentre.org/
entExam.txt">
```

for external entities saved outside of the XML document, in the text element.

Parameter entities have a similar declaration, with the exception of an extra % character. The declaration of a parameter entity will be

```
<!ENTITY % NameOfEntity "This is an example of parameter entity
declaration">
```

If you want to insert your text into an XML document, you will need to refer to it by the name of the entity, inside of `&...;` delimiters. As such, if you defined your general internal entity as

```
<!ENTITY adInfo   "Replace with sales/address info">
```

You will to refer to

```
&adInfo;
```

There is no space between &name and ;

As in Example 3-12, Martin Luther King's famous speech, "I have a dream . . ." can be created and inserted as an external entity. First, declare it.

Example 3-12

```
<!ENTITY LutherSpeech SYSTEM: "http://www.learningcentre.org/
Luther.txt">
```

You will refer it in the XML document as

```
<famousSpeech> Martin Luther said &LutherSpeech;</famousSpeech>
```

During processing of the XML document the text file Luther.text will replace the entity LutherSpeech.

Parameter entities are referenced as

```
%parEntName
```

Parameter entities only occur inside of a DTD Document.

3.8 ENCODING

When declaring an XML document, as you know, the XML prolog is mandatory.

```
<?xml version="1.0"?>
```

However, along with the XML declaration you can define an optional encoding attribute representing legal character encoding. There are several encoding values, parsers must support at least universal characterset transformation format (UTF) UTF-8 and UTF-16 Unicode.

With an encoding attribute, the XML prolog takes the following form:

```
<?xml version="1.0" encoding="UTF-8" standalone ="yes">
```

The standalone attribute can have values of yes or no. The value yes states required entity declarations are within the XML document, and the value no states that the XML document has an external DTD.

In changing encoding value you can incorporate different character sets, enabling you to write XML documents in different languages as in Example 3-13.

Example 3-13

```
<?xml version="1.0" encoding="ISO-8859-2"?>
```

supports Slavic, Latin languages such as Slovenian, Croatian, and Bosnian (if the browser and operational system support the character sets as well), as in

```
<?xml version="1.0" encoding="windows-1250"?>
<?xml-stylesheet type="text/css" href="slovene.css"?>
```

An example of Russian encoding is

```
<?xml version="1.0" encoding="K016-R"?>
```

EXERCISES

3.1 In the following example, what mistakes have been made? How many errors are there?

```
<?xml version=_1.0_?>
<!-- Address Book/>
<addressbook>
   <persons>
     <name>Tech Cafe</name>
     <adress>2500 Lawrence Expressway</adress>
     <city>Sunnyvale</city>
     <@state>CA</@state>
     <Country>US</Country>
     <zip>94087</ZIP>
   </person>
</addressbook>
```

3.2 What is prolog in the following XML document?

```
<?xml version="1.0" ?>
<weather_forecast>
    <date>01.01.2003</date>
    <weather>snow</weather>
    <temperature>32F</temperature>
</weather_forecast>
```

3.3 Find the errors in the following XML document:

```
<!-- Ship Manifest -->
<?xml version="1.0" >
<fleet>
  <ship>Hood</ship>
  <Country>UK</country>
  <type>Destroyer</type>
  <19 year of production>1934</19 year of production>
</fleet>
```

3.4 Look at the dialog below of Caesar and Antony from the play *Julius Caesar* and make an XML document for it. Name the file `caesar.xml`. Create two .css files to best present the dialog (a) as though it were a modern screenplay (`caesar_screen.css`) and (b) as though it were a web replica of an old manuscript (`caesar_manus.css`).

CAESAR

Let me have men about me that are fat;

Sleek-headed men and such as sleep o' nights:

Yond Cassius has a lean and hungry look;

He thinks too much: such men are dangerous.

ANTONY

Fear him not, Caesar; he's not dangerous;

He is a noble Roman and well given.

CAESAR

Would he were fatter! But I fear him not:

Yet if my name were liable to fear,

I do not know the man I should avoid

So soon as that spare Cassius. He reads much;

He is a great observer and he looks

Quite through the deeds of men: he loves no plays,

As thou dost, Antony; he hears no music;

Seldom he smiles, and smiles in such a sort

As if he mock'd himself and scorn'd his spirit

That could be moved to smile at any thing.

Such men as he be never at heart's ease

Whiles they behold a greater than themselves,

And therefore are they very dangerous.

I rather tell thee what is to be fear'd

Than what I fear; for always I am Caesar.

Come on my right hand, for this ear is deaf,

And tell me truly what thou think'st of him.

3.5 A construction order for lumber includes characters that could be misunderstood by a parser. Rewrite the following using `PCDATA`, once by name, and a second time by number.

Lumber grade for 2 x 4s should be Std & Btr or above
Lumber > 4 × 14 should be #1 FOHC
Lumber > 2 × 6 & < 4 × 12 should be #2 & Btr or better

3.6 Add two additional famous people to the famous people example described earlier in the chapter (example 3-9). One person should be an artist, another a Nobel Prize winner.

3.7 Write and name an entity for an XML document (not yet for the DTD) for the following information:

Your Order Has Been Sent.
Your seller will ship within two business days. Books.com will send a confirmation of your purchase via email. Please refer any questions related to your shipment to the seller at sales@usedbooks.com.

3.8 Write an XML prolog incorporating encoding for the Japanese language, defined by the international organization for standards (ISO) as ISO-2022-JP.

3.9 NAMESPACES

The use of namespaces is not mandatory in XML but helps to ensure uniqueness among XML elements. In the next exercise there are several apartments for rent. The document includes common information such as the amount of the rents, how many bedrooms and bathrooms are in the apartment, and the apartment addresses. If there were several apartment or real estate web sites in XML, and if a user were moving from one apartment for rent site to another, there could be some confusion with the parser as to which site's definition of `<rent>`, `<beds>`, `<baths>`, `<address>` elements is correct. When two documents containing identical elements from different sites or sources merge, the elements are said to collide. Namespaces keep the documents and their element definitions separate by adding an identifier to differentiate one document's elements from another document's elements.

As discussed in Chapter 1, XHTML, namespace is a collection of names identified by a uniform resource identifier (URI). The Internet contains many points of content. A URI allows you to identify any of those points of content. The most common form of a URI is the web page address, which is a form or subset of URI called uniform resource locator (URL). Additionally, qualified names from XML namespaces may contain a single colon, separating the name into a namespace prefix and a local part. The combination of the URI namespace and the document's local part produces identifiers that are universally unique.

The namespace is often declared in the root element of the document but may be in any element. The namespace cannot be used until after it has been declared. An example of using the URL to the W3C site as a namespace is Example 3-14.

Example 3-14

```
<?xml version="1.0"?>
<?xml-stylesheet type="text/css" href="wine.css"?>
<wine
   xmlns="http://www.w3c.org">
<name>Kraski Teran</name>
```

A company's human resource department may have several XML applications. As such, namespace may look more like Example 3-15.

Example 3-15

```
<?xml version="1.0"?>
<?xml-stylesheet type="text/css" href="globalSales.css"?>
<sales xmlns:local="http://www.company.com"
   xmlns:regional="http://www.EU.company.com"
   xmlns:global="http://www.global.company.com">
```

Namespace is used in additional XML technologies, such as extensible stylesheet language (XSL), and will be discussed again in later chapters.

EXERCISES

As mentioned in the chapter introduction, it is important to practice keying the basic XML structure before moving on to the XML-related technologies. Below is an example of how you might track apartments for rent.

3.9 Key the file (name it `apartment.xml`), making adjustments to allow for possible searching options on a web site.

```
<?xml version="1.0"?>
<?xml-stylesheet type="text/css" href="apartment.css"?>
<apartment
   xmlns="http://www.bonanzaApartments.com">
   <offer>
     <availDate>07/01</availDate>
     <information>
       <rent>1600.00</rent>
       <beds>1 Bed</beds>
       <baths>1 Bath</baths>
     </information>
     <location>
       <address>997 Palm Drive</address>
       <cityState>Millbrae, CA</cityState>
     </location>
   </offer>
```

```
    <offer>
      <availDate>07/15</availDate>
      <information>
        <rent>1400.00</rent>
        <beds>1 Bed</beds>
        <baths>1 Bath</baths>
      </information>
      <location>
        <address>824 Acorn Street</address>
        <cityState>Daly City, CA</cityState>
      </location>
    </offer>
    <offer>
      <availDate>06/29</availDate>
      <information>
        <rent>1300.00</rent>
        <beds>2 Bed</beds>
        <baths>1 Bath</baths>
      <location>
        <address>1961 Central Avenue</address>
        <cityState>Hayward, CA</cityState>
      </location>
    </offer>
    <offer>
      <availDate>07/01</availDate>
      <information>
        <rent>1600.00</rent>
        <beds>2 Bed</beds>
        <baths>1.5 Bath</baths>
      </information>
      <location>
        <address>4210 National Drive</address>
        <cityState>San Jose, CA</cityState>
      </location>
    </offer>
</apartment>
```

Key the .css file (`apartment.css`):

```
offer{
    display:block;
    width: 350px;
    background-color: silver;
    color: navy;
    text-align:center;
     }
availDate, rent{
```

```
          display:block;
          font-family:Arial, sans-serif;
          font-size:12;
          font-weight:bold;
                 }
      beds, baths{
          display:block;
          font-family:Arial;
          font-size:12;
          font-weight:normal;
            }
      address{
          display:block;
          font-family:Arial;
          font-size:11;
          font-weight:bold;
            }
     cityState{
          display:block;
          font-family:Arial;
          font-size:11;
          font-weight:bold;
            }
```

3.10 Review the files you created above. Make any adjustments to the files you think would simplify the code and offer better presentation of the information to clients interested in renting an apartment. Combine selectors where possible to reduce the CSS file size. Make any adjustments to combine or add attributes to XML for simpler maintenance and keying of the .css file.

3.11 The next document pertains to looking up and potentially transferring medication between physicians and a pharmacy over the Internet or a medical center Intranet. Name the files `healthnut.xml` and `healthnut_intra.css`. The next document pertains to looking up and potentially transferring medication between physicians and a pharmacy over the Internet or a medical center Intranet. Key the and two .css documents. Name the files healthnut.xml, healthnut_intra.css, and healthnut_kiosk.css. In one, the XML document will be for in-house, intranet use by physicians. In the other, the XML document will be for general information on a patient kiosk. Each should present with the audience in mind. Kiosks generally have larger screens, around 21 inches, do not have keyboards, and are touch-screen controlled. As such, your in-house Intranet output will be for a typical 15-inch monitor with keyboard, and your kiosk will be larger, with edited information, and you will need enough room for fingers to punch buttons and for novice users to interact with a simple interface. Add the style sheet link and use `<span>`.

```
<?xml version="1.0"?>
<!-- Non Prescription Section @ healthnut.com -->
<drug
    xmlns:nonpresc="http://www.healthnut.com">
      <name>aspirin</name>
      <content>0.4 g. acetisalicil acid, 0.24 g.
            ascorbine acid </content>
      <therapy>analgetic</therapy>
      <contraindication> ulcer, pregnancy
          </contraindication>
      <interaction_other_drugs>antireumatics
      </interaction_other_drug>
      <dosage>1-2 pills per day </dosage>
      <analogon="substitute">andol</analogon>
      <price="USD">5</price>
      <available>yes</available>
</drug>
```

3.12 The following XML document is describing ski jump competition. Name the file `skijump.xml`. Key the document and add a .css file, using two ski-related graphics from the web. Use `class` and <span> as you determine.

```
<?xml version="1.0"?>
<!-- Quarter Final Scores-Slovenia -->
<skijump_competition
   xmlns:Slovenia="http://www.olympicTrialScore.org">
   <athlete>Primoz Peterka</athlete>
   <country>Slovenia</country>
    <events>
     <length>130</length>
    </events>
    <results>
     <mark_first_judge>18.5</mark_first_judge>
     <mark_second_judge>17.5</mark_second_judge>
     <mark_third_judge>19.5</mark_third_judge>
     <mark_fourth_judge>18.5</mark_fourth_judge>
     <average>18.5</average>
     </results>
     <awards>
      <eventRank>1</eventRank>
      <overallRank>3</overallRank>
     </awards>
</skijump_competition>
```

3.13 Build an XML document that could be used for inventory system for maintenance of technological equipment. Create style sheets so that output will be used on:

(a) a handheld PDA with a 4" × 4" screen, and

(b) a web site to be used for e-commerce orders.

The elements of the document are:

Model Number

Part Number

Part Name

Availability in Local Warehouse

Warehouse Location

Supplier

Commerce Server URL

3.14 Build an XML document and a simple style sheet to be used for transferring water pollution data from a wastewater treatment plant to a pollution information center. Name the file `treatment_plant.xml`.

The data that will be transferred are

(a) Location

(b) Time

(c) pH value

(d) biological oxygen demand (BOD) value

(e) Content of heavy metals in water

3.10 XML HIERARCHICAL STRUCTURE

So far, you have worked with XML documents from the perspective of semantic, structure, and style. This focus helps you to determine what data needs to be associated with content, its organization, and its presentation. You know the basic semantic rules necessary for an XML parser to identify a well-formed or a valid document. You know how a XML file looks and, in a short time, will have no problem getting XML to do what you used to do with HTML.

The difference between XML and HTML, though, is that with XML, this basic understanding is only the beginning. XML, as stated earlier, is about data manipulation. A good place to begin understanding XML data capabilities is with understanding the document tree structure of XML.

The term *document tree* is used as a metaphor for understanding the relationships and order of the document (Figure 3-1).

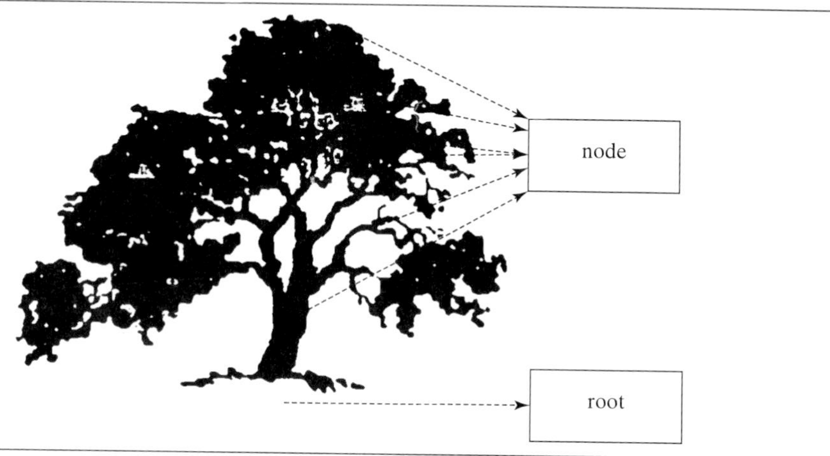

Figure 3-1 Document Tree as a Metaphor.

A document tree has only one root.

A document tree may have an unbounded number of nodes, at any level of the tree. In this example, `<trunk>`, `<limb>`, `<branch>`, `<twig>`, `<leaf>`, could, in turn, have many multiples of themselves. The limitation of high numbers of nodes is an increase in processing time.

The hierarchy of a document tree can be represented as in Figure 3-2.

The document tree, made of one root and multiple nodes, is referred to in the parent-child hierarchy for the purpose of planning, organizing, and accessing data. The relationships between the parents, children, and siblings allow for ease of navigation between nodes, ease of adding additional nodes, and ease of manipulating data within nodes. This hierarchical approach to data organization becomes critical in XML developing the document object model (DOM) and extensible stylesheet language transformation (XSLT) (Figure 3-2).

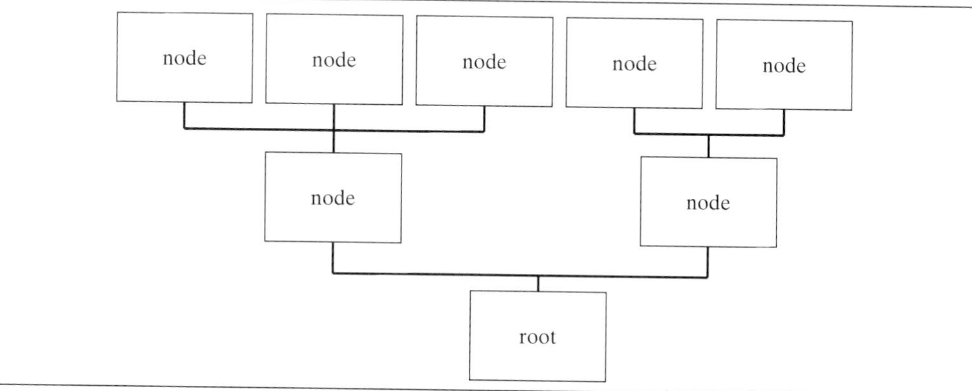

Figure 3-2 Hierarchy of a Document Tree.

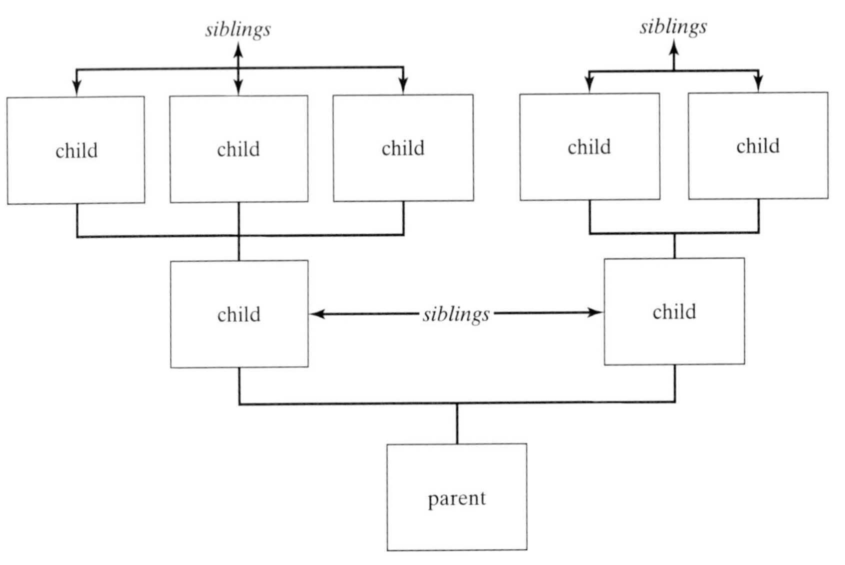

Figure 3-3 Parent-Child Hierarchy.

The document tree and code in Figure 3-4 begin to explain and show the importance of planning and organizing the XML document.

The layout for the document tree has been adjusted due to available space on the page. As you can see, there is one root element `<flight>` and 16 nodes. Those nodes without < and > are text nodes and can be manipulated in the same manner as the XML elements. The code for this document tree would be in Example 3-16.

Example 3-16

```
<?xml version="1.0"?>
<flight>
<number>084<plane>Boeing 747</plane></number>
<company>Air France</company>
<from>Paris<departure>13:20</departure></from>
<to>San Francisco<arrival>16:25</arrival></to>
<status>on time</status>
</flight>
```

You will key the code for your document, but the browser will build the document tree and determine if it is well formed. The effectiveness of processing the XML document is determined by the way you organize and nest elements. New developers have a tendency to develop "flat files" as shown in Example 3-17.

Example 3-17

```
<?xml version="1.0"?>
<flight>
<number>084</number>
<plane>Boeing 747</plane>
<company>Air France</company>
<from>Paris</from>
<departure>13:20</departure>
<to>San Francisco</to>
<arrival>16:25</arrival>
<status>on time</status>
</flight>
```

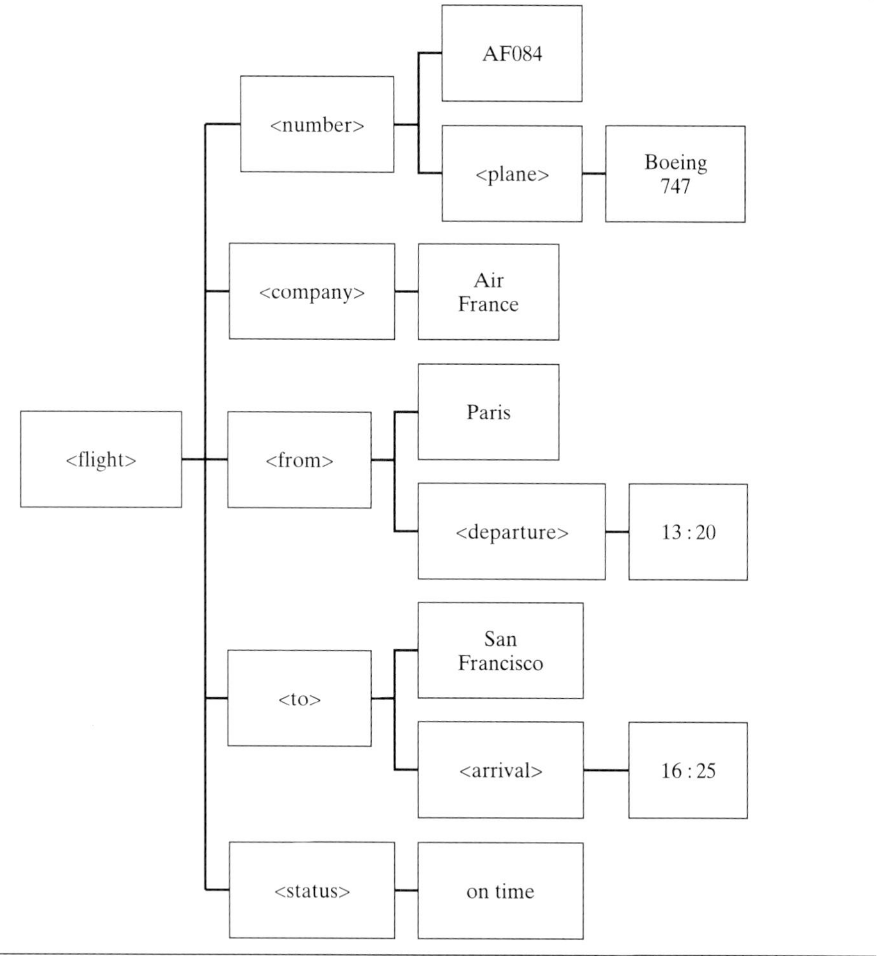

Figure 3-4 Example Document Tree Incorporating XML Elements.

Although this file will parse as well-formed, its structure is not set up for effective data manipulation. Important to developing XML applications is understanding how the user may want to access information.

For now, key both examples of the Air France code; the first example is nested, the second is not. View the source code for each in your browser and notice the differences in the respective document trees. Were the document larger or more complex, you can readily see the difference in how the trees would look, and later you will understand how that difference translates into more effective XML applications.

3.11 XML PARSERS

Parsers are tools that analyze XML documents for correct syntax. There are two types of parsers:

1. Non-validating parsers that ensure a data object is well-formed
2. Validating parsers that use a DTD to ensure the validity of a well-formed data object's form and content

Parsers do nothing to suggest how the XML document's structure could be organized better or the elements named more effectively. The parser's job is to check if the document is made according to the syntax rules of XML 1.0.

Parsers start from the top of an XML document, looking at the first elements (typically within the prolog), checking to see if the element meets XML syntax rules. If the syntax is not correct, possibly because of a tag not properly closed, a message error appears and parsing stops. After the error is corrected, the parser runs again until it locates another error. If there are no errors, an array is built with data about the type of node, and the parser proceeds to the next element, again to check if it is well formed. When the parser reaches a non-empty element, it checks all of the element's child nodes as it does for all other nodes, again saving the information about the node into the array.

When the parser comes to the end of the document and determines that the document is well formed, it produces a parse tree (a set of arrays) that can be passed on to the XML processor. The arrays can be handed off to an application using object properties via an application programming interface (DOM as an example) or as a class an application can refer to.

A validating parser additionally compares each element in the parse tree to its associated DTD. The parser may:

1. Build a logic structure from the DTD and match the document against this structure
2. Iterate through the XML document again and match the elements against the DTD

In addition to a tree-based parser, an event-driven parser executes a call-back to the application for each class of XML data (elements with or without attributes, processing instructions, comments, notation). An event-driven parser doesn't maintain the element tree structure or any data after it parses. The event-driven method, however, requires modest system resources.

3.12 MODELING

The ability of a parser to check for syntax errors potentially saves time in application development. XML will not run if the code is not exactly correct. Parsers can greatly increase the functionality of the code, but what about the functionality of the application? You determine how well an XML application functions for the user. Your constant question should be: **What will we/they do with the data?**

Good XML application design begins by thinking about all possible applications of the data. As an example,

You are hired to develop an Intranet application. You are given a list of the information to be collected and accessed on the Intranet. The list includes

1. Name
2. Social Security Number
3. Birth Date
4. Age
5. Height
6. Weight
7. Fingerprints
8. Nationality
9. Street Address
10. City, State
11. Phone Number
12. Email Address

It seems simple enough to create an XML document with these 12 common items. However, read the three possible Intranet applications below and determine which 4 of the 12 items is the most important for the user to access.

1. The human resources organization of a start-up company
2. The homicide division of a police department
3. The event planners for a holiday cruise ship

At first glance, the human resources organization is simple; some of the questions are illegal to ask. However, what if it turned out the start-up used fingerprint identifiers for secure access? In the context of a homicide investigation, name, height, weight, nationality, and fingerprints are critical data. Do you see how different the priorities of the homicide division would be from the itinerary of a cruise ship roster?

In all of these cases, the strength of the XML application is in its design. The parser helps you to keep the syntax for the document to run, but you develop the application for the document to be used. Parsing errors can be corrected easily enough. Errors in the planning phase can be difficult and expensive to correct.

Even in the simplest applications, it is important to determine what data you will need, how you will access the data, what names make the most effective elements, and how the data will be used. A constant focus on "What is the purpose? Who is the audience?" will help you to design from the user's perspective.

Here is a very simple Example 3-18.

Example 3-18

```
<vegetable>tomato</vegetable>
<price>$1.49 per pound</price>
<vegetable>potato</vegetable>
<price>$.69 per pound</price>
```

This is a well-formed document but not optimal as an application. If the user wanted to find the price of a vegetable, it would be difficult because the items are not separated. Finding a price would be easier with this approach as in Example 3-19.

Example 3-19

```
<product>
<vegetable>tomato</vegetable>
<price>$1.49 per pound</price>
</product>
<product>
<vegetable>potato</vegetable>
<price>$.69 per pound</price>
</product>
```

This again well-formed document allows for separation of product, but what if the user wanted to add, calculate, or average prices? The content of `<price>` is a string, not a number. An attribute is one possible solution, as in Example 3-20.

Example 3-20

```
<product>
<vegetable>tomato</vegetable>
<price currency="$" weightUnit="pound">1.49</price>
</product>
<product>
```

```
<vegetable>potato</vegetable>
<price currency="$" weightUnit="pound">.69</price>
</product>
```

If you decided to do a mathematical operation with price, you will have only numbers, not numbers as a part of a string where you will need to extract a number. If you decide to change currency or weight units, the attributes described allow for ease of editing. There are several possible solutions to how the code for this simple XML application could be designed. The best solution would be the one that meets the needs and expectations of the user.

EXERCISES

3.15 The Household Appliance Manufacturing Company is selling products on the web (www.hamshop.com). Create an XML document showing what they will be selling. Name the document `hamshop.xml`. Format the site taking into consideration the following information:

The HAM Company has two main customer groups. The first is large construction companies who typically order for tract home projects and apartment buildings. Although there may be hundreds of homes and apartments on each of their projects, the construction companies typically ask for delivery in multiples of 15. The second customer group is retail customers who expect to see more information about the features of each appliance and receive more help from the site in the decision-making process.

The construction companies place large orders on account, typically with a purchase order number. The retail customers prefer to use Visa, Master Card, or American Express.

Refrigerators, freezers, washing machines, dryers, microwave ovens
For every kind of product the following data should be available:
Type
Brand
Model Name
Model Number
Dimension
Available Colors
Energy Consumption Information
Price
Delivery Time
Web Site of Service and Additional Information from the Manufacturer

3.16 Print the XML document you created above. Label the nodes as parent, first child, and last child.

3.17 Create an XML document with the following information. Name the document `IS_EU_Slovenia.xml`. Format the document as a table (`IS_EU_Slovenia.css`) for presentation purposes on an international conference web site.

Here is a short report on a survey about interest in services of the Information Society: European Union (EU) and Slovenia. In July 1999 a telephone survey (n = 1,000) was conducted by Research Internet in Slovenia (RIS) in cooperation with project Incopernicus of the Institute for Economic Research. Questions about interest in various services of the information society were included in the survey. The questions originated in *Eurobarometer* (*EB* 50.1), which at the end of the year 1998 measured such opinion in countries of the EU. The question ran: "Next, we will state some services of the information society and you can tell us whether you are interested in using each of them or not." The June results were surprisingly high for such questions and it was assumed the cause was the influence of holiday time, and so the survey was repeated in September, but the high scores remained. Table 3-2 shows percentages of interest, both June's and September's, and for the EU the average from *EB* 50.1 (end of year 1998).

Table 3-2 Example Data for Exercise 3-17.

Information Service	Slovenia	EU (average)
Online medical diagnosis	54.2/54.5	41.9
Contact with MPs	18.7/15.6	10.9
Education	55.2/50.4	33.9
Providing of consumer's rights information	63.7/55.6	33.4
Official/administrative services	54.5/58.6	47.8

Interest in information society (Source: *EB* 50.1, RIS)

3.18 An information technology (IT) company recently decided to make an Internet survey for feedback on a large IT fair. Name the file `ITfair.xml`. The following information needs to be on the questionnaire. Format the document with CSS (`ITfair.css`) for use on a kiosk with a 21-inch screen with a touch-screen keyboard on the bottom 7". You will later transfer results out to participating vendors.

First, build an XML document for a questionnaire to include

Participant Name
Organization
Position
Email

What three things most interested you in the IT fair?
What three vendors were the most helpful?
What product or vendors would you have liked to see that were not here?
Did you purchase items or attend for informational purposes?
How would you rate this IT fair in comparison to others you attend?
How did you hear about the fair?
Did you have any obstacles in registering, eating, finding your way around?
Please list any additional comments.

3.19 An outside contractor started the following XML document and style sheet (`spareParts.xml` and `spareParts.css`). The style sheet needs to be edited to make it very clear for ordering in warehouse environments and subcontractor shops. The XML document needs to be organized differently.

The priority of the client is to be able to access product by part number and to have the part type show immediately after. Once a number and type have been identified, the client wants to know if the product is available, and where it is located. Later plans include the ability to search by article designation and by type with its definition attached.

```
<?xml version ="1.0"?>
<?xml-stylesheet type="text/css" href="spareParts.css"?>
<!-- www.spareParts.com partial listing stockcheck prototype -->
<spare_parts
      xmlns="http://www.spareParts.com">
   <part_no>104524</part_no>
   <type>FLP-45-4</type>
   <article_designation>Sub-base</article_designation>
   <description>With barbed fitting PK-4, for valves
   </description>
   <location>Union City Warehouse</location>
   <on_hand period="monthlyCount">120 cases @ 48 ct</on_hand>
   <part_no>104520</part_no>
   <type>VLH-345-1/2</type>
   <article_designation>Single pilot pneumatic
   soft-start valve</article_designation>
   <description>Normally closed, slow start-up valve
   </description>
   <location>Union City Warehouse</location>
   <on_hand period="monthlyCount">80 cases @ 36 ct</on_hand>
   <part_no>104521</part_no>
   <type>MFE-3-1/2</type>
   <article_designation>Solenoid valve
   </article_designation>
   <description>Start-up valve for delayed pressure
```

```
   </description>
   <location>Oakland Warehouse</location>
   <on_hand period="monthlyCount">40 cases @ 24 ct</on_hand>
   <part_no>104508</part_no>
   <type>CEP-1/4-NPT-B</type>
   <article_designation>End plate</article_designation>
   <description>For manifold mounting of valves Type
   CJ-, CJM-, CL-, CM-... </description>
   <location>Richmond Warehouse</location>
   <on_hand period="monthlyCount">66 cases @ 48 ct</on_hand>
</spare_parts>
```

The existing CSS code is

```
spare_parts {
display:block;
width:250px;
text-align:center;
}
part_no{
display:block;
font-family:Arial;
font-size:16pt;
font-weight:bold;
}
type{
display:block;
font-family:Arial;
font-size:16pt;
font-weight:bold;
}
article_designation{
display:block;
font-family:Arial;
font-size:14pt;
font-style:oblique;
font-weight:bolder;
}
description{
display:block;
font-family:Arial;
font-size:12pt;
font-style:italic;
}
```

CHAPTER SUMMARY

1. Three files are typically processed by an XML compliant application, the XML document, the style sheet, and the schema or DTD.
2. An XML element name must start with a letter or an underscore. Numbers, hyphens, periods, or additional underscores can follow, and there is no limit to characters per element.
3. Colons are permitted only for specifying namespaces.
4. Whitespace and symbols are illegal in an element name.
5. Non-empty elements must have a start and end tag.

   ```
   <sales> </sales>
   ```

6. XML supports empty elements, typically used to add non-text content to a document. XML empty elements must still contain a forward slash.

   ```
   <logo src="company.gif" />
   ```

7. XML tags must be nested correctly.

   ```
   <partNumber>..<partName>..</partName>..</partNumber>
   ```

   Incorrect nesting will not parse, as in

   ```
   <partNumber>..<partName>..</partNumber>..</partName>
   ```

8. XML documents begin with the XML declaration that specifies the XML version used. The XML declaration, while not mandatory for XHTML, is mandatory in an XML document. The initial portion of a document, preceding the first element, is the prolog. The prolog contains only declarations, whitespace, comments, and processing instructions.
9. XML is case sensitive. All declarations and markup must match in case. This applies throughout XML processing. Additionally, the name XML is reserved.
10. Attributes consist of a name and a value and must appear in the start tag or the empty-element tag. The attribute name paired with its quoted value, is an attribute specification.

    ```
    <anthology proverb="journey">
    ```

    The attribute value may use `" "` or `' '`, but it must always be quoted and follow the same character restrictions as element names.
11. Comments in XML match comments in XHTML. Comments cannot nest inside of a markup and cannot come before the XML declaration.

```
<?xml version="1.0"?>
<!-- Comment. -->
```

12. All XML documents consist of characters. There are two types of character data in XML documents.

    PCDATA, which has to be parsed

    CDATA, which is not parsed

    Elements consist of PCDATA and attributes of CDATA
13. There are two type of entities, general and parameter. General entities are used in XML documents and parameter entities are used in DTDs.
14. Along with the XML declaration you can define an optional encoding attribute representing legal character encoding. There are several encoding values; the parser must support at least UTF-8 and UTF-16 Unicode.
15. The use of namespaces is not mandatory in XML but helps to ensure uniqueness among XML elements.
16. The document tree, made of one root and multiple nodes, is referred to in the parent-child hierarchy for the purpose of planning, organizing, and accessing data. The relationships between the parents, children, and siblings allow for ease of navigation between nodes, ease of adding additional nodes, and ease of manipulating data within nodes.
17. Parsers are tools that analyze XML documents for correct syntax. There are two types of parsers.

    Non-validating parsers that ensure a data object is well formed
    Validating parsers that use a DTD to ensure the validity of a well-formed data object's form and content
    Parsers do nothing to suggest how the XML document's structure could be organized better or the elements named more effectively. The parser's job is to check if the document is made according to the syntax rules of XML 1.0.

18. Good XML application design begins by thinking about all possible applications of the data.

SELF-ASSESSMENT

To move on to the next chapter, you should feel comfortable that you understand and can do the following:

1. Plan and create a well-nested XML document web site.
2. Check to see if an XML document is well formed or valid.

3. Work with processing instructions, attributes, entities, comments, PCDATA, and CDATA.
4. Display XML using CSS.
5. Present a document tree from an XML document.
6. Demonstrate an understanding of namespaces.
7. Transfer, using modeling, a commercial problem into an XML document.

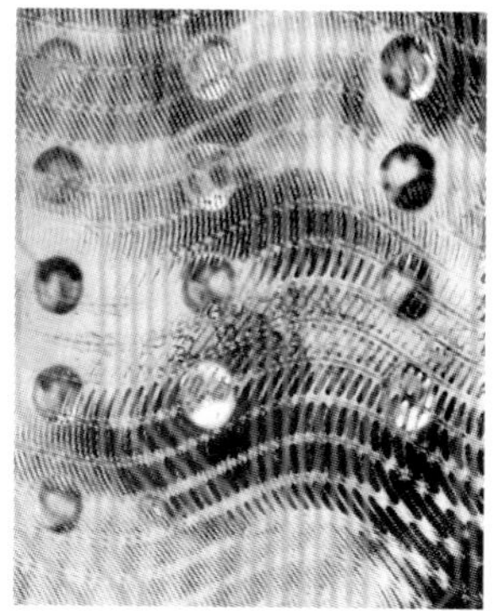

4 Document Object Model

CHAPTER OBJECTIVES

By reading the information and practicing the code in this chapter, you will understand and be able to

1. Create XML documents based on the document object model hierarchical tree structure. Navigate and modify XML documents using document object model (DOM).
2. Prepare XML documents using DOM nodes root, children, and siblings.
3. Develop DOM objects to be accessed for data manipulation purposes.
4. Work with node properties and methods in simple applications.
5. Use JavaScript with Microsoft ActiveX technology and ActiveX XML island to manipulate XML documents.
6. Apply node properties and methods for traversing XML documents and modifying the document tree.

4.1 MANIPULATING DATA

Commercial customers rarely go to a URL to see what a company's web site looks like. Commercial customers go to a commercial site to do business with a company. The decisions that go into commercial site development are nearly identical to the decisions a company makes to add a physical operation such as a store, plant, or service center. Commercial customers care about the same issues in either an online or an in-person delivery format. They use language such as knowledgeable staff, easy to get around, stock what I need, reasonable prices, product availability, helpful information, and fast service to describe a positive business experience with a company or organization.

The ability to provide the type and level of services to meet customer expectations begins with, but goes beyond screen design and text or graphic presentation. Customers want to be able to access the information, products, and services they are looking for. Extensible hypertext markup language (XHTML) or extensible markup language (XML), with cascading style sheets (CSS) or extensible style language (XSL) (outside of extensible style language transformation [XSLT]), allow for sophisticated presentation, but they do not allow companies and customers to sort, move, or modify information.

The document object model (DOM) allows data to be read, searched, modified, manipulated, added, and deleted from an XML document.

Until now you have used XML to present information to be read by the user. Current web sites use a combination of this presented information and HTML-based forms for users to key in data to be collected. This presentation/form collection model does not begin to satisfy the needs of either the company or the user in commercial web site development. It is not enough to display information; users want to find, combine, and access information as they need it. As mentioned earlier, users want to do business within a site. Additionally, companies want to offer their services, products, and expertise in various formats for targeted audiences. Sophisticated or innovative presentation limits options between the parties and slows interactive information sharing, resulting in much of the customer transactions still taking place offline.

DOM allows for web-based transactions that significantly improve the capabilities of commercial web sites. With DOM, you develop a model to manipulate the data in a document. First, an XML document(s) is created. Second, using DOM, applications are designed and developed to either access data from the XML document, collect or sort data from existing databases, or allow multiple users to access, combine, and manipulate data or modify data output platforms.

DOM is an application programming interface (API) for HTML, XHTML, and XML documents, providing a standardized, versatile view of a document's contents. DOM defines the logical structure of the document's data and the way the document data is accessed and manipulated. DOM may also be used to manage this data. Important to this process is the concept, throughout development, that the document, its data, and the multiple output possibilities will not be confined to the average 15-inch monitor. XML data, managed by DOM, may be output on multiple platforms and formats where presentation may include a 2-inch monitor, a Braille-based user agent, a voice-based Internet connection in a vehicle, and more. Most data found in an XHTML or XML document can be accessed, modified, added, or deleted using the DOM.

The World Wide Web Consortium (W3C) DOM is language and platform neutral, interfaces are defined for different objects and a common vocabulary is used for manipulating the XML document. Applications written in C, Java, JavaScript, Visual Basic, Perl, or Python utilize the same methods (commands) whether the user is viewing the site with Netscape, Internet Explorer, or Opera, the script will work when implemented with DOM.

This chapter focuses on DOM Level 1. Information about DOM Level 2 and DOM Level 3 is located on the companion web site (www.prenhall.com/carey) and is updated as the technologies evolve. The purpose of DOM Level 1, according to the W3C, is to concentrate on core HTML and XML document models and functionality for document navigation and manipulation.

DOM Level 2 includes a style sheet object model and defines the functionality for manipulating a document's style information. DOM Level 2 additionally enables traversals on a document, define an event model, and provide support for XML namespaces.

DOM Level 3 addresses document loading and saving, content models such as DTDs and Schemas (with validation support). DOM Level 3 also addresses document views and formatting, key events, and event groups.

Future DOM levels may specify some interface with the possibly underlying window system, including some ways to prompt the user. They may also contain a query language interface, and address multithreading and synchronization, security, and repository. Additional information regarding the purpose of DOM and future capabilities may be found at the w3.org web site.

4.2 DOM LEVEL 1

DOM is based on an XML file hierarchical tree structure that can be represented as an object collection. Using DOM, you can access different parts of an XHTML or XML document to change and modify data. One thing to keep in mind, though, is that large XML files require memory of approximately the document size × 10, for processing. In other words, a 100K file can require about 1MB of memory for processing; this can be a problem, depending on your computer and available memory. The processing of these large XML documents can take significant time because of the memory requirements of processing DOM.

Two alternative technologies to DOM are SAX and XSLT (DOM and SAX can also be used together).

Simple API for XML (SAX) is simpler and was developed to avoid memory and time problems that may appear when using DOM. SAX does not require the entire XML document to be saved in memory during processing, is event-based, gives read only access, and is preferable for use with large documents. However, SAX does not allow the same level of in-depth modification available with DOM.

XSL Transformation Language (XSLT) is a declarative language, based on DOM, and represents a tool for processing XML documents on a high level. However, it does not have the modify, search, replace flexibility of DOM, resulting in a simple, strong technology highly dependent on its application use and its limited, linear approach to passing through a search.

4.3 DOM NODES

As you know, XML documents follow a logical structure resembling a tree, or a group of trees. When DOM is used to manipulate an XML document, it parses the file, breaking it into individual elements, attributes, entities, processing instructions, and comments. Next, DOM creates (in memory) a representation of the XML file as a node tree. DOM treats every item in the document as a **node**, from an element to a single character of content. A node is defined as any part of the document, whether it be element, attribute, entity, content, or comment. An entire document can become part of a node tree, rather than only its nodes. DOM interacts with the different nodes of the tree(s), accessing and modifying content as designed by the developer.

The Air France document tree (Figure 4-1) from the previous chapter is a good place to begin to see how nodes are accessed.

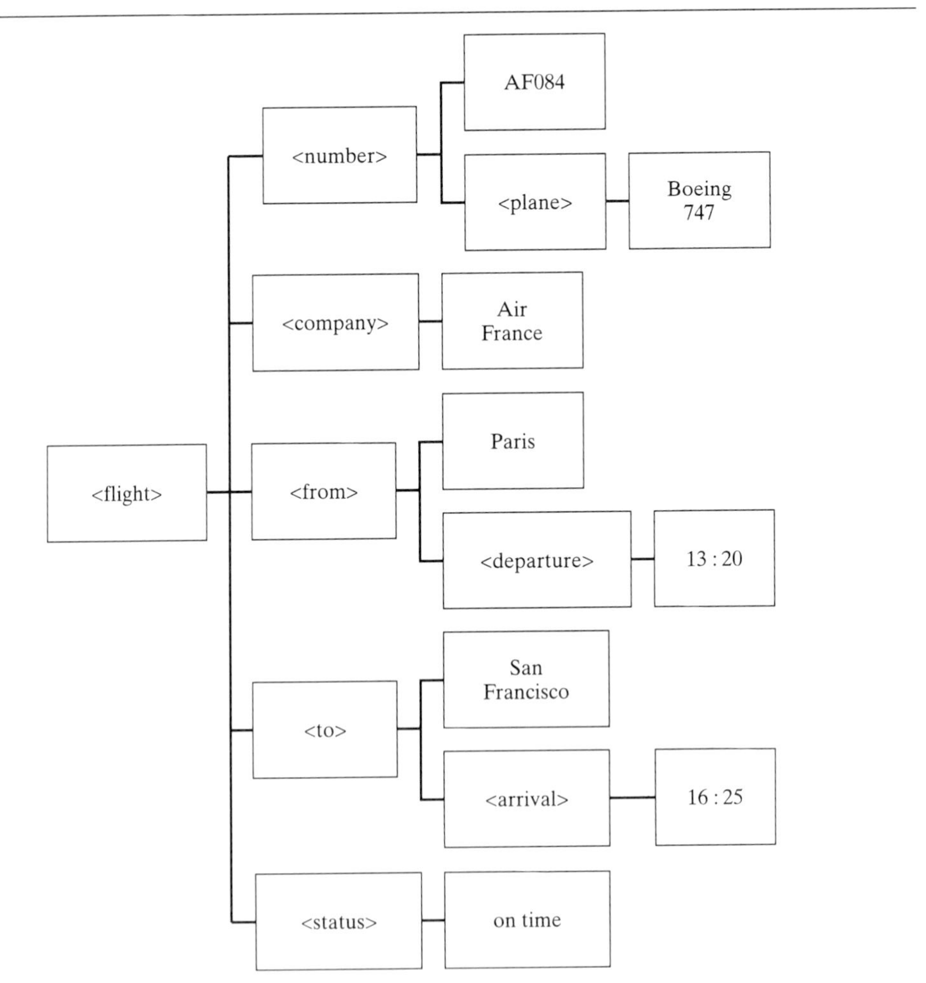

Figure 4-1 Tree Diagram of an XML Document.

From the tree diagram you can see that:

1. The root element has five children
2. The first child is <number>
3. The last child is <status>
4. Siblings are <number>, <company>, <from>, <to>, and <status> because they have the same parent, <flight>
5. The next sibling to the first child is <company>
6. The previous sibling to the last child is <to>
7. The next sibling to the next sibling of the first child is <from>
8. The first child of the root element has two children

   AF 084, which is the content of <number>
   And <plane> with one content child, Boeing 747

9. <company> has only one child, it's content, Air France
10. <from> has two children, content Paris and <departure>, with its content child 13:20
11. <to> has two children, content San Francisco and <arrival> with its content child 16:25
12. <status> has one content child, on time

If you want to find a specific element, there are several possible approaches:

1. You can make a list of all children of the root element <flight> and say, "find the 5th child."
2. You can say, "Find the last child of the root element."
3. You can say, "Find an element with the tag name <status>." If there is more one than element, you will receive a list.

If you want to find the content of <status> you might request

1. the first child of the 5th child of root element <flight>
2. the first child of the last child of root element <flight>
3. the first child of the element with the tag name <status>

You can make changes to the XML document tree such as

1. Add a comment element before the second child of root <flight>
2. Delete the last child of <flight>
3. Change the content of <status> to delayed
4. Copy the entire tree and add it to another XML document

EXERCISES

4.1 Draw a document tree for following XML document:

```
<?xml version="1.0"?>
<countryList>
<country>
<name>Slovenia</name>
<capital>Ljubljana</capital>
<population>2 million</population>
</country>
<country>
<name>Italy</name>
<capital>Rome</capital>
<population>56 million</population>
</country>
</countryList>
```

4.2 What is the root element in the following document?

```
<?xml version="1.0"?>
<example>
<!--Example for parent-child relationship-->
<company>
<name>Inova</name>
<address zip="3320">Velenje</address>
<phone>386 3 5875476</phone>
<fax>386 3 5874949</fax>
<email>inova@siol.net</email>
</company>
</example>
```

4.3 Which elements in the document above are

(a) the first child of root element
(b) the last child of root element
(c) the next sibling of first child of `<company>`
(d) the previous sibling of last child of `<company>`

4.4 Construct an XML document if you know that

(a) the root element of the document is `<phoneList>`
(b) the first child of `root` is comment, "example of how to construct XML using parent-children relationships."
(c) the last child of the root element has the tag name `<contact>` and the following children:

first child `<name>Stropnik</name>`

next sibling to first child `<address>Ljubljana</address>`

last child `<phoneNumber>386 1 8913345</phoneNumber>`

previous sibling to last child `<street>Jamova 42</street>`

The DOM, as an API, allows you all of the above described activities.

4.4 THE DOM TREE

In DOM, nodes represent objects with functions and identities. These objects represent both the structure of the document and the behavior of the document and its objects. Nodes act as interfaces and objects to represent and manipulate a document. DOM identifies these interfaces and their objects, semantics, relationships, and collaboration.

The words *nodes* and *objects* may be referred to interchangeably. The term *interface* is not related to the interface between the user and computer. Rather, interface refers to behavior with objects. One interface may work with multiple objects, acting as a kind of umbrella over object behavior. As an example, you may want to add data to several objects. Rather than set up each object to add data, an interface can be used to add data to multiple objects.

Because most XML documents are dynamic, it is preferable to use models that describe intrinsic parts of a document and allow modification of the document. In the W3C DOM, the concept of the tree and object are integrated into a single model. DOM does not specify all documents must be implemented as trees or how relationships between objects will be implemented. The tree refers to the structural model used to represent the document. If more than one document object model is used to represent one document, one shared structural model will be created.

Each tree model contains

1. Zero or one `DOCTYPE` nodes
2. One root element node that serves as the document's root element tree
3. Zero or more comments or processing instructions

To review, with the tree model, the document is represented as a collection of nodes. In this structure, each node has a parent. All nodes may also have a series of child nodes. This model allows for multiple approaches to processing an XML document. You may analyze the document as a whole, search for certain types of elements, and/or search and modify certain content. Processing instruction changes, adding a DTD, deleting a record, or any number of possibilities exist using the tree model and DOM.

4.5 BUILDING DOM

Document tree nodes may include the objects listed below. The W3C specifies these DOM objects can be accessed for data manipulation purposes.

Authors' Note: To review the definition of any term listed below, refer to Chapter 3, Extensible Markup Language.

1. Document

   The document object represents the whole document and may have the following children:

   One Element (called root)
   Processing Instruction
   Comment
   Document Type

2. Document Fragment

   A fragment of the document. It may have several nodes and may have the following children:

   Element
   Processing Instruction
   Comment
   Text
   CDATA
   Entity Reference

3. Document Type

   Allows access to the entities and notation contained in the DTD. It may have the following children:

   Notation (Notation declares external, non-XML content and the external application that handles that content. Attribute-type notation is often declared in a DTD to specify the non-XML data that will be within the XML document).

   Entity

4. Element

   The majority of nodes of the document will be element. It may have the following children:

   Element (if nested)
   Text

Comment
Processing Instruction
CDATASection
Entity Reference

5. Attribute

   In DOM, for attribute you will use Attr, to avoid confusion with an attribute keyword in the interface definition language (IDL) interface. Attributes may have the following children:

   Text and Entity Reference
6. Processing Instruction (may not have children)
7. Comment (may not have children)
8. Text (may not have children. Its content is a string value.)
9. CDATASection (may not have children)
10. Entity (may not have children)
11. Notation (may not have children)

4.5.1 Examples of DOM Nodes

Example 4-1

```
<?xml version="1.0"?>
<!DOCTYPE example SYSTEM "example.dtd">
  <?xml-stylesheet type="text/css" href="example.css"?>
<example>
  <!--example of node types-->
  <first type="simple">example</first>
</example>
```

The first line in Example 4-1 is the XML declaration.

`<!DOCTYPE example SYSTEM "example.dtd">` specifies the document type definition.

`<?xml-stylesheet type="text/css" href="example.css"?>` is a processing instruction.

`<example>` is the root element.

`<!--example of node types-->` is the comment.

`<first type="simple">example</first>` is an element with two nodes; `type="simple"`, is an attribute; and `example`, is a text element.

`</example>` closes the root.

4.6 DOM NODE PROPERTIES AND METHODS

All DOM nodes have properties and methods. These properties and methods allow for navigation through the DOM tree to access data and to modify the tree by adding or deleting nodes.

Every node has a node name, node value, and node type. Every node type may have the following properties and methods. Please study the definitions below; later you will implement these properties and methods in building your first DOM application.

4.6.1 The Node Object

The node object represents any node in the node tree. A node may be an element node, a text node, or any of the node types explained on the previous pages. All node types have properties and methods. Table 4-1 and 4-2 list the general properties and methods for all node types.

Table 4-1 Node Properties.

Name and Description
`attributes`
Returns a `NamedNodeMap` containing all attributes for this node
`childNodes`
Returns a `nodeList` containing all the child nodes for this node
`firstChild`
Returns the first child node for this node
`lastChild`
Returns the last child node for this node
`nextSibling`
Returns the next sibling node. Two nodes are siblings if they have the same parent node
`nodeName`
Returns the `nodeName`, depending on the type
`nodeType`
Returns the `nodeType` as a number
`nodeValue`
Returns, or sets, the value of this node, depending on the type
`ownerDocument`

Table 4-1 Node Properties. (continued)

Returns the document
`parentNode`
Returns the parent node for this node
`previousSibling`
Returns the previous sibling node. Two nodes are siblings if they have the same parent node

Table 4-2 Node Methods.

Name and Description
`appendChild(newChild)`
Appends the node `newChild` at the end of the child nodes for this node
`cloneNode(boolean)`
Returns an exact clone of this node. If the boolean value is set to true, the cloned node contains all the child nodes as well
`hasChildNodes()`
Returns true if this node has any child nodes
`insertBefore(newNode,refNode)`
inserts a new node, `newNode`, before the existing node, refNode
`removeChild(nodeName)`
Removes the specified code, nodeName
`replaceChild(newNode, oldNode)`
Replaces the `oldNode`, with the `newNode`

4.6.2 Node Types

All nodes are separated into different types. Table 4-3 lists these types and what the `.nodeName` and `.nodeValue` properties return.

Table 4-3 Node Types.

nodeType	nodeName	nodeValue
1 element	tagName	null
2 attribute	name	value
3 text	#text	content of node
4 CDATASection	#cdatasection	content of node

Table 4-3 Node Types. (continued)

nodeType	nodeName	nodeValue
5 entity reference	entity reference name	null
6 entity	entity name	null
7 processing instruction	target	content of node
8 comment	#comment	text
9 document	#document	null
10 document type	doctype name	null
11 document fragment	#document fragment	null
12 notation	notation name	null

If a is an element with the name `<address>` then `a.nodeName` will return `address` and `a.nodeValue` will return `null`.

If `b` is a node of type comment, such as, `<!--This is a comment-->`, then `b.nodeName` will return `#comment`. Additionally, `b.nodeName` and `b.nodeValue` will return `This is a comment`, the text of the comment.

If `c` is a node, in this case a processing instruction, `<?receive instruction?>`, then `c.nodeName` will return receive and `c.nodeValue` will return `instruction`.

For identification of DOM node types, see Table 4-4.

Table 4-4 Node Types—Named Constants.

Node Type	Named Constant
1	ELEMENT_NODE
2	ATTRIBUTE_NODE
3	TEXT_NODE
4	CDATA_SECTION_NODE
5	ENTITY_REFERENCE_NODE
6	ENTITY_NODE
7	PROCESSING_INSTRUCTION_NODE
8	COMMENT_NODE
9	DOCUMENT_NODE
10	DOCUMENT_TYPE_NODE
11	DOCUMENT_FRAGMENT_NODE
12	NOTATION_NODE

For the purpose of DOM document properties, see Table 4-5.

Table 4-5 Document Properties.

Name and Description
`documentElement`
Returns the root element of the document. There will be many cases when you choose to begin searching from the root element, as such, `documentElement` is a very important property
`doctype`
Returns the DTD or Schema for the document
`implementation`
Returns the implementation object for this particular document

EXERCISE

4.5 Using the XML document below (line numbers are for identification purposes). Fill in Table 4-6.

```
1. <?xml version="1.0"?>
2. <!DOCTYPE SnowReport PUBLIC weather/report>
3. <?xml-stylesheet type="text/css" href=" snowreport.css"?>
4. <!--These are not real data-->
5. <snowReport>
6. <location>Rogla</location>
7. <image>
8. <![CDATA["<img src='rogla.gif'>"]]></image>
9. <snowHeight>210cm</snowHeight>
10. </snowReport>
```

Table 4-6 Example Data for Exercise 4-5.

item line #	node type	node name	node value
1	7	xml	version="1.0"
2			
3			
4			
5			
6			
7			

Table 4-6 Example Data for Exercise 4-5. (continued)

item line #	node type	node name	node value
8			
9			
10			

4.7 GETTING STARTED

You can use the properties and methods in the previous tables to navigate and modify the DOM tree. The following examples explore their use.

The first example works with the properties `nodeName`, `nodeValue`, and `nodeType`.

As explained in Table 4-1, Node Properties,

`nodeName` returns the name of the node

`nodeType` returns the type of the node

`nodeValue` returns the value of the node

1. If a is the following element:

   `<capital>Washington</capital>`

   then,

   `a.nodeName` will be `<capital>`

   `a.nodeType` will be `1`

   `a.nodeValue` will be `null`

2. If `b` is the following comment:

   `<!--This is a comment-->`

   then,

   `b.nodeName` will be `#comment`

   `b.nodeType` will be 8

   `b.nodeValue` will be `This is a comment`

When you want to use the properties and methods of DOM nodes, you will load the XML document into memory to make the DOM document tree. The specifics of loading are not defined in the W3C DOM specification. As such, you will, for this text, use a solution developed by Microsoft and used in Internet Explorer 5 (IE5) or above, the current browser with native DOM Libraries.

Microsoft implemented DOM ActiveX, a set of technologies from Microsoft that enable interactive content for the web.

To load for use with IE5 or above, there are three possibilities.

1. to load using ActiveX, from the hard drive
2. to load using ActiveX, as a string, but only for very small XML documents
3. to load using XML Island as a signal to IE that you want to manipulate an XML document

Using DOM as an API requires you to write code that uses DOM specified properties and methods of `node` for navigation and manipulation of a document tree. The text examples will use JavaScript as the script language. If you do not know JavaScript, see the companion web site for a tutorial on those parts of JavaScript you need to develop DOM applications (typically basic JavaScript, loops, if statements, alert, and document.write)

4.7.1 DOM and JavaScript with Microsoft ActiveX

DOM with Microsoft ActiveX begins with an HTML document. The code that loads an XML document and makes a document tree in memory is

```
<script language="JavaScript">
var xmlDoc = new ActiveXObject("Microsoft.XMLDOM")
xmlDoc.async=false
xmlDoc.load("example.xml")
```

Authors' Note: In some documentation, `ActiveXObject("MSXML.DOMdocument")` is acceptable.

To understand this code, it can be broken down by line as in

1. `<script language="JavaScript">`
   identifies the scripting language as JavaScript.
2. `var xmlDoc = new ActiveXObject ("Microsoft.XMLDOM")`
   instantiates a Microsoft DOM object and assigns it to reference `xmlDOC`.
3. `xmlDoc.async=false`
   defines the way the document is loaded. Setting a document's `async` property to false results in a synchronous load (this means the browser will not continue processing until the document is fully loaded).
4. `xmlDoc.load("example.xml")`
   loads the file, `example.xml`, which must be in the same directory as your application. When `load` returns, the document should be fully loaded and parsed.
5. The filename extension for the JavaScript is .html

4.7.2 Subset of DOM with Microsoft ActiveX

If you are working with a small XML document (XML code is 30 to 50 lines or less, you will need to experiment with this), it is possible to parse and load the tree document as a string. You would use this option less often than the ActiveXObject above or the XML island below (Example 4-2).

Example 4-2

```
<script language="JavaScript">
var tstring="<flight>"
tstring=tstring+"<number>AF084</number>"
tstring=tstring+"<from>Paris</from>"
tstring=tstring+"<to>San Francisco</to>"
tstring=tstring+"</flight>"
var ourDoc=new ActiveXObject("Microsoft.XMLDOM")
ourDoc.async=false
ourDoc.loadXML(tstring)
alert(ourDoc.xml)
...
</script>
```

Authors' Note: Remember to save the JavaScript as an .html file.

In Example 4-6, `loadXML` was used to load and parse the document, which was created as a string. The alert (`ourDoc.xml`) will display the entire XML document, created in the described scenario.

4.7.3 DOM and JavaScript with XML Island

The same purpose can be met using XML island with an HTML document. The code, using XML island, to load an XML document and make a document tree in memory is Example 4-3.

Example 4-3

```
<html>
<xml id="island" src="example.xml"></xml>
<script>
 ourDoc=island
```

followed by your application code.

To use XML island, your document must be well formed. If there is a DTD, it must be valid or the Microsoft parser, MSXML, will refuse to load it.

To access the document for display or other purposes, declare the variable

```
ourDoc=island
```

4.8 PARSING AND LOADING

Loading an XML document creates the document tree and parses the document in memory. When loading, it is highly recommended that you utilize the `parseError` properties to extract error information from the Microsoft XML parser to save a lot of time. If you do not ask a parser to extract error information, and the XML document does have an error, running the application will return information suggesting something is wrong with the application. You will spend time searching the application for the error, when more times than not, you will discover an unclosed tag in your original XML document that you did not see earlier.

The `parseError` object is used to extract error information from the Microsoft XML parser.

If you attempt to open an XML document, the XML parser may generate an error. By accessing the `parseError` object, the exact error code, the error text, and the line causing the error can be retrieved and will display as in Table 4-7.

Table 4-7 Parse Error Properties.

Name and Description
`errorCode`
Returns a long integer error code
`reason`
Returns a string explaining the reason for the error
`line`
Returns a long integer representing the inline position for the error
`linePos`
Returns a long integer representing the line position for the error
`srcText`
Returns a string containing the line that caused the error
`url`
Returns the URL pointing the loaded document

The `parseError` object is not a part of the W3C DOM recommendation.

4.8.1 File Error(s)

For an example of file error, the following is loaded into a non-existing file and displayed as Example 4-4.

Example 4-4

```
<script>
var falseDoc = new ActiveXObject("Microsoft.XMLDOM")
falseDoc.async=false
falseDoc.load("nonexisting.xml")
document.write("<br />Error Code: ")
```

```
document.write(falseDoc.parseError.errorCode)
document.write("<br />Error Reason: ")
document.write(falseDoc.parseError.reason)
document.write("<br />Error Line: ")
document.write(falseDoc.parseError.line)
</script>
```

The error message, from attempting to load the non-existent document is

```
Error Code: -2146697210
Error Reason: The system cannot locate the object specified.
Error Line: 0
```

4.8.2 XML Errors

In Example 4-5, the parser loads an XML document as a string that is not well formed.

Example 4-5

```
<script language="JavaScript">
var tstring="<flight>"
tstring=tstring+"<!--Comment example of loading using string-->"
tstring=tstring+"<number>AF084</number>"
tstring=tstring+"<from>Paris</from>"
tstring=tstring+"<to>San Francisco</to>"
tstring=tstring+"<flight>"
var ourDoc=new ActiveXObject("Microsoft.XMLDOM")
ourDoc.async=false
ourDoc.loadXML(tstring)
document.write("<br />Error Code: ")
document.write(ourDoc.parseError.errorCode)
document.write("<br />Error Reason: ")
document.write(ourDoc.parseError.reason)
document.write("<br />Error Line: ")
document.write(ourDoc.parseError.line)
</script>
```

The error message, from attempting to load the not-well-formed document is

```
Error Code: -1072896685
Error Reason: The following tags were not closed: flight, flight.
Error Line: 0
```

In Example 4-6, `flight_error.xml` loads and parses with an error.

Example 4-6

```
<?xml version="1.0"?>
<flight>
```

```
<!--Comment example of loading with an error-->
</number>AF084</number>
<from>Paris</from>
<to>San Francisco</to>
</flight>

<script>
var xmlDoc = new ActiveXObject("Microsoft.XMLDOM")
xmlDoc.async=false
xmlDoc.load("flight_error.xml")

document.write("<br />Error Code: ")
document.write(xmlDoc.parseError.errorCode)
document.write("<br />Error Reason: ")
document.write(xmlDoc.parseError.reason)
document.write("<br />Error Line: ")
document.write(xmlDoc.parseError.line)
</script>
```

The error message, from attempting to load the document with an error is

```
Error Code: -1072896659
Error Reason: End tag 'number' does not match the start tag 'flight'.
Error Line: 4
```

EXERCISES

4.6 Write JavaScript code to load the XML document below asynchronously, as a string. Parse the document and identify errors found by the parser. Correct the identified errors and parse until the document is error free.

```
<?xml version="1.0"?>
<particles>
<name>proton</names>
<mass unit="GEV">1</mass>
<charge>positive</charge>
<lifetime>stable</lifetime>
<family>barion</family>
</particles>
```

4.7 Refer to Exercise 3-3 in Chapter 3, XML.Write code to use an XML island for loading the XML document. Detect errors displayed by the parsing process.

4.8 Write JavaScript code to load the XML document from Exercise 3-2 (Chapter 3) using ActiveX technology. Loading must be asynchronous and errors will not be displayed. After the document is loaded and parsed, find the root element of the document and display its name using alert.

4.9 Write JavaScript code to load and parse two different XML documents; Exercise 3-11 and 3-12 (Chapter 3). Use ActiveX technology, loading will be asynchronous, the errors do not have to be displayed. Find the root elements of both documents and display their names using `alert`.

4.9 APPLYING NODE PROPERTIES AND METHODS

4.9.1 Accessing the Document Tree

At this point, you will begin to apply node properties and methods for traversing the XML document.

1. First, you will see how to get information about nodes using `nodeName`, `nodeType`, and `nodeValue` properties.
   Beginning with the XML document saved as `example.xml`.

Example 4-7

```
<?xml version="1.0"?>
<example>
<!-- This is a comment-->
<?processing instruction?>
<first>element</first>
</example>
```

You need a piece of code in JavaScript to write the names, types, and values of nodes that are children of the root element. As you can see in the code above, the root element is `example` and has three children; comment, a processing instruction, and `<first>`.

To solve the problem, you need to find the root element and all of its children, then using node properties `nodeName`, `nodeType`, and `nodeValue`, get the name, type, and value of the root's children. The root element can be defined with the property `documentElement` of the document node.

If you give the name `myDoc` to a variable that will hold the document tree, then you can get the root element with the code:

`root=myDoc.documentElement` (the name `root` is arbitrary, it can be any name allowed in JavaScript).

To get the number of the root element's children, you will use the node property `childNodes`, which retrieves the number of children of the node on which it is applied, and a list of those children. The number of children is the length of `childNodes`. `childNodes` contains information that is updated if the document tree is changed (removed node, added node). The list starts with `zero item(0)`, the first `child`. The code for this is

```
rootlist=root.childNodes
x=rootlist.length
```

The children, in this case, items of `childNodes` are

`rootlist.item(0)` — first child
`rootlist.item(1)` — second child
`rootlist.item(2)` — third child

At this point, you have applied the properties `nodeName`, `nodeType`, and `nodeValue` to get the name, type, and value of each node in the document. The complete code is as follows:

```
<script>
var myDoc=new ActiveXObject("Microsoft.XMLDOM")
myDoc.async=false
myDoc.load("example.xml")
if (myDoc.parseError!=0)
{
 alert(myDoc.parseError.reason);
}
root=myDoc.documentElement
rootList=root.childNodes
l=rootList.length
alert(myDoc.xml)
for (i=0;i<l;i++)
{
j=i+1
document.write("<br />"+j+" node"+"<br />")
document.write("Name of node is "+rootList.item(i).nodeName+"<br />")
document.write("Type of node is "+rootList.item(i).nodeType+"<br />")
document.write("Value of node is "+rootList.item(i).nodeValue+"<br />")
}
</script>
```

Running the code in IE displays the following information:

```
1 node
Name of node is #comment
Type of node is 8
Value of node is This is a comment

2 node
Name of node is process
Type of node is 7
Value of node is application
```

```
3 node
Name of node is first
Type of node is 1
Value of node is null
```

Another approach to the same problem is to use the parent-child relationship rather than `childNodes`. The loading and parsing of the document remains the same as in the previous example. After finding the root element, you would use the properties `firstChild`, `nextSibling`, and `lastChild` to get the nodes and then use the properties `nodeName`, `nodeType`, and `nodeValue` on those nodes.

Example 4-8

```
<script>
var myDoc=new ActiveXObject("Microsoft.XMLDOM")
myDoc.async=false
myDoc.load("example.xml")
if (myDoc.parseError!=0)
{
 alert(myDoc.parseError.reason);
}
root=myDoc.documentElement
a=root.firstChild
a1=a.nextSibling
a2=root.lastChild
document.write("Name of node is "+a.nodeName+"<br />")
document.write("Type of node is "+a.nodeType+"<br />")
document.write("Value of node is "+a.nodeValue+"<br />")
document.write("Name of node is "+a1.nodeName+"<br />")
document.write("Type of node is "+a1.nodeType+"<br />")
document.write("Value of node is "+a1.nodeValue+"<br />")
document.write("Name of node is "+a2.nodeName+"<br />")
document.write("Type of node is "+a2.nodeType+"<br />")
document.write("Value of node is "+a2.nodeValue+"<br />")
</script>
```

2. The next example illustrates the properties `parentNode` and `ownerDocument` to make small changes in the previous example code. You want to determine which node is the parent of the first child, declared with

   ```
   a=root.firstChild
   ```

   If you apply `parentNode` to the first child and look for `nodeName`, then the node name is the name of the parent. As an example,

   ```
   parentName=a.parentNode.nodeName
   ```

displays the name of the parent with an alert statement.

Similarly, you can find the document to which a node belongs. Applying `ownerDocument` to all children and the root element will return the document.

Example 4-9

```
<script>
var myDoc=new ActiveXObject("Microsoft.XMLDOM")
myDoc.async=false
myDoc.load("example.xml")
if (myDoc.parserError!=0)
{
 alert(myDoc.parserError.reason);
}
root=myDoc.documentElement
a=root.firstChild
a1=a.nextSibling
a2=root.lastChild

document.write("Name of parent node is "+a.parentNode.nodeName+"
<br />")
document.write("Name document node is
"+root.ownerDocument.nodeName+"<br />")
document.write("Name of document node is
"+a.ownerDocument.nodeName+"<br />")
document.write("Name of document node is
"+a1.ownerDocument.nodeName+"<br />")
document.write("Name of document node is
"+a2.ownerDocument.nodeName+"<br />")
</script>
```

And the IE result is

```
Name of parent node is example
Name of document node is #document
Name of document node is #document
Name of document node is #document
Name of document node is #document
```

EXERCISES

4.10 Find and display the names, types and values of all children of the root element of following XML document. Use attributes `firstChild`, `lastChild`, `nextSibling`, `previousSibling`. Use `alert` for displaying the results and the XML document.

```
<drafting>
<!--client's data-->
<client>
<lastName>Wages</lastName>
<firstNames>Nancy, Mason</firstNames>
<address>110 Pine Street, Paso Robles</address>
<jobSiteAddress>110 Pine Street, Paso Robles</jobSiteAddress>
</client>
<!--information on status-->
<status>
<jobType>remodel/addition</jobType>
<clientSketch>Nancy brought in a floorplan sketch and a photograph of a
house she likes</clientSketch>
<floorplan_ElevSketch1>Completed 1/15</floorplan_ElevSketch1>
<clientApproval1>1/22, add patio door to Master Bedroom
</clientApproval1>
<floorplan_ElevProof2>Completed 2/15</floorplan_ElevProof2>
<clientApproval2>Approved 3/1</clientApproval2>
<floorplanCAD>Completed 3/22</floorplanCAD>
<roofplanCAD>Completed 3/22</roofplanCAD>
<elevationsCAD>Completed 3/22</elevationsCAD>
<fdnplanCAD>in progress</fdnplanCAD>
<cross_sectionsCAD>in progress</cross_sectionsCAD>
</status>
</drafting>
```

4.11 Find the following data on the Internet (use the CIA fact book at www.cia.gov): population, GDP per capita, expected lifetime. Form an XML document with content for the following countries: Bosnia, Angola, and USA. Write JavaScript code to find the population of USA, GDP of Bosnia, and the life expectancy in Angola.

4.12 Write an XML document with the content of URLs of your 10 favorite developer web sites. Write JavaScript code to look for the web site address of your favorite site. The name of the site you are looking for should be input using a prompt command and the result should be displayed using the alert command.

4.9.2 Modifying the Document Tree

Until now you used properties to access different nodes on the document tree. Next, you will learn to modify the document tree using methods `appendChild`, `removeChild`, `insertBefore`, and others.

1. In the document `flight.xml`, you may want to add a new node element `<status>on time</status>`. The original code is

```
<?xml version="1.0"?>
<flight>
<!--Comment example of loading using string-->
<number>AF084</number>
<from>Paris</from>
<to>San Francisco</to>
</flight>
```

To add a new node, you can use the method `appendChild` and the form `appendChild(newNode)`. The new element will have one child, its content, `on time`. As such, you will create and add two nodes, the new element and its content. First, you create a new text node with the code

```
var nTxt=myDoc.createTextNode("on time")
```

Next, add the new node element `<status>` with the code

```
var nNd=myDoc.createElement("status")
```

Then, append the new element to the root element with the code

```
root.appendChild(nNd)
```

To append the text node to the new node status, key

```
nNd.appendChild(nTxt)
```

To see how the XML document looks after this modification, add the code

```
alert(myDoc.xml)
```

The complete code will be Example 4-9.

Example 4-10

```
<script>
var myDoc=new ActiveXObject("Microsoft.XMLDOM")
myDoc.async=false
myDoc.load("flight.xml")
if (myDoc.parseError!=0)
{
 alert(myDoc.parseError.reason);
}
root=myDoc.documentElement
var nTxt=myDoc.createTextNode("on time")
var nNd=myDoc.createElement("status")
root.appendChild(nNd)
```

```
nNd.appendChild(nTxt)
alert(myDoc.xml)
</script>
```

Authors' Note: The XML document is created only in memory. At present, it is not possible to save this XML document, using JavaScript, without changing the security setting of IE. More about saving data changes is covered on the companion web site because of rapid changes in implementation.

2. To remove a node from the XML document, again the code begins with

```
<?xml version="1.0"?>
<flight>
<!--Comment example of loading using string-->
<number>AF084</number>
<from>Paris</from>
<to>San Francisco</to>
</flight>
```

To remove, for example, the comment node, you see it is the first child of the root. You can use the node method `removeChild(nodeName)` where `nodeName` is the name of the node to be removed. You can use the `removeChild` method to the root node, such as

```
root.removeChild(root.firstChild)
```

The complete code is Example 4-10.

Example 4-11

```
<script>
var myDoc=new ActiveXObject("Microsoft.XMLDOM")
myDoc.async=false
myDoc.load("flight.xml")
if (myDoc.parseError !=0)
{
 alert(myDoc.parseError.reason)
}
root=myDoc.documentElement
//displaying document before removing
alert(myDoc.xml)
root.removeChild(root.firstChild)
//displaying document after selected node was removed
alert(myDoc.xml)
</script>
```

3. Changing an XML document using DOM could also include, as an example, adding a date before the last child of the root element to the previous example. This is

possible by using the node method `insertBefore(newNode, refNode)`, where the new node is the node to be inserted and `refNode` is the node after the new node.

If you wanted to insert element <date>01 31 2003</date>, you would create a new text node, create a new element node, insert a new element node before the last child, and append the text node to the new node. As always, it is good practice to display the XML document before and after inserting nodes to make sure your code is correct. The key portion of your code will be

The creation of the text node

```
var nText = myDoc.createTextNode("01 31 2003")
```

The creation of the element node

```
var nNode= myDoc.createElement("date")
```

Inserting the new node before the last child

```
root.insertBefore(nNode,root.lastChild)
```

Appending the text node to the new node

```
nNode.appendChild(nText)
```

The complete code is Example 4-12.

Example 4-12

```
<script>
var myDoc=new ActiveXObject("Microsoft.XMLDOM")
myDoc.async=false
myDoc.load("flight.xml")
if (myDoc.parseError!=0)
{
 alert(myDoc.parseError.reason);
}
alert(myDOC.xml)
root=myDoc.documentElement
var nText=myDoc.createTextNode("01 31 2003")
var nNode= myDoc.createElement("date")
root.insertBefore(nNode,root.lastChild)
nNode.appendChild(nText)
alert(myDoc.xml)
</script>
```

4.9.3 Manipulating and Replacing Nodes from Two Documents

There will be many occasions when more than one document participates in data manipulation. The first example below accesses an element in the first document and adds it to the second, taking it out of the first. The second example accesses a selected element in the first document and replaces that element in the second document. To add an element to the second document and retain it in the first, consider the following two XML documents:

```
<?xml version="1.0"?>
<catalog>
<partName>belt</partName>
<partID>123</partID>
<quantity>12</quantity>
</catalog>
```

and

```
<?xml version="1.0"?>
<workOrder>
<activity>replacement</activity>
<partName>belt</partName>
</workOrder>
```

To begin, add the element `partID` from the first XML document to the end of the second XML document. Use the append method `appendChild(newChild)`

The element `partID` is the next sibling to the first child of the root element in the first document. Define the new node as

```
var newNode=root1.firstChild.nextSibling
```

where `root1` is the root element of the first document to be loaded using ActiveX and named `Doc1`. As such

```
root1=Doc1.documentElement
```

If the second document is loaded using ActiveX and named `Doc2`, its root element can be named `root2`, as in

```
root2=Doc2.documentElement
```

To append a new element at the end of the second document, use the following code:

```
root2.appendChild(newNode)
```

To ensure the modification is taking place, display both files before and after appending using `alert(Doc1.xml)`, and `alert(Doc2.xml)`, respectively.

Since you have two XML documents, you need to make two ActiveX objects. The complete code is Example 4-12.

Example 4-13

```
<script>
var Doc1= new ActiveXObject("Microsoft.XMLDOM")
var Doc2= new ActiveXObject("Microsoft.XMLDOM")
Doc1.async=false
Doc2.async=false
Doc1.load("catalog.xml")
Doc2.load("workOrder.xml")
root1=Doc1.documentElement
root2=Doc2.documentElement
alert(Doc1.xml)
alert(Doc2.xml)
var newNode=root1.firstChild.nextSibling
alert(newNode.xml)
root2.appendChild(newNode)
alert(Doc1.xml)
alert(Doc2.xml)
</script>
```

4. To add an element to the second document, so that it does not remain in the first document, use the `replaceChild` method with the form `replaceChild(newChild.oldChild)`

   For example, if you want to replace the last child of the second document with the next sibling of first child of the first document, you

   Define the new child

   ```
   newNode=root1.firstChild.nextSibling
   ```

   Define the old child

   ```
   oldNode=root2.lastChild
   ```

   Replace nodes in second document

   ```
   root2.replaceChild(newNode,oldNode)
   ```

   The complete code is Example 4-13.

Example 4-14

```
<script>
var Doc1= new ActiveXObject("Microsoft.XMLDOM")
var Doc2= new ActiveXObject("Microsoft.XMLDOM")
Doc1.async=false
Doc2.async=false
Doc1.load("catalog.xml")
Doc2.load("workOrder.xml")
root1=Doc1.documentElement
root2=Doc2.documentElement
alert(Doc1.xml)
alert(Doc2.xml)
var newNode=root1.firstChild.nextSibling
alert(newNode.xml)
var oldNode=root2.lastChild
root2.replaceChild(newNode,oldNode)
alert(Doc1.xml)
alert(Doc2.xml)
</script>
```

In running this code, you see that `<partName>` is removed from the first document. This happens because a node may have only one parent, and that parent is now in the second document. To avoid this problem, a copy of a node to replace the node in the second document can be made using the `cloneNode` and `appendChild` methods.

The `cloneNode()` method makes a copy of the node. If the node's parameters are set to true, a copy will be made of the node's subnodes as well. For this to take place, you first clone the node

```
newNode=root1.firstChild.cloneNode(true)
```

and then append it to the second document with

```
root2.appendChild(newNode)
```

The complete code is Example 4-14.

Example 4-15

```
<script>
var Doc1= new ActiveXObject("Microsoft.XMLDOM")
var Doc2= new ActiveXObject("Microsoft.XMLDOM")
Doc1.async=false
Doc2.async=false
Doc1.load("catalog.xml")
Doc2.load("workOrder.xml")
root1=Doc1.documentElement
```

```
root2=Doc2.documentElement
alert(Doc1.xml)
alert(Doc2.xml)
var newNode=root1.firstChild.cloneNode(true)
alert(newNode.xml)
root2.appendChild(newNode)
alert(Doc1.xml)
alert(Doc2.xml)
/*if we put deep parameter to false only node will be cloned*/
var newNode=root1.firstChild.cloneNode(false)
alert(newNode.xml)
root2.appendChild(newNode)
alert(Doc1.xml)
alert(Doc2.xml)
</script>
```

CHAPTER SUMMARY

1. DOM is a model for manipulating documents by building a document tree and manipulating data with node methods and properties.
2. DOM allows for web-based transactions to take place that significantly improve the capabilities of commercial web sites. With DOM, you develop a model to manipulate the data in a document. First, an XML document(s) is created. Second, using DOM, applications are designed and developed to either access data from the XML document, collect or sort data from existing databases, or allow multiple users to access, combine, and manipulate data or modify data output platforms.
3. DOM defines the logical structure of the document's data and the way the document data is accessed and manipulated. DOM may also be used to manage this data.
4. Most data found in an XHTML or XML document can be accessed, modified, added, or deleted using the Document Object Model.
5. The purpose of DOM Level 1, according to the W3C, is to concentrate on core HTML and XML document models and functionality for document navigation and manipulation. DOM Level 2 includes a style sheet object model and defines the functionality for manipulating a document's style information. DOM Level 2 additionally enables traversals on a document, define an event model, and provide support for XML namespaces. DOM Level 3 addresses document loading and saving, content models such as DTDs and Schemas (with validation support). DOM Level 3 also addresses document views and formatting, key events and event groups. Future DOM levels may specify some interface with the possibly underlying window system, including some ways to prompt the user.

6. A solid understanding of hierarchical trees and parent child relationships is crucial for developing DOM applications.
7. DOM is language-independent; you can use different languages when developing DOM applications (Java, JavaScript, C++, VBScript, Python).
8. XML documents follow a logical structure resembling a tree, or a group of trees. When DOM is used to manipulate an XML document, it parses the file, breaking it into individual elements, attributes, entities, processing instructions and comments. Next, DOM creates (in memory) a representation of the XML file as a node tree. DOM treats every item in the document as a node, from the level of an element to a single character of content. A node is defined as any part of the document, whether it be element, attribute, entity, content, or comment. An entire document can become part of a node tree, rather than only its nodes. DOM interacts with the different nodes of the tree(s), accessing and modifying content as designed by the developer.
9. Searching the document tree begins with the root element and can follow with several possible approaches; if there are only few elements you can use `firstChild`, `lastChild` properties of nodes.
10. In DOM, nodes represent objects with functions and identities. These objects represent both the structure of the document and the behavior of the document and its objects. Nodes act as interfaces and objects to represent and manipulate a document. DOM identifies these interfaces and their objects, semantics, relationships, and collaboration.
11. In the W3C DOM, the concept of the tree and object are integrated into a single model. DOM does not specify all documents must be implemented as trees or how relationships between objects will be implemented. The tree refers to the structural model used to represent the document. If more than one document object model is used to represent one document, one shared structural model will be created.
12. Each tree model contains: zero or one DOCTYPE nodes; one root element node that serves as the document's root element tree; zero or more comments or processing instructions.
13. If there are only few elements you can use `firstChild`, `lastChild` properties of nodes.
14. XML documents can be changed using `appendChild`, `removeChild`, `cloneNode`, and other methods.
15. The modified document tree is in memory and can not be saved using JavaScript without changing IE settings.

SELF-ASSESSMENT

To move on to the next chapter, you should feel comfortable that you understand and can do the following:

1. Create an XML document and draw a tree model for that document. Name all elements of the document in parent-child terminology.
2. Describe the main DOM node properties and methods.
3. Create XML documents with different node types, and make a table in which nodeType, nodeName, and nodeValue will be displayed.
4. Use ActiveX technology, and XML islands to load a XML document, using JavaScript for coding.
5. Write an XML document, load and parse it. Change the document so that there will be some errors and test it.
6. Write down your XML document and access elements of the document using the `childNodes` property, `firstChild`, `lastChild` and `getElementsByTagName`.
7. Modify a document tree using the `createElement` and `appendChild` methods.

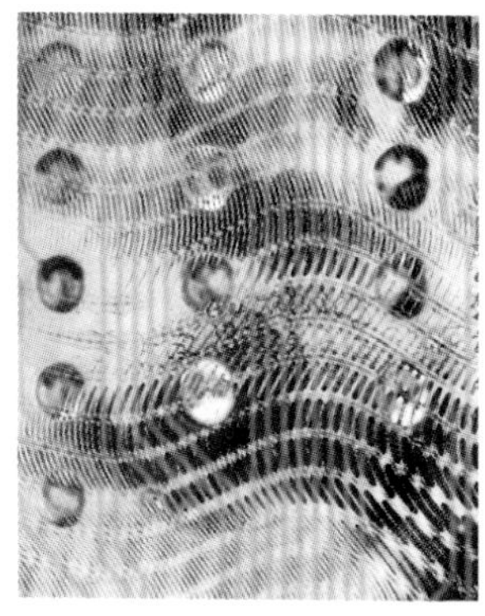

5 DOM with Larger Documents

CHAPTER OBJECTIVES

By reading the information and practicing the code in this chapter, you will understand and be able to

1. Navigate and manipulate larger documents using node list objects.
2. Develop applications using document object properties and methods and element objects.
3. Navigate and modify larger documents using the `getElementsByTagName` method.
4. Create medium complexity applications using document object model (DOM) methods.
5. Apply style to output from DOM results.

5.1 WORKING WITH LARGER DOCUMENTS

Real applications require more complex code to cover more complex needs of the user. As mentioned earlier, the user expects to interact with a commercial XML application and to be able to sort, search, modify, and so on. In addition, the amount of data, the size of the document, and the structure of the application all intertwine, requiring more sophisticated and complex modeling and code. As a result, simple parent-child relationships may not be effective methods in larger and more complex applications.

DOM properties, `firstChild`, `lastChild`, `nextSibling`, `previousSibling`, work well to access nodes in small XML documents. If a document is large, with many nested elements, use of the parent-child relationship approach can be cumbersome. With larger documents, it is easier to use the `childNodes` property of nodes. `childNodes` is a node list that carries information about the number of children of the node and an ordered list of those children.

5.1.1 The `nodeList` Object

The `nodeList` object represents a node and its child nodes as a node tree (Table 5-1).

Table 5-1 Property and Method for the nodeList Object.

Name and Description
`length`
`NodeList` property. Returns the number of nodes in a `nodeList`
`item`
`NodeList` method. Returns a specific node in the `nodeList`. The `length` of `childNodes` returns the number of children and the children are listed in the item. As an example, if you have node `root` then
`root.childNodes` contains information about the children of that node.

`root.childNodes.length` returns the number of children. If the node `root` has four children, then the children nodes can be accessed using item
`firstchild=root.childNodes.item(0)`
`secondchild=root.childNodes.item(1)`
`thirdchild=root.childNodes.item(2)`
`fourthchild=root.childNodes.item(3)`

Children are nodes with their own children. If you apply a property on their nodes, you can access their children. This approach may be used for any node in the document tree. It is easier to use the `childNodes` property for larger documents because you can use JavaScript for traversing nodes rather than implementing large expressions such as

```
myDoc.documentElement.firstChild.lastChild.nextSibling
```

The following example shows how the `childNodes` property accesses nodes:

```
<property>
  <propertyDescription>
    <propertyName>Critical Current Density
    </propertyName>
      <propertyUnits>kA/cm<sup>2</sup></propertyUnits>
```

```
  </propertyDescription>
  <propertyValue>3040</propertyValue>
    <parameter>
       <parameterName>Magnetic Field</parameterName>
       <parameterValue>0</parameterValue>
       <parameterUnits>T</parameterUnits>
    </parameter>
    <parameter>
       <parameterName>Temperature</parameterName>
       <parameterValue>3</parameterValue>
       <parameterUnits>K</parameterUnits>
    </parameter>
</property>
```

Your objective, using the code above, is to write code to display the number of children in the document, and the names of each node. To do this, use the `childNodes` property of node objects. The most important part of the code is

```
rootNoList=root.childNodes
```

which represents the node list of `root` element's children.

```
x=rootNoList.length
```

returns the number of `root` element's children.

```
rootChild=rootNoList.item(i)
```

returns each child from the list, beginning with 0.

The complete code, in JavaScript, is in Example 5-1.

Example 5-1

```
<script>
var myDoc=new ActiveXObject("Microsoft.XMLDOM")
myDoc.async=false
myDoc.load("propertiesMat.xml")
if (myDoc.parseError !=0)
{
  alert(myDoc.parseError.reason)
}
root=myDoc.documentElement
alert(myDoc.xml)
rootNoList=root.childNodes
x=rootNoList.length
alert("The document has "+x+" children")
for (i=0;i<x;i++)
```

```
{
 rootChild=rootNoList.item(i)
 rootChildNoList=rootChild.childNodes
 xch=rootChildNoList.length
 alert((i+1)+ " The root's child has "+xch+" children")
  for(j=0;j<xch;j++)
    {
    nameChild=rootChildNoList.item(j).nodeName
    alert("The name of "+(j+1)+" child is "+nameChild)
    }
}
</script>
```

The first part of this JavaScript example loads and parses the document. After the number of root element's children is found, the for-loop starts from 0 to until the number of child -1 is executed. In the loop, `childNodes` is applied on nodes representing children of root elements, so that the information about their children is obtained. In the nested loop, `for(j=0;j++;xch)`, the names of the children are displayed. This information is displayed using the alert command.

EXERCISES

5.1 Write the code to find the root element and number of children for the following XML document (use `childNodes`).

```
<televisionShows>
  <program>
    <item>
      <day>Sunday</day>
      <channel>2</channel>
      <startTime>16:30</startTime>
      <endTime>19:30</endTime>
      <showTitle>World Series Game 2</showTitle>
    </item>
    <info>
      <category>Sports</category>
      <actor>n/a</actor>
      <criticRating>n/a</criticRating>
    </info>
  </program>
  <program>
    <item>
      <day>Sunday</day>
      <channel>4</channel>
      <startTime>19:00 </startTime>
```

```
      <endTime>20:00</endTime>
      <showTitle>Comedy Review</showTitle>
    </item>
    <info>
      <category>Comedy</category>
      <actor>WC Fields</actor>
      <actor>Laurel and Hardy</actor>
      <actor>Burns and Allen</actor>
      <actor>Steve Allen</actor>
      <criticRating>4</criticRating>
    </info>
  </program>
  <program>
    <item>
      <day>Sunday</day>
      <channel>5</channel>
      <startTime>19:00 </startTime>
      <endTime>20:00</endTime>
      <showTitle>A Fish Called Wanda</showTitle>
    </item>
    <info>
      <category>Comedy</category>
      <actor>John Cleese</actor>
      <actor>Kevin Kline</actor>
      <actor>Jamie Curtis</actor>
      <criticRating>3</criticRating>
      <MPARating>G</MPARating>
    </info>
  </program>
  <program>
    <item>
      <day>Sunday</day>
      <channel>36</channel>
      <startTime>18:00 </startTime>
      <endTime>20:00</endTime>
      <showTitle>Honey I Shrunk the Kids</showTitle>
    </item>
    <info>
      <category>Fantasy</category>
      <actor>Rick Moranis</actor>
      <criticRating>3</criticRating>
      <MPARating>G</MPARating>
    </info>
  </program>
  <program>
    <item>
```

```
      <day>Sunday</day>
      <channel>BRV</channel>
      <startTime>18:00 </startTime>
      <endTime>20:30</endTime>
      <showTitle>The Lion in Winter</showTitle>
    </item>
    <info>
      <category>Drama</category>
      <actor>Katherine Hepburn</actor>
      <criticRating>4</criticRating>
      <MPARating>n/a</MPARating>
    </info>
  </program>
  <program>
    <item>
      <day>Sunday</day>
      <channel>STZ</channel>
      <startTime>18:15</startTime>
      <endTime>20:00</endTime>
      <showTitle>Austin Powers: The Spy Who Shagged Me
      </showTitle>
    </item>
    <info>
      <category>Comedy</category>
      <actor>Mike Murphy</actor>
      <criticRating>n/a</criticRating>
      <MPARating>R</MPARating>
    </info>
  </program>
</televisionShows>
```

5.2 Write the code to find and display all programs in the previous XML document with an `MPARating` and display the values.

Write code to modify the previous XML document as follows:

(a) delete `criticRating` from last item record,
(b) change the content of `MPARating` in the item that is the previous sibling to last item from n/a to R
(c) insert node `<MPARating>G</MPARating>` before `<criticRating>` in the second item.

5.2 THE DOCUMENT OBJECT

The document object is the root element in the node tree. All nodes in the node tree are child nodes of the document object. The document object is required in all XML documents. Table 5-2 lists document object properties and methods.

Table 5-2 Properties and Methods of the Document Object.

Document Properties
`documentElement`
Returns the root element of the document. If, as an example, the root element is `catalog` and the variable refers to the document you named `retailCatalog.xml`, then: `retailCatalog.documentElement.nodeName` will return `catalog`
`doctype`
Returns the DTD or Schema for the document
`implementation`
Returns the implementation object for the document
Document Methods
`createAttribute(attributeName)`
Creates an attribute node with the specified attribute name
`createCDATASection(text)`
Creates a CDATASection, containing the specified text
`createComment(text)`
Creates a comment node, containing the specified text
`createDocumentFragment()`
Creates an empty document fragment object
`createElement(tagName)`
Creates an element with the specified tag name
`createEntityReference(referenceName)`
Creates an entity reference with the specified reference name
`createProcessingInstruction(target,text)`
Creates a processing instruction node, containing the specified target and text
`createTextNode(text)`
Creates a text node containing the specified text
`getElementsByTagName(tagName)`
Returns the specified node, and all its child nodes, as a node list

Document methods create XML documents using code. In the next example, the XML document is created with one root element, one comment, one processing instruction, and an element with text, using the above-described methods. The code is straightforward, and there is no need for detailed description.

Example 5-2

```
<script>
var newDoc= new ActiveXObject("Microsoft.XMLDOM")
var newCom=newDoc.createComment("Creating XML using code")
var newCData=newDoc.createCDATASection("bull.jpg")
var
newPI=newDoc.createProcessingInstruction("xsltarget","application")
var newRoot=newDoc.createElement("report")
var newElem=newDoc.createElement("name")
newDoc.appendChild(newRoot)
newDoc.appendChild(newPI)
newRoot.appendChild(newCData)
newDoc.appendChild(newCom)
newRoot.appendChild(newElem)
var newText=newDoc.createTextNode("John Smith")
newElem.appendChild(newText)
newDoc.appendChild(newPI)
alert(newDoc.xml)
</script>
```

The result will be

```
<report>
<![CDATA[bull.jpg]]>
<name>John Smith</name>
<report>
<!--Creation xml using code-->
<?xsltarget,application?>
```

EXERCISES

5.3 Small changes in code result in differences in the document and its application. Look carefully at the example below, and write the XML document that will be created with this code. Run the code on your browser to compare the results.

```
<script>
var newDoc= new ActiveXObject("Microsoft.XMLDOM")
var newCom=newDoc.createComment("Creating XML using code")
var newCData=newDoc.createCDATASection("bull.jpg")
var
newPI=newDoc.createProcessingInstruction("xsltarget","application")
var newRoot=newDoc.createElement("report")
var newElem=newDoc.createElement("name")
newDoc.appendChild(newRoot)
```

```
newRoot.appendChild(newPI)
newRoot.appendChild(newCData)
newRoot.appendChild(newCom)
newRoot.appendChild(newElem)
var newText=newDoc.createTextNode("John Smith")
newElem.appendChild(newText)
alert(newDoc.xml)
</script>
```

5.4 Write the code that will change the content value of element `status` from `on time` to `delayed` in the following XML document:

```
<?xml version="1.0"?>
<flight>
<!--Comment example of loading using string-->
  <number>AF084</number>
  <from>Paris</from>
  <to>San Francisco</to>
  <status>on time </status>
</flight>
```

5.2.1 The Element Object

The element object represents the element nodes in the document. If the element node contains text, the text is represented in a text node. Table 5-3 shows the purpose of property and method for the element object.

Table 5-3 Property and Method for the Element Object.

Element Property
`tagName`
Returns, or sets, the name of the node. If `a` is an element with the tag name `<customer>` then `a.tagName` will return `customer`. You use the `tagName` property to get the tag names of all elements that are children of the root element.

The code to use `tagName` to return the names of elements that are children of the root element is Example 5-3.

Example 5-3

```
<script>
var myDoc=new ActiveXObject("Microsoft.XMLDOM")
myDoc.async=false
myDoc.load("flight1.xml")
if (myDoc.parseError !=0)
```

```
{
  alert(myDoc.parseError.reason);
}
root=myDoc.documentElement
alert(myDoc.xml)
childList=root.childNodes
numchild=childList.length
alert("The root node has "+numchild+" children")
for(i=1;i<numchild;i++)
{a=childList.item(i)
b=a.tagName
alert(b)
}
</script>
```

EXERCISE

5.5 Using the code in the previous example, change the line that reads

```
for(i=1;i<numchild;i++)
```

to

```
for(i=0;i<numchild;i++)
```

Run the modified code and explain the results. What happened? Why?

5.2.2 `getAttribute` Method

Table 5-4 defines the purpose of the getAttribute method.

Table 5-4 The getAttribute Method.

Element Method
`getAttribute(attributeName)`
Returns the value of the specified attribute. If the node has the form `<price currency="SIT">3000</price>` then `a.getAttribute("currency")` will return SIT

As an example of the `getAttribute` method, in the XML document

```
<?xml version="1.0"?>
<flight>
<!--Comment example of loading using string-->
<number>AF084</number>
```

```
<from>Paris</from>
<to>San Francisco</to>
<status>on time </status>
<price currency="Euro">2000</price>
</flight>
```

You want to display the value of the currency. The code to accomplish this is Example 5-4.

Example 5-4

```
<script>
var myDoc=new ActiveXObject("Microsoft.XMLDOM")
myDoc.async=false
myDoc.load("flight2.xml")
if (myDoc.parseError !=0)
{
  alert(myDoc.parseError.reason);
}
root=myDoc.documentElement
a=root.lastChild
b=a.getAttribute("currency")
</script>
```

EXERCISE

5.6 Write the code needed to display the price of a flight in the form amount currency (example $1000)

The `getAttributeNode(attributeName)` returns the specified attribute node as an object. If you have an element,

```
<price currency="Euro">2000</price>
```

the expression `a.getAttributeNode("currency")` will return object. The value of that object can be found using the `nodeValue` property of nodes. Use

```
a.getAttributeNode.nodeValue("currency")="Euro"
```

5.2.3 `getAttributeNode` Method Example

The following code, Example 5-5, illustrates the use of the method `getAttributeNode` for displaying the node name, node value, and node type of attribute node `currency` in the XML document `flight`.

Example 5-5

```
<script>
var myDoc=new ActiveXObject("Microsoft.XMLDOM")
myDoc.async=false
myDoc.load("flight2.xml")
if (myDoc.parseError !=0)
{
  alert(myDoc.parseError.reason);
}
root=myDoc.documentElement
a=root.lastChild
b=a.getAttributeNode("currency")
alert(b)
alert("The node value is "+b.nodeValue)
alert("The node name is "+b.nodeName)
alert("The node type is "+b.nodeType)
</script>
```

5.2.4 `getElementsByTagName(tagName)` Method Example

`getElementsByTagName`

returns the specified node, and all its child nodes, as a node list.
If the root element has three elements with the tag name `parameter` then

```
root.getElementsByTagName("parameter")
```

will return a node list containing the number of elements with tag name `parameter` and an ordered list of children.

The number of elements can be accessed with

```
root.getElementsByTagName("parameter").length
```

and the elements can be accessed using the `item` property of `nodeList`. As such

```
root.getElementsByTagName("parameter").item(0)
```

returns the first element with the tag name `parameter`;

```
getElementsByTagName("parameter").item(1)
```

returns the second element with the tag name `parameter`;

```
getElementsByTagName("parameter").item(2)
```

returns the third element with the tag name `parameter`.

The method getElementsByTagName gives only elements with desired tag names that are subnodes of the node you are applying the method to. In the example below, there are two applications of getElementsByTagName. One is applied to the entire document, and one is applied to the root element. The tag name is keyed in using a prompt. In Example 5-6 look for an element with the tag name root and parameter. The XML document is propertiesMat.xml.

Example 5-6

```
<script>
var myDoc=new ActiveXObject("Microsoft.XMLDOM")
myDoc.async=false
myDoc.load("propertiesMat.xml")
if (myDoc.parseError !=0)
{
  alert(myDoc.parseError.reason)
}
root=myDoc.documentElement
var a=prompt("Please enter the tag name of the element(s) you are
looking for","")
ListElemWithName=myDoc.getElementsByTagName(a)
document.write("There are "+ListElemWithName.length +" elements with
the tag name "+a+" in the document"+"<br />")
ListElemWithName1=root.getElementsByTagName(a)
document.write("<br />"+"The root node has "+ListElemWithName1.length
+" elements with the tag name "+a+"<br />")
</script>
```

EXERCISE

5.7 Write the code to search for elements (which are subnodes of the element parameter) with a specified tag name. Try different names and analyze the results.

5.2.5 Searching for a Specified Tag Name

In the following, Example 5-7, you are searching the tree for an element with a specified tag name. When the element(s) is found, the node displays its name, value, and type. If the node has children, the first child (text) is displayed.

Example 5-7

```
<script>
var myDoc=new ActiveXObject("Microsoft.XMLDOM")
myDoc.async=false
myDoc.load("propertiesMat.xml")
if (myDoc.parseError !=0)
```

```
{
  alert(myDoc.parseError.reason);
}
root=myDoc.documentElement
var a=prompt("Please enter the tag name of the element you are looking
for","")
ListElemWithName=myDoc.getElementsByTagName(a)
document.write("There are "+ListElemWithName.length +" elements(s)
with the tag name "+a+" in the document"+"<br />")
x=ListElemWithName.length
for(i=0;i<x;i++)
{
fElem=ListElemWithName.item(i)
document.write("<br />"+"The name of the element(s) is
"+fElem.nodeName)
document.write("  The type of the element is "+fElem.nodeType)
document.write("  The value of the element is "+fElem.nodeValue+"
<br />")
document.write(" The value of the child is
"+fElem.firstChild.nodeValue+"<br />")
}
</script>
```

5.2.6 Scanning All Elements Using `childNodes`

In the following, Example 5-8, scan all elements in the XML documents using the `childNodes` method. To execute, two loops first scan the root element's subnode; then scan the subnodes and display information about the nodes.

Example 5-8

```
<script>
var myDoc=new ActiveXObject("Microsoft.XMLDOM")
myDoc.async=false
myDoc.load("propertiesMat.xml")
if (myDoc.parseError !=0)
{
  alert(myDoc.parseError.reason);
}
root=myDoc.documentElement
alert(myDoc.xml)
rootNoList=root.childNodes
x=rootNoList.length
alert("The document has "+x+" children")
for (i=0;i<x;i++)
{
 rootChild=rootNoList.item(i)
```

```
 rootChildNoList=rootChild.childNodes
 xch=rootChildNoList.length
 alert((i+1)+ " root'child has "+xch+" children")
  for(j=0;j<xch;j++)
    {
    nameChild=rootChildNoList.item(j).nodeName
    alert("The name of the "+(j+1)+" child is "+nameChild)
    }
}
</script>
```

5.2.7 Using the removeAttribute(attributeName) Method

removeAttribute(attributeName)removes the specified attribute's value. If the attribute has a default value, that value will be inserted. As an example, if a is the following element:

```
<energy unit="Joule">150</energy>
```

using the removeAttribute(attributeName) on element a:

```
a.removeAttribute
```

will remove the attribute unit

In the following, Example 5-9, the attribute currency will be removed.

Example 5-9

```
<script>
var myDoc=new ActiveXObject("Microsoft.XMLDOM")
myDoc.async=false
myDoc.load("flight2.xml")
if (myDoc.parseError !=0)
{
  alert(myDoc.parseError.reason);
}
alert(myDoc.xml)
root=myDoc.documentElement
a=root.lastChild
b=a.getAttribute("currency")
alert(b)
a.removeAttribute("currency")
alert(myDoc.xml)
</script>
```

The `removeAttributeNode(attributeNode)` method removes the specified attribute node. If the attribute node has a default value, this attribute is inserted.

The method `removeAttributeNode` takes as a parameter an attribute object, the attribute you want to remove. The method `removeAttributeNode` returns the attribute object that was removed.

If a is the following element,

```
<energy unit="Joule">150</energy>
```

in order to get the attribute object of that attribute, use the method `getAttributeNode`:

```
b=a.getAttributeNode("unit")
```

and to remove the node use the method `removeAttributeNode(attributeObject)` on element `b`:

```
c-a.removeAttributeNode(b)
```

The attribute will be removed, although the attribute object will remain in `c`, as shown in Example 5-10

Example 5-10

```
<script>
var myDoc=new ActiveXObject("Microsoft.XMLDOM")
myDoc.async=false
myDoc.load("flight2.xml")
if (myDoc.parseError !=0)
{
  alert(myDoc.parseError.reason)
}
alert(myDoc.xml)
root=myDoc.documentElement
a=root.lastChild
b=a.getAttributeNode("currency")
c=a.removeAttributeNode(b)
alert("The value of the removed node is "+c.nodeValue)
alert("The name of the removed node is "+c.nodeName)
alert("The type of the removed node is "+c.nodeType)
alert(myDoc.xml)
</script>
```

5.2.8 Inserting a New Attribute

The `setAttribute(attributeName, attributeValue)` inserts a new attribute. The `setAttribute` method take two parameters, the name of the attribute you want to set and the value you want to give it. If you have element a,

```
<mass>35</mass>
```

then using the `setAttribute` method on a

```
a.setAttribute(unit, kg)
```

creates an attribute unit with whose value is kg. The element will look like

```
<mass unit="kg">35</mass>
```

If an attribute unit already exists, such as

```
a = <mass unit="gr">350<mass>
```

applying the method

```
a.setAttribute(unit,kg)
```

results in

```
<mass unit="kg">350</mass>
```

5.2.9 Creating or Modifying Attributes

The following, Example 5-11, demonstrates creating or modifying an attribute.

Example 5-11

First, the XML file is `units.xml`

```
<?xml version="1.0" ?>
<physunit>
  <mass>15</mass>
  <energy unit="Gev">200</energy>
  </physunit>
```

Next, the example code

```
<script>
var myDoc=new ActiveXObject("Microsoft.XMLDOM")
myDoc.async=false
myDoc.load("units.xml")
if (myDoc.parseError !=0)
{
  alert(myDoc.parseError.reason)
}
root=myDoc.documentElement
alert(myDoc.xml)
a=root.firstChild
a.setAttribute("unit","kg")
```

```
alert(myDoc.xml)
b=root.lastChild
b.setAttribute("unit","Joule")
alert(myDoc.xml)
</script>
```

The `setAttributeNode(attributeNodeName)` inserts a new attribute node. This method takes one parameter. As in the previous example, if the attribute already exists, it is replaced by a new one, but the method returns the old attribute. In this case you first create the attribute object

```
newAttribute= myDoc.createAttribute("unit")
```

then define it's value

```
newAttribute.value=kCal
```

and apply to element a

```
c=a.setAttributeNode(newAttribute)
```

a will get attribute

```
unit="kcal"
```

and c will contain the old attribute object (if it existed under the same name).

Example 5-12

```
<script>
var myDoc=new ActiveXObject("Microsoft.XMLDOM")
myDoc.async=false
myDoc.load("units.xml")
if (myDoc.parseError !=0)
{
  alert(myDoc.parseError.reason);
}
root=myDoc.documentElement
alert(myDoc.xml)
a=root.firstChild
NewAttr=myDoc.createAttribute("unit")
NewAttr.nodeValue="pound"
alert(myDoc.xml)
a.setAttributeNode(NewAttr)
alert(myDoc.xml)
b=root.lastChild
NewAt=myDoc.createAttribute("unit")
NewAt.nodeValue="BTU"
c=b.setAttributeNode(NewAt)
```

```
alert(myDoc.xml)
alert(c.nodeName)
alert(c.nodeValue)
alert(c.nodeType)
</script>
```

EXERCISES

5.8 On the web, find and download images of five of your favorite places in the world. Save the images in the same directory. Create an XML file with records of names of these favorite locations, a short description of each location, and images of each, saved as a CDATA section. Write JavaScript code to find the name of one of your locations you would travel to first and display images of it.

5.9 On the web, find a speech (audio file) of Martin Luther King, Jr., (or another famous person). Create an XML document with elements that will reference photographs and interesting facts, opinions, or events related to Dr. King or the person you selected. Write the JavaScript code to display image(s) of Dr. King and play the audio file.

5.10 Suppose you have an XML document with 12 instances of `<client>`. How will you find the ninth element and display its content? How can you find the number of elements with that name? Write the code to display the content of the seventh element with name client and the contents of the element before it and after it.

5.11 Using DOM, create the following XML document, then display the document using `alert()`. Next, using parent-child relationships, find and display the order number and the invoice number.

```
<?xml version="1.0"?>
<order>
 <orderNumber>756</orderNumber>
 <deliverTo>Praxis Development</deliverTo>
 <address>Los Gatos</address>
 <zip>93495</zip>
 <street>Los Gatos-Almaden Boulevard</street>
 <invoiceNumber>634</invoiceNumber>
</order>
```

5.12 Write code to calculate using data from the XML document below

(a) the total cost of fuel for the months of April, May, and June
(b) the total cost of groceries for March, May, and June
(c) the average phone cost for all months

```
<?xml version="1.0"?>
<?xml-stylesheet type="text/xsl" href="SumExam.xsl"?>
<expenses>
    <month>
      <name>March</name>
        <bill>
          <grocery>234</grocery>
          <fuel>98</fuel>
          <phone>112</phone>
          <utility>89</utility>
        </bill>
    </month>
    <month>
      <name>April</name>
        <bill>
          <grocery>264</grocery>
          <fuel>107</fuel>
          <phone>102</phone>
          <utility>95</utility>
        </bill>
     </month>
      <month>
        <name>May</name>
          <bill>
            <grocery>227</grocery>
            <fuel>128</fuel>
            <phone>212</phone>
            <utility>78</utility>
          </bill>
     </month>
     <month>
        <name>June</name>
          <bill>
            <grocery>204</grocery>
            <fuel>198</fuel>
            <phone>90</phone>
            <utility>78</utility>
          </bill>
    </month>
</expenses>
```

5.13 Starting with the following data about tea products (see Chapter 1, exercise 1.8), write code to search for teas by name. When the requested tea is returned, the name, size, and price should be displayed.

Product, Size, Price
Green Teas
Chinese Green Tea, Plain Tea Bags, 30 ea. $4.49
Green Organic Whole-Leaf Tea Bags,15 ea. $3.99
Green and Mild Citrus Tea Bags, 20 ea. $1.99
Green Decaf & Cherry Jubilee Tea Bags, 20 ea. $2.59
Black Teas and Whole-Leaf Teas
Caribbean Tea Bags, 18 ea. $3.59
Indian Tea Bags, 18 ea. $3.59
Mediterranean Tea Bags, 18 ea. $3.49
Scottish Tea Bags, 18 ea. $3.59
Black Forest Berry Whole-Leaf Tea Bags, 15 ea. $3.99
Decaf Ceylon Whole-Leaf Tea Bags, 15 ea. $3.99
Herbal and Therapeutic Teas
Caffeine-Free Chamomile Tea Bags, 30 ea. $3.77
Caffeine Free Echinacea & Goldenseal Tea Bags, 24 ea. $7.59
Caffeine-Free Ginger Root Tea Bags, 24 ea. $3.29
Caffeine-Free Ginger-Peppermint Tea Bags, 24 ea. $3.57

5.14 In the XML document below are some famous Slovenian wines. Write the code to search for white wines costing less than $20 and display their name, region, and price.

```
<?xml version="1.0"?>
<wines>
 <item>
  <name>zelen</name>
  <region>Vipava</region>
  <type>white</type>
  <price>$20</price>
 </item>
 <item>
  <name>refosk</name>
  <region>Koper</region>
  <type>red</type>
  <price>$18</price>
 </item>
 <item>
  <name>silvanec</name>
  <region>Maribor</region>
  <type>white</type>
  <price>$19</price>
 </item>
```

```
  <item>
   <name>sipon</name>
   <region>Ormoz</region>
   <type>white</type>
   <price>$18</price>
  </item>
</wines>
```

5.15 Write a program to perform the same search as in the previous exercise but with a differently structured XML document. Compare both documents (both are well formed), and discuss the relevance of document organization for problem solving.

```
<?xml version="1.0"?>
<wines>
   <name>zelen</name>
   <region>Vipava</region>
   <type>white</type>
   <price>$20</price>
   <price>$18</price>
   <region>Koper</region>
   <type>red</type>
   <name>refosk</name>
   <name>silvanec</name>
   <region>Maribor</region>
   <type>white</type>
   <price>$19</price>
   <name>sipon</name>
   <region>Ormoz</region>
   <type>white</type>
   <price>$18</price>
</wines>
```

5.16 Write code to find and display marks for XML and Web Design from the following XML document:

```
<?xml version="1.0"?>
<studentMark>
<marks Java="83" XML="85" UserAnalysis="89" WebDesign="71">
</marks>
</studentMark>
```

5.17 From Table 5-5 create an XML document containing the schedule of in-house training seminars. Your records should contain seminar topic, date, location, time as described in the following table. Organize the XML document so that it will be easy to write application code. Write code to display occupancy of Conference 12.

Table 5-5 Example Data August/September Training Schedule for Exercise 5-17.

Topic	Date	Location	Time
User Analysis and Interface Design	8/1	Conference 12	9:30–11:30
Specifications and Documentation	8/8	Conference 12	9:30–11:30
Developing First Prototypes	8/15	Studio 10	9:00–12:00
Planning and Implementing First Test	8/22	Conference 12	9:30–11:30
Developing Final Prototype	8/29	Studio 10	9:00–12:00
Finalizing Budget and Timeline	9/5	Conference 12	9:30–11:30
Scheduling and Managing Product Build	9/12	Conference 12	9:30–11:30
Planning and Implementing Testing	9/17	Conference 12	9:30–12:00

5.18 Create an XML document containing data, found on the web, about 12 cars for sale (name, year, price, mileage, color). Write code using DOM to display all data as a table, sorted by price (ascending from lowest to highest).

5.19 In the following XML document, the address of a medical image is saved.

```
<?xml version="1.0"?>
<test>
<image><![CDATA["<img src='APAbdomen2.gif'>"]]>
</image>
</test>
```

The syntax `<img src='APAbdomen2.gif'>` will open the `image.gif`, using the JavaScript `write.document` method. Write the code to find and display the image (see the companion web site for the .gif file). See the code and explanation below to guide your document. After your code is complete, test and run the document to view the image on a browser.

```
<?xml version="1.0"?>
<test>
<image><![CDATA["<img src='APAbdomen2.gif'>"]]></image>
</test>
```

Use DOM `getElementsByTagName` to get the element with tag name `image`. The statement is

```
med=root.getElementsByTagName("image");
```

The statement

```
imMd=med.item(0).firstChild.nodeValue;
```

gets the content of <image>. The image is then displayed using `document.write`. Next, complete the document

```
<html>
<script>
 source = new ActiveXObject("Microsoft.XMLDOM")
 source.async=false
 source.load("exampleMed.xml")
 if (source.parseError !=0)
{
  alert(source.parseError.reason)
}
  root=source.documentElement
  med=root.getElementsByTagName("image")
  imMd=med.item(0).firstChild.nodeValue
document.write(imMd)
</script>
</html>
```

5.20 Transfer the data from Table 5-6 to an XML document and write the code to display the distance between cities. The search should be accomplished by keying names of cities using a prompt command.

Table 5-6 Distance (Miles) Data for Exercise 5-20.

Cities	Denver	Sacramento	Atlanta	Honolulu
Denver	0	892	1202	3344
Sacramento	892	0	2079	2458
Atlanta	1202	2079	0	4488
Honolulu	3344	2458	4488	0

In one possible solution to the problem, the table can be represented as

```
<?xml version="1.0"?>
<Distance>
<!--DistanceDenver node contains nodes which give the distance from
Denver to other cities. The same notation is used throughout the
document-->
<DistanceDenver>
<Sacramento>892</Sacramento>
<Atlanta>1202</Atlanta>
<Honolulu>3344</Honolulu>
</DistanceDenver>
<DistanceSacramento>
```

```
<Denver>892</Denver>
<Atlanta>2079</Atlanta>
<Honolulu>2458</Honolulu>
</DistanceSacramento>
<DistanceAtlanta>
<Sacramento>2079</Sacramento>
<Denver>1202</Denver>
<Honolulu>3344</Honolulu>
</DistanceAtlanta>
<DistanceHonolulu>
<Sacramento>2458</Sacramento>
<Atlanta>4488</Atlanta>
<Denver>3344</Denver>
</DistanceHonolulu>
</Distance>
```

Because distances between the cities are nested inside an element combining distance with the name of the city, and because the user does not know that the name of the cities should be keyed, the string `a ="Distance"+firstcity` is used to generate the tag name `DistanceDenver` through `distanceHonolulu`, depending on what the user is searching for. The code to find the distance between selected cities is as follows:

```
<html>
<script>
//loading XML document, forming ActiveX object, parsing document
alerting errors
 source = new ActiveXObject("Microsoft.XMLDOM")
 source.async=false
 source.load("distance.xml")
 if (source.parseError !=0)
{
alert(source.parseError.reason)
}
/*Input the names of the cities for which you want to find the
distances. Use the prompt instruction to input names */
var firstCity=prompt("Key in the name of the first city")
var secondCity=prompt("Key in the name of the second city")
//finding root node of the document
/*String a will be the same as in the XML document, for example
DistanceAtlanta*/
var a="Distance"+firstCity
//finding root node of the document
  root=source.documentElement
/*Looking for an element with a name in the variable secondCity using
```

```
the method getElementsByTagName. If there is more than one node with
the same name, return the number of nodes with the variable z */
  var firstCityList =root.getElementsByTagName(secondCity)
  z=firstCityList.length
/*Because you are looking for the distance between only two cities, you
are looking for the second city which is child of a (DistancefirstCity,
like DistanceAtlanta and so on). You create an if statement asking if
for the secondCity parent node. */
   for(i=0;i<z;i++)
    {
     if(firstCityList.item(i).parentNode.nodeName==a)
       {
          distance=firstCityList.item(i).firstChild.nodeValue
          alert("The distance between "+firstCity+" and "+secondCity+"
is "+distance+" miles.")
       }
     }
</script>
</html>
```

5.21 Use another form of an XML document and write the code to accomplish the same function as the code above. Compare and discuss both solutions.

5.22 Use DOM to sort the structures in Table 5-7 by height, in ascending order

Table 5-7 Building or Structure Location and Height Data for Exercise 5-22.

Structure	Location	Height (meters)
Bank of Manhattan	New York	283
Chrysler Building	New York	319
Eiffel Tower	Paris	300
Empire State Building	New York	381
Rockefeller Center	New York	259
Wall Street Building	New York	290
Woolworth Building	New York	241

One possible solution is

```
<?xml version="1.0"?>
<buildings>
  <BankofManhattan>
    <Location>New York</Location>
    <Height>283</Height>
  </BankofManhattan>
```

```
  <ChryslerBuilding>
    <Location>New York</Location>
    <Height>319</Height>
  </ChryslerBuilding>
  <EiffelTower>
    <Location>Paris</Location>
    <Height>300</Height>
  </EiffelTower>
  <EmpireStateBuilding>
    <Location>New York</Location>
    <Height>381</Height>
  </EmpireStateBuilding>
  <RockefellerCenter>
    <Location>New York</Location>
    <Height>259</Height>
  </RockefellerCenter>
  <WallStreetBuilding>
    <Location>New York</Location>
    <Height>290</Height>
  </WallStreetBuilding>
  <WoolworthBuilding>
    <Location>New York</Location>
    <Height>241</Height>
  </WoolworthBuilding>
</buildings>
```

The XML document, as shown, does not define meters as the unit of measurement. The height element allows for a more responsive sort. However, units of measurement are often needed in cases where products are ordered in varying allotments.

Authors' Note: This example also shows elements starting in uppercase. The code runs, however you will need to remember element names; matching throughout a project is critical. Typically, beginning an element in lower case, then capitalizing the first letter of each word, beginning with the second word, allows for consistency and easy-to-read elements.

The code to sort buildings in the collection is

```
<script>
source=new ActiveXObject("Microsoft.XMLDOM")
source.async=false
source.load("Buildings.xml")
if (source.parseError !=0) {
 alert(source.parseError.reason);
 }
```

```
 root=source.documentElement
var HeightList=root.getElementsByTagName("Height");
z= HeightList.length;
//The values of height will be saved in the array defined below
var height = new Array(10)
for(i=0;i<z;i++) {
  height[i]=HeightList.item(i).firstChild.nodeValue;
  }
// You will sort the array using the sort() method
 height.sort()
document.write("<table border='2'>")
document.write("<tr><th>Building</th><th>Location</th><th>Height
</th></tr>")
/* You have sorted array height[] but not the other element. You need to
find which buildings have a corresponding height. To do that you will
use a loop in which you will compare the heights and use a parent-child
relationship to find which building corresponds to that height.*/
for(i=0;i<z;i++)
{
 for(j=0;j<z;j++)
  {
   if(height[i]==HeightList.item(j).firstChild.nodeValue)
{
 var building=HeightList.item(j).parentNode.nodeName;
var
location=HeightList.item(j).parentNode.firstChild.firstChild.nodeValue;
document.write("<tr><th>"+building+"</th><th>"+location+"
</th><th>"+height[i]+"</th></tr>")
}
}
}
document.write("</table>")
</script>
```

5.23 You have two XML documents, one contains information about new homes for sale, the other about resale homes in different counties. Write the code to find available houses in both documents using the search word "area." If the searched area is found, all data should be displayed.

The first XML Document

```
<?xml version="1.0"?>
<adNewHomes>
  <adDetail>
    <property>University Square</property>
    <area>San Mateo County</area>
```

```
    <developer>Summer Hill Homes</developer>
    <location>Exit University, off 101. Right on Donahoe </location>
    <price>from the high $500's</price>
    <adText>Ponderosa Series. 3 and 4 BR homes with Craftsman details
     from 1,761 to 2,024 sq ft. </adText>
    <hours>11-5 Thurs-Sun</hours>
    <phone>650/466-8700</phone>
  </adDetail>
  <adDetail>
    <property>Sonsara</property>
    <area>Contra Costa County</area>
    <developer>Taylor Woodrow Homes</developer>
    <location>Moraga. Camino Ricardo and Morago Way </location>
    <price>from the high $800's</price>
    <adText>3 to 5 BR homes with great views. Luxury Homes in a great
location.
     </adText>
    <hours>10-5 Daily</hours>
    <phone>925/431-2800</phone>
  </adDetail>
  <adDetail>
    <property>Vintners Green</property>
    <area>Alameda County</area>
    <developer>Greystone Homes</developer>
    <location>I-680 to 84. Rt on 84, go several mi. 84 turns into
Holmes. Left on Alden Lane.</location>
    <price>from the mid $600's</price>
    <adText>3, 4 and 5 bedroom single-family homes. </adText>
    <hours>11-5 Daily</hours>
    <phone>925/442-3200</phone>
  </adDetail>
  <adDetail>
    <property>Dublin Ranch</property>
    <area>Alameda County</area>
    <developer>Shore Homes</developer>
    <location>680 at Dublin Canyon</location>
    <price>from the $400-700's</price>
    <adText>Master planned community, 3-6 BR Shore Home. </adText>
    <hours>11-7 Tues-Sun</hours>
    <phone>925/779-9000</phone>
  </adDetail>
</adNewHomes>
```

The second XML document

```
<?xml version="1.0"?>
<adResaleHomes>
```

```
  <adDetail>
    <area>San Mateo County</area>
    <listingOffice>Chin Properties</listingOffice>
    <listingAgent>Rose Chin</listingAgent>
    <agentPhone>650/409-5555</agentPhone>
    <location>280 and San Mateo Blvd</location>
    <price>$949,950</price>
    <adText>Beautiful view overlooking Scenic 280. </adText>
    <bed>4</bed>
    <bath>2.5</bath>
    <extras>Custom details throughout</extras>
  </adDetail>
  <adDetail>
    <area>Santa Clara County</area>
    <listingOffice>Century Central</listingOffice>
    <listingAgent>Dan McGee</listingAgent>
    <agentPhone>408/309-5544</agentPhone>
    <location>Alamaden Road and Hwy 85</location>
    <price>$639,950</price>
    <adText>Remodeled kitchen. Close to light rail, good schools.
</adText>
    <bed>3</bed>
    <bath>2.5</bath>
    <extras>Custom Cabinets</extras>
  </adDetail>
  <adDetail>
    <area>Alameda County</area>
    <listingOffice>Red Lantern Real Estate </listingOffice>
    <listingAgent>Bill Lee</listingAgent>
    <agentPhone>510/329-3200</agentPhone>
    <location>680 and Mission Blvd</location>
    <price>$749,950</price>
    <adText>Mission School District. 4 miles to BART. Clean.</adText>
    <bed>3</bed>
    <bath>2</bath>
    <extras>Hot tub on private deck</extras>
  </adDetail>
  <adDetail>
    <area>Alameda County</area>
    <listingOffice>Household Properties</listingOffice>
    <listingAgent>Sue Coates</listingAgent>
    <agentPhone>510/790-2419</agentPhone>
    <location>Mowry and 4th</location>
    <price>$549,950</price>
    <adText>1.5 mi to BART station. Great yard.</adText>
    <bed>3</bed>
```

```
    <bath>2</bath>
    <extras>Pool</extras>
  </adDetail>
</adResaleHomes>
```

Because you want to search two documents with almost the same structure, use a function, searching, with both files. The function to be set in the head of the documents is the following:

```
function houses(fileName, stringName,text)
{
```

The parameters to be used when the functions are called are `fileName` (name of the XML document that is searched), `stringName` (the string array that contains the names of information that have to be displayed), and `text` (contains title to be displayed before outputting the results of the search). First, the ActiveXObject is created and the XML document is loaded, parsed, and errors, if any, are displayed.

```
xmA= new ActiveXObject("Microsoft.XMLDOM")
xmA.async=false
xmA.load(fileName)
if(xmA.parseError!=0)
{
alert(xmA.parseError.reason)
}
```

The root element and the element with the tag name area is found using the `getElementsByTagName` method.

```
rootA=xmA.documentElement
areaA=rootA.getElementsByTagName("area")
document.write("<h2>"+"<br />"+text+"<br />"+"</h2>")
```

The number of elements with the tag name `area` is found and the specified area is searched for.

```
hitsA=areaA.length
for(i=0;i<hitsA;i++)
{
```

If an area with that name is found, the parent node of element `area` is found, because all relevant data to be displayed are children of the parent node.

```
if(areaA.item(i).firstChild.nodeValue==sarea)
{parA=areaA.item(i).parentNode
```

```
document.write("<br />"+"The number of hits is "+i+"<br />")
nCh=parA.childNodes.length
```

The information the customer is looking for is displayed.

```
for(j=0;j<nCh;j++)
{
 chA=parA.childNodes.item(j).firstChild.nodeValue
 document.write("<br />"+stringName[j]+" is "+chA+"<br />")
}
}
}
}
{
document.write("Sorry, there are currently no homes available for sale
in that area.")
}
```

The function is called in the body of the XML document.

The search term is keyed, using the prompt command

```
sarea=prompt("Key in the county in which you are searching for a home")
```

The name of the information in the first XML document is defined using `array`, and the text to be displayed before hits to be output are declared is

```
strA=new Array("property","area","developer", "location", "price",
"adText", "hours","phone")
textA="Here are your search results for new homes:"
```

The function for the first document is called

```
homes("home.xml",strA,textA)
```

The names of the information, in the first XML document, are defined using `array`, and the text to be displayed before hits to be output are declared is

```
strB=new Array("area","listing office", "listing agent", "agent
phone", "location", "price", "adText", "bed", "bath", "extras")
textB="Here are your search results for resale homes:"
```

The function for searching the second document is

```
homes("homeB.xml",strB,textB)
</script>
```

The complete code is

```
<html>
<head>
<script>
function homes(fileName, stringName,text)
{
xmA= new ActiveXObject("Microsoft.XMLDOM")
xmA.async=false
xmA.load(fileName)
var k=0
if(xmA.parseError!=0)
{
alert(xmA.parseError.reason)
}
rootA=xmA.documentElement
areaA=rootA.getElementsByTagName("area")
document.write("<h2>"+"<br />"+text+"<br />"+"</h2>")
hitsA=areaA.length
for(i=0;i<hitsA;i++)
{
if(areaA.item(i).firstChild.nodeValue==sarea)
{parA=areaA.item(i).parentNode
k++
document.write("<br />"+"The number of hits is "+k+"<br />")
nCh=parA.childNodes.length
for(j=0;j<nCh;j++)
{
 chA=parA.childNodes.item(j).firstChild.nodeValue
 document.write("<br />"+stringName[j]+" is "+chA+"<br />")
}
}
}
if(k==0)
{
document.write("Sorry, there are currently no homes available for sale
in that area.")
}
}
</script>
</head>
<body>
<script>
sarea=prompt("Key in the county in which you are searching for a home")
strA=new Array("property","area","developer", "location", "price",
"adText", "hours","phone")
```

```
textA="Here are your search results for new homes:"
homes("homeA.xml",strA,textA)
strB=new Array("area","listing office", "listing agent", "agent
phone", "location", "price", "adText", "bed", "bath", "extras")
textB="Here are your search results for resale homes:"
homes("homeB.xml",strB,textB)
</script>
```

5.3 ADDING STYLE WITH CSS

Eventually, XSL and DOM Level 2 will allow more choices related to style and XML documents using DOM. At this time, it is possible to link to cascading style sheets (CSS) within `document.write`, although this technique is not recommended when other options are implemented. The use of alert boxes in this chapter does not present as well as output with style; however, it is important to understand working with DOM and getting data manipulation possibilities right first. Using alert boxes allows you to gain skills in working with XML and DOM without spending too much time managing CSS properties and rules. The ideas of modeling, of understanding the users' needs, what the behavior of the sort should be, and what the priorities are for the way data will be sorted is the first set of steps to working well with XML and DOM. Understanding how to build the XML document, how to set up the DOM sort, and how to debug, is the second set of steps. Adding style as an interface is the third step. The companion web site contains information about DOM Level 2 and additional information about XSL formatting objects as they are implemented. In the meantime, here is one way to add style to your working XML document and DOM sort.

```
document.write("<html><head><link rel='stylesheet' type='text/css'
href='fileName.css'></head></html>")
document.write("<body>")
document.write("<h2>"content"</h2>")
```

CHAPTER SUMMARY

1. Searching the document tree begins with the root element and can follow with several possible approaches; if the XML document is large and has a clear structure, you can use the `childNodes` property. The list `childNodes` is updated as the document tree changes.
2. If the structure is not well organized, the best approach is `getElementsByTagName`, to return all children of the node on which the method is applied.
3. DOM properties, `firstChild`, `lastChild`, `nextSibling`, `previousSibling`, work well to access nodes in small XML documents. If a document is large, with many nested elements, use of the parent-child relationship approach can be cumbersome.

With larger documents, it is easier to use the `childNodes` property of nodes. `childNodes` is a node list that carries information about the number of children of the node and an ordered list of those children.

4. Children are nodes with their own children. If you apply a property on their nodes, you can access their children. This approach may be used for any node in the document tree.
5. The document object is the root element in the node tree. All nodes in the node tree are child nodes of the document object. The document object is required in all XML documents.
6. Document methods create XML documents using code.
7. Attributes can be treated in a similar way as elements.
8. Document objects and methods allow dynamic creation of XML using code.
9. The element object represents the element nodes in the document. If the element node contains text, the text is represented in a text node.
10. Element methods allow processing of attributes in an XML document.
11. The method `getElementsByTagName` gives only elements with desired tag names that are subnodes of the node to which you are applying the method.
12. DOM is an efficient tool to navigate and modify XML documents. However, if the XML document is huge, problems can arise because DOM is memory-demanding. In the case of a large-scale XML documents, the event-based Simple API for XML (SAX) is more efficient.
13. If you do not have basic programming skills, it may be simpler to use XSLT. However, understanding the tree structure of XML documents is important for any application modifying and navigating XML documents.
14. DOM is not the optimal solution for all problems, although sometimes it is used in connection with other tools such as SAX and XSLT.

SELF-ASSESSMENT

To move on to the next chapter, you should feel comfortable that you understand and can do the following:

1. Create an XML document using attributes. Manipulate the document using attribute properties and methods.
2. Develop using `childNodes` and `getElementsByTagname`. Discuss the advantages and disadvantages of each method.
3. Using document object methods, you can create XML documents with different types of nodes such as attribute, comment, processing instructions, and so on.
4. Develop larger scale, more complex, dynamic applications using DOM.

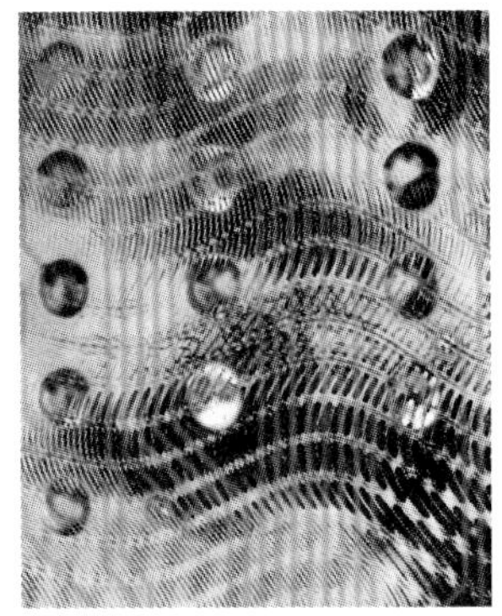

6 Extensible Stylesheet Language: Transformation

CHAPTER OBJECTIVES

By reading the information and practicing the code in this chapter, you will understand and be able to

1. Differentiate between document object mode (DOM) and extensible stylesheet language transformation (XSLT), determine which works best under specific criteria, and work with XSLT as an option to DOM.
2. Develop, with XSLT, a declarative language.
3. Use XPath language to address and locate sections of an XML document.
4. Work with frequently used XSLT elements.
5. Develop, simple XSLT applications, transform existing XML documents to HTML or to another XML document.
6. Determine appropriateness and develop with XSLT tools.

6.1 XML STRUCTURE TRANSFORMATION

In previous chapters you became acquainted with DOM and simple API for XML (SAX); with navigating and modifying XML documents. DOM and SAX require a solid knowledge of scripting or programming languages and an understanding of the tree structure of XML documents. Next, you will learn XSLT, a different approach to building XML applications, without scripting, programming, or working with document trees.

XSLT is a language for transforming the structure of an XML document. The most common application of XSLT is converting XML to XHTML for display on browsers capable of presenting HTML but not all of XML. The growth of electronic commerce and the subsequent increased data exchange between companies is resulting in higher demands for XSLT as well. XSLT's data conversion capabilities are important in the context of multiple organizations and multiple documents with different forms. Extracting and combining data from various XML documents and generating a new XML document is possible with XSLT.

Consider a network with six members, each using different databases. If the group determines to exchange data in a classical way, they will develop thirty interfaces (in general cases n(n–1) where n is the number of members of the group). If, instead, data moves from each database to a common XML file, is transformed, combined, and returned, the group's interfaces reduce from 30 to 12; six to transform the XML document to the six different database formats and six to transform database formats in XML. XSLT, as a high-level language, makes exchanging data simple, as diagrammed in Figure 6-1.

As another example, two companies each have a different XML document, although there is overlap in the data. The documents are in different forms, one focuses on elements, the other on attributes. For the documents to be combined, one must accept the other or there needs to be a way to extract and transform data from each of the documents and build a new document for joint use. This new document and its combined data can easily be created with XSLT.

Additional XSLT application areas include wireless, where starting with XML, XSLT produces wireless markup language (WML), and WebTV.

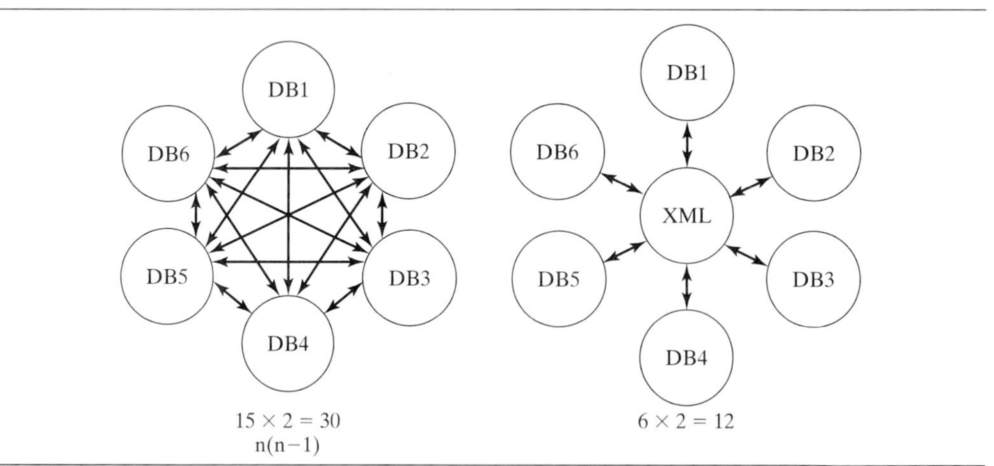

Figure 6-1 Data Transfer Example; Classical Solution and XML.

Before XSLT was developed, the only way to process XML documents was to write custom code for every application. To retrieve data from an XML document and process it, an application programming interface (API) had to be used, in this case either SAX or DOM. SAX is an event-based interface, and DOM is tree-based. The parser builds a tree-like structure of the document in memory. The problem with the SAX and DOM approach in this context is if you want to handle a new kind of XML document, you have to write a custom application to take into account the concrete structures of the XML document.

In the examples cited above, where data needs to be transformed, but the databases have some shared similarities, it is possible to describe what is needed using a declarative language, rather than writing custom applications using the procedural languages SAX or DOM.

XSLT is a **declarative language**, it describes the transfer, it does not provide procedural instructions. XSLT relies on a parser to convert the XML document into a tree structure. XSLT then manipulates that tree structure, not the document. As a high-level, declarative language, XSLT navigates around a node tree, selects nodes, and manipulates these nodes. An XSLT processor applies an XSLT style sheet to an XML source document and produces a results document.

There are several XSLT processors available including

1. Microsoft MSXML3-.0, which can be downloaded from www.microsoft.com/downloads/default.asp
2. xt is an open source XSLT processor (a Java application) developed by James Clark. www.jclark.com/xml/xt.html
3. Saxon is an open source XSLT processor (a Java application) developed by Michael Kay. http://saxon.sorceforge.net
4. An XSLT helper tool to help you test XSLT applications in Internet Explorer (IE) is available at www.finetuning.com/tutorials.html
5. Xalan Apache XSLT processor can be found at http://xml.apache.org/xalan-j/index.html

XSLT is written in XML syntax; there is no need for special parsers in the browser. Although XSLT is primarily designed for transformation of XML documents to HTML, XML, WML, or other type of documents, it is possible to perform some calculations such as determining an average as in

```
<?xml version="1.0"?>
<xsl:stylesheet version="1.0" xmlns:xsl="http://www.w3.org/1999/XSL/
Transform">
 <xsl:template match="/company">
<html>
```

```
 <body>
 <xsl:variable name="total"
 select="sum(//employee/distance)" />
<xsl:text>total is </xsl:text>
<xsl:value-of select="$total" />
<xsl:variable name="number"  select="count(//employee)"   />
<xsl:text> The number of employee is </xsl:text>
<xsl:value-of select="$number" />
<p>
<xsl:value-of select="($total div $number)" />
<xsl:variable name="average" select="($total div $number)" />
</p>
</body>
</html>
</xsl:template>
</xsl:stylesheet>
```

As you can see, XSLT uses XML namespaces. Important to XSLT, namespaces allow you to mix tags from different vocabularies. Namespace is defined with the statement:

```
<xsl:stylesheet version="1.0" xmlns:xsl="http://www.w3.org/1999/XSL/
Transform">
```

XSLT, as a declarative language, has no side effects. This means, regardless of how many times you call functions, the values and results remain the same.

6.2 HOW XSLT WORKS

XSLT is a **rule-based** language. This means the typical style sheet consists of a sequence of template rules describing how a particular element type or other construct should be processed. The following guidelines overview how XSLT works:

1. You have an XML source document; the XSLT processor makes a tree from this document.
2. At the same time, a tree from the style sheet is made and transforms the source document to an output document that can be XML, XHTML, WML, or a text file that can be PDF, .rtf, or another text extension. This output process is controlled by the XSLT element `<xsl:output>`. It is possible to produce different output formats, for example, starting from one XML source document and producing two output documents; one XHTML for presentation on the web and a WML document for sending to a wireless application protocol (WAP) device.
3. The XSLT processor starts to process a source document from its root element and looks to the style sheets tree for a matching template. If there is such a template, its

rules are applied to write the results in the result tree. This procedure is repeated from node to node of the source document. If there is no matching template, the XSLT processor moves to another node. The result of the transformation process is then translated into the output document(s) (XML, WML, XHTML, text).

4. Style sheets contain a number of template rules. The rules are expressed as an `<xsl:template>` element. A template specifies the transformation to be applied to a specific part of the source document. The `match` attribute is used to define which nodes the template rule(s) applies to.

6.3 XPATH

XSLT intensively uses the XPath language (defined as a separate specification at World Wide Web Consortium [W3C]) to address and locate sections of XML documents. Learning XPath basics will help you to locate XML elements using XSLT. XPath uses the term *node* to refer to any part of the XML document. To begin an XPath search, you will first define a starting point. There are two possibilities.

1. To begin from the document root, which is not the same as the root of the XML document but virtually represents the entire document. The document root is specified with "/". If you want to match the document root, using XPath, declare

```
<xsl:template match"/">
```

2. To begin from another node of the document, the starting node is called the context node.

   There are two possibilities to define the LocationPath, using XPath terminology `PathExpr`, to select nodes:

3. An absolute path, for when you start from the document root, as in

```
/company/name
```

which reads the select node `name`, is a child of `company`, which is a child of document root. As a second example, the expression

```
//flight
```

selects all `flight` elements in the document. Using the absolute path for searching can be time-consuming, especially with large documents, because the XSLT processor must search the entire document.

4. The second search possibility, using context node, removes the sign "/" for document roots such as

```
location
```

which reads all elements will be selected that are children of `location`, which is a child of the context node.

The expression

```
location/temperature
```

selects all `temperature` elements that are children of `location`, which is a child of the context node.

XPath allows you to select attributes using the `@` sign in front of an attribute name. As an example,

```
//@color
```

selects any attribute in the XML document with the name `color`. The expression

```
@color
```

selects attributes with the name `color`, from the context node.

With XPath, you can also use a more specific location path to satisfy conditions such as selecting elements with children or attributes, or selecting a child with a specific value. This more specific selection takes place using `[ ]`. As an example,

```
flight[company]
```

selects all `flight` elements that are children of the context node and have `company` as a `child` element.

```
flight[@status]
```

selects all `flight` elements that are children of the context node and have a `status` attribute.

```
flight[company='AirFrance']
```

selects all `flight` elements that are children of the context node and that have a child, `company`, with a value, `AirFrance`.

XPath expressions allow several functions, with the form

```
function()
```

The parameter of the function must be inserted in the parentheses ( ). An example of functions follows, more information about XPath is available on the companion web site.

When working with nodes, you use the following node functions:

1. name() returns the name of the node. If you want to find the names of all nodes which are children of element country, you would code:

```
<xsl:template match="country">
  <xsl:for-each select="*">
   <xsl:value-of select="name()" />
  <xsl:for-each>
</xsl:template>
```

2. processing-instruction returns the contents of a processing instruction.
3. comment() returns the text in the comment element.
4. text() returns the content of an XML element.

In using XPath, you work with node sets that are collections of nodes. To find data about the nodes in the node set, you use the following functions:

1. position(), which defines the position of the node in the node set.
2. last(), which returns the position of the last node in the node set.
3. count(), which returns the number of node elements with a specified name, as in

```
<xsl:value-of select="count(company)" />
```

which returns the number of elements with the name company in the node set.
There are times when it is useful to use a numerical function specified in XPath, as in

1. number(), which converts PCDATA text into a number, and
2. function sum, which adds together all numeric values of specified elements in a node set. For example, if you have the XML document,

```
<expenses>
<food>123</food>
<phone>23</phone>
<food>223</food>
<phone>12</phone>
</expenses>
```

then

```
<xsl:value-of select="sum(/expenses/food)" />
```

will return

```
346
```

and

```
<xsl:value-of select="sum(/expenses/phone)" />
```

returns

```
35
```

This "warm-up" to XPath focuses on preparing you to explore XSLT. As mentioned, more information about XPath can be found on the companion web site (www.prenhall.com/carey).

EXERCISE

6.1 For the XML document below, find the absolute and relative path (context node is `month`) to:

(a) nodes with the name `production`
(b) nodes with the names `stockValue`
(c) nodes with the name `sales`

```
<report>
  <month>
    <name>April</name>
    <production>112</production>
    <sales>123,000</sales>
    <employeeNum>112</employeeNum>
    <stockValue>28</stockValue>
  </month>
  <month>
    <name>May</name>
    <production>108</production>
    <sales>131,000</sales>
    <employeeNum>109</employeeNum>
    <stockValue>37</stockValue>
  </month>
</report>
```

6.4 XSLT TRANSFORMATION

With the XML document Example 6-1

Example 6-1

```
<?xml version="1.0"?>
<weatherReport>
<location>
  <name>Moscow</name>
    <temperature>27</temperature>
    <conditions>hazy</conditions>
```

```
    <winds>NW 7mph</winds>
    <relativeHumidity>100%</relativeHumidity>
</location>
<location>
  <name>Ljubljana</name>
    <temperature>37</temperature>
    <conditions>cloudy</conditions>
    <winds>SW 6mph</winds>
    <relativeHumidity>93%</relativeHumidity>
</location>
<location>
  <name>Los Gatos</name>
    <temperature>50</temperature>
    <conditions>cloudy</conditions>
    <winds>SE 12mph</winds>
    <relativeHumidity>74%</relativeHumidity>
</location>
</weatherReport>
```

To transform this XML document into an XHTML document, using XSLT, follow these steps

1. Write XSLT code to transform the XML document. Save the file as `.xsl` (for example, `weatherReport.xsl`).
2. To reference the XML source document add

   ```
   <?xml-stylesheet type="text/xsl" href="weatherRep.xsl"?>
   ```

3. Call from the IE browser with, as an example, the latest version of MSXML (3.0 at the time of this writing). The output result depends how you designed the style sheet to format.

These steps are not the only possible solution for transformation. You can use additional XSLT processors, such as Saxon or xt, to transform your XML document to XHTML or write a small script program that uses a transform function (`xml.transform(xsl)`). This second and third option is explored later in the chapter. For now, the XSLT code for transforming an XML document to XHTML will be broken down to better understand the code and how matching takes place.

XSLT is an XML document, as such, it begins with the XML prolog

```
<?xml version="1.0"?>
```

The root element of your style sheet is

```
<xsl:stylesheet version="1.0"
  xmlns:xsl="http://www.w3.org/1999/XSL/Transform">
```

The `xsl:stylesheet` element has two attributes:

1. the XSLT version information
2. the `xmlns:xsl`, the namespace for the XSL transformation recomendation.

To output as an XHTML document the next line in code is

```
<xsl:output method="html">
```

The XSLT element `<xsl:output>` defines the output format. If it is omitted, the output document will be HTML type by default. There is no default value of an output element. If the value is omitted, the XSLT processor will look to the tag with which the output element began. If it is `<html>` the output document will be HTML; otherwise it will be XML. To further confuse things is the question should you use XHTML instead of HTML with XSLT. In XSLT, XHTML will be treated as an XML document.

Next, you will start the first template to match the root node. This template creates the main XHTML elements. In the XSL document, the root node is the XML document, not <weatherRep> as is usual in XML documents. The document root is represented with a slash symbol. The template example matching the root element is

```
<xsl:template match="/">
```

Add standard XHTML tags `html` and `body` in which the templates insert how your output formats. The first template inside of `<html>` is the `<xsl:apply-templates>` element to indicate which nodes of the original document is processed. As an example,

```
<html>
  <body>
    <xsl:apply-templates/>
  </body>
</html>
</xsl:template>
```

If you add the end tag,

```
</xsl:stylesheet>
```

Running the code on IE, returns the result Moscow27hazyNW 7mph100% Ljubljana37cloudySW 6mph93%Los Gatos50cloudySE 12mph74%

Although the results show temperature, their presentation is not impressive because you have not specified how each node from the source will be processed. In this case, the document was processed using the default value of `<xsl:apply-templates>`.

To better organize the output, it is possible to add templates to process the nodes of the source document. This can be done in several steps to observe changes in output.

The first step is to add the XSL code template to process the node city in the document. Example 6-2.

Example 6-2

```
<xsl:template match="name">
<p>The name of the city is</p>
</xsl:template>
```

The result of the transformation is:

The name of the city is
27hazyNW 7mph100%
The name of city is
37cloudySW 6mph93%
The name of city is
50cloudySE 12mph74%

This output is a little more clear but still far away from what you would require. As you can see, the content of all nodes that are children from the <location> node, except name, are shown as a string and <p> content is displayed, but not the content of node <name>.

Adding the element

```
<xsl: value-of select="." />
```

inside of <p>, under <xsl:template match="name"> displays the content of <name>.

Running the code on an IE browser returns the result:

The name of the city is Moscow
27hazyNW 7mph100%
The name of the city is Ljubljana
37cloudySW 6mph93%
The name of the city is Los Gatos
50cloudySE 12mph74%

If you add templates to match other children of node <location> such as Example 6-3

Example 6-3

```
<xsl:template match="temperature">
<p>The temperature is
<xsl:value-of select="." />
</p>
```

```
</xsl:template>
<xsl:template match="conditions">
<p>The conditions are
<xsl:value-of select="." />
</p>
</xsl:template>
<xsl:template match="winds">
<p>The wind is
<xsl:value-of select="." />
</p>
</xsl:template>
<xsl:template match="relativeHumidity">
<p>The relative humidity is
<xsl:value-of select="." />
</p>
</xsl:template>
```

The result will be

The name of the city is Moscow
The temperature is 27
The conditions are hazy
The wind is NW 7 mph
The relative humidity is 100%
The name of the city is Ljubljana
The temperature is 37
The conditions are cloudy
The wind is SW 6 mph
The relative humidity is 93%
The name of the city is Los Gatos
The temperature is 50
The conditions are cloudy
The wind is SE 12 mph
The relative humidity is 74%

There are several ways to run your XSLT code.

1. You can open an XML document in IE
2. Write short JavaScript code using ActiveX technology and the `transformNode` method.

Here is an example how to accomplish the second method, using JavaScript.

```
<script>
var xmlDoc = new ActiveXObject("Microsoft.XMLDOM")
```

```
xmlDoc.async=false
xmlDoc.load("Exam_JS.xml")
var xslDoc = new ActiveXObject("Microsoft.XMLDOM")
xslDoc.async=false
<!--you load the XSL document and then with the method transformNode
you transfer the XML document into HTML-->
xslDoc.load("Exam_JS.xsl")
document.write(xmlDoc.transformNode(xslDoc))
</script>
```

6.5 XSLT ELEMENTS

The commonly used element `xsl:stylesheet` is the outermost element of a style sheet and fulfills the same role as `<xsl:transform>`. As an example,

```
<xsl:stylesheet version="1.0"
  xmlns:xsl="http://www.w3.org/1999/XSL/Transform">
```

As you can see, the element includes at least one namespace declaration.

Additional elements include

Elements defining template rules and controlling how they are invoked such as `<xsl:template>`, `<xsl:apply-templates>`, and `<xsl:call-template>`

Elements defining style sheet structure such as `<xsl:stylesheet>`, `<xsl:includes>`, and `<xsl:import>`

Elements generating output include `<xsl:value-of>`, `<xsl:element>`, `<xsl:attribute>`, `<xsl:comment>`, `<xsl:processing-instruction>`, and `<xsl:text>`

Elements defining variables and parameters include `<xsl:variable>`, `<xsl:param>`, and `<xsl:with-param>`

Elements copying information from the source to the result include `<xsl:copy>` and `<xsl:copy-of>`

Elements for conditional processing and iteration include `<xsl:if>`, `<xsl:choose>`, `<xsl:when>`, `<xsl:otherwise>`, and `<xsl:for-which>`

Elements controlling sorting and numbering include `<xsl:sort>`, and `<xsl:number>`

The element controlling the final output format is `<xsl:output>`

The `<xsl:stylesheet>` may contain XSLT elements referred to as top-level elements (Table 6-1).

Table 6-1 XSLT Top-level Elements

Element Names
<xsl:attribute-set>
<xsl:preserve-space>
<xsl:namespace-alias>
<xsl:import>
<xsl:templates>
<xsl:param>
<xsl:key>
<xsl:decimal-format>
<xsl:strip-space>
<xsl:output>
<xsl:include>
<xsl:variable>

In practice, almost all of your application code will be inside `<stylesheet>` tags.

```
<xsl:stylesheet version="1.0" xmlns:xsl="http://www.w3.org/1999/XSL/
Transform">
...
...
code
</xsl:stylesheet>
```

6.5.1 <xsl:output>

The `<xsl:output>` is a top-level element (the child of `<xsl:stylesheet>`), which controls format of the style sheet output.

Elements may have several attributes. The attribute method defines what the output file generates during the transformation of the source document. As such

```
<xsl:output method="html">
```

generates an HTML file and

```
<xsl:output method="text">
```

generates a plain text, RTF, or PDF file.

Attribute encoding defines character encoding for the output document. As an example,

```
<xsl:output method="xml" encoding="UTF-16" />
```

specifies output of the document that uses universal character set transformation format UTF-16 encoding.

It is not necessary to include an <xsl:output> element in the style sheet. XML is the default value of the attribute method of <xsl:output>. If the first output is HTML, then the value of the attribute method is HTML.

<xsl:output>, as a top-level element and child of <xsl:stylesheet>, may appear any number of times in a style sheet. <xsl:output> is concerned with how your result tree is transformed into an output file. If the XSLT processor allows you do something else with the result tree, for example passing it to the application as a DOM document, then the output element is irrelevant.

6.5.2 <xsl:apply-templates>

With <xsl:apply-templates> it is possible to define a set of nodes of the source document to be processed. This element, which is an instruction, selects a template rule for each node. The attributes `select` and `mode` are optional. `select` is commonly used, `mode` is rarely used.

<xsl:apply-templates> may contain the elements <xsl:sort> and <xsl:with-param>.

As an example,

```
<xsl:apply-templates>
<xsl:sort select="partName" />
</xsl:apply-templates>
```

To explicitly define the node to be processed use the `select` attribute. As an example,

```
<xsl:templates select="//location" />
```

selects all elements in the document with the name `location`.

The following example shows using the select attribute to access nodes in the XML document `weatherReport`:

```
<?xml version="1.0"?>
<xsl:stylesheet version="1.0"
 xmlns:xsl="http://www.w3.org/1999/XSL/Transform">
<xsl:template match="location">
<html>
<body>
<p><xsl:apply-templates select="name" /></p>
<p><xsl:apply-templates select="temperature" /></p>
<p><xsl:apply-templates select="conditions" /></p>
<p><xsl:apply-templates select="winds" /></p>
<p><xsl:apply-templates select="relativeHumidity" /></p>
```

```
</body>
</html>
</template>
</stylesheet>
```

If no attribute is selected in the instruction `<xsl:apply-templates>`, then the built-in template rules default. How the built-in template rule acts depends on the type of processed node.

1. If the node type is `root`, the instruction apply-templates processes each child of the `root` node using the mode specified in the call `<xsl:apply-templates>`.
2. If the node type is `element`, the instruction apply-templates processes each child of the `element` node using the mode specified on the call `<xsl:apply-templates>`.
3. If the node type is `text`, the instruction `<xsl:apply-templates>` copies the text value of the node to the output. The result is the same as the element `<xsl:value-of select=".">`.
4. If the node type is `attribute`, the instruction `<xsl:apply-templates>` copies the value of the attribute to the output. The result is the same as the element `<xsl:value-of select=".">`.
5. If the processed node is of type `processing instruction`, `comment`, or `namespace`, the built-in template rule does not act.

If you have the following XML document Example 6-4,

Example 6-4

```
<?xml version="1.0"?>
<applyExample>
<!--This is example of acting default xsl:apply-template on different
types of nodes-->
<?processing instruction?>
<line>Do you see this text?</line>
</applyExample>
```

then the following style sheet

```
<?xml version="1.0"?>
<xsl:stylesheet version="1.0"
 xmlns:xsl="http://www.w3.org/1999/XSL/Transform">
<xsl:template match="line">
<html>
<body>
<xsl:apply-templates/>
</body>
</html>
```

```
</xsl:template>
</xsl:stylesheet>
```

will generate the output document

```
Do you see this text?
```

There are elements `<xsl:for-each>` and `<xsl:value-of>`, which accomplish the same functions as `<xsl:apply-templates>`. However, if the document has a structure that is difficult to navigate, as an example, when elements to be processed may contain children of different types in an unpredictable sentence, it is better to use `<xsl:apply-templates>`.

`<xsl:template>` is the key element in any XSLT style sheet and takes the form

```
<xsl:template match="/city">
```

If the match attribute of `<xsl:template>` is absent, there must a `name` attribute to define a named template to be invoked using the `<xsl:call-template>` instruction. `<xsl:template>` has an attribute priority with a number value. This optional attribute determines which template is called if there is more than one template in a document matching a particular node. The attribute value pattern specifies the node to which the template applies. As a top-level element, `<xsl:template>` is a child of `<xsl:stylesheet>`.

6.5.3 `<xsl:value-of>`

If you want to write text (the string value of an expression) to the result tree, use the instruction `<xsl:value-of>`. `<xsl:value-of>` has two possible attributes, `select`, which is mandatory to specify the value to be output, and `disable-output-escaping`, which is optional and has two possible values, `yes` and `no`. If the value is `yes`, special characters are output. The default value `no`. `<xsl:value-of>` is the most common way to write text to the result tree and is used in most style sheets. As an example,

`<xsl:value-of select=".">` inserts `PCDATA` from the `context` node into output.

6.5.4 `<xsl:for-each>`

If you need to repeat an operation several times, for example, to display the contents of elements with the same tag name that appear several times in the XML document, use `<xsl:for-each-instruction>`. This instruction acts much like a loop instruction in procedural languages. It selects a set of nodes defined as the value of attribute `select`. This attribute is mandatory and the instruction takes the form

```
<xsl:for-each select="//item"> as in Example 6-5.
```

Example 6-5

```
<?xml version="1.0"?>
<spareParts>
 <item>
    <partName>valve</partName>
    <partNumber>HV-152</partNumber>
    <partImage>valve.jpeg</partImage>
    <quantity>150</quantity>
 </item>
 <item>
    <partName>belt</partName>
    <partNumber>HB-342</partNumber>
    <partImage>belt.jpeg</partImage>
    <quantity>50</quantity>
 </item>
 <item>
    <partName>gear</partName>
    <partNumber>HG-431</partNumber>
    <partImage>gear.jpeg</partImage>
    <quantity>102</quantity>
 </item>
 <item>
    <partName>sensor</partName>
    <partNumber>Hs-142</partNumber>
    <partImage>sensor.jpeg</partImage>
    <quantity>251</quantity>
  </item>
</spareParts>
```

Assume you want to develop the XSLT code to display all of the above elements in a table. First, you would need to develop the XSLT code to display a table. This code might look like

```
<?xml version="1.0"?>
<xsl:stylesheet version="1.0" xmlns:xsl="http://www.w3.org/1999/XSL/
Transform">
<xsl:template match="/">
<html>
 <body>
  <table border="2">
   <tr>
     <th>Part Name</th>
     <th>Part Number</th>
     <th>Part Image</th>
     <th>Quantity</th>
```

```
    </tr>
    <tr>
      <td>-</td>
      <td>-</td>
      <td>-</td>
     <td>-</td>
    </tr>
  </table>
</body>
</html>
</xsl:template>
</xsl:stylesheet>
```

The result is

Part Name	Part Number	Part Image	Quantity

The table is created in <body>, but it does not present any elements. Running this code displays only the table, names of columns, and empty cells. To place results into the cells, you can make a slight change to the code with the two instructions:

```
<xsl:value-of select="spareParts/item/partName" />
```

and

```
<xsl:value-of select="spareParts/item/partImage" />
```

which cause the output contents of elements `partName` and `partImage` to be placed into the table cells as in Example 6-6.

Example 6-6

```
<?xml version="1.0"?>
<xsl:stylesheet version="1.0"
xmlns:xsl="http://www.w3.org/1999/XSL/Transform">
<xsl:template match="/">
<html>
 <body>
  <table border="2">
   <tr>
     <th>Part Name</th>
     <th>Part Number</th>
     <th>Part Image</th>
     <th>Quantity</th>
   </tr>
```

```
    <tr>
    <td><xsl:value-of select="spareParts/item/partName" /></td>
    <td>-</td>
    <td><xsl:value-of select="spareParts/item/partImage" /></td>
    <td>-</td>
    </tr>
  </table>
</body>
</html>
</xsl:template>
</xsl:stylesheet>
```

Running the code in IE produces the result

Part Name	Part Number	Part Image	Quantity
Valve		valve.jpeg	

Next, you could improve the code by adding

```
<xsl:value-of select="spareParts/item/partNumber" />
<xsl:value-of select="spareParts/item/quantity" />
```

as in Example 6-7.

Example 6-7

```
<?xml version="1.0"?>
<xsl:stylesheet version="1.0" xmlns:xsl="http://www.w3.org/1999/XSL/
Transform">
<xsl:template match="/">
<html>
  <body>
 <table border="2" bgcolor="yellow">
   <tr>
     <th>Part Name</th>
     <th>Part Number</th>
     <th>Part Image</th>
     <th>Quantity</th>
   </tr>
   <tr>
   <td><xsl:value-of select="spareParts/item/partName" /></td>
   <td><xsl:value-of select="spareParts/item/partNumber" /></td>
   <td><xsl:value-of select="spareParts/item/partImage" /></td>
   <td><xsl:value-of select="spareParts/item/quantity" /></td>
   </tr>
 </table>
```

```
</body>
</html>
</xsl:template>
</xsl:stylesheet>
```

The code displays the values of the first item from the XML document in the cells of the first row, such as

Part Name	Part Number	Part Image	Quantity
valve	HV-152	valve.jpeg	150

You will want to see all elements in the XML document, as such use the instruction

1. `<xsl:for-each select="sparePart/item">` after the table tag;
2. `<table border="2">` and the closed tag `</xsl:for-each>` before the end tag; and
3. `</table>` so that instructions

```
<tr>
   <td><xsl:value-of select="partName" /></td>
   <td><xsl:value-of select="partNumber" /></td>
   <td><xsl:value-of select="partImage" /></td>
   <td><xsl:value-of select="quantity" /></td>
</tr>
```

are repeated as many times as there are element items in the source document. In this way, all elements display in the table. The final code is Example 6-8.

Example 6-8

```
<?xml version="1.0"?>
<xsl:stylesheet version="1.0" xmlns:xsl="http://www.w3.org/1999/XSL/
Transform">
<xsl:template match="/">
<html>
 <body>
  <table border="2">
 <xsl:for-each select="spareParts/item">
   <tr>
   <td><xsl:value-of select="partName" /></td>
   <td><xsl:value-of select="partNumber" /></td>
   <td><xsl:value-of select="partImage" /></td>
   <td><xsl:value-of select="quantity" /></td>
   </tr>
 </xsl:for-each>
```

```
 </table>
</body>
</html>
</xsl:template>
</xsl:stylesheet>
```

Running the code in IE produces the result

valve	HV-152	valve.jpeg	150
belt	HB-342	belt.jpeg	50
gear	HG-431	gear.jpeg	102
sensor	Hs-142	sensor.jpeg	251

If you have a more complex problem that is difficult to solve in the framework of XSLT, you can combine DOM and XSLT by writing a piece of code in JavaScript. The first part uses DOM to perform required task and the second uses the `transformNode` method to transform the XML document to HTML. For example, if you want to find the number of spare parts with stock counts of less than 150, it would be not easy to write using only XSLT. However, with both DOM and XSLT using JavaScript, the code would be

```
<script>
var xmlDoc = new ActiveXObject("Microsoft.XMLDOM")
xmlDoc.async=false
xmlDoc.load("Exam_DOMXSLT.xml")
var xslDoc = new ActiveXObject("Microsoft.XMLDOM")
xslDoc.async=false
xslDoc.load("Exam_DOMXSLT.xsl")
root=xmlDoc.documentElement
quantityList=root.getElementsByTagName("quantity")
qlength=quantityList.length
s1=0
for(i=0;i<qlength;i++)
{
quantity=quantityList.item(i).firstChild.nodeValue
if(quantity<150)
{
s1++
}
}
document.write("<br> There are "+s1+" elements with quantity less than
150<br /><br />")
document.write(xmlDoc.transformNode(xslDoc))
</script>
```

EXERCISE

6.2 Write the code that presents the content of all elements partName, partNumber, and quantity in the following table.

The number of rows that return depend on the number of elements returned.

Part Name	Part Number	Quantity

6.5.5 <xsl:sort>

If you want to sort elements from the source document and present that sort list in a results document, use <xsl:sort>. This XSLT element sorts nodes when using <xsl:apply-templates> or <xsl:for-each> and has the following form:

```
<xsl:sort select="expression"
 lang="lang"
 data-type="text" or "number"
 order="ascending" or "descending"
 case-order="upper-first" or "lower-first" />
```

The attribute select chooses the element with which you sort the source document. The default values are

```
lang="en"
data-type="text"
order="ascending"
case-order="upper-first" when lang is set to "en"
```

If you wanted to sort spareParts.xml by partName, you could use the default values of attributes and add the following to your code:

```
<xsl:sort select="partName" />
```

Inserting this code after

```
<xsl:for-each select="partName" />
```

results in the following XSL documents Example 6-9.

Example 6-9

```
<?xml version="1.0"?>
<xsl:stylesheet version="1.0" xmlns:xsl="http://www.w3.org/1999/XSL/
Transform">
<xsl:template match="/">
<html>
```

```
 <body>
  <table border="2">
 <xsl:for-each select="spareParts/item">
 <xsl:sort select="partName" />
   <tr>
     <td><xsl:value-of select="partName" /></td>
     <td><xsl:value-of select="partNumber" /></td>
     <td><xsl:value-of select="partImage" /></td>
     <td><xsl:value-of select="quantity" /></td>
   </tr>
 </xsl:for-each>
 </table>
</body>
</html>
</xsl:template>
</xsl:stylesheet>
```

Running this code on IE generates the output

belt	HB-342	belt.jpeg	50
gear	HG-431	gear.jpeg	102
sensor	Hs-142	sensor.jpeg	251
valve	HV-152	valve.jpeg	150

To sort the same document by element `quantity`, with numeric data, and to sort it in descending order, define the `sort` element as

```
<xsl:sort select="quantity" data-type="number" order="descending" />
```

The code is Example 6-10.

Example 6-10

```
<?xml version="1.0"?>
<xsl:stylesheet version="1.0" xmlns:xsl="http://www.w3.org/1999/XSL/
Transform">
<xsl:template match="/">
<html>
 <body>
  <table border="2">
<xsl:for-each select="spareParts/item">
<xsl:sort select="quantity" data-type="number" order="descending" />
   <tr>
     <td><xsl:value-of select="partName" /></td>
```

```
      <td><xsl:value-of select="partNumber" /></td>
      <td><xsl:value-of select="partImage" /></td>
      <td><xsl:value-of select="quantity" /></td>
    </tr>
  </xsl:for-each>
  </table>
</body>
</html>
</xsl:template>
</xsl:stylesheet>
```

Running this code on IE generates the following output:

sensor	Hs-142	sensor.jpeg	251
valve	HV-152	valve.jpeg	150
gear	HG-431	gear.jpeg	102
belt	HB-342	belt.jpeg	50

If some elements have the same name, you could add one more <xsl:sort> to sort by other elements. In this case, output is sorted first by the element in the first <xsl:sort> and second by the element in the second <xsl:sort>. For example, if you add new items to the spare parts example with the same product name, sensor, the new XML document is Example 6-11.

Example 6-11

```
<?xml version="1.0"?>
<?xml-stylesheet type="text/xsl" href="sparePart3Sort2.xsl"?>
<spareParts>
<item>
 <partName>sensor</partName>
 <partNumber>HsD-149</partNumber>
 <partImage>sensorD.jpeg</partImage>
 <quantity>281</quantity>
</item>
<item>
 <partName>valve</partName>
 <partNumber>HV-152</partNumber>
 <partImage>valve.jpeg</partImage>
 <quantity>150</quantity>
</item>
<item>
 <partName>sensor</partName>
 <partNumber>HsC-42</partNumber>
```

```
  <partImage>sensorC.jpeg</partImage>
  <quantity>51</quantity>
 </item>
 <item>
  <partName>belt</partName>
  <partNumber>HB-342</partNumber>
  <partImage>belt.jpeg</partImage>
  <quantity>50</quantity>
 </item>
 <item>
  <partName>sensor</partName>
  <partNumber>HsB-182</partNumber>
  <partImage>sensorB.jpeg</partImage>
  <quantity>257</quantity>
 </item>
 <item>
  <partName>gear</partName>
  <partNumber>HG-431</partNumber>
  <partImage>gear.jpeg</partImage>
  <quantity>102</quantity>
 </item>
 <item>
  <partName>sensor</partName>
  <partNumber>HsA-242</partNumber>
  <partImage>sensorA.jpeg</partImage>
  <quantity>151</quantity>
 </item>
 <item>
  <partName>sensor</partName>
  <partNumber>Hs-142</partNumber>
  <partImage>sensor.jpeg</partImage>
  <quantity>251</quantity>
 </item>
 </spareParts>
```

You then add the second `<xsl:sort select="partNumber">`. The sort selection of the code is

```
<xsl:sort select="partName" />
<xsl:sort select="partNumber" />
```

As an example,

```
<?xml version="1.0"?>
<xsl:stylesheet version="1.0" xmlns:xsl="http://www.w3.org/1999/XSL/
```

```
Transform">
<xsl:template match="/">
<html>
 <body>
  <table border="2">
 <xsl:for-each select="spareParts/item">
  <xsl:sort select="partName" />
 <xsl:sort select="partNumber" />
   <tr>
     <td><xsl:value-of select="partName" /></td>
     <td><xsl:value-of select="partNumber" /></td>
     <td><xsl:value-of select="partImage" /></td>
     <td><xsl:value-of select="quantity" /></td>
   </tr>
 </xsl:for-each>
 </table>
</body>
</html>
</xsl:template>
</xsl:stylesheet>
```

Running this code for a modified XML document produces the output

belt	HB-342	belt.jpeg	50
gear	HG-431	gear.jpeg	102
sensor	Hs-142	sensor.jpeg	251
sensor	HsA-242	sensorA.jpeg	151
sensor	HsB-182	sensorB.jpeg	257
sensor	HsC-42	sensorC.jpeg	51
sensor	HsD-149	sensorD.jpeg	281
valve	HV-152	valve.jpeg	150

EXERCISES

6.3 Write the code that sorts the `spartParts.xml` document by `partName` and then by `quantity`, in ascending order.

6.4 Write the code to transform the XML document `films.xml` (below) to an HTML document displaying the following data: film title, director, category, and theater, as a table.

```
<?xml version="1.0"?>
<?xml-stylesheet type="text/xsl" href="films.xsl"?>
<filmProject>
<todaysFilms>
  <film>
    <filmTitle>Nights of Cabiria</filmTitle>
    <year>1957</year>
    <actor>Giulietta Masina</actor>
    <director>Federico Fellini</director>
  </film>
  <info>
    <MPARating>not rated</MPARating>
    <category>Drama</category>
    <subtitles>English subtitles</subtitles>
    <criticRating>4*</criticRating>
  </info>
  <schedule>
    <theater>Saratoga Cinema</theater>
    <times>
      <startTime>16:00</startTime>
      <startTime>18:00</startTime>
      <startTime>20:00</startTime>
      <startTime>22:00</startTime>
    </times>
    <ticketPrice>7.50</ticketPrice>
  </schedule>
</todaysFilms>
<todaysFilms>
  <film>
    <filmTitle>Grand Illusion</filmTitle>
    <year>1937</year>
    <actor>Jean Gabin</actor>
    <director>Jean Renoir</director>
  </film>
  <info>
    <MPARating>not rated</MPARating>
    <category>Drama</category>
    <subtitles>English subtitles</subtitles>
    <criticRating>4*</criticRating>
  </info>
  <schedule>
    <theater>Saratoga Cinema</theater>
    <times>
      <startTime>15:00</startTime>
      <startTime>18:00</startTime>
      <startTime>21:00</startTime>
```

```
    </times>
    <ticketPrice>8.00</ticketPrice>
  </schedule>
</todaysFilms>
<todaysFilms>
  <film>
    <filmTitle>Cinema Paradiso</filmTitle>
    <year>1990</year>
    <actor>Philippe Noiret</actor>
    <director>Giuseppe Tornatore</director>
  </film>
  <info>
    <MPARating>PG</MPARating>
    <category>Drama</category>
    <subtitles>English subtitles</subtitles>
    <criticRating>4*</criticRating>
  </info>
  <schedule>
    <theater>Saratoga Cinema</theater>
    <times>
      <startTime>12:00</startTime>
      <startTime>15:00</startTime>
      <startTime>18:00</startTime>
      <startTime>21:00</startTime>
    </times>
    <ticketPrice>9.50</ticketPrice>
  </schedule>
</todaysFilms>
<todaysFilms>
  <film>
    <filmTitle>Desert Hearts</filmTitle>
    <year>1987</year>
    <actor>Helen Shaver</actor>
    <actor>Patricia Charbonneau</actor>
    <director>Donna Deitch</director>
  </film>
  <info>
    <MPARating>R</MPARating>
    <category>Comedy</category>
    <subtitles>no subtitles</subtitles>
    <criticRating>4*</criticRating>
  </info>
  <schedule>
    <theater>Saratoga Cinema</theater>
    <times>
      <startTime>16:00</startTime>
```

```
        <startTime>18:00</startTime>
        <startTime>20:00</startTime>
        <startTime>22:00</startTime>
      </times>
      <ticketPrice>9.00</ticketPrice>
    </schedule>
  </todaysFilms>
</filmProject>
```

6.5 Write the XSLT code to sort your `films.xml` document by ticket price in descending order.

6.6 Write the XSLT code to transform `films.xml` into an XML document in which there is only one actor, one start time (first of the day), and information about subtitles.

CHAPTER SUMMARY

1. XSLT is a language for transforming the structure of an XML document. XSLT is primarily intended for communication between software systems. The most common application of XSLT is converting XML to XHTML for display on browsers capable of presenting HTML, but not all of XML.
2. XSLT is a declarative language, it describes the transfer, it does not provide procedural instructions. XSLT relies on a parser to convert the XML document into a tree structure. XSLT then manipulates that tree structure, not the document. As a high-level, declarative language, XSLT navigates around a node tree, selects nodes, and manipulates these nodes. An XSLT processor applies an XSLT style sheet to an XML source document and produces a results document.
3. XSLT is a tool for transforming XML documents. As a language, XSLT is written in XML syntax; there is no need for special parsers in the browser.
4. XSLT is a rule-based language. This means the typical style sheet consists of a sequence of template rules describing how a particular element type or other construct should be processed.
5. XSLT intensively uses the XPath language (defined as a separate specification at W3C) to address and locate sections of XML documents.
6. The main features of XPath important to the application of XSLT are absolute and relative path, document root, context node, function sum, count, and position.
7. XSLT is an XML document. As such, it begins with the XML prolog `<?xml version="1.0"?>`

   The root element of the style sheet is `<xsl:stylesheet version="1.0"`

   `xmlns:xsl="http://www.w3.org/1999/XSL/Transform">`

8. The xsl:stylesheet element has two attributes:

   (a) the XSLT version information
   (b) the xmlns:xsl, the namespace for the XSL transformation recommendation.

9. The XSLT element <xsl:output> defines the output format, if it is omitted, the output document is HTML type by default. There is no default value of an output element. If the value is omitted, the XSLT processor looks to the tag with which the output element began. If it is <html> the output document will be HTML; otherwise it will be XML.
10. In the XSL document, the root node is the XML document, not <weatherRep> or whatever element name was selected for the root element as is usual in XML documents. The document root is represented with a slash symbol. The template example matching the root element is <xsl:template match="/">
11. Add standard XHTML tags html and body in which the templates insert how your output formats. The first template inside of <html> is the <xsl:apply-templates> element to indicate which nodes of the original document are processed.
12. To better organize the output, it is possible to add templates to process the nodes of the source document.
13. There are several ways to run your XSLT code. You can open an XML document in IE or write short JavaScript code using ActiveX technology and the transformNode method.
14. The commonly used element xsl:stylesheet is the outermost element of a style sheet and fulfills the same role as <xsl:transform>.
15. In practice, almost all of your application code are inside <stylesheet> tags.
16. The <xsl:output> is a top-level element (the child of <xsl:stylesheet>), which controls format of the style sheet output.
17. Elements may have several attributes. The attribute method defines what the output file generates during the transformation of the source document.
18. With <xsl:apply-templates> it is possible to define a set of nodes of the source document to be processed. This element, which is an instruction, selects a template rule for each node. The attributes select and mode are optional. select is commonly used; mode is rarely used.
19. If you want to write text (the string value of an expression) to the result tree, use the instruction <xsl:value-of>. <xsl:value-of> has two possible attributes select, which is mandatory to specify the value to be output, and disable-output-escaping, which is optional and has two possible values, yes and no. If the value is yes, special characters are output. The default value is no. <xsl:value-of> is the most common way to write text to the result tree and is used in most style sheets.

20. If you need to repeat an operation several times, for example to display the contents of elements with the same tag name that appear several times in the XML document, use `<xsl:for-each-instruction>`. This instruction acts much like a loop instruction in procedural languages. It selects a set of nodes defined as the value of the mandatory attribute `select`.
21. If you have a more complex problem that is difficult to solve in the framework of XSLT, you can combine DOM and XSLT by writing a piece of code in JavaScript. The first part uses DOM to perform the required task and the second uses the `transformNode` method to transform the XML document to html.
22. If you want to sort elements from the source document and present that sort list in a results document, use `<xsl:sort>`. This XSLT element sorts nodes when using `<xsl:apply-templates>` or `<xsl:for-each>`.

SELF-ASSESSMENT

To move on to the next chapter, you should feel comfortable that you understand and can do the following:

1. Demonstrate an understanding of the differences between XSLT, DOM SAX, procedural, and declarative languages.
2. Demonstrate an understanding how XSLT works and how style sheet template rules transform from one document type to another.
3. Be able to use XPath to define absolute and relative path, demonstrating an understanding of the terms *document root* and *context node.*
4. Use the basic XSLT elements `<xsl:stylesheet>`, `<xsl:template>`, `<xsl:apply-templates>`, `<xsl:for-each>`, `<xsl:output>`, and `<xsl: value-of select>`.

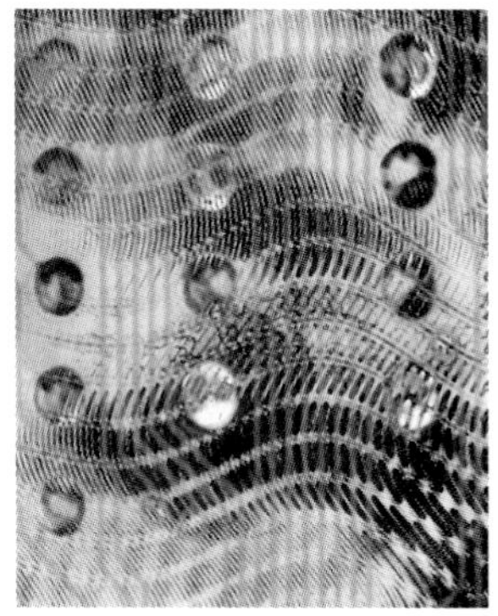

7 XSLT—Toward More Complex Applications

CHAPTER OBJECTIVES

By reading the information and practicing the code in this chapter, you will understand and be able to

1. Work with additional and more sophisticated elements and functions.
2. Develop medium complexity extensible stylesheet language transformation (XSLT) applications and transform existing extensible markup language (XML) documents to hypertext markup language (HTML) or to another XML document.
3. Determine appropriateness and develop with XSLT tools.
4. Execute some arithmetic operations and use `xsl:variable` in XSLT applications.
5. Format numerical results output using `format-number`.

7.1 ADDITIONAL ELEMENTS

Additional elements used in development of more complex XSLT applications include conditional statements for selection and functions for simple arithmetic calculation. The first of these additional elements is

7.1.1 `<xsl:element>`

When you want to output an element node to the output destination (especially when the element name is to be calculated at run-time) use the `<xsl:element>` instruction. `<xls:element>` has a mandatory attribute `qname` (qualified name, a valid XML name with an optional namespace prefix). The value for qname is the name of the element that is generated by the <xsl:element> instruction. The instruction <xsl:element> can have an optional attribute namespace, the value of which is the namespace URI of the generated name. The contents of the generated elements of <xsl:element> are the nodes produced between the xsl:element start and end tags. As an example, beginning with

```
<?xml version="1.0"?>
<?xml-stylesheet type="text/xsl" href="comment1.xsl"?>
<insert>
example
</insert>
```

you want to transform another XML document in which the element

```
<first>start</first>
```

needs to be nested in the element test, whose content is the same as the insert element in the source document. The style sheet for this transformation is

```
<?xml version="1.0"?>
<xsl:stylesheet version="1.0" xmlns:xsl="http://www.w3.org/1999/XSL/
Transform">
<xsl:output method="xml" />
<xsl:template match="/">
<test>
<xsl:element name="first">
<xsl:value-of select="'start'" />
</xsl:element>
<xsl:value-of select="/insert" />
</test>
</xsl:template>
</xsl:stylesheet>
```

As you can see, the element test is inserted after <xsl:template match="/"> and first is created using <xsl:element>.

Since you want to create an XML document that can be saved, you should use the XSLT processor rather than the Internet Explorer (IE) processor. For example, if you named the source document source.xml, the XSL document transform.xsl, and the result document result.xml, then the command line in Saxon

```
saxon source.xml transform.xsl>result.xml
```

creates the following XML document:

```
<?xml version="1.0" encoding="utf-8"?>
<test>
<first>start</first>
example
</test>
```

You must be careful with the content of elements created with `<xsl:element>`. If the content is a string, as with "start" in the previous example, you need to include double quotations marks as in

```
<xsl:value-of select="'first'" />
```

If you use only one set of quotation marks, as in

```
<xsl:value-of select="first" />
```

the code produces an empty first element as in

```
<?xml version="1.0" encoding="utf-8"?>
<test>
<first />
example
</test>
```

7.1.2 `<xsl:attribute>`

To output an attribute name and value in a result tree, use `<xsl:attribute element>`. This element has two attributes, `name` and `namespace`. `name` is mandatory and has a value `Qname` to define the name of the attribute that will be generated. `namespace` is optional; its value is the namespace uniform resource identifier (URI) of the generated attribute. `<xsl:attribute>` takes the form

```
<xsl:attribute name ={Qname}>
   body
</xsl:attribute>
```

If you begin with the source code as in Example 7-1

Example 7-1

```
<?xml version="1.0"?>
<?xml-stylesheet type="text/xsl" href="comment1.xsl"?>
<insert>
example
</insert>
```

and want to add an element mass with the attribute `unit="Mev"`, use the code

```
<?xml version="1.0"?>
<xsl:stylesheet version="1.0" xmlns:xsl="http:// www.w3.org/1999/XSL/
Transform">
<xsl:output method="xml" />
<xsl:template match="/">
<test>
<xsl:element name="mass">
<xsl:attribute name="unit">Mev</xsl:attribute>
<xsl:value-of select="13.5" />
</xsl:element>
<xsl:value-of select="/insert" />
</test>
</xsl:template>
</xsl:stylesheet>
```

The `<xsl:attribute>` must be used when the element is added to the result tree and before any child is added to that node. The sequence

```
<xsl:element name="mass">
<xsl:value-of select="13.5" />
<xsl:attribute name="unit">Mev</xsl:attribute>
```

generates an error because the child (`content`) must be added to the element `mass`. The resulting XML file takes the following form, obtained using the Saxon extensible stylesheet language (XSL) processor

```
<?xml version="1.0" encoding="utf-8"?>
<test>
<mass unit="Mev">13.5</mass>
example
</test>
```

The next example is a little more complicated. If the XML source document has the form of Example 7-2,

Example 7-2

```
<?xml version="1.0"?>
<?xml-stylesheet type="text/xsl" href="elcreation.xsl"?>
<student name="John Focht"
   javaMark="80"
   xmlMark="90"
   xhtmlMark="89">
</student>
```

and you want to transform the XML document so that attributes become elements at the same time, the XSLT code to accomplish this is

```
<?xml version="1.0"?>
<xsl:stylesheet version="1.0" xmlns:xsl="http://www.w3.org/1999/XSL/
Transform">
<xsl:output method="xml" />
<xsl:template match="student">
<student>
<xsl:for-each select="@*">
<xsl:element name="{name()}">
<xsl:value-of select="." />
</xsl:element>
</xsl:for-each>
</student>
</xsl:template>
</xsl:stylesheet>
```

The code

```
<xsl:for-each select="@*">
```

selects all attributes, and the code

```
<xsl:element name="{name()}">
```

creates the new elements with the same names as the attributes in the XML source code. Using Saxon, as described in the previous example, returns the following result:

```
<?xml version="1.0" encoding="utf-8"?>
<student>
  <name>JohnFocht</name>
    <javaMark>80</javaMark>
    <xmlMark>90</xmlMark>
    <xhtmlMark>89</xhtmlMark>
</student>
```

7.1.3 <xsl:processing-instruction>

Sometimes you will want to generate a processing instruction in the output of your XML document. To accomplish this, use <xsl:processing-instruction> with the form

```
<xsl:processing instruction name =QName>
        template-body
</xsl:processing-instruction>
```

As an example, if you want to add a (CSS) style sheet to the output file with the form

```
<xml-stylesheet type="text/css" href:comment.css>
```

write the code

```
<xsl:processing-instruction name="xml-stylesheet">
type="text/css" href="comment.css"
<xsl:processing-instruction>
```

If you want to add a comment instruction to the output document, use `<xsl:comment>` with the form

```
<xsl:comment>
  body
</xsl:comment>
```

Beginning with the XML source document of Example 7-3

Example 7-3

```
<?xml version="1.0"?>
<?xml-stylesheet type="text/xsl" href="comment1.xsl"?>
<insert>
  example
</insert>
```

The following code creates a comment, a processing instruction, and an element test in which the content is equal to the content of the `insert` element in the source document

```
<?xml version="1.0"?>
<xsl:stylesheet version="1.0" xmlns:xsl="http://www.w3.org/1999/XSL/
Transform">
<xsl:output method="xml" />
<xsl:template match="/">
<xsl:processing-instruction name="xml-stylesheet"> type="text/css"
href="comment.css"
</xsl:processing-instruction>
<xsl:comment> This is a COMMENT</xsl:comment>
<test>
<xsl:element name="first">
<xsl:value-of select="'start'" />
</xsl:element>
<xsl:value-of select="/insert" />
</test>
</xsl:template>
</xsl:stylesheet>
```

Using Saxon, returns the following result

```
<?xml version="1.0" encoding="utf-8"?>
<?xml-stylesheet type="text/css" href="comment.css"?>
<!-- This is a COMMENT-->
<test>
<first>start</first>
example</test>
```

7.1.4 <xsl:text>

If you want to output literal text, use the <xsl:text> instruction. Its form is

```
<xsl:text>
  text
</xsl:text>
```

The XML source document, in the following example:

```
<?xml version="1.0"?>
<?xml-stylesheet type="text/xsl" href="text.xsl"?>
<insert>
  example
</insert>
```

is transformed to an HTML document and displays the string

```
This is a test example
```

The code needed for this transformation is Example 7-4.

Example 7-4

```
<?xml version="1.0"?>
 <xsl:stylesheet version="1.0" xmlns:xsl="http://www.w3.org/1999/XSL/
Transform">
 <xsl:template match="/">
 <html>
 <body>
 <p>
 <xsl:text>This is a text example</xsl:text>
 </p>
 </body>
 </html>
 </xsl:template>
</xsl:stylesheet>
```

7.1.5 <xsl:variable>

If you want to declare a variable, you can use <xsl:variable> with the form

```
<xsl:variable name=Qname select=expression>
  body
</xsl:variable>
```

<xsl:variable> has two attributes, name and select. name is mandatory, its value is the name of the variable. select is optional, its value is the expression equivalent to the value of the parameter. If the select attribute is omitted, the value of variable is the content of <xsl:variable>. You can specify the value of the variables in different ways. As an example,

```
<xsl:variable name="state" select="'California'" />
```

or

```
<xsl:variable name="state">California</xsl:variable>
```

If you use the select attribute to assign the value to the variable, a string value must be enclosed in additional quotes, or the wrong output results. If <xsl:variable> appears at the top level of the style sheet, it is a global variable. If <xsl:variable> appears as an instruction, within a template-body, it is a local variable.

As a declarative language, XSLT variables cannot change their values after they have been initiated. If you want to access variables anywhere in the style sheet, use a dollar sign followed by the variable name. As an example, if you have defined a variable conversion as

```
<xsl:variable name="conversion">3.38</xsl:variable>
```

later, when you want to use this variable, you need to use $ before the name. As such, the instruction

```
<xsl:value-of select="$conversion" />
```

returns the value

```
3.38
```

Using attribute select you can assign the value, which is the content of an element from the XML document, for example,

```
<xsl:variable name="price" select="/item/carPrice" />
```

assigns the value from element carPrice.

In XSLT, you can execute some arithmetic operations. You can use `<xsl:variable>` to convert temperatures, as an example, to convert a weather report from Fahrenheit to centigrade using the conversion factor

```
temCel= (temFah-32)/1.8
```

The style sheet to transform the XML source document to HTML and convert the temperatures is Example 7-5.

Example 7-5

```
<?xml version="1.0"?>
<xsl:stylesheet version="1.0" xmlns:xsl="http://www.w3.org/1999/XSL/
Transform">
<xsl:variable name="a">32</xsl:variable>
<xsl:variable name="b">1.8</xsl:variable>
<xsl:template match="/">
<html>
<body>
<table border="2">
   <tr>
     <th>Name</th>
     <th>Conditions</th>
     <th>Temperature</th>
     <th>Winds</th>
     <th>Relative Humidity</th>
   </tr>
<xsl:for-each select="//location">
<xsl:variable name="temp"
 select="temperature" />
   <tr>
     <td><xsl:value-of select="name" /></td>
     <td><xsl:value-of select="conditions" /></td>
     <td><xsl:value-of select="($temp div$b-$a div$b)" /></td>
     <td><xsl:value-of select="winds" /></td>
     <td><xsl:value-of select="relativeHumidity" /></td>
    </tr>
</xsl:for-each>
</table>
</body>
</html>
</xsl:template>
</xsl:stylesheet>
```

Running the code in IE returns the output

Name	Conditions	Temperature	Winds	Relative Humidity
Moscow	hazy	–2.7777777777777785	NW 7 mph	100%
Ljubljana	cloudy	2.777777777777775	SW 6 mph	93%
Los Gatos	cloudy	10	SE 12 mph	74%

The results table above outputs with a different format if the following code is changed:

1. original code from above

```
<td><xsl:value-of select="($temp div$b-$a div$b)" /> </td>
```

2. substituted code

```
<td><xsl:value-of select="format-number(($temp div$b-$a
div$b),'##0.00')" /></td>
```

3. result of substituted code is Example 7-6:

Example 7-6

Name	Conditions	Temperature	Winds	Relative Humidity
Moscow	hazy	–2.78	NW 7 mph	100%
Ljubljana	cloudy	2.78	SW 6 mph	93%
Los Gatos	cloudy	10.00	SE 12 mph	74%

Authors' Note: We suggest running code first without formatting. Results can then be improved per the exact number of digits returned.

In the above example, formatting was changed by keying

1. `format-number(`
2. the expression containing the number to be formatted
3. `, '` (comma, space, single quote)
4. `0` for each digit that should appear
5. `#` for each digit that should only appear when not zero (and not significant)
6. `.` to separate the integer part of a number from the fractional part
7. `,` to separate groups of digits in the integer part
8. `%` to display the number as a percentage

Using JavaScript, you can obtain the same result with

```
<script>
var xmlDoc = new ActiveXObject("Microsoft.XMLDOM")
xmlDoc.async= false
xmlDoc.load("exampleJS.xml")
var xslDoc = new ActiveXObject("Microsoft.XMLDOM")
xslDoc.async=false
xslDoc.load("exampleJS.xsl")
document.write(xmlDoc.transformNode(xslDoc))
</script>
```

7.1.6 <xsl:if> <xsl:choose>

If you want to offer an option of choice in your code, there are two XSLT options:

<xsl:if> and <xsl:choose>
<xsl:if> takes the form:

```
<xsl:if test="Boolean expression">
```

The XSLT <xsl:if> is simpler, it evaluates the expression in the test attribute. If the expression is true, the contents of <xsl:if> is evaluated. As an example, to display the spare parts from the XML document, `spareParts.xml`, with a current quantity higher than 210, use the variable `total` to test if the condition is fulfilled. The variable is defined with the expression

```
<xsl:variable name="total" select="quantity" />
```

Executing the code causes a <for-each> loop variable to get values that are content quality elements and tests with the expression:

```
<xsl:if test="($total >210)">
```

If there are more than 210 items of certain products, the data about those parts are displayed in the form of a table as in Example 7-7.

Example 7-7

```
<?xml version="1.0"?>
<xsl:stylesheet version="1.0" xmlns:xsl="http://www.w3.org/1999/XSL/
Transform">
 <xsl:template match="/spareParts">
<html>
 <body>
<h2><p><xsl:text>Spare parts which have more than 210 pieces in stock
</xsl:text></p></h2>
<table border="2">
   <tr>
```

```
        <th>Part Name</th>
        <th>Part Number</th>
        <th>Part Image</th>
        <th>Quantity</th>
      </tr>
<xsl:for-each select="//item">
<xsl:variable name="total"
 select="quantity" />
<xsl:if test="($total>210)">
  <tr>
   <td><xsl:value-of select="partName" /></td>
   <td><xsl:value-of select="partNumber" /></td>
   <td><xsl:value-of select="partImage" /></td>
   <td><xsl:value-of select="quantity" /></td>
  </tr>
</xsl:if>
</xsl:for-each>
</table>
</body>
</html>
</xsl:template>
</xsl:stylesheet>
```

The previous example displays

Spare parts which have more than 210 pieces in stock

Part Name	Part Number	Part Image	Quantity
sensor	Hs-142	sensor.jpeg	251

The following code is an example of using `<xsl:choose>` to select the spare parts with the selected part numbers HV-152 and HG-431. As you can see, the expression test is evaluated and set to true if the content of `partNumber` element is equal to HV-152 or HG-431. In this case, the characteristics of spare part are sent to the output. Only data of selected spare parts are displayed as in example 7-8.

Example 7-8

```
<?xml version="1.0"?>
<xsl:stylesheet version="1.0" xmlns:xsl="http://www.w3.org/1999/XSL/
Transform">
<xsl:template match="/spareParts">
<html>
<body>
<h2>
  <p>
  <xsl:text>An example of using the choose XSLT element for selecting
```

```
spare parts:</xsl:text>
  </p>
  </h2>
<p>
  <b><xsl:text>The following elements meet your request:</xsl:text>
  </b></p><br></br>
  <table border="2">
  <tr>
  <th>Part Name</th>
  <th>Part Number</th>
  <th>Part Image</th>
  <th>Quantity</th>
  </tr>
  <xsl:for-each select="//item">
  <xsl:choose>
  <xsl:when test="(partNumber='HV-152')">
  <tr>
  <td>
  <xsl:value-of select="partName" />
  </td>
  <td>
  <xsl:value-of select="partNumber" />
  </td>
  <td>
  <xsl:value-of select="partImage" />
  </td>
  <td>
  <xsl:value-of select="quantity" />
  </td>
  </tr>
  </xsl:when>
   <xsl:when test="(partNumber='HG-431')">
  <tr>
  <td>
  <xsl:value-of select="partName" />
  </td>
  <td>
  <xsl:value-of select="partNumber" />
  </td>
  <td>
  <xsl:value-of select="partImage" />
  </td>
  <td>
  <xsl:value-of select="quantity" />
  </td>
  </tr>
```

```
</xsl:when>
<xsl:otherwise></xsl:otherwise>
</xsl:choose>
</xsl:for-each>
</table>
</body>
</html>
</xsl:template>
</xsl:stylesheet>
```

Running the code in IE returns the result

An example of using the choose XSLT element for selecting spare parts

The following elements meet your request:

Part Name	Part Number	Part Image	Quantity
valve	HV-152	valve.jpeg	150
gear	HG-431	gear.jpeg	102

In the following example, the use of function sum is demonstrated. With the command `<xsl:value-of select="sum(//item/quantity)/>` the sum of all numbers representing the quantity of spare parts in stock is calculated and sent to output as in Example 7-9.

Example 7-9

```
<?xml version="1.0"?>
<xsl:stylesheet version="1.0" xmlns:xsl="http://www.w3.org/1999/XSL/
Transform">
<xsl:template match="/spareParts">
<html>
 <body>
   <h2>An example of how to use function sum() in XSLT</h2>
   <p><b><xsl:text>There are   </xsl:text>
    <xsl:value-of select="sum(//item/quantity)" />
    <xsl:text> parts in stock.</xsl:text></b></p>
  </body>
</html>
</xsl:template>
</xsl:stylesheet>
```

Running the code in IE returns the result

```
An example of how to use function sum() in XSLT
There are 553 parts in stock.
```

EXERCISES

7.1 Write the code to transform `releaseMeetings.xml` to HTML, and display it as a table sorted by `meetingTopic` element.

The listed meetings are tied to a major product release. This meeting schedule will be strictly followed in the 30-day pre-release period.

```
<releaseMeetings>
  <meeting>
    <day>Monday</day>
    <room>2</room>
    <startTime>9:30</startTime>
    <endTime>10:30</endTime>
    <meetingTopic>Marketing Status</meetingTopic>
    <participants>IC</participants>
    <participants>Marcom</participants>
    <participants>Direct Sales</participants>
  </meeting>
  <meeting>
    <day>Tuesday</day>
    <room>2</room>
    <startTime>9:30</startTime>
    <endTime>10:30</endTime>
    <meetingTopic>Weekly Update</meetingTopic>
    <participants>IC Project Managers</participants>
    <participants>Technical Writer</participants>
    <participants>IT Project Contact</participants>
  </meeting>
  <meeting>
    <day>Monday</day>
    <room>3</room>
    <startTime>3:30</startTime>
    <endTime>4:00</endTime>
    <meetingTopic>Budget</meetingTopic>
    <participants>IC Program Manager</participants>
    <participants>VP Commerce</participants>
  </meeting>
  <meeting>
    <day>Friday</day>
    <room>1</room>
    <startTime>1:00</startTime>
    <endTime>2:30</endTime>
    <meetingTopic>Weekly Wrap-Up</meetingTopic>
    <participants>IC Project Managers</participants>
    <participants>IT Analyst</participants>
```

```
    <participants>IT Lead Developer</participants>
    <participants>IC Program Manager</participants>
  </meeting>
  <meeting>
    <day>Friday</day>
    <room>2</room>
    <startTime>11:00</startTime>
    <endTime>11:45</endTime>
    <meetingTopic>Documentation</meetingTopic>
    <participants>IC Project Managers</participants>
    <participants>IT Analyst</participants>
    <participants>IT Lead Developer</participants>
    <participants>Technical Writer</participants>
  </meeting>
</releaseMeetings>
```

7.2 Write the code to find which meetings, in `releaseMeetings.xml`, the Internet commerce (IC) Project Managers will attend.

7.3 Write the code to find which meetings, in `releaseMeetings.xml`, will be held on Fridays; please note their start time and room number.

7.4 Later in the text you will send messages to mobile phones. For now, determine four lines of text to send to Weekly Update meeting participants reminding them of the meeting on their mobile. Write a code that will transform `releaseMeetings.xml` to a new XML file with this short note of information. Next, write the code to transform that new file to an HTML document, displaying the four lines of text you selected.

7.5 In the following XML document, `employee.xml`, locate the employee assigned to workspace C455 and display her/his name and all elements nested in the `setup` element.

```
<HREmpRecords>
<employee>
  <name>
    <last>Crowe</last>
    <first>Sharon</first>
    <suffix></suffix>
  </name>
  <status>
    <dateOfHire>1-12-01</dateOfHire>
    <ssn>549-55-5116</ssn>
    <EmpID>798</EmpID>
    <vested>3</vested>
```

```
      <empType>exempt</empType>
    </status>
    <location>
      <position>Sr. Technical Writer</position>
      <dept>Internet Commerce</dept>
      <section>Project Management</section>
      <hiringManager>Pat Kim</hiringManager>
      <workspace>C455</workspace>
    </location>
    <setup>
      <phone>741-5466</phone>
      <fax>741-4467</fax>
      <networkPass>798IC</networkPass>
      <email>scrowe</email>
      <pager>509-5445</pager>
      <laptop>Dell 800</laptop>
    </setup>
  </employee>
  <employee>
    <name>
      <last>Li</last>
      <first>Wei</first>
      <suffix></suffix>
    </name>
    <status>
      <dateOfHire>12-29-00</dateOfHire>
      <ssn>017-54-5596</ssn>
      <EmpID>763</EmpID>
      <vested>3</vested>
      <empType>exempt</empType>
    </status>
    <location>
      <position>Project Manager</position>
      <dept>Internet Commerce</dept>
      <section>IT</section>
      <hiringManager>Pat Kim</hiringManager>
      <workspace>C459</workspace>
    </location>
    <setup>
      <phone>741-2541</phone>
      <fax>741-5666</fax>
      <networkPass>763IC</networkPass>
      <email>wli</email>
      <pager>509-6523</pager>
      <laptop>Dell 650</laptop>
    </setup>
```

```
</employee>
<employee>
  <name>
    <last>Sadlowski</last>
    <first>David</first>
    <suffix>Jr.</suffix>
  </name>
  <status>
    <dateOfHire>1-15-01</dateOfHire>
    <ssn>557-98-4116</ssn>
    <EmpID>804</EmpID>
    <vested>3</vested>
    <empType>non-exempt</empType>
  </status>
  <location>
    <position>Developer</position>
    <dept>Internet Commerce</dept>
    <section>IT</section>
    <hiringManager>Pat Kim</hiringManager>
    <workspace>C452</workspace>
  </location>
  <setup>
    <phone>741-3255</phone>
    <fax>741-5666</fax>
    <networkPass>804IC</networkPass>
    <email>dsadlowski</email>
    <pager>509-1212</pager>
    <laptop>Dell 800</laptop>
  </setup>
</employee>
</HREmpRecords>
```

7.6 Transform the `employee.xml` document, from the previous example, to a new XML document to be used on the corporate Intranet directory. The directory will display the following information:

name
position
department
phone
email address

7.7 Transform the `employee.xml` document, from the previous example, to a new XML document to be used by Tech Support for scheduled upgrades. The schedule will display the following information:

name
email
workspace
networkPass
laptop

7.8 Create an XML document, `buildings.xml`, containing data describing the buildings in the following table:

Table 7-1 Skyscraper Statistics Example Data

Building of Structure	Location	Height (meters)
Bank of Manhattan	New York	283
Chrysler Building	New York	319
Eiffel Tower	Paris	300
Empire State Building	New York	381
Rockefeller Center	New York	259
Wall Street Building	New York	290
Woolworth Building	New York	241

7.9 Use XSLT to transform document into HTML, sorted with highest to lowest (descending) order and location.

7.10 Using document object model (DOM) and XSLT find the lowest building in New York. Sort the whole document by the name of the building.

7.11 The following document was started to assist in tracking students participating in information technology (IT) training and their subsequent employment. Complete the document and nest differently, if warranted. Write code to search for women over 40, with a high school education, who are employed after completing the IT training program.

```
<participants>
  <person>
    <name>Pahovnik</name>
    <personID>2312967</personID>
    <gender>f</gender>
    <unemployedBefore>5</unemployedBefore>
    <formalEducation>High school</formalEducation>
    <age>43</age>
    <addTraCourse>Digital Media</addTraCourse>
    <employedAfter>yes</employedAfter>
```

```
</person>
<person>
  <name>Hribar</name>
  <personID>120978</personID>
  <gender>f</gender>
  <unemployedBefore>3</unemployedBefore>
  <formalEducation>High School</formalEducation>
  <age>23</age>
  <addTraCourse>Web Design</addTraCourse>
  <employedAfter>yes</employedAfter>
</person>
<person>
  <name>Kovac</name>
  <personID>281053</personID>
  <gender></gender>
  <unemployedBefore>2</unemployedBefore>
  <formalEducation>College</formalEducation>
  <age>47</age>
  <addTraCourse>Internet Services</addTraCourse>
  <employedAfter>no</employedAfter>
</person>
<person>
  <name>Hudovernik</name>
  <personID>1311970</personID>
  <gender>m</gender>
  <unemployedBefore>5</unemployedBefore>
  <formalEducation>Primary School</formalEducation>
  <age>30</age>
  <addTraCourse>Computer Basics</addTraCourse>
  <employedAfter>no</employedAfter>
</person>
<person>
  <name>Potocnik</name>
  <personID>1712960</personID>
  <gender>f</gender>
  <unemployedBefore>3</unemployedBefore>
  <formalEducation>High School</formalEducation>
  <age>42</age>
  <addTraCourse>Web Design</addTraCourse>
  <employedAfter>no</employedAfter>
</person>
<person>
  <name>Leskosek</name>
  <personID>2810943</personID>
  <gender>m</gender>
  <unemployedBefore>6</unemployedBefore>
```

```
    <formalEducation>High School</formalEducation>
    <age>57</age>
    <addTraCourse>Computer Network</addTraCourse>
    <employedAfter>yes</employedAfter>
  </person>
  <person>
    <name>Hudarin</name>
    <personID>2311956</personID>
    <gender>m</gender>
    <unemployedBefore>2</unemployedBefore>
    <formalEducation>University</formalEducation>
    <age>45</age>
    <addTraCourse>Digital Media</addTraCourse>
    <employedAfter>yes</employedAfter>
  </person>
</participants>
```

7.12 Using DOM and XSLT, find the number of successful participants and transform source XML document to HTML. Show data in the form of a table with the following columns: person, formal education, unemployment, and employed after.

`person`, `formalEducation`, `unemployment`, and `newEmployment`, which must have the same value as `employedAfter`.

The number of successful participants (who found a job after training) should be found, and the percentage of their success in obtaining employment should be calculated and displayed.

7.13 Find a stock report on the Internet. Write an XML document with all relevant data. Process the XML document and transform it to an HTML document that displays results in a table sorted by company name.

7.14 Two companies use the same data, although it is saved in two different XML documents. Write code to transform one XML document in another and vice versa:

The Company A document has the following form:

```
<companyA>
  <itemCustomer>
    <customer address="Saratoga">ABCD Ltd.</customer>
    <orderNumber date="101201">1234</orderNumber>
    <productName quantity="20">computer</productName>
    <amount pricePerUnit="2000">40,000</amount>
  </itemCustomer>
  <itemCustomer>
    <customer address="Los Gatos">Praxis</customer>
    <orderNumber date="161101">1201</orderNumber>
```

```
    <productName quantity="2">printer</productName>
    <amount pricePerUnit="1000">2,000</amount>
  </itemCustomer>
  <itemCustomer>
    <customer address="Palo Alto">QWER</customer>
    <orderNumber date="211201">1331</orderNumber>
    <productName quantity="3">scanner</productName>
    <amount pricePerUnit="800">2,400</amount>
  </itemCustomer>
  <itemCustomer>
    <customer address="Oakland">CDg, Inc.</customer>
    <orderNumber date="111201">341</orderNumber>
    <productName quantity="10">fax</productName>
    <amount pricePerUnit="250">2,500</amount>
  </itemCustomer>
</companyA>
```

and the Company B document has the following form:

```
<companyB>
  <customer>
    <customerName>ABCD Ltd.</customerName>
    <customerAddress>Saratoga</customerAddress>
    <orderNum>1234</orderNum>
    <orderDate>101200</orderDate>
    <product>computer</product>
    <quantity>20</quantity>
    <amountTotal>40,000</amountTotal>
    <pricePerUnit>2,000</pricePerUnit>
  </customer>
  <customer>
    <customerName>Praxis</customerName>
    <customerAddress>Los Gatos</customerAddress>
    <orderNum>1201</orderNum>
    <orderDate>161100</orderDate>
    <product>printer</product>
    <quantity>2</quantity>
    <amountTotal>2,000</amountTotal>
    <pricePerUnit>1,000</pricePerUnit>
  </customer>
  <customer>
    <customerName>QWER</customerName>
    <customerAddress>Palo Alto</customerName>
    <orderNum>1331</orderNum>
    <orderDate>211200</orderDate>
    <productName>scanner</productName>
```

```
    <quantity>3</quantity>
    <amountTotal>2,400</amountTotal>
    <pricePerUnit>800</pricePerUnit>
  </customer>
  <customer>
    <customerName>CDg, Inc.</customer>
    <customerAddress>Oakland</customerAddress>
    <orderNumber>341</orderNumber>
    <orderDate>111201<orderDate>
    <productName>fax</productName>
    <quantity>10</quantity>
    <amount>2,500</amount>
    <pricePerUnit>250</pricePerUnit>
  </customer>
</companyB>
```

7.15 In the following XML document:

```
<?xml version="1.0"?>
<?xml-stylesheet type="text/xsl" href="SalesAver.xsl"?>
<company>
  <month>March
    <sales>135,000</sales>
  </month>
  <month>April
    <sales>145,000</sales>
  </month>
  <month>May
    <sales>185,000</sales>
  </month>
  <month>June
    <sales>165,000</sales>
  </month>
  <month>July
    <sales>125,000</sales>
  </month>
  <month>August
    <sales>105,000</sales>
  </month>
</company>
```

Find the average monthly sales using function `count` and `sum`.

Solution: The average value is equal to the sum of monthly sales divided by the number of months. To find total sales, sum sales for the months using function `sum` defined with the expression

```
sum(//month/sales)
```

The value is assigned to the variable total with the statement

```
<xsl:variable name="total" select="sum(//month/sales)" />
```

The number of months can be calculated using function `count` defined as

```
count(//month)
```

Assigned to the variable number with statement.

```
<xsl:variable name="number" select="count(//month)" >
```

The result

```
<?xml version="1.0"?>
<xsl:stylesheet version="1.0" xmlns:xsl="http://www.w3.org/1999/XSL/
Transform">
 <xsl:template match="/company">
<html>
 <body>

<xsl:variable name="total"
 select="sum(//month/sales)" />
<p><xsl:text>Total sales were </xsl:text></p>
<xsl:value-of select="$total" />
<xsl:variable name="number"  select="count(//month)" />
<p><xsl:text> The number of months was </xsl:text></p>
<xsl:value-of select="$number" />
<p>
<xsl:text> The average sale was </xsl:text>
<xsl:value-of select="($total div $number)" />
</p>
</body>
</html>
</xsl:template>
</xsl:stylesheet>
```

Running the code on IE returns the following result:

```
Total sales were 860000
The number of months was 6
The average sale was 143333.33333333334
```

The results above, output with a different format if the following code is changed:

1. original code from above

```
<xsl:value-of select="($total div $number)" />
```

2. substituted code

```
<xsl:value-of select="format-number(($total div
$number),'##00,000.00')" />
```

3. result of substituted code

```
Total sale were 86,0000
The number of months was 6
Average sale was 143,333.33
```

CHAPTER SUMMARY

1. When you want to output an element node to the output destination (especially when the element name is to be calculated at run-time), use the `<xsl:element>` instruction.`<xls:element>` has a mandatory attribute `qname` (qualified name, a valid XML name with an optional namespace prefix).
2. The value for `qname` is the name of the element that is generated by the `<xsl:element>` instruction. The instruction `<xsl:element>` can have an optional attribute `namespace`, the value of which is the namespace URI of the generated name. The contents of the generated elements of `<xsl:element>` are the nodes produced between the `xsl:element` start and end tags.
3. To output an attribute name and value in a result tree, use `<xsl:attribute element>`. This element has two attributes, `name` and `namespace`. `name` is mandatory and has a value `Qname` to define the name of the attribute that is generated. `namespace` is optional, its value is the namespace URI of the generated attribute.
4. The `<xsl:attribute>` must be used when the element is added to the result tree and before any child is added to that node.
5. Sometimes you will want to generate a processing instruction in the output of your XML document. To accomplish this, use `<xsl:processing-instruction>`.
6. If you want to add a comment instruction to the output document, use `<xsl:comment>`.
7. If you want to output literal text, use the `<xsl:text>` instruction.
8. If you want to declare a variable, you can use `<xsl:variable>`. `<xsl:variable>` has two attributes, `name` and `select`. `name` is mandatory; its value is the name of the variable. `select` is optional; its value is the expression equivalent to the value of the parameter. If the `select` attribute is omitted, the value of variable is the content of `<xsl:variable>`.
9. If you want to offer an option of choice in your code, there are two XSLT options, `<xsl:if>` and `<xsl:choose>`. The XSLT `<xsl:if>` is simpler; it evaluates the expression in the test attribute. If the expression is true, the contents of `<xsl:if>` is evaluated.

10. Although XSLT is primarily designed for the transformation of XML documents to XHTML, HTML, or WML, it is possible to perform some calculations using functions such as `sum` and `count`.
11. XSLT enables simple calculation with output formatted using `formatnumber`.

SELF-ASSESSMENT

To move on to the next chapter, you should feel comfortable that you understand and can do the following:

1. Use other XSLT elements, to include `<xsl:element>`, `<xsl:attribute>`, `<xsl:processing-instruction>`, and `<xsl:text>`. Develop a more complex application transforming a source XML document into another XML document.
2. Use XSLT elements `<xsl:variable>`, `<xsl:if>`, and `<xsl:choose>` in a more complex application including testing using arithmetic operation.
3. Use XPath function `sum` and `count` in different applications.
4. Be able to analyze different problems, understand user needs, and develop complex application using XSLT elements for transforming XML files into XHTML, HTML, wireless markup language (WML), and XML documents. Know how to produce different type of documents from a source XML file, and use the functions XSLT offers.

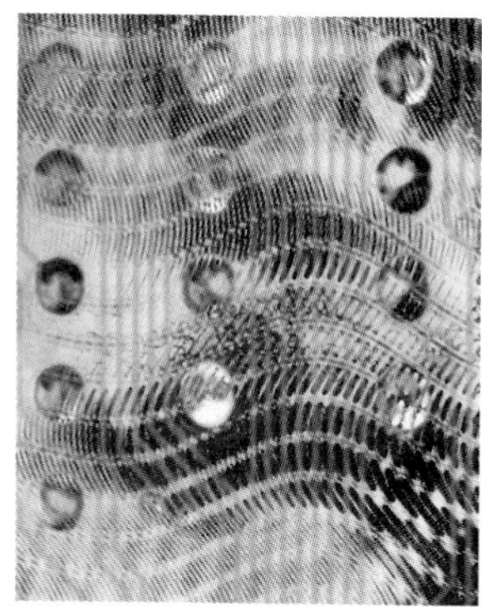

8 Simple API for XML

CHAPTER OBJECTIVES

By reading the information and practicing the code in this chapter, you will understand and be able to

1. Differentiate between document object mode (DOM) and simple API for XML (SAX), determine which works best under specific criteria, and work with SAX as an option to DOM.
2. Develop with SAX, an event-based simple application programming interface (API) for extensible markup language (XML).
3. Work with frequently used SAX methods.
4. Develop simple applications using SAX for navigating through large XML documents.
5. Select and develop SAX tools from the companion web site.

8.1 EVENT-BASED SEARCH

The SAX approach to the document search is much different than DOM (pronounced *sax* as a word, not as an acronym). With SAX, the XML document is not considered as a complex tree structure but as a linear, flat text document, monitored from start to end on an event basis. Events appear when there is change taking place in a document. As an example, if you read the XML document

```
<?xml version="1.0"?>
<DOMandSAX>
<philosophyDOM>tree based</philosophyDOM>
<philosophySAX>events based</philosophySAX>
<drawbackDOM>memory demanding</drawbackDOM>
<drawbackSAX>read only</drawbackSAX>
</DOMandSAX>
```

You can report about the appearance of the following events:

```
startDocument()
startElement("DOMandSAX")
startElement(philosophyDOM)
characters("tree based")
endElement("philosophyDOM")
startElement("philosophySAX")
characters("events based")
endElement("philosphySAX")
startElement(drawbackDOM)
characters("memory demanding")
endElement(drawbackDOM)
startElement(drawbackSAX)
characters("read only")
endElement(drawbackSAX)
endElement(DOMandSAX)
endDocument()
```

A similar algorithm is used in SAX. The XML documents contain elements defined by start and end tags and characters inside of those tags. If a parser runs from the start to the end of an XML document, it finds start tags, then characters, then end tags. This event-based interface has several advantages when compared to the more sophisticated DOM approach for processing XML documents.

1. Since the entire source document does not load into memory, there are no problems related to the size of the XML document.
2. Since SAX is not creating a complex tree structure, as in DOM, and simply scans the document in one pass, SAX is faster than DOM.
3. SAX is effective as an application when you need only a small portion of information returned from the XML document.
4. If you are an experienced Java programmer, you will easily transition to SAX to develop your applications.
5. SAX interfaces are supported by the most popular XML parsers.

SAX has some disadvantages as well.

1. At the time of this writing, current browsers are not supporting SAX.
2. Tools documentation is minimal, large amounts of time can be spent setting up.
3. SAX is not designed to change documents like DOM is; however, there are ways to use SAX to write XML documents.
4. SAX is difficult for developing applications with complex searches because without the document in memory, there is no document tree, making it difficult to access nodes.
5. SAX is developed in Java, and at this time there is no active support of SAX in other languages (some support for Python, VB, and C).
6. With DOM, you work with the XML document and Notepad. SAX requires tools that take time to set up and time with which to keep current.

8.2 THE STRUCTURE OF SAX

To use SAX, you need to download a SAX parser, such as Xerces from www.apache.org or xp from James Clark (www.jclark.com/xml/xp/). Some parsers do not include SAX classes. If not, these classes must to be downloaded as well (www.megginson.com/SAX/). You also need a Java Development kit (www.java.sun.com). SAX tools are changing quickly, check the companion web site (www.prenhall.com/carey) Tools Resource Center for additional tool information and download instructions.

Authors' Note: Updating your path and classpath is problematic with SAX. Again, please check the web site Tools Resource Center for step-by-step instructions. Parser documentation does not contain guidelines to take you through the process of effectively preparing to implement SAX. Although setting up can be complicated because of changing technologies, once you are ready, SAX can be used to create a simple application.

Starting from the XML document at the start of this chapter (on the philosophy of SAX and DOM), you can create code that will write the start of the document, the names of all document elements, and the end of the document.

SAX is structured as a number of Java Interfaces. The main interface that most SAX applications implement is the public interface ContentHandler implementing classes XMLReaderAdapter, XMLFilterImpl, and DefaultHandler. Because you will develop simple SAX applications use only some classes from the DefaultHandler class. They are

(a) `startDocument()` receive notification of the beginning of document.
(b) `endDocument()` receive notification of the end of document.
(c) `startElement(java.lang.String uri, java.lang.String localName, java.langString rawName, Attributes attributes)` receive notification of the start of an element.

(d) `endElement (java.lang.String uri, java.lang.String localName, java.lang.String rawName)` receive notification of the end of an element.
(e) `characters(char[] ch, int start int length)` receive notification of character data inside an element.

With the previous methods you can write small applications in Java. The following pages describe possible applications. As you know, to use SAX interfaces you also use Java, so to begin, create a Java class called `XMLDocReader`. Because several SAX interfaces must be implemented, include the import statement at the top of the code.

First, use the `startDocument` method to register the start of the document and to display "The start of the document" using `System.out.println`. Next, use the `startElement` method to detect the appearance of elements and to display the tag name of elements. Finally, use `endDocument` to display the message, "The end of the document." Your code will be Example 8-1.

Example 8-1

```
import org.xml.sax.*;
import org.xml.sax.helpers.DefaultHandler;
import org.apache.xerces.parsers.SAXParser;
public class DocReaderSax extends DefaultHandler
 {
 public void startDocument ()
      {
       System.out.println("The start of the document ");
      }
 public void startElement(String uri, String localName, String rawName,
        Attributes attributes)
      {
       System.out.println("The name of the element is " +rawName);
      }
   public void endDocument()
     {
       System.out.println("The end of the document  ");
     }
   public static void main(String[] args)
     {
         try {
            DocReaderSax SAXHandler = new DocReaderSax();
            SAXParser parser = new SAXParser();
            parser.setContentHandler(SAXHandler);
            parser.setErrorHandler(SAXHandler);
            parser.parse(args[0]);
         }
           catch (Exception e) {
```

```
                e.printStackTrace(System.err);
            }
        }
    }
```

The program is creating new class DocReaderSax using a parser that is an object of the org.apache.xerces.parsers.SAXParser class. At the same time, import the SAXParser class and a DefaultHandler interface that implements the required callback methods. This is done in the first three lines of the code.

```
import org.xml.sax.*;
import org.xml.sax.helpers.DefaultHandler;
import org.apache.xerces.parsers.SAXParser;
```

The main class of this program, the DocReaderSax class, is derived with

```
public class DocReaderSax extends DefaultHandler
```

When the parser register starts the event message, the start of the document is displayed.

```
startDocument method
 public void startDocument ()
   {
     System.out.println("The start of the document ");
   }
```

When the event start of element registers using the startElement method, the name of the element is sent to output.

```
public void startElement(String uri, String localName, String rawName,
        Attributes attributes)
  {
    System.out.println("The name of the element is " +rawName);
  }
```

When the end of the document is registered, using method endDocument, the message at the end of document is sent to output, as in

```
 public void endDocument()
   {
     System.out.println("The end of the document  ");
   }
```

Parsing of the document is done using the `parse` method of the parser object. The name of the file that will be parsed is specified by the user. The Java exception will be thrown. In the main method use

```
public static void main(String[] args)
  {
    try {
        DocReaderSax SAXHandler = new DocReaderSax();
        SAXParser parser = new SAXParser();
        parser.setContentHandler(SAXHandler);
        parser.setErrorHandler(SAXHandler);
        parser.parse(args[0]);
    }
      catch (Exception e) {
          e.printStackTrace(System.err);
    }
  }
}
```

Next, run the code using

`c:>java DocReaderSax example.xml` (`example.xml` is the name of file to be parsed).

The results will be

```
The start of document
The name of the element is DOMandSAX
The name of the element is philosophyDOM
The name of the element is philosophySAX
The name of the element is drawbackDOM
The name of the element is drawbackSAX
The end of the document
```

In the next example, move a step forward to find and send to output the contents of all elements.

First, use the `startDocument` method to register the start of document and to display, "The start of the document" using `System.out.println`.

Next, to find and display the content of the elements use the `characters` method and the `endDocument` method to register the end of the document and to display the message, "The end of the document." The code is Example 8-2.

Example 8-2

```
import org.xml.sax.*;
import org.xml.sax.helpers.DefaultHandler;
import org.apache.xerces.parsers.SAXParser;
```

```
public class ConReaderSax extends DefaultHandler
{
 public void startDocument ()
   {
    System.out.println("The start of the document ");
   }
     public void endDocument()
     {
       System.out.println("The end of the document  ");
     }
    public void characters(char characters[], int start, int length)
     {
       for (int i=start;i< start+length; i++)
        {
          System.out.print(characters[i]);
        }
     }
    public static void main(String[] args)
     {
       try {
              ConReaderSax SAXHandler = new ConReaderSax();
              SAXParser parser = new SAXParser();
              parser.setContentHandler(SAXHandler);
              parser.setErrorHandler(SAXHandler);
              parser.parse(args[0]);
        }
          catch (Exception e) {
              e.printStackTrace(System.err);
        }
  }
}
```

As you can see, the code is slightly modified. To get the contents of the XML document you used the `characters` method, which has three parameters, an array of type characters, the start location in the array, and the length of the text. The text is generated in the for-loop, where characters are printed.

```
public void characters(char characters[], int start, int length)
     {
       for (int i=start;i< start+length; i++)
     {
      System.out.print(characters[i]);
     }
     }
```

The output is

```
The start of the document
tree based
events based
memory demanding
read only
The end of the document
```

8.3 FIND CONTENT, SEND TO OUTPUT

In the following XML document, the goal is to find and send to output the contents of the following elements: `lastName` and `address`, `jobType`, and `clientSketch`. Begin, as in Example 8-3, by keying the XML document, `CADdrafting.xml`.

Example 8-3

```
<construction_clients>
  <drafting>
    <client>Wages</client>
      <lastName>Wages</lastName>
      <firstNames>Nancy, Mason</firstNames>
      <address>110 Pine Street, Paso Robles</address>
      <jobSiteAddress>110 Pine Street, Paso Robles
      </jobSiteAddress>
    </client>
    <status>
      <jobType>remodel/addition</jobType>
      <clientSketch>Nancy brought in a floorplan sketch and a
photograph of a house she likes </clientSketch>
      <floorplan_ElevSketch1>Completed 1/15 </floorplan_ElevSketch1>
      <clientApproval1>1/22, add patio door to Master Bedroom
</clientApproval1>
      <floorplan_ElevProof2>Completed 2/15 </floorplan_ElevProof2>
      <clientApproval2>Approved 3/1</clientApproval2>
      <floorplanCAD>Completed 3/22</floorplanCAD>
      <roofplanCAD>Completed 3/22</roofplanCAD>
      <elevationsCAD>Completed 3/22</elevationsCAD>
      <fdnplanCAD>in progress</fdnplanCAD>
      <cross_sectionsCAD>in progress</cross_sectionsCAD>
    </status>
  </drafting>
  <drafting>
    <client>Brown</client>
      <lastName>Brown</lastName>
      <firstNames>Don, Janelle</firstNames>
```

```
      <address>500 4th Avenue, San Jose 95123</address>
      <jobSiteAddress>330 Rancho Road, Hollister </jobSiteAddress>
    </client>
    <status>
      <jobType>new construction</jobType>
      <clientSketch>Janelle brought in a packaged plan with sketches
for changes</clientSketch>
      <floorplan_ElevSketch1>Completed 129 </floorplan_ElevSketch1>
      <clientApproval1>2/4, add 2 feet to porch in front. Reduce bath
#3 to 1/2 bath and add cabinetry/storage to replace tub unit.
</clientApproval1>
      <floorplan_ElevProof2>Completed 2/29</floorplan_ElevProof2>
      <clientApproval2>Approved 3/14</clientApproval2>
      <floorplanCAD>Completed 3/20</floorplanCAD>
      <roofplanCAD>Completed 3/20</roofplanCAD>
      <elevationsCAD>Completed 3/21</elevationsCAD>
      <fdnplanCAD>Completed 3/22</fdnplanCAD>
      <cross_sectionsCAD>Completed 3/22
      </cross_sectionsCAD>
    </status>
  </drafting>
  <drafting>
    <client>Minsberg</client>
      <lastName>Minsberg</lastNames>
      <firstNames>Stephanie, Art</firstName>
      <address>367 Stevens Creek #4, Santa Clara 94555 </address>
      <jobSiteAddress>900 Lake Blvd., Lake Tahoe, CA 92663
</jobSiteAddress>
    </client>
    <status>
      <jobType>new construction</jobType>
      <clientSketch>Stephanie and Art brought in floorplan made with
HomePlan Software and photographs of the lot with measured location of
trees. </clientSketch>
      <floorplan_ElevSketch1>Completed 1/28 </floorplan_ElevSketch1>
      <clientApproval1>CCRs in change, bring down under 1,200 SQ FT,
take the 175 SQ FT loss from fourth 4th bed and nominal other bedrooms.
Try to keep front room and kitchen as sketch. </clientApproval1>
      <floorplan_ElevProof2>Completed 2/19 </floorplan_ElevProof2>
      <clientApproval2>Approved 2/24</clientApproval2>
      <floorplanCAD>Completed 3/10</floorplanCAD>
      <roofplanCAD>Completed 3/10</roofplanCAD>
      <elevationsCAD>Completed 3/11</elevationsCAD>
      <fdnplanCAD>Completed 3/14</fdnplanCAD>
      <cross_sectionsCAD>Completed 3/14 </cross_sectionsCAD>
    </status>
```

```
  </drafting>
</construction_clients>
```

Next, search for elements `lastName`, `address`, `jobType`, and `clientSketch`. First, use the `startDocument` method to register the start of the document and to display, "The start of the document" using `System.out.println`. Next, you need the `startElement` method to register the element and to check if its tagname is equal to `lastName`, `address`, `jobType`, or `clientSketch`. Here you use an if statement. If the condition is fullfilled, the integer `i` will be set to `1` and `0` in all other cases. To find and display the content of the required elements, use the `characters` method in which you test the value of integer `i`. If it is `1`, the content will be displayed. Finally, use the `endDocument` method to register the end of the document and to display the message, "The end of the document."

The code is

```
import org.xml.sax.*;
import org.xml.sax.helpers.DefaultHandler;
import org.apache.xerces.parsers.SAXParser;
public class FindSax extends DefaultHandler
{
 int is=0;
 public void startDocument ()
   {
    System.out.println("The start of the document ");
   }
 public void endDocument()
   {
   System.out.println("The end of the document  ");
   }
 public void startElement(String uri, String localName, String rawName,
     Attributes attributes)
   {
     if(rawName.equals("lastName")||rawName.equals("address")||
rawName.equals("jobType")||rawName.equals("clientSketch"))
      {
       is=1;
      }
      else
      {
       is=0;
      }
   }
    public void characters(char characters[], int start, int length)
   {
      if(is>0)
```

```
{
       for (int i=start;i< start+length; i++)
        {
          System.out.print(characters[i]);
        }
}
     }
    public static void main(String[] args)
     {
       try {
            FindSax SAXHandler = new FindSax();
            SAXParser parser = new SAXParser();
            parser.setContentHandler(SAXHandler);
            parser.setErrorHandler(SAXHandler);
            parser.parse(args[0]);
        }
          catch (Exception e) {
              e.printStackTrace(System.err);
       }
   }
}
```

To select only elements using tag name `lastName`, you have to use if ()/else constructed first in the `startElement` method and next in the void characters method.

```
public void startElement(String uri, String localName, String rawName,
    Attributes attributes)
  {
   if(rawName.equals("lastName"))
     {
      is=1;
     }
      else
     {
      is=0;
     }
 }
   public void character (char characters[], int start, int length)
   {
     if(is>0)
{
       for (int i=start;i< start+length; i++)
        {
          System.out.print(characters[i]);
       }
}
```

The result is

```
The start of the document
Wages
110 Pine Street, Paso Robles
remodel/addition
Nancy brought in a floorplan sketch and a photograph of a house she
likes
Brown
500 4th Avenue, San Jose 95123
new construction
Janelle brought in a packaged plan with sketches for change
Minsberg
367 Steven Creek #4, Santa Clara 94555
new construction
Stephanie and Art brought in floorplan made with HomePlan Software and
photographs of the lot with measured location and trees
The end of the document
```

EXERCISES

8.1 Write the code needed to output the status data from the previous XML document (`CADdrafting.xml`) if the last name is Brown.

8.2 For the next exercise, first create the following XML document (Example 8-4) and save it as `finData.xml`. Instructions follow to assist in working this problem.

Example 8-4

```
<?xml version="1.0"?>
<silValFin>
 <semConMan>
    <company>
      <name>Append</name>
      <exchange>N</exchange>
      <tickerSymbol>APND</tickerSymbol>
      <last>39.63</last>
      <firstYearReturn>9.8</firstYearReturn>
      <high>55.38</high>
      <low>20.00</low>
      <earningPerShare>1.7</earningPerShare>
      <priceEarningRatio>18</priceEarningRatio>
      <marketCapitalizator>7236</marketCapitalizator>
      <relativeStrength>108</relativeStrength>
    </company>
    <company>
```

```
      <name>SemiGlobal</name>
      <exchange>N</exchange>
      <tickerSymbol>SG</tickerSymbol>
      <last>27.94</last>
      <firstYearReturn>-44.3</firstYearReturn>
      <high>85.94</high>
      <low>17.13</low>
      <earningPerShare>+3.76</earningPerShare>
      <priceEarningRatio>7</priceEarningRatio>
      <marketCapitalizator>48676</marketCapitalizator>
      <relativeStrength>105</relativeStrength>
    </company>
  </semConMan>
  <computSoft>
    <company>
      <name>Avantage</name>
      <exchange>N</exchange>
      <tickerSymbol>AVTG</tickerSymbol>
      <last>23.94</last>
      <firstYearReturn>42.8</firstYearReturn>
      <high>27.00</high>
      <low>8.91</low>
      <earningPerShare>2.00</earningPerShare>
      <priceEarningRatio>12</priceEarningRatio>
      <marketCapitalizator>8853</marketCapitalizator>
      <relativeStrength>106</relativeStrength>
    </company>
    <company>
      <name>Pluto</name>
      <exchange>N</exchange>
      <tickerSymbol>PLU</tickerSymbol>
      <last>2.19</last>
      <firstYearReturn>-93.9</firstYearReturn>
      <high>48.31</high>
      <low>.50</low>
      <earningPerShare>-61.60</earningPerShare>
      <priceEarningRatio>n/a</priceEarningRatio>
      <marketCapitalizator>703</marketCapitalizator>
      <relativeStrength>159</relativeStrength>
    </company>
  </computSoft>
  <telcomAndNetwork>
    <company>
      <name>WorldCall</name>
      <exchange>N</exchange>
      <tickerSymbol>WCAL</tickerSymbol>
```

```
      <last>10.13</last>
      <firstYearReturn>+19.7</firstYearReturn>
      <high>12.88</high>
      <low>5.38</low>
      <earningPerShare>0.44</earningPerShare>
      <priceEarningRatio>23</priceEarningRatio>
      <marketCapitalizator>347</marketCapitalizator>
      <relativeStrength>111</relativeStrength>
    </company>
    <company>
      <name>Verinext</name>
      <exchange>N</exchange>
      <tickerSymbol>VRNXT</tickerSymbol>
      <last>3.13</last>
      <firstYearReturn>-37.5</firstYearReturn>
      <high>22.00</high>
      <low>1.75</low>
      <earningPerShare>+0.11</earningPerShare>
      <priceEarningRatio>28</priceEarningRatio>
      <marketCapitalizator>441</marketCapitalizator>
      <relativeStrength>91</relativeStrength>
    </company>
  </telcomAndNetwork>
  <biotechAndMedPro>
    <company>
      <name>Avail</name>
      <exchange>N</exchange>
      <tickerSymbol>AVIL</tickerSymbol>
      <last>50.44</last>
      <firstYearReturn>+153.6</firstYearReturn>
      <high>70.61</high>
      <low>17.94</low>
      <earningPerShare>-5.49</earningPerShare>
      <priceEarningRatio>n/a</priceEarningRatio>
      <marketCapitalizator>11519</marketCapitalizator>
      <relativeStrength>93</relativeStrength>
    </company>
    <company>
      <name>XScope</name>
      <exchange>NY</exchange>
      <tickerSymbol>XSP</tickerSymbol>
      <last>53.00</last>
      <firstYearReturn>-16.3</firstYearReturn>
      <high>122.50</high>
      <low>42.25</low>
      <earningPerShare>n/a</earningPerShare>
```

```
        <priceEarningRatio>n/a</priceEarningRatio>
        <marketCapitalizator>278178</marketCapitalizator>
        <relativeStrength>89</relativeStrength>
      </company>
   </biotechAndMedPro>
  </silValFin>
```

For this exercise, use SAX to find the average value of the relative strength parameter. At the same time, for each company, send the following data to output:

Company Name
Ticker Symbol
The Last Stock Value
Relative Strength

To solve this problem

To find the average value, put initial values for variables average, total, and company to 0.
Next, use method `startElements` to set flags to 1 if you want to print the tagname of the elements to 3 to calculate the average of the `RelativeStrength` element and to increase the counter `ncompany`.
Using the method characters, print the tagname of elements that you selected and sum the values of `relativeStrength`.
Finally, in the `endDocument` divide the sum by the number of companies, to calculate and display the average.
The code is

```
import org.xml.sax.*;
import org.xml.sax.helpers.DefaultHandler;
import org.apache.xerces.parsers.SAXParser;
class SaxAver extends DefaultHandler {
 float Average=0;
float total=0;
int flag = -1;
int ncompany = 0;
public void startElement(String uri, String localName, String rawName,
Attributes attributes) {
    if(localName.equals("name")) {
      flag = 1;
System.out.print(localName+" = ");
   }
    else if(localName.equals("tickerSymbol")) {
      flag = 1;
```

```
System.out.print(localName+" = ");
   }
    else if(localName.equals("last")) {
      flag = 1;
System.out.print(localName+" = ");
   }
    else if(localName.equals("relativeStrength")) {
      flag = 3;
System.out.print(localName+" = ");
   }
    else if(localName.equals("company"))
ncompany++;
 }
  public void endElement(String uri, String localName, String rawName)
{
    flag = -1;
 }
  public void characters(char characters[], int start, int length) {
    String chData = (new String(characters, start,length)).trim();
if(chData.indexOf("\n") < 0 && chData.length() > 0) {
       if(flag >= 0){
System.out.println(chData);
 if(flag>=3) {
   total=Integer.parseInt(chData);
Average+=total;
 }
   }
   }
 }
 public void endDocument() {
    Average /=ncompany;
System.out.println("The average relative strength= "+Average);
 }
 public static void main(String[] args) {
    try {
 SaxAver SAXHandler = new SaxAver();
SAXParser parser = new SAXParser();
parser.setContentHandler(SAXHandler);
parser.setErrorHandler(SAXHandler);
parser.parse(args[0]);
   }
    catch(Exception e) {
 e.printStackTrace(System.err);
   }
 }
}
```

8.3 Using the XML document from the previous example (`finData.xml`), write the code to display

Company name
The ratio of the high value of stock to low value of stock higher than 4

8.4 Using `finData.xml`, write code to display

Company name
High value of stock
Market capitalizator if the price earning ratio is not available

CHAPTER SUMMARY

1. SAX is another API for navigation of XML documents. It is event based, registering events, rather than creating a document tree. As such, there are no memory problems, SAX can be used for parsing huge XML files.
2. SAX is read only, you can not modify document as with DOM. If the document is large as well as complex, it is difficult to use SAX because the user has to take care of all elements.
3. SAX is a common interface implemented for many different XML parsers.
4. To get the start and end of a document, you can use `startDocument` and `endDocument` methods, which have no arguments and are invoked when a parser finds the beginning and end of the document.
5. To get the start and end of XML element, use `startElement` and `endElement` methods. To get the content of an element, use the characters method.
6. Using methods for handling a document, you can develop different applications. Depending on application criteria, choose methods and write code that solves the problem.
7. SAX is a Java-based API. To write serious applications, you need a good understanding of Java.
8. The decision of when to use Java or SAX depends on the type of application.

SELF-ASSESSMENT

1. Demonstrate an understanding and be able to explain the main differences between SAX and DOM.
2. Demonstrate an understanding of events and how to use them in the development of SAX applications.
3. Demonstrate an understanding of handling methods such as `startDocument`, `endDocument`, `startElement`, `endElement`, and the characters method.

4. Write a simple Java application of SAX using the SAX interface and methods.
5. Analyze the problem with an application, and determine which to use, DOM or SAX, and argue your decision.
6. Write an application that extracts some information from an XML document and makes a mathematical operation on data such as the calculation of average values.

9 Extensible Stylesheet Language

CHAPTER OBJECTIVES

By reading the information and practicing the code in this chapter, you will understand and be able to

1. Apply style formatting using extensible stylesheet language (XSL).
2. Work with frequently used formatting objects.
3. Develop simple applications using formatting objects.
4. Use a formatting object to PDF (FOP) tool for transforming extensible markup language (XML) into portable document format (PDF) documents.
5. Select and develop using a combination of XSL and scalable vector graphics (SVG) as shown on the companion web site.

9.1 SOURCE CONTENT OUTPUT

The World Wide Web Consortium (W3C) defines XSL as "a language for expressing style sheets." XSL style sheets determine how the source content, from the XML document, should be formatted for output on browsers, hand-held devices, books, and other user agents. XSL provides a comprehensive model and vocabulary for developing style sheets using XML syntax.

XSL formatting objects are not implemented in any current browsers. Partial implementation is possible with James Tauber's FOP, which converts XML documents, using XSL formatting objects, into PDF files (shown later in this chapter). No web browsers currently display a document written with XSL formatting objects in the way cascading style sheets (CSS) displays extensible hypertext markup language (XHTML) or XML.

This chapter introduces the intent of XSL. Using XSL to apply style, formatting, and layout options to your web site is covered on the companion web site as they are implemented. Updates on browser compatibility are also regularly maintained on the companion web site (www.prenhall.com/carey) along with visual design considerations.

XHTML and CSS or XML and CSS link together to render style. XML with XSL separates semantic, structure, and style following the same approach to design; however, the XML/XSL combination is more powerful in its processing and capabilities. XSL is a bit daunting at first, the W3C specification includes over 100 pages of possible formatting options.

Although there are many similarities between CSS and XSL, XSL is designed for multiple output platforms, including large-scale documentation. As such, there are many options for detailed positioning on pages, creating master pages, and what seems like countless combinations. The approach you may decide to take is to continue to assess customer needs, develop XML documents with the focus of data manipulation, and as it becomes implemented, select portions of XSL to use for applying style.

The good news is that XSL will, when implemented, be powerful enough to allow you to effectively format complex web-based applications. The other good news is that if you need a simple application for an Intranet or an announcement for a client site, it is acceptable to continue with CSS. Memorizing available declarations for either CSS or XSL isn't the role of the developer. Planning and creating effective interfaces, then researching and applying style to allow the interface to meet the users' expectations makes for clean web applications. Style supports your purpose and the interaction between the client and the user.

With XSL, there are two aspects of the presentation process:

1. **Tree transformation** (constructing a result tree from the XML source tree)
2. **Formatting** (interpreting the result tree and producing the formatted results)

Tree transformation gives XSL an added dimension to CSS. As you know from previous chapters, source trees and result trees make sorting and multiple output configurations possible. Transformation also allows the structure of the result tree to be significantly different from the structure of the source tree. As a result, the XML source document can be manipulated in many different forms, supporting the idea of XML acting as a data bank, as discussed in the first chapter.

Formatting semantics are included in the result tree, expressed in terms of a catalog of classes of **formatting objects**. Formatting objects have to do with abstractions such as page, form, or table. Each of the nodes of the result tree are formatting objects. Presentation of the abstractions is a result of **formatting properties** (similar to CSS) applied to formatting objects.

The vocabulary of formatting objects supported by XSL is the set of `fo:` element types. Theoretically, there is more to formatting such as the **formatting object tree** and the **refined formatting object tree**. However, in this early stage of XSL you are to focus on basic semantics and application (more about XSL is available on the companion web site).

Formatting takes place with the generation of a tree of geometric areas, called the **area tree**. These areas are positioned on a sequence of one or more pages and have a position on the page specifying what to display in the area. These areas may be nested.

Rendering takes this area tree and causes a presentation to appear on the browser window or other output device.

These rectangular areas (Figure 9.1) have a **content rectangle**, which may include child areas and optional padding and border. The outer bound of the border is called the border rectangle, the outer bound of the padding is called the padding rectangle, and the outer border of the content is called the content rectangle.

Each area has a set of traits (a mapping of names to values). Individual traits may be used for rendering the area (**rendering traits**) or for defining constraints on formatting (**formatting traits**) or both.

9.2 FORMATTING

The four classes of XSL properties include:

1. CSS properties by copy (unchanged from CSS2 semantics)
2. CSS properties with extended values
3. CSS properties broken apart and/or extended
4. XSL only properties

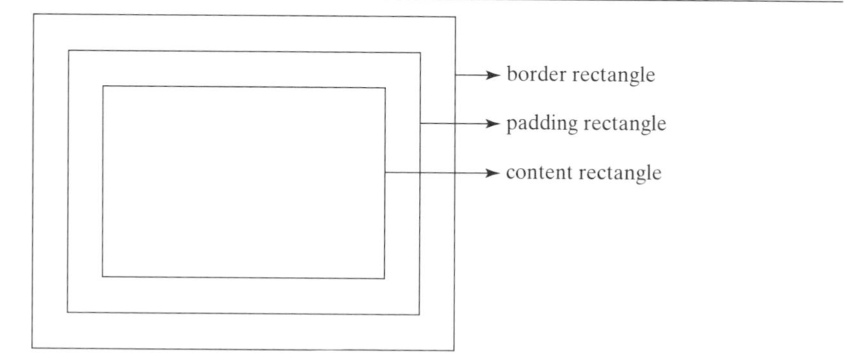

Figure 9-1 Rectangular Areas.

New properties include an extended page layout model, a comprehensive area model (extends the CSS2 box formatting model), internationalization and writing modes, and linking.

The XSL namespace is

```
http://w3.org/1999/XSL/Format
```

The date, 1999, is the year the URI was allocated to the W3C. It is not indicative of any XSL version number or version year. The XML namespace must be included for XSL processor to recognize the correct elements and attributes. XSL namespace elements are recognized only in the style sheet, not in the XML source document.

If you want to extend elements and attributes beyond this namespace, you must add a separate namespace rather than extend the W3C namespace. An XSL namespace element may include any attribute not from the XSL namespace if the expanded name of the attribute has a non-null namespace URI. Inclusion of these attributes cannot change the behavior or function of XSL elements as defined by the W3C. An XSL processor ignores attributes without giving an error, if it doesn't recognize the namespace URI.

The syntax developed by the W3C, used for naming XSL elements, attributes, and functions includes

1. Names are all in lowercase.
2. Hyphens are used to separate words.
3. Dots are used to separate names for the components of complex datatypes.
4. Abbreviations are used only if they already appear in the syntax of a related language such as XML or HTML.

9.3 XSL-FO

XSL is more flexible than CSS and can be used to transform languages into different media. Using XSL formatting objects (XSL-FO) you can develop sophisticated layout models. However, XSL-FO is still in development and changes outside of the abstract model discussed earlier in this chapter, in addition to implementation issues with browsers, are expected.

In XSL-FO there are currently 56 formatting objects, most of which include the prefix `fo`. These objects include more than 200 properties, most of which can be found on the companion web site. Areas, rectangular boxes that can contain text, empty space, and images make the base of formatting object model.

During the processing, the formatting object document is broken in pages. Each page contains areas. Basic areas are

1. Region
2. Block areas

3. Line areas
4. Inline areas

Regions contain blocks, blocks contain lines, and line areas contain inline areas. If you use page terminology you can say a page has three regions header, body, and footer. Block areas include paragraphs or list items, line areas include characters, symbols, and footnote references.

Formatting objects in an XSL-FO document determines the order of appearance of the elements on a page. Formatting properties specify page size color, font size, and so on. Formatting is the process in which description converts to presentation. Examples of formatting objects and their definitions are located on the companion web site. As an example,

1. The `fo:root` node is the top node of an XSL result tree composed of formatting objects.
2. The `fo:page-sequence` formatting object specifies how to create a sub-sequence of pages within a document, such as a financial statement or a quarterly summary within a year-end report. The content of these pages comes from flow children of the `fo:page-sequence`.
3. The `fo:flow objects` provide the flowing content distributed into pages.

These examples are important objects in XSL, and yet if XSL is closely related to CSS, why is it that they seem foreign? XSL is significantly more complex than CSS in its formatting capabilities. The following `fo` objects may seem more familiar:

4. The `fo:inline` formatting object formats a portion of text with a background or encloses it in a border.
5. The `fo:list-block` flow object formats a list.
6. The `fo:list-item` formatting objects contains the label and body of an item in a list.
7. The `fo:list-item-body` formatting objects contains the content of the body of a list-item.
8. The `fo:table` flow object formats the tabular material of a table.
9. Additional `fo` objects related to tables include `fo:table-and-caption`, `fo:table-body`, `fo:table-caption`, `fo:table-cell`, `fo:table-column`, `fo:table-footer`, `fo:table-header`, `and` `fo:table-row`, all with definitions close to those of CSS and XHTML.

With a document tree and formatting objects, the multitude of possible data and document combinations a user requests can be returned as readable, usable information.

9.3.1 Tree Example

In the following XSL document tree example, the root of the document is `fo:root`. It has two children, `fo:layout-master-set` and `fo:page-sequence`. The `fo:layout-master-set` can have more `fo:simple-page-master` children. The `fo:simple-page-master` can have following region child elements: `fo:region-before`, `fo:region-after`, `fo:region-body`, `fo:region-start`, and `fo:region-end`.

The formatting object can have one or more `fo:page` sequence elements. The `fo:paqe-sequence` can have three different child elements: `fo:title`, which is optional and contains the inline element that can be used as the title of the document; `fo:static-content`, used for creating headers and footers, and `fo:flow`, which contains the data to be placed on each page.

The `fo:root` object is the top node of the formatting tree and is declared with the expression

```
<fo:root xmlns:fo="http://www.w3.org/1999/XSL/Format">
```

Figure 9-2 represents the tree example just described.

The `fo:layout-master-set` formatting object contains all "masters" used in the document, which you can use to specify how each page will actually be built.

The `fo:layout-master-set` contains `fo:single-page-master` where you will insert data from the page specification in the attributes page-height, page-width, margin-top, margin-left, and margin-right. Here you also define the region area of the page.

Each `fo:page-sequence` represents a sequence of pages formatted the way you determined.

The XSL document starts with the page master `fo:simple-page-master`.

`fo:simple-page-master` has the following properties: margin-top, margin-bottom, margin-left, margin-right, space-before, space-after, start-indent, end-indent, master-name, page-height, page-width, reference-orientation, and writing-mode.

There are five regions on each page: region-body, region-after, region-before, region-body, region-start, region-end. These regions are a little confusing and, as such, are diagrammed on the web site.

The regions on the pages are created using the following XSL formatting objects; `fo:region-before`, `fo:region-after`, `fo:region-body`, `fo:region-start`, and `fo:region-end`. With these formatting objects you can use the following properties: common border, padding, and background properties, common margin properties for blocks, clip, column-count, column-gap, display-align, extent, overflow, region-name, reference-orientation, and writing-mode.

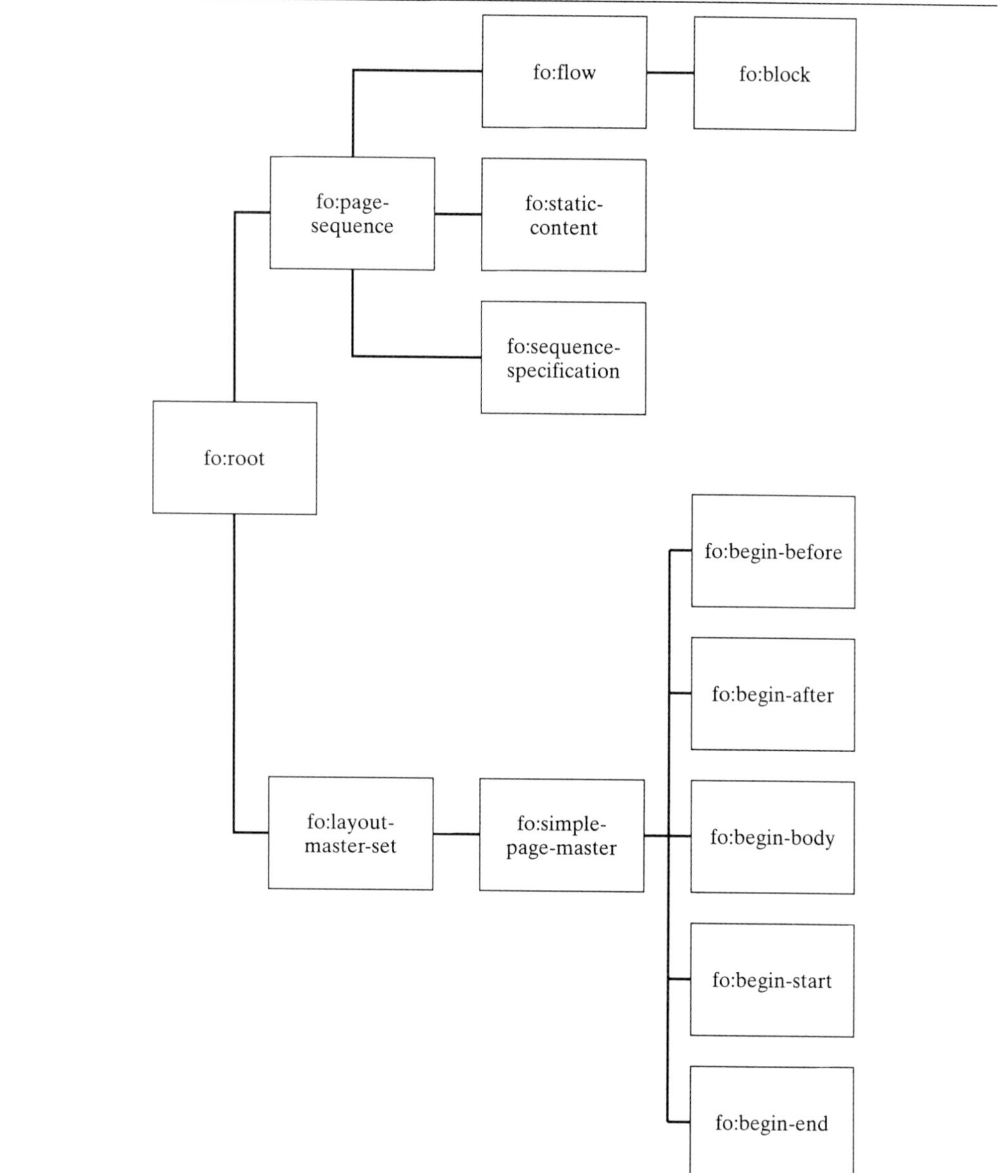

Figure 9-2 XSL Document Tree.

The `fo:page-sequence` elements are used when the XSL processor is creating pages of output documents. Each `fo:page-sequence` object references either an `fo:page-sequence-master` or a page master. The actual layout of pages is specified by those masters.

The following properties apply to the `fo:page-sequence object`; country, format, language, letter-value, grouping separator, grouping-size, id, initial-page-number, force-page-count, and master-name.

Next, specify the contents of the pages using the `fo:flow` elements.

You can use three kinds of flow objects; `fo:title`, `fo:static`, and `fo:flow`. `fo:flow` has a single property, `fo:flow-name`.

To create headers and footers use `fo:static-content` objects. To create block level content use `fo:block` with the properties: common accessibility properties (source-document, role), common aural properties, common border, padding, and background properties, background-attachment, common font properties (font-family, font-size, font-stretch, font-size-adjust, font-style, font-variant, font-weight), common hyphenation properties (country, language, script), and common margin properties for blocks (margin-top, margin-bottom).

You can add blocks into an XSL document, as in Example 9-1.

Example 9-1

```
<?xml version="1.0"?>
<fo:root xmlns:fo="http://www.w3.org/1999/XSL/Format">
  <fo:layout-master-set>
  <fo:simple-page-master master-name="page"
            page-height="29.7cm"
            page-width="21cm"
            margin-top="1cm"
            margin-bottom="2cm"
            margin-left="2.5cm"
            margin-right="2.5cm">
          <fo:region-body margin-top="2.5cm" />
          <fo:region-before extent="2.5cm" />
        <fo:region-after extent="1.5cm" />
  </fo:simple-page-master>
  </fo:layout-master-set>
  <fo:page-sequence master-name="page">
          <fo:flow>
          <fo:block font-size="18pt" font-family="arial"
line-height="30pt" text-align="center">
            First line
        </fo:block>
          <fo:block font-size="30pt" font-family="sans-serif"
line-height="24pt" text-align="center">
            Second line
          </fo:block>
        </fo:flow>
  </fo:page-sequence>
</fo:root>
```

9.4 INLINE-LEVEL FORMATTING OBJECTS

In addition to block objects, you can also create inline objects. Inline objects are typically used to format the part of the text that follows the normal flow in the page. For example, you can make the first character in a paragraph larger, the whole first line smaller, insert page numbers into text, and so on.

The inline formatting objects are; fo:bidi-override, fo:character, fo:leader, fo:page-number, fo:page-number-citation, fo:initial-property-set, fo:external-graphic, fo:instream-foreign-object, fo:inline, and fo:inline-container.

Graphics can be added with the fo:external-graphic object, which is used to embed an image in a document. The size of the image in the document can be set with the content, height, content-width, and scaling properties.

The following example adds graphics to the block:

```
<fo:flow>
  <fo:block>
   <fo:external-graphic src="vel.jpg" />
</fo:block>
```

If you wanted to create tables, there are nine formatting objects for creating tables; fo:table and-caption, fo:table, fo:table-column, fo:table-row, fo:table-cell, fo:table-caption, fo:table-header, fo:table-footer, and fo:table-body.

To create a table use the following sequence:

1. Create a fo:table object.
2. Format each column with an fo:table-column object.
3. Create a table body object.
4. Create table-row and table-cell for each cell in each row.

In the following example (Example 9-2), create a 2x2 table with the words XML, XSLT, XSL, XSFL in the cells.

Example 9-2

```
<?xml version="1.0"?>
<fo:root xmlns:fo="http://www.w3.org/1999/XSL/Format" >
    <fo:layout-master-set>
      <fo:simple-page-master master-name="page"
        page-height="11.0in"
        page-width="8.5in"
        margin-top="1.0mm"
        margin-bottom="1.0in"
        margin-left="1.5mm"
        margin-right="1.0mm">
```

```
    <fo:region-body margin-top="1.0in"
      margin-bottom=".5in"
      margin-left="0in"
              margin-right="0in" />
    <fo:region-before extent="1.0in" />
    <fo:region-after extent="0.5in" />
    </fo:simple-page-master>
  </fo:layout-master-set>
  <fo:page-sequence master-name="page">
    <fo:static-content flow-name="xsl-region-before">
    <fo:block font-size="18pt"
      font-family="sans-serif"
      line-height="24pt"
      space-after.optimum="15pt"
      background-color="red"
      color="yellow"
      text-align="center"
      padding-top="3pt">
      The XSLT, XPath and XSLF
    </fo:block>
    </fo:static-content>
    <fo:static-content flow-name="xsl-region-after">
    <fo:block font-size="14pt"
      font-family="sans-serif"
      line-height="20pt"
      space-after.optimum="15pt"
      background-color="blue"
      color="white"
      text-align="center"
      padding-top="3pt">
      Institute for Symbolic Analysis
    </fo:block>
    </fo:static-content>
    <fo:flow flow-name="xsl-region-body">
    <fo:block font-size="18pt"
      font-family="sans-serif"
      line-height="24pt"
      space-after.optimum="15pt"
      background-color="blue"
      color="white"
      text-align="center"
      padding-top="3pt">
      How to use table elements
    </fo:block>
    <fo:table>
    <fo:table-column column-number="1" column-width="20mm">
```

```
        </fo:table-column>
        <fo:table-column column-number="2" column-width="20mm">
        </fo:table-column>
        <fo:table-column column-number="3" column-width="20mm">
        </fo:table-column>
        <fo:table-body>
        <fo:table-row line-height="15mm">
        <fo:table-cell column-number="1">
        <fo:block font-family="sans-serif" font-size="12pt">
          XML
        </fo:block>
        </fo:table-cell>
        <fo:table-cell column-number="2">
        <fo:block font-family="sans-serif" font-size="14pt">
          XSLT
        </fo:block>
        </fo:table-cell>
        </fo:table-row>
        <fo:table-row line-height="15mm">
        <fo:table-cell column-number="1">
        <fo:block font-family="sans-serif" font-size="12pt">
          XSL
        </fo:block>
        </fo:table-cell>
        <fo:table-cell column-number="2">
        <fo:block font-family="sans-serif" font-size="14pt">
          XSLF
        </fo:block>
        </fo:table-cell>
        </fo:table-row>
        </fo:table-body>
        </fo:table>
        </fo:flow>
      </fo:page-sequence>
</fo:root>
```

9.5 XSL AND PDF OUTPUT

XML with XSL documents is not currently supported by any browser. XML and XSL can currently output to PDF files.

This PDF output seems a little complicated at first, but it does allow you to experiment with XSL and formatting objects. Additionally, PDF will remain an output you will use in web development, its read-only status is excellent for transporting documents over the Internet and Intranets without concern over adjustments to document content.

The first step in working with XSL to PDF is to define what the output is to look like. After determining style, transform the XML source document into an XML formatting document (`fo`). Typically, this transformation takes place using XSLT. If the `fo` document is small, you may decide to handcode rather than transform to an XML `fo` document. Both possibilities will be shown in the chapter.

Once you have the `fo` document, use Apache's tool, FOP (the only software tool implementing some of the features of XSL-FO, but not all). Using FOP you can transform your `fo` document into a PDF document, which can be opened and read using Adobe Acrobat Reader.

The crucial steps to this process are

1. Defining how the output will look
2. Developing the XSLT code to transform the source XML document into a `fo` document
3. Transforming the `fo` document into a PDF file using Apache FOP
4. Opening the PDF document with Adobe Acrobat Reader

As an example,

```
<?xml version="1.0"?>
<pdfToXml>
<title>Converting XML to a PDF document</title>
<text>Simple to do with some experience</text>
</pdfToXml>
```

As you know, first you determine how the output should look. In this example, the text is written on a page with the following dimensions and criteria:

1. width 800 pt
2. height 610 pt
3. top margin 45 pt
4. bottom margin 30 pt
5. left margin 40 pt
6. right margin 35 pt
7. header 20 pt and footer 15 pt
8. text in the header in XSLT, XPath, and XSL-FO
9. text in the footer is "Institute for Symbolic Analysis"

The content of element title is

10. font family sans serif
11. font style bold
12. character size 14 pt
13. text center aligned

The content of the element text is

14. font family sans-serif
15. font style italic
16. character size 10 pt

Since the document small, you can develop the `fo` document without using XSLT. The `fo` document must to be an XML document. With a standard prolog and namespace declaration, the code is

```
<?xml version="1.0"?>
<fo:root xmlns:fo="http://www.w3.org/1999/XSL/Format" >
  <fo:layout-master-set>
  <fo:simple-page-master master-name="page"
    page-height="800pt" page-width="610pt" margin-top="45pt"
    margin-bottom="30pt"
    margin-left="40pt"
    margin-right="35pt">
  <fo:region-body margin-top="20pt"
    margin-bottom="15pt"
    margin-left="0in"
    margin-right="0in" />
  <fo:region-before extent="20pt" />
  <fo:region-after extent="15pt" />
  </fo:simple-page-master>
  </fo:layout-master-set>
  <fo:page-sequence master-name="page">
  <fo:static-content
    flow-name="xsl-region-before">
  <fo:block>The XSLT, Path and XSLF</fo:block>
  </fo:static-content>
  fo:static-content
    flow-name="xsl-region-after">
  <fo:block>Institute for Symbolic Analysis</fo:block>
  </fo:static-content>
  <fo:flow name="a">
  <fo:block  font-size="14pt" line-height="38pt"
    font-family="sans-serif">
    Converting XML to a PDF document
  </fo:block>
  <fo:block  font-size="12pt" line-height="26pt"
    font-family="courier" background-color="red" font-style ="italic">
    Simple to do with some experience.
  </fo:block>
  </fo:flow>
```

```
  </fo:page-sequence>
</fo:root>
```

9.5.1 Adding XSLT

The fo document was created directly from small document. If the document were larger, you would have used XSLT to transform the XML to an fo document.

The following XSL document (Example 9-3) demonstrates XSLT transformation.

Example 9-3

```
<?xml version="1.0"?>
<xsl:stylesheet version="1.0"
xmlns:xsl="http://www.w3.org/1999/XSL/Transform"
xmlns:fo="http://www.w3.org/1999/XSL/Format">
<xsl:template match="/">
<fo:root>
  <fo:layout-master-set>
  <fo:simple-page-master master-name="page"
    page-height="800pt" page-width="610pt" margin-top="45pt"
    margin-bottom="30pt"
    margin-left="40pt"
    margin-right="35pt">
  <fo:region-body margin-top="20pt"
    margin-bottom="15pt"
    margin-left="0in"
    margin-right="0in" />
  <fo:region-before extent="20pt" />
  <fo:region-after extent="15pt" />
  </fo:simple-page-master>
  </fo:layout-master-set>
  <fo:page-sequence master-name="page">
  <fo:static-content
    flow-name="xsl-region-before">
  <fo:block>The XSLT, Path and XSLF</fo:block>
  </fo:static-content>
  <fo:static-content
    flow-name="xsl-region-after">
  <fo:block>Institute for Symbolic Analysis</fo:block>
  </fo:static-content>
  <fo:flow>
  <xsl:apply-templates/>
  </fo:flow>
  </fo:page-sequence>
  </fo:root>
  </xsl:template>
```

```
<xsl:template match="pdfToXml/title">
<fo:block font-size="14pt" line-height="38pt"
  font-family="sans-serif">
<xsl:value-of select="." />
</fo:block>
</xsl:template>
<xsl:template match="pdfToXml/text">
<fo:block  font-size="12pt" line-height="26pt"
  font-family="sans-serif" background-color="red" font-style
="italic">
<xsl:value-of select="." />
</fo:block>
</xsl:template>
</xsl:stylesheet>
```

Transformation of XML source document in `fo` document takes place with an XSLT processor such as Saxon (see companion web site for installation procedures and location of Saxon).

EXERCISES

9.1 The following code creates a PDF file (see the companion web site PDF example). Look at the code and see what adjustments you can make to increase readability of the document. Some properties will work, others will not. Try adding color, changing margins, and working with the fonts or font-weight.

```
<?xml version="1.0"?>
<fo:root xmlns:fo="http://www.w3.org/1999/XSL/Format" >
  <fo:layout-master-set>
  <fo:simple-page-master master-name="page"
    page-height="11.0in" page-width="8.5in" margin-top="1.0mm"
    margin-bottom="1.0in"
    margin-left="1.5mm"
    margin-right="1.0mm">
  <fo:region-body margin-top="1.0in"
    margin-bottom=".5in"
    margin-left="0in"
    margin-right="0in" />
  <fo:region-before extent="1.0in" />
  <fo:region-after extent="0.5in" />
  </fo:simple-page-master>
  </fo:layout-master-set>
  <fo:page-sequence master-name="page">
  <fo:static-content
    flow-name="xsl-region-before">
```

```
<fo:block>The XSLT, Path and XSLF</fo:block>
</fo:static-content>
<fo:static-content
  flow-name="xsl-region-after">
<fo:block>Institute for Symbolic Analysis</fo:block>
</fo:static-content>
<fo:flow>
<fo:block  font-size="12pt" font-weight="bold" line-height="38pt"
  font-family="arial">
  Observations
</fo:block>
<fo:list-block>
<fo:list-item line-height="20mm">
<fo:list-item-label>
<fo:block font-family="arial" font-size="14pt">
  1.
</fo:block>
</fo:list-item-label>
<fo:list-item-body>
<fo:block font-size="12pt" line-height="20pt" text-align="left"
  font-family="arial">

  Development of the web site is synonymous with the development of
the sales and support divisions within RPC. Not about creating a site,
but about expanding RPC. Users do business with the site in the same
way they do business with sales and support. Potential employees and
investors do business with the site in the same way they would do
business with human resources and finance.

Users view the site as though talking with sales, support, or an
engineer. They have the same needs and expectations. They are not
interested in using the site, but rather in doing business with RPC.

</fo:block>
</fo:list-item-body>
</fo:list-item>
</fo:list-block>
<fo:list-block>
<fo:list-item line-height="20mm">
<fo:list-item-label>
<fo:block font-family="arial" font-size="14pt">
  2.
</fo:block>
</fo:list-item-label>
<fo:list-item-body>
<fo:block font-size="12pt" line-height="20pt" text-align="left"
  font-family="arial">
```

```
 Simple, clean, consistent navigation is needed to allow for
understanding and accessibility of clients and RPC. The focus is on the
relationship with RPC and the client. It simply happens to take place
over the web.
 Current navigation is not consistent. First page navigates by
category, folders on the left and icon navigation by product confuses
users as to where they need to go to do business.

  </fo:block>
  </fo:list-item-body>
  </fo:list-item>
  </fo:list-block>
  <fo:list-block>
  <fo:list-item line-height="20mm">
  <fo:list-item-label>
  <fo:block font-family="arial" font-size="14pt">
    3.
  </fo:block>
  </fo:list-item-label>
  <fo:list-item-body>
  <fo:block font-size="12pt" line-height="20pt" text-align="left"
    font-family="arial">

  Users are comfortable with the RPC catalog and the small suite of
products they order. Even larger customers indicate they repeat order
like products. The ability to rely on the site as an extension of the
sales and support force may increase site use and encourage
understanding of a larger breadth of products.

  </fo:block>
  </fo:list-item-body>
  </fo:list-item>
  </fo:list-block>
  <fo:list-block>
  <fo:list-item line-height="20mm">
  <fo:list-item-label>
  <fo:block font-family="arial" font-size="14pt">
    4.
  </fo:block>
  </fo:list-item-label>
  <fo:list-item-body>
  <fo:block font-size="12pt" line-height="20pt" text-align="left"
    font-family="arial">

  Customers talk highly of the BrandX support as it offers access areas
for higher-level information and technical support. It seems as though
```

```
they have access to engineers. BrandX training gives them confidence in
product understanding with a moderate investment of time.

  </fo:block>
  </fo:list-item-body>
  </fo:list-item>
  </fo:list-block>
  <fo:list-block>
  <fo:list-item line-height="20mm">
  <fo:list-item-label>
  <fo:block font-family="arial" font-size="14pt">
    5.
  </fo:block>
  </fo:list-item-label>
  <fo:list-item-body>
  <fo:block font-size="12pt" line-height="20pt" text-align="left"
    font-family="arial">

  Although quite a bit of work has been done in the site over the past
month, an overall design concept will allow content to be presented
more consistently and will allow more focus on content development.

  </fo:block>
  </fo:list-item-body>
  </fo:list-item>
  </fo:list-block>
  </fo:flow>
  </fo:page-sequence>
</fo:root>
```

9.2 Using FOP, make a PDF document to contain verses from Oscar Wilde's poem, *The Ballad of Reading Gaol*. Define the outlook of the document. Build an XML document to hold the text, write XSLT for transforming, and use FOP to create the PDF file.

Yet each man kills the thing he loves,
By each let this be heard,
Some do it with a bitter look,
Some with a flattering word,
The coward does it with a kiss,
The brave man with a sword!
Some kill their love when they are young,
And some when they are old;
Some strangle with the hands of Lust,
Some with the hands of Gold:

The kindest use a knife, because
The dead so soon grow cold.
Some love too little, some too long,
Some sell, and others buy;
Some do the deed with many tears,
And some without a sigh:
For each man kills the thing he loves,
Yet each man does not die.
I know not whether Laws be right,
Or whether Laws be wrong;
All that we know who lie in gaol
Is that the wall is strong;
And that each day is like a year,
A year whose days are long.

9.3 Starting with the XML document below, make a PDF document in which the report is shown in a table with a student names in every row and marks for XML, Java, and XHTML.

```
<?xml version="1.0"?>
<report>
  <student>
    <name>Focht</name>
    <marks XML="87" Java="78" XHTML="90"/>
  </student>
  <student>
    <name>Jimenez</name>
    <marks XML="89" Java="78" XHTML="90"/>
  </student>
  <student>
    <name>Smith</name>
    <marks XML="82" Java="76" XHTML="95"/>
  </student>
  <student>
    <name>Bunin</name>
    <marks XML="86" Java="89" XHTML="95"/>
  </student>
</report>
```

9.4 Create an XML document with the content emergency procedures, and produce a PDF document to be distributed via email, presenting the procedures as:

The first page has title and information about medical emergency, security, and assault.

The second page has title and information about fire and bomb attack.

The third page has title and information about sexual harassment.

All pages must have a header with the text "Emergency Procedures" and footer with "Network Computing Security Department."

```
<emergency_procedures>
  <medical_emergency>
    <procedure>Immediately dial *8. Give your name, location, number of
people involved, details of medical emergency. Await further
instruction and advice.</procedure>
  </medical_emergency>
  <security>
    <procedure>dial *8, or from a public or mobile phone, ring the
police at 911. Report any threat. Important: Do NOT endanger your
life.</procedure>
  </security>
  <assault>
    <procedure>dial *8, or from a public or mobile phone, ring the
police at 911. Do not wash, shower, change clothes, or clean up in any
way until after talking to the police and going to the hospital. You
could destroy vital evidence. Don't drink alcohol or take tranquilizers
or other drugs, you want to give a clear account of what happened. Try
to remember everything you can about your attacker. Remember, you are
the victim. You have nothing to feel guilty or ashamed about. Police
officers are aware that a person who has been assaulted, sexually or
otherwise, is likely to be suffering from emotional shock. They will do
all they can to make things as comfortable as possible for you.
</procedure>
  </assault>
  <harassment>
    <procedure>in an emergency dial *8. If you are being harassed on
site, call security at *111. Report all incidents of harassment to a
contact officer, where confidentiality is ensured. Sexual harassment is
not always violent-it takes many different forms. Sexually oriented
comments, jokes, abuse, gestures, and the display of sexually offensive
materials are all examples of sexual harassment.</procedure>
  </harassment>
  <fire>
    <procedure>Do NOT panic. dial *8. Report the location and details
of the fire. Alert other occupants by calling "FIRE." Attend to other
human life in danger. If appropriate, select the correct fire
extinguisher and dispense of the contents on the fire, only if
appropriate. If you are uncertain or are unable to extinguish the fire,
```

```
leave via the fire escape; do not use the elevator. Do NOT endanger
your life or the life of others. If in doubt, leave the building or
area immediately.</procedure>
  </fire>
  <bomb_threat>
    <procedure>Attempt to gain as much information as possible. Where
is the bomb located? When is it set to go off? What does it look like?
Do NOT hang up-keep the line open, even if the other party hangs up, Do
NOT hang up. Immediately go to another phone and dial *8. If you find a
bomb, or suspect you have, DO NOT TOUCH IT. Ask all persons to leave
the area within the building. Seal the area as best possible (block the
entrance). Immediately go to another area and call *8. Await further
instructions.
  </procedure>
  </bomb_threat>
</emergency_procedures>
```

9.5 Update your resume as an XML document, and transform it to a PDF file using XSLT and FOP.

CHAPTER SUMMARY

1. No web browsers currently display a document written with XSL formatting objects in the way CSS displays XHTML or XML.
2. Partial implementation is possible with James Tauber's FOP, which converts XML documents, using XSL formatting objects, into PDF files.
3. XML with XSL separates semantic, structure, and style following the same approach to design; however, the XML/XSL combination will be more powerful in its processing and capabilities.
4. Although there are many similarities between CSS and XSL, XSL is designed for multiple output platforms, including large scale documentation. As such, there are many options for detailed positioning on pages, creating master pages, and what seems like countless combinations.
5. There are several formatting objects and multiple properties for styling output documents from an XML document. With XSL, there are two aspects of the presentation process, tree transformation (constructing a result tree from the XML source tree) and formatting (interpreting the result tree and producing the formatted results. Formatting is performed by the formatter).
6. Formatting semantics are included in the result tree, expressed in terms of a catalog of classes of formatting objects. Each of the nodes of the result tree are formatting objects. Formatting properties (similar to CSS) are applied to formatting objects, providing the vocabulary for presentation intent.

7. Formatting objects may be block-level or inline-level (following the definition developed for CSS) according to how they are typically stacked by the formatter.
8. The FO document has a tree structure with the `fo:root` element on top and with two children, `fo:layout-master-set` and `fo:page-sequence`.
9. The `fo:layout-master-set` has `fo:simple-page-master` child elements that describe the page on which the content is placed. The content of the source document is placed using the `fo:page-sequence` object.
10. `fo:page-sequence` has the following child elements: `fo:sequence specification`, `fo:static-content`, and `fo:flow`.
11. `fo:page` specifies in which order master pages must be used. For simple documents, you have only one master page; for complex document there may be more than one master page.
12. `fo:static-content` is used to place information that is to appear on all pages of document (such as header and footer).
13. `fo:flow` object contains the content of document using `fo:blocks`, which is placed on the document in a specified sequence.
14. To present the content of a source XML document, use XSLT to create a fo document. After the fo document is created, it can be transformed to the desired output document.
15. Browsers currently do not support XSL-FO. The only working software tool is Apache's FOP, which can transform an FO document into a PDF file. This tool does not implement all elements of XSL-FO.

SELF-ASSESSMENT

1. Demonstrate an understanding of the tree structure of `fo` documents and the main elements of the tree, `fo:layout-master-set` and `fo:page-sequence`.
2. Demonstrate an understanding of `fo:simple-page-master`, its main properties, and how to use and define them in applications.
3. Demonstrate an understanding of creating five regions and corresponding formatting objects: `fo:region-before`, `fo:region-after`, `fo:region-body`, `fo:region-start`, and `fo:region-end`, and how to write code using these objects.
4. Use `fo:page-sequences` for specifying the page sequence of a document using the main properties of this object.
5. Create headers and footers using `fo:static-content` object and its properties.
6. Use `fo:flow` objects with different `fo:block` elements to design pages in accordance with user requirements.
7. Write an application for creating lists in output documents and simple tables using fo objects.

8. Transform a source XML document to a FO document using XSLT and Apache's FOP tool for transforming FO document to PDF documents.
9. Develop small applications, starting from user analysis, modelling the XML document using XSLT for transforming and generating PDF output using FOP.

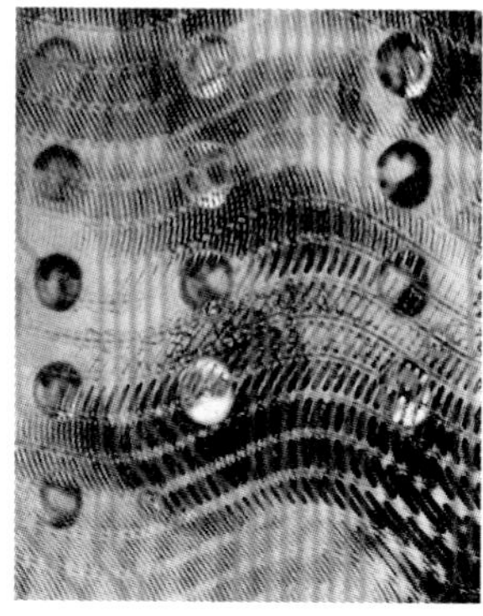

10 Server Side XML

CHAPTER OBJECTIVES

By reading the information and practicing the code in this chapter, you will understand and be able to

1. Develop server side extensible markup language (XML) applications.
2. Utilize Active Server Page (ASP) technology to develop simple applications on the server side.
3. Use document object mode (DOM) and extensible stylesheet language transformation (XSLT) on the server side within the framework of ASP.
4. Transform XML into hypertext markup language (HTML) and send to the client side.
5. Use active data object (ADO) for database manipulation using the XML framework of ASP.
6. Develop code using the additional technologies covered on the companion web site (www.prenhall.com/carey) such as JavaServer Pages (JSP).

10.1 SERVER TECHNOLOGIES

As you know, the Internet has changed dramatically in the last few years. Companies' expectations have shifted from a presence on the web to secure transactions and sophisticated interface design. The Internet is based on media for communicating information, developing partnerships, and conducting trading. The jobshift resulting from transitioning economies changes the way we work and live. More people are working, buying, accessing, learning, and communicating online.

XML plays an important role in this transition because of its simplicity, reliability, and ease of transmission of data from one web site, protocol, and platform to another.

At this time, one of the technologies used for server-side programming is active server pages (ASP), developed by Microsoft. ASP is a server-side scripting environment that enables you to embed scripting commands inside an HTML document. The default scripting language in ASP is VBScript. You can use other languages, such as JavaScript, as well. One important feature of ASP is that the result of the document processing is returned as a plain HTML document to the user. This means any user with any browser can open the resulting document regardless of the level of the user's browser support. As an example, if the source document is XML, ASP returns information in the form of an hypertext markup language (HTML) document.

Authors' Note: The text demonstrates ASP using JavaScript, continuing the example set in the DOM chapter. The same code and exercises are available on the companion web site (www.prenhall.com/carey) using VBScript, Microsoft's scripting language. Additionally, the same code and exercises are also on the web site replacing ASP with JavaServer Pages (JSP), from Sun Microsystems. ASP and JSP, JavaScript and VBScript all do a good job. The decision of which to use is based on requirement specifications of your client, company, and browser compatibility. Whatever your personal preference or politics, Internet Explorer (IE) 5.5 and 6 support XML more vigorously than competing browsers. As a developer, you will most likely have the opportunity to work with both ASP and JSP as well as VBScript and JavaScript.

It is much easier to write server-side applications using ASP than to use technologies such as common gateway interface CGI, because ASP is simpler to develop. Security, an important issue on the Internet is tighter with ASP technology. It is not possible to download an ASP document because the ASP processor interprets the ASP document every time it is called, sending the resulting HTML file to the client.

ASP technology is based on the component object model (COM).

To manage interaction between a web server and the user's browser, ASP provides a collection of objects and components. There are six core objects in the Active Server Pages Object model: Request, Response, Application, Session, Server, and Object Context. For client server applications, the most important are core objects Request and Response.

The Request object is used to pass information with an HTTP request and to access data. The Request object has five collections (which store information in a similar way as an array): `QueryString`, `Form`, Cookies, ClientCertificate. In your applications use `QueryString` and `form` to get data from the user.

QueryString is simple way of sending data to a server. Information is added after the end of the URL and is passed to the server. As an example,

```
http://www.mojpes.net/test.asp?searchkey=weather
```

Because collections store information as a pair of name and value, ASP understands `searchkey` as name and `weather` as value. The pair are stored in the collection for later access. To access the information write the following command:

```
Request.QueryString("searchkey")
```

You can send more than one name/value pair using & (ampersand) as a delimiter. As an example,

```
http://mojpes.net/test.asp?searckey=weather&name=flight&company=
AdriaAirways&destination=Paris
```

transmits three pairs: `searchkey` with value `weather`; `name` with value `flight`, and `company` with value `AdriaAirways`. The pairs are saved in the collection and can be accessed in an application with `Request.QueryString("searchkey")`, `Request.QueryString("name")`, and `Request.QueryString("company")` respectively.

Another way to send information to a server is to add it in same way to the link specified in an anchor tag, as in

```
<a href="http://mojpes.net/test.asp?searchkey="weather">nice web site
about dogs</a>
```

When you click on the link, the added information is sent to the server. You can invoke it in the same way as in previous examples.

Another way to send data is to use the `form` and `get` method. The information from the examples above can be sent, as in

```
<form action="test.asp" method="get">
Key searchkey <input type="text" name="searchkey"><br />
<input type=submit value=Submit>
</form>
```

`test.asp`, in this case, is an application document using the information you will send.

`QueryString` and `get` methods are not the best way to send information. The information is accessible to the public, and you are limited in the size of the information sent. The best way to send information is to use forms using the `post` method, as in

```
<form action="test.asp" method="post">
Key searchkey <input type="text" name="searchkey"><br />
```

```
<input type=submit value=Submit>
</form>
```

The information sent with the `post` method can be retrieved with the expression

```
Request.Form("searchkey")
```

Because communication between the client and server is bidirectional, you need to use a Response object method. The most frequently used method is `Response.Write`, as in

```
Response.Write("Welcome to our web site")
```

which sends the string Welcome to our web site to the user's browser. In your application, use this method to send the results of the processed document to the user. In applications using XML documents on the server side use methods from the server object connected with processing XML documents, such as

```
Server.CreateObject
```

which instantiates a new instance of an object (usually the first command you have to execute to start document processing), and the `MapPath` method, which returns the string that contains the actual path to the file for which you are looking.

If you understand the above explained methods and can write code in scripting languages, such as JavaScript or VBScript, you will be able to write small ASP applications (an understanding of DOM and XSLT is also necessary).

10.2 ACTIVE SERVER PAGE FILES

The ASP file is relatively easy to write. ASP files contain HTML tags and sometimes server scripts located in <% %> tags. Applications utilizing ASP are based on DOM and XSLT. To begin, you need a basic understanding of ASP syntax.

First, you need to know how to load an XML document, parse it, and create a document tree to use DOM for manipulation of the XML document and to send information to the client side. This procedure is similar to loading an XML document using ActiveX technology on the client side. As an example,

```
var yourDoc=Server.CreateObject("Microsoft.XMLDOM")
```

instantiates a Microsoft DOM object and assigns it `reference yourDoc`
Loading is done synchronously

```
yourDoc.async=false
```

the document should be validated;

```
yourDoc.validateOnParse=true
```

loading of the XML document `example.xml` is executed;

```
yourDoc.load(Server.MapPath("example.xml"))
```

enabling you to find the root element of `yourDoc`;

```
root=yourDoc.documentElement
```

At this point, you can use other DOM interfaces for manipulation of the document on the server side.

If rather than DOM, you decide to use XSLT for transforming the XML document into an HTML document (the result is sent to the browser as a plain HTML file and can be opened on browsers not supporting XML) on the server side, the procedure is similar to the DOM example. First, you create two objects to load the XML and XSL documents, then transform the XML (using XSLT) to HTML, which will be send to the client. As an example,

loading and creating document tree for the XML document;

```
yourXML = Server.CreateObject("Microsoft.XMLDOM")
yourXml.async=false
yourXml.load(Server.MapPath("example.xml"))
```

loading and creating an XSL document;

```
yourXsl=Server.CreateObject("Microsoft.XMLDOM")
yourXsl.async=false
yourXsl.load(Server.MapPath("example.xsl"))
```

Transforming the XML to HTML is accomplished with the statement

```
yourHTML = yourXml.transformNode(yourXsl)
```

To send the HTML document to the client, add the instruction

```
Response.Write(yourHTML)
```

Now you are ready to develop a small application (Example 10-1).

Example 10-1

```
<?xml version="1.0"?>
<product>
```

```
<name>computer</name>
<price>$2,000</price>
<inStock>yes</inStock>
</product>
```

is saved on a server as `example.xml`.

Using DOM, find the name `price` and `inStock` elements, sending their contents to the browser. This can be accomplished using JavaScript in an ASP file. The code is

```
<%@ Language="JavaScript"%>
<%
var yourDoc= Server.CreateObject("Microsoft.XMLDOM")
yourDoc.async=false
yourDoc.load(Server.MapPath("example.xml"))
root=yourDoc.documentElement
strHtml=""
a=root.firstChild.firstChild.nodeValue
b=root.firstChild.nextSibling.firstChild.nodeValue
c=root.lastChild.firstChild.nodeValue
strHtml=a+"<br />"+b+"<br />"+c
Response.Write(strHtml)
%>
```

Looking at the code above, you can see DOM was used to find root element and its children. Values are saved in the string `strHtml`, which is sent to the client with the `Response.Write` instruction.

Open the following XML document, keyed earlier in the text and saved as `spareParts.xml`. In the following example use `spareParts.xml` and XSL to transform the XML into HTML on the server side, sending the result to the client.

```
<?xml version="1.0"?>
<?xml-stylesheet type="text/xsl" href="sparePart3.xsl"?>
<spareParts>
<item>
 <partName>valve</partName>
 <partNumber>HV-152</partNumber>
 <partImage>valve.jpeg</partImage>
 <quantity>150</quantity>
</item>
<item>
 <partName>belt</partName>
 <partNumber>HB-342</partNumber>
 <partImage>belt.jpeg</partImage>
 <quantity>50</quantity>
```

```
</item>
<item>
 <partName>gear</partName>
 <partNumber>HG-431</partNumber>
 <partImage>gear.jpeg</partImage>
 <quantity>102</quantity>
</item>
```

The XSL document to transform XML is

```
<?xml version="1.0"?>
<xsl:stylesheet version="1.0" xmlns:xsl="http://www.w3.org/1999/XSL/
Transform">
<xsl:template match="/">
<html>
 <body>
  <table border="2">
<xsl:for-each select="spareParts/item">
   <tr>
   <td><xsl:value-of select="partName" /></td>
   <td><xsl:value-of select="partNumber" /></td>
   <td><xsl:value-of select="partImage" /></td>
   <td><xsl:value-of select="quantity" /></td>
  </tr>
 </xsl:for-each>
 </table>
</body>
</html>
</xsl:template>
</xsl:stylesheet>
```

The ASP file that creates both tree documents, transforms the source XML into an HTML document, and sends it to the browser is Example 10-2.

Example 10-2

```
<%@ Language ="JavaScript"%>
<%
yourXml=Server.CreateObject("Microsoft.XMLDOM")
yourXml.async=false
yourXml.load(Server.MapPath("sparePart3.xml"))
yourXsl=Server.CreateObject("Microsoft.XMLDOM")
yourXsl.async=false
yourXsl.load("sparePart3.xsl")
Response.Write(yourXml.transformNode(yourXsl))
%>
```

As you can see, the code has two parts. Loading XML and XSL documents uses the load function, as in

```
yourXml=Server.CreateObject("Microsoft.XMLDOM")
yourXml.async=false
yourXml.load(Server.MapPath("sparePart3.xml"))
yourXsl=Server.CreateObject("Microsoft.XMLDOM")
yourXsl.async=false
yourXsl.load(Server.MapPath("sparePart3.xsl"))
```

and transforms XML into HTML and sends the HTML to the client, as in

```
Response.Write(yourXml.transformNode(yourXsl)).
%>
```

To avoid problems, if one of the loaded files is not well-formed, you must improve the code by adding an instruction to warn if an error occurs during parsing, as in

```
<%@ Language="JavaScript"%>
<%
var yourXml=Server.CreateObject("Microsoft.XMLDOM")
var yourXsl=Server.CreateObject("Microsoft.XMLDOM")
  yourXml.async=false
  yourXsl.async=false
  yourXml.load(Server.MapPath("sparePart3.xml"))
  yourXsl.load(Server.MapPath("sparePart3.xsl"))
 if (yourXml.parseError==0 && yourXsl.parseError==0)
{
    Response.Write(yourXml.transformNode(yourXsl))
}
 else
    {
    Response.Write("Could not generate XHTML document")
  }
%>
```

10.3 MORE COMPLEX ASP

Next, you will use ASP technology to navigate XML documents on the server side and send the results to the client side. The following XML document (Example 10-3) describes a portion of the employee records from a Human Resources department.

Example 10-3

```
<?xml version="1.0"?>
<HREmpRecords>
```

```
<employee>
  <name>
    <last>Crowe</last>
    <first>Sharon</first>
    <suffix></suffix>
  </name>
  <status>
    <dateOfHire>1-12-01</dateOfHire>
    <ssn>549-55-5116</ssn>
    <EmpID>798</EmpID>
    <vested>3</vested>
    <EmpType>exempt</EmpType>
  </status>
  <location>
    <position>Sr. Technical Writer</position>
    <dept>Internet Commerce</dept>
    <section>Project Management</section>
    <hiringManager>Pat Kim</hiringManager>
    <workspace>C455</workspace>
  </location>
  <setup>
    <phone>741-5466</phone>
    <fax>741-4467</fax>
    <networkPass>798IC</networkPass>
    <email>scrowe</email>
    <pager>509-5445</pager>
    <laptop>Dell 800</laptop>
  </setup>
</employee>
<employee>
  <name>
    <last>Li</last>
    <first>Wei</first>
    <suffix></suffix>
  </name>
  <status>
    <dateOfHire>12-29-00</dateOfHire>
    <ssn>017-54-5596</ssn>
    <EmpID>763</EmpID>
    <vested>3</vested>
    <EmpType>exempt</EmpType>
  </status>
  <location>
    <position>Project Manager</position>
    <dept>Internet Commerce</dept>
    <section>IT</section>
```

```
      <hiringManager>Pat Kim</hiringManager>
      <workspace>C459</workspace>
    </location>
    <setup>
      <phone>741-2541</phone>
      <fax>741-5666</fax>
      <networkPass>763IC</networkPass>
      <email>wli</email>
      <pager>509-6523</pager>
      <laptop>Dell 650</laptop>
    </setup>
  </employee>
  <employee>
    <name>
      <last>Sadlowski</last>
      <first>David</first>
      <suffix>Jr.</suffix>
    </name>
    <status>
      <dateOfHire>1-15-01</dateOfHire>
      <ssn>557-98-4116</ssn>
      <EmpID>804</EmpID>
      <vested>3</vested>
      <EmpType>non-exempt</EmpType>
    </status>
    <location>
      <position>Developer</position>
      <dept>Internet Commerce</dept>
      <section>IT</section>
      <hiringManager>Pat Kim</hiringManager>
      <workspace>C452</workspace>
    </location>
    <setup>
      <phone>741-3255</phone>
      <fax>741-5666</fax>
      <networkPass>804IC</networkPass>
      <email>dsadlowski</email>
      <pager>509-1212</pager>
      <laptop>Dell 800</laptop>
    </setup>
  </employee>
  </HREmpRecords>
```

You are to develop an application enabling users to search the document by family name, return the name, phone and fax number, and the email address of the requested employee. The code for this search must run on the server side; the result will be sent to the user. ASP technology can solve this problem. One possible approach is to use DOM. To begin, you identify three modules (parts) to solving the problem:

1. Sending searched data from the client to the server
2. Processing the XML document to get the required data
3. Sending the required data to the user on the client side

In answer to 1, an XHTML document is running on the client side. You can use the get method to send search keywords to the server. One possible approach is

```
<html>
<body>
<form action="employee1.asp" method="get">
Please type the name you are looking for:
<input type="text" name="fname"><br /><br />
<input type="submit" value="Submit">
</form>
</body>
</html>
```

saved on the server as `employee.html`.

In answer to 2, searching the `employee.xml` document, on the server, can be accomplished with

```
<%@ Language="JavaScript"%>
<%
//loading XML document
 source = Server.CreateObject("Microsoft.XMLDOM")
 source.async =false
 source.load(Server.MapPath(("employee.xml"))
//getting family name
fname=Request.QueryString("fname")
//searching for root and other elements using getElementsByTagName
  root=source.documentElement
  a=root.getElementsByTagName("name")
  a1=root.getElementsByTagName("fax")
  a2=root.getElementsByTagName("email")
 l=a.length
for(i=0;i<l;i++)
{
b=a.item(i).firstChild.nodeValue
//if the last name is found, sending the result to the client side
if(b==fname)
{
```

```
fax=a1.item(i).firstChild.nodeValue
email=a2.item(i).firstChild.nodeValue
Response.Write("The search result is:"+"<br />")
Response.Write("<br />"+"The fax number of Ms/Mr "+b+" is "+fax+"
<br />")
Response.Write("<br />"+"The email address of Ms/Mr "+b+" is "+email)
}
}
%>
```

In answer to 3, sending data to the user on the client side can be done using `Response.Write`, with simple styling. To accomplish this, first save the previous code as an ASP file. Next, to run the code on the server side, you need

1. The XML document containing data to be processed.
2. The HTML document to be used, on the client side, for input data.
3. The ASP document to process data on the server side and send the results to the client side.

These files must be in the same folder. To test your examples, you can use the Internet information server (IIS) or personal web server (PWS) on your PC. Other testing options include access to space on a commercial server supporting ASP or free space on servers for testing. There are several web sites offering this type of service. In this example, you will use `www.brinkster.com`. (Tools Resource Center is on the companion web site.)

The steps to the process are

1. Go to the web site where your `.html` file is located.
2. The `.html` file will be downloaded to your computer and the form will be executed.
3. The input will be sent to the `.asp` file, on the server, which will process the `.xml` file and send the search result back to your computer using `Response.Write`.
4. Write code to search the XML document from the previous example, find a person by Social Security Number (SSN), and output the following data: last name, first name, SSN, hiring date, position, and workspace.

10.4 SEARCHING ON THE SERVER

The next example (Example 10-4) is a little more complicated. You need to develop code to run on the server side, using ASP technology, to enable users on the client side to search for jobs available in different businesses, such as software.

To solve the problem, you can use DOM or XSLT. First try a DOM solution. To begin, generate XML documents. The first describes a legend (like a table of contents) for the jobs, and the second describes the job offerings.

Example 10-4

1. Legend

```
<?xml version="1.0"?>
<legend>
  <adm>Administrative</adm>
  <asy>Assembly</asy>
  <atr>Auto Repair</atr>
  <ban>Banking</ban>
  <byr>Buyer/Planer</byr>
  <chi>Childcare/Nannies</chi>
  <chm>Chemist</chm>
  <cnr>Counselor</cnr>
  <con>Construction</con>
  <csa>Customer Service Agent</csa>
  <dba>Database Administrator</dba>
  <dis>Dispatch</dis>
  <drv>Driver</drv>
  <edt>Editor</edt>
  <edu>Education</edu>
  <elc>Electrician</elc>
  <eng>Engineer</eng>
  <fin>Finance/Accounting</fin>
  <gra>Graphics</gra>
  <han>Handler(baggage,ramp,package)</han>
  <hr>Human Resources</hr>
  <ins>Instructor/Training</ins>
  <itl>Installer</itl>
  <lan>LAN/Network Admin.</lan>
  <law>Law Enforcement/Security</law>
  <lbr>Librarian</lbr>
  <mcn>Machinist</mcn>
  <med>Medical (Doctor,Nurse,Dentist</med>
  <mer>Merchandiser</mer>
  <mgr>Manager/ProjectLeader</mgr>
  <mkt>Marketing</mkt>
  <mnt>Maintenance</mnt>
  <opr>Data Processing Operator</opr>
  <pa>Application Programmer/Analyst></pa>
  <par>Paralegal</par>
  <pnr>Planner</pnr>
```

```
  <ppm>Property Manager</ppm>
  <pro>Web Producer</pro>
  <qa>Quality Assurance/Tester</qa>
  <rec>Recruiter</rec>
  <rst>Restaurant</rst>
  <sci>Scientist</sci>
  <sls>Sales</sls>
  <soc>Social Services</soc>
  <sya>Systems Administrator</sya>
  <sys>Systems Programmer Support</sys>
  <tch>Technician</tch>
  <tec>Customer/Tech Support</tec>
  <web>Web Developer/Webmaster</web>
  <whs>Warehouse/Shipping/Receiving</whs>
  <wrt>Technical/Copy Writer</wrt>
</legend>
```

2. Job Offerings

```
<?xml version="1.0"?>
<employerIndex>
  <accounting>
     <company>
      <name>Accounting Solution</name>
      <city>San Francisco</city>
      <job>FIN</job>
      <contact>www.accsol.com</contact>
    </company>
    <company>
      <name>Mohler, Nixon</name>
      <city>Campbell</city>
      <job>FIN</job>
       <job>MGR</job>
      <contact>www.mohlernixon.com</contact>
    </company>
  </accounting>
  <biotech>
    <company>
      <name>Connetics Corporation</name>
      <city>Palo Alto</city>
      <job>ADM</job>
      <job>FIN</job>
      <contact></contact>
    </company>
    <company>
      <name>Allergan</name>
```

```
      <city>Irvine</city>
      <job>CHM</job>
      <job>SCI</job>
      <contact></contact>
    </company>
  </biotech>
  <computerHwNet>
    <company>
      <name>Nokia</name>
      <city>Mountain View</city>
      <job>HR</job>
      <job>ENG</job>
      <job>SYS</job>
      <contact>www.nokia.com</contact>
    </company>
    <company>
      <name>Quantum</name>
      <city>Milpitas</city>
      <job>ENG</job>
      <contact>www.quantum.com</contact>
    </company>
  </computerHwNet>
  <ComputerSW>
    <company>
      <name>Netpace</name>
      <city>Union city</city>
      <job>WEB</job>
      <job>SYS</job>
      <contact>careers@netpace.com</contact>
    </company>
    <company>
      <name>Adobe Systems</name>
      <city>San Jose</city>
      <job>ADM</job>
      <job>ENG</job>
      <job>GRA</job>
      <job>MGR</job>
      <job>MKT</job>
      <contact>jobs@adobe.com</contact>
    </company>
  </ComputerSW>
</employerIndex>
```

Next, develop an application with several steps.

1. Develop the XHTML to run on the client side to enable the user to select job opportunity business area.
2. The choice is to be sent to the server; you can use the `post` method, with the following form:

```
<html>
<body>
<form action="EmployIndex.asp" method="post">
Please type the business area in which you would like to find a job:
<input type="text" name="iname"><br /><br />
<input type="submit" value="Submit">
</form>
</body>
</html>
```

3. Next, develop an ASP document to process both XML documents, find job listings in the selected business area, and send the search results to the client. One possible solution is

```
<%@ Language="JavaScript"%>
<%
// here the search keyword sname gets, from the client sent by the post
method
sname = Request.Form("iname")
// you process the two XML documents
var legXml=Server.CreateObject("Microsoft.XMLDOM")
var empXml=Server.CreateObject("Microsoft.XMLDOM")
legXml.async=false
legXml.load(Server.MapPath("legend.xml"))
empXml.async=false
empXml.load(server.MapPath("employInd.xml"))
rleg=legXml.documentElement
remp=empXml.documentElement
// finding business area
typeBusiness=remp.getElementsByTagName(sname)
jobAvail=typeBusiness.item(0).getElementsByTagName("job")
jobNum=jobAvail.length
if(jobNum==0)
{
document.Write("<br />"+"Sorry, there are no job offerings in
"+(sname)+"<br />")
}
for(i=0;i<jobNum;i++)
{
jobAcr=jobAvail.item(i).firstChild.nodeValue
```

```
jobAcrlow=jobAcr.toLowerCase()
//transferring job acronym in job name
jobName=rleg.getElementsByTagName(jobAcrlow).item(0).firstChild.
nodeValue
//finding elements to be sent to the user, on the client site
par=jobAvail.item(i).parentNode
comName=par.firstChild.firstChild.nodeValue
city=par.firstChild.nextSibling.firstChild.nodeValue
contact=par.lastChild.firstChild.nodeValue
//sending the data to the user
Response.Write("<br />"+"Company: "+comName+"<br />")
Response.Write("<br />"+"City: "+city+"<br />")
Response.Write("<b>"+"<br />"+"Job: "+jobName+"</b>"+"<br />")
Response.Write("<br />"+"Contact: "+contact+"<br />")
}
%>
```

EXERCISE

10.1 Using the previous example, write the code to find a job, searching by job name, in any business area and send the return hits back to the user.

10.5 SENDING DATA TO THE USER

In the next example (Example 10-5), `findata.xml` (created in Chapter 8, Simple API for XML) describes financial data about companies. Write code to find a specific company, and send its financial data back to the user.

Example 10-5

1. Open `findata.xml`
2. Again, develop three pieces of code. First, the XHTML for input, which can be saved on the server as `finData.html`

```
<html>
<body>
<form action="finData.asp" method="post">
Please key the name of the company you are looking for:
<input type="text" name="fname"><br /><br />
<input type="submit" value="Submit">
</form>
</body>
</html>
```

3. Searching the XML document (saved on the server as `finData.xml`) is accomplished with the code

```
<%@ Language="JavaScript"%>
<%
//loading XML document
source = Server.CreateObject("Microsoft.XMLDOM")
source.async=false
source.load(Server.MapPath("finData.xml"))
//defining array with names
var strName = new Array("name", "exchange", "tickerSymbol", "last",
"firstYearReturn", "high", "low", "earningPerShare",
"priceEarningRatio", "marketCapitalizator", "relativeStrength")
//getting company name
cname=Request.Form("fname")
//search for root and other elements using getElementsByTagName
  root=source.documentElement
  a=root.getElementsByTagName("name")
  l=a.length
  for(i=0;i<l;i++)
{
b=a.item(i).firstChild.nodeValue
//if the last name is found, send the result to the client side
if(b==cname)
{
companyRec=a.item(i).parentNode
numChild=companyRec.childNodes.length
for(j=0;j<numChild;j++)
{
el=companyRec.childNodes.item(j).firstChild.nodeValue
Response.Write(strNam[j]+" is "+el+"<br />)
}
}
}
%>
```

10.6 ASP AND XSLT

The following example (Example 10-6) shows how you can use XSLT to navigate your XML document and display the results. Referring, once again, to the XML document showing job availability (a sample portion of the document is shown below, refer to your saved document `employInd.xml`).

Example 10-6

```
<?xml version="1.0"?>
<?xml-stylesheet type="text/xsl" href="jobs.xsl"?>
<employerIndex>
<accounting>
```

```
<company>
 <name>Accounting Solution</name>
 <city>San Francisco</city>
 <job>FIN</job>
 <contact>www.accsol.com</contact>
</company>
<company>
 <name>Mohler, Nixon</name>
 <city>Campbell</city>
 <job>FIN</job>
 <job>MGR</job>
 <contact>www.mohlernixon.com</contact>
</company>
```

1. First, write the XSL code to show all jobs offered by the different companies:

```
<?xml version="1.0"?>
<xsl:stylesheet version="1.0" xmlns:xsl="http://www.w3.org/1999/XSL/
Transform">
<xsl:template match="/">
<html>
<body>
<table border="2">
 <tr>
     <th>Name</th>
     <th>City</th>
     <th>Job</th>
     <th>Contact</th>
 </tr>
<xsl:for-each select="//company">
 <tr>
   <td><xsl:value-of select="name" /></td>
   <td><xsl:value-of select="city" /></td>
   <td><xsl:value-of select="job" /></td>
   <td><xsl:value-of select="contact" /></td>
 </tr>
</xsl:for-each>
</table>
</body>
</html>
</xsl:template>
</xsl:stylesheet>
```

2. If you want to have the XML document on the server side and to send the XHTML file to the client side, write the ASP code

```
<%@ Language="JavaScript"%>
<%
 yourXml=Server.CreateObject("Microsoft.XMLDOM")
 yourXml.async=false
 yourXml.load(Server.MapPath("employInd.xml"))
 yourXsl.Server.CreateObject("Microsoft.XMLDOM")
 yourXsl.async=false
 yourXsl.load(Server.MapPath("employInd.xsl")
Response.Write(yourXml.transformNode(yourXsl))
%>
```

There are two parts to this process:

1. Loading both files synchronously.
2. Transforming the XML document to plain XHTML and sending it to the client side using the Response object from ASP.

EXERCISES

10.2 Using the XML document `employInd.xml`, XSLT, and ASP, write the code to find available jobs in the fields of accounting and biotechnology. Send them in the form of an XHTML file to the user, on the client side. The results should be formatted in a table.

10.3 Solve the same problem above using DOM. Compare the two ways of solving the problem

10.4 Write code to find all jobs in the field of science located in Irvine. Display the name of the company and contact information so the user can open the corporate web site to obtain more information

10.5 Earlier in the chapter you worked with the XML document `finData.xml`. In this exercise, using `finData.xml`, display all data, sorted by relative strength, in descending order.

First, key the XSL document

```
<?xml version="1.0"?>
<xsl:stylesheet version="1.0" xmlns:xsl="http://www.w3.org/1999/XSL/
Transform">
<xsl:template match="/">
<html>
 <body>
 <table border="2">
 <tr>
     <th>Name</th>
```

```
      <th>Last</th>
      <th>High</th>
      <th>Low</th>
      <th>Relative Strength</th>
 </tr>
<xsl:for-each select="//company">
<xsl:sort select="relativeStrength" data-type="number"
order="descending" />
 <tr>
   <td><xsl:value-of select="name" /></td>
   <td><xsl:value-of select="last" /></td>
   <td><xsl:value-of select="high" /></td>
   <td><xsl:value-of select="low" /></td>
   <td><xsl:value-of select="relativeStrength" /></td>
 </tr>
 </xsl:for-each>
 </table>
</body>
</html>
</xsl:template>
</xsl:stylesheet>
```

Sorting is accomplished with

```
<xsl:sort select ="relativeStrength" data-type="number"
order="descending"" />
```

The ASP document to process both documents on the server side is

```
<%
yourXml=Server.CreateObject("Microsoft.XMLDOM")
yourXml.async=false
yourXml.load(Server.MapPath("finData.xml"))
yourXsl=Server.CreateObject("Microsoft.XMLDOM")
yourXsl.async=false
yourXsl.load(Server.MapPath("finData.xsl"))
Response.Write(yourXml.transformNode(yourXsl))
%>
```

As you can see it has two parts:

Loading XML and XSL documents using load function

```
yourXml=Server.CreateObject("Microsoft.XMLDOM")
yourXml.async=false
yourXml.load(Server.MapPath("finData.xml"))
```

```
yourXsl=Server.CreateObject("Microsoft.XMLDOM")
yourXsl.async=false
yourXsl.load(Server.MapPath("finData.xsl"))
```

and transforming XML to HTML and sending to client with the instruction

```
Response.Write(yourXml.transformNode(yourXsl)).
%>
```

10.6 Develop code to sort the previous `finData.xml` document by new index ratio high/low value of stock in ascending order, on the server side, using ASP. The data to be displayed include

company name
earning per share
high
low
index=high/low
Solve the problem using DOM and XSLT

10.7 Develop code to calculate the average relative strength factor for all companies (in `finData.xml`), and display all data about those companies with relative strength larger than the average value. The application needs to run on a server using ASP technology.
Solve the problem using DOM.

10.8 If you begin with the following XML document, how would you go about deleting the last two children of the document, on the server side?

```
<?xml version="1.0"?>
<ExampleDOM>
<country>Slovenia</country>
<population>2,000,000</population>
<area>25,000</area>
<capital>Ljubljana</capital>
<GDP>10,900</GDP>
</ExampleDOM>
```

To solve this problem, use DOM and the `removeChild` method. The ASP document to accomplish this has the following form:

```
<%@ Language="JavaScript"%>
<html>
<%
 source = Server.CreateObject("Microsoft.XMLDOM")
 source.async =false
 source.load(Server.MapPath("exampleDOM.xml"))
```

```
 root=source.documentElement
  a=root.childNodes
  x=a.length
Response.Write("An example of using ASP and DOM"+"<br />")
Response.Write("<br />"+"The document has "+x+" children"+"<br />")
 xrem=root.removeChild(root.lastChild)
  a=root.childNodes
  x=a.length
 Response.Write("<br />"+"The document has "+x+" children"+"<br />")
xrem=root.removeChild(root.lastChild)
Response.Write("<br />"+"The document has "+x+" children"+"<br />")
  a=root.childNodes
  x=a.length
 Response.Write("<br />"+" The document has "+x+" children")
 %>
</html>
```

10.7 ASP AND DATABASES

Databases, the manipulation of database content, and the exchange of data is one of the major strengths of XML. Retrieving and sending data to the client or another server is possible using XML. Databases are important to most web-based applications; however, manipulating and saving data in and out of databases is not yet fully implemented.

In the following example (Example 10-7) use ASP to extract data from simple database on the server side and send them as XML document to the client. To develop that code use VBscript, which is the default language for ASP.

Example 10-7

First you have to define that you will send the XML document with the statement:

```
<%ResponseContentType="application/xml"%>
```

Next, send the prolog and root element of the XML document

```
<?xml version="1.0"?>
<dbExample>
```

To access data, use active data objects (ADO), which allows connection to the database using ADO objects:

```
DIM adoConnect
DIM adoRecordset
Set adoConnect =Server.CreateObject("ADODB.Connection")
adoConnect.open "Provider=Microsoft.Jet.OLEDB.4.0;"_
& "Data Source=c:\coldCall.mdb"
```

In the next example, coldCall.mdb (an Access database file) contains data about potential new clients.

Table 10-1 Data for coldCall.mdb.

ID	Client
1	Mateja Hribar
2	Steve Contreras
3	Gita Hazemi
4	Rory Condon
5	Jean McIntosh
6	Joshua Rascov

In the code below new is the name of database table; client is the element name. To get the data, use a SQL statement. To get all records, use a loop.

```
Set adoRecordset=adoConnect.Execute("SELECT * FROM new")
Do While Not adoRecordset.EOF
    Response.Write("<client>"+ adoRecordset("client")+"</client>")
    adoRecordset.MoveNext
Loop
```

The completed code is

```
<%Response.ContentType="application/xml "%>
<?xml version="1.0"?>
<dbExample>
<%
DIM adoConnect
DIM adoRecordset
Set adoConnect =Server.CreateObject("ADODB.Connection")
adoConnect.open "Provider=Microsoft.Jet.OLEDB.4.0;"_
& "Data Source=c:\coldCall.mdb"
Set adoRecordset=adoConnect.Execute("SELECT * FROM new")
Do While Not adoRecordset.EOF
    Response.Write("<client>"+ adoRecordset("client")+"</client>")
    adoRecordset.MoveNext
Loop
adoRecordset.Close
set adoRecordset = Nothing
%>
</dbExample>
```

EXERCISE

10.9 If you have access to a proprietary database application, create the following database. The filename is `purchaseStudio`; the table name is `accessories`.

Table 10-2 Data for Exercise 9-9.

ID	Product	Model Number	Price Each	Quantity
1	40GB Ultra DMA/100 Hard Drive	B8989	$89.99	1
2	IDE/ATAPI Internal Zip Drive	i38883	$75.99	2
3	10X CD-R	F267	$3.95	3
4	Zip disks-10 pack	i566	$69.99	1
5	3100 Touch Scan	A44	$49.00	1
6	CD Writable	CD222	$199.99	1

Practice returning XML files to the client for the purpose of

(a) listing products ordered
(b) finding model number for the zip drive and zip disks

CHAPTER SUMMARY

1. Server-side programming becomes more and more important because of the fast growth of different applications (e-commerce, business-to-business B2B, and searching for information).
2. There are several technologies that can be used for server-side programming; CGI, ASP, and JSP.
3. ASP technology is based on the component object model (COM).
4. To manage interaction between a web server and the user's browser, ASP provides a collection of objects and components. There are six core objects in the Active Server Pages Object model: Request, Response, Application, Session, Server, and Object Context. For client server applications, the most important are core objects, Request and Response.
5. The result of processing an XML document with ASP is a plain HTML document that can be opened in any browser on the client side. You start with an XML document on the server side, process it, and send the resulting HTML file to the user.
6. ASP is a server-side scripting environment that enables you to embed scripting commands inside an HTML document. The default language for ASP is VBScript, although you can use JavaScript as well.
7. Typical applications using ASP have the following components:

   (a) Sending the data from client to server using `QueryString`, `get`, or `post` methods
   (b) Processing data and documents on the server side using different technologies
   (c) Sending resulting documents to the client using the Response object method from ASP

8. `QueryString` and `get` methods are not the best way to send information. The information is accessible to the public, and you are limited in the size of the information sent. The best way to send information is with forms using the `post` method.
9. When processing XML documents on the server side, you can use all available technologies used on the client side such as DOM, XSLT, and SAX.
10. The need for outputting documents to different devices (mobile phone, web, large screen) strongly supports the use of XSLT because it is easy to generate different output documents from one XML source document, such as HTML files for web and WML for use on wireless devices.
11. XML will be more and more important on the server side because it can easily process and transform and because it can be used for data exchange between different databases.

SELF-ASSESSMENT

1. Demonstrate an understanding of ASP technology and how ASP can be used for small- and large-scale web site development.
2. Be able to send data and information to an ASP server.
3. Plan, create, and edit a small ASP application.
4. Be able to load files and create a document tree using ASP.
5. Create an application using DOM in an ASP environment.
6. Create an application using XSLT, on the server side, in an ASP environment. Determine the main points in the development of this type of application.
7. Demonstrate sending information or data from the server to the client.
8. Develop complete applications using ASP technology, including sending data to the server, processing an XML document on the server side, and sending information back to the client.

11 XML Schema and Document Type Definition

CHAPTER OBJECTIVES

By reading the information and practicing the code in this chapter, you will understand and be able to

1. Develop schema or a document type definition (DTD) to create valid, medium complexity extensible markup language (XML) documents.
2. Select and utilize schema data types.
3. Create DTD elements, attributes, and entities.
4. Develop XML documents following an existing schema or DTD.
5. Validate XML documents in accordance with a DTD.

11.1 VALIDATING XML DOCUMENTS

As you know from previous chapters, for an XML document to be well-formed, it must adhere to the syntax rules of XML 1.0. You can process and modify well-formed XML files using document object model (DOM), simple application programming interface (API) for XML (SAX), or extensible style sheet language transformation (XSLT), but for commercial applications in areas such as e-commerce and business-to-business (B2B), it is important that XML documents follow a defined structure as well. To define the structure of a document and to test the XML file to see that it follows this structure, there are two possible approaches, schemas and DTDs. DTDs have been around longer and evolve from standard generalized markup language (SGML). Schemas have several advantages over DTDs, although they are not implemented at this time.

1. Schemas are easier to learn because they are written in XML.
2. Schemas support data types and namespaces.
3. Because they are written in XML, schemas are extensible in the same way XML documents are and, as such, can be customized, modified, and easily parsed with the XML parser.

The purpose of a schema is to define a class of XML documents. As such, the term *instance document* is often used to describe an XML document conforming to a particular schema. This defining purpose can be achieved, then, with a schema, an instance document, and additionally with streams of bytes sent between applications, such as fields in a database. In this chapter you will refer to instances and schemas as if they are documents and files and use schemas to describe the content and structure of an XML document to determine its validity.

Sometimes schemas and DTDs are developed after the XML document is built; this is common when an existing XML application needs to be validated. There may be cases where, in working with a client, you develop a clear vision of how the XML document needs to be put together and building the XML document first will make for a stronger interface. However, when developing larger-scale commercial applications, building the schema or DTD first allows you to check validation errors in the XML document as you develop it.

As an example, a company is exchanging information in the form of XML documents for the purpose of data related to invoices and orders. During the transmission process, the company realizes small parts of data were lost, possibly from the user not completing the key-in information correctly. How would you begin to resolve the problem? Developing a schema for the documents may solve the problem by defining and checking validity of the structure of the document.

11.1.1 Complex and Simple Data Types

Before defining an entire schema, this section defines complex and simple data types. **Complex type elements** contain other elements or attributes as in:

```
<product>
<productName>printer</productName>
<price>2,450.00</price>
<productionDate>2001-12-20</productionDate>
</product>
```

where three elements are contained, `productName`, `price`, and `productionDate`. Or as in

```
<unitName code="12/34">valve</unitName>
```

where there is one attribute, `code`.

Simple type elements do not have subelements and contain simple data as a string, number, or date. As an example,

`<productName>printer</productName>` -contains the string `printer`
`<price>2,450</price>` -contains the number `2,450`
`<productionDate>2001-12-20</productionDate>` -contains the date `2001-12-12`

Complex types, in a schema document, are declared by the user. However, several simple types are declared in the XML schema specification. A sample of the most commonly used simple types follows:

`string`—string of text
`boolean`—with values `true` or `false`
`float`—floating point number
`double`—double precision 64-bit floating point
`integer`—integer number
`date`—date in YYYY-MM-DD format
`binary`—text-encoded binary data
`uriReference`—URI such as http://www.yahoo.com

You also have the option to create simple-type elements using built-in simple types. As an example, if the value of your element `marks` can be an integer in the range of 1 to 10, you can define it as a simple type using constraining facets `minInclusive` and `maxInclusive`.

```
<xsd:simpleType name="marks">
<xsd:restriction base="xsd:integer">
  <xsd:minInclusive value="1" />
  <xsd:maxInclusive value="10" />
</xsd:restriction>
</xsd:simpleType>
```

If element `marksReal` may have any real value larger than 5 and less than 10, you can define your simple type using facets `minExclusive` and `maxExclusive` in the following way:

```
<xsd:simpleType name="marksReal">
<xsd:restriction base="xsd:float">
  <xsd:minExclusive value="5" />
  <xsd:maxExclusive value="10" />
</xsd:restriction>
</xsd:simpleType>
```

If you want to create simple-type element code, as a string with the following form:

two characters from the set [A–Z], underscore, three digits you can use facet `pattern` and declare

```
<xsd:simpleType name="code">
 <xsd:restriction base="xsd:string">
 <xsd:pattern value="\[A-Z]{2}_d(3)" />
 </xsd:restriction>
</xsd:simpleType>
```

EXERCISES

11.1 Create your own simple type for element `evaluationMark`, which has a minimal value 10 and a maximum value of less than 100.

11.2 Create your own simple type for element `partNumber`, which consists of four digits, underscore, and two characters from the set `[A-G]`

11.2 DECLARING ELEMENTS

In XML schema, complex types allow elements in their content and may carry attributes. Simple types cannot have element content or carry attributes. It is possible to define new types (simple and complex) and declare elements and attributes with specific names and types (again simple and complex) to appear in document instances.

New complex types are defined using the `complexType` element. These definitions contain a set of element declarations, element references, and attribute declarations. The declarations are not types, they associate a name and constraint to govern the appearance of that name and its constraints. In other words, you create an element order and determine that it may occur a maximum of 10 times, where it is placed in the document hierarchy, and what type of data it contains. In declaring the element, you declare what constraints will be followed in order for the XML document to be validated.

Elements are declared using the `element` element, and attributes are declared using the `attribute` element.

Elements are declared as in Example 11-1.

Example 11-1

```
<xsd:element name="product" type="productType" />
<xsd:complexType name="productType">
<xsd:sequence>
  <xsd:element name="productName" type="xsd:string" />
  <xsd:element name="price" type="xsd:float" />
```

```
  <xsd:element name="productionDate" type="xsd:string">
</xsd:sequence>
</xsd:complexType>
```

The schema is developed as an XML document. To define the structure, determine which elements are of complex type and which are of simple type. Next, declare complex-type elements in the terms of other complex element attributes and simple-types elements. All schema elements have the prefix `xsd:` (which is conventional; you can use others). Elements are declared with `<xsd:element>` and attributes with `<xsd:attribute>`.

`<xsd:element>` has the form

```
<xsd:element name="elementName" type="typeName">
```

`elementName` is the name of the element in the source XML document, such as `product`, `productName`, `price`, and `productionDate` in the Example 11-1.

`typeName` is named if you determine the element is of a complex type or a simple type. If you use simple types already built into the XML schema specification, then you use names from the simple-type list defined early in the chapter.

In this case, the type of simple-type elements is

`<productName>` is string,
`<price>` is float
`<productionDate>` is date

The order of appearance of elements in the document is defined by `<xsd:sequence>`. Elements in the document must be in the same order as their declarations appear in the schema document. As such

```
<xsd:sequence>
<xsd:element name="productName" type="xsd:string" />
<xsd:element name="price" type="xsd:float" />
<xsd:element name="productionDate" type="xsd:string" />
</xsd:sequence>
```

defines the elements in the XML document that must appear in the following order:

```
<productName>printer</productName>
<price>2,450.00</price>
<productionDate>2001-12-20</productionDate>
```

If the sequence is defined differently, such as

```
<xsd:sequence>
<xsd:element name="price" type="xsd:float" />
<xsd:element name="productionDate" type="xsd:string" />
<xsd:element name="productName" type="xsd:string" />
</xsd:sequence>
```

The elements in the XML document must appear in the following sequence:

```
<price>2,450.00</price>
<productionDate>2001-12-20</productionDate>
<productName>printer</productName>
```

11.3 MORE ON TYPES

Sometimes, you will use complex types or simple types only once in a document. In this case, you do not need to name the type but can declare an **anonymous type definition** inside of an element definition. As an example, you have complex-type element `order`, which you determine can appear 12 times in your XML document.

```
<order>
<customer>ABC</customer>
<address>San Jose</address>
<orderDate>2000-11-23</orderDate>
<product>PLC</product>
<quantity>12</quantity>
</order>
```

The complex type element can be defined, without naming, as in Example 11-2.

Example 11-2

```
<xsd:element name="order" minOccurs="12" maxOccurs="12" />
<xsd:complexType>
<xsd:sequence>
<xsd:element name="customer" type="xsd:string" />
<xsd:element name="address" type="xsd:string" />
<xsd:element name="orderDate" type="xsd:date" />
<xsd:element name="quantity" type="xsd:integer" />
</xsd:sequence>
</xsd:complexType>
```

In the above example, how many element types are declared? How many attribute types?

11.4 DECLARING ATTRIBUTES

To specify how many times certain elements appear in a document use attributes.

`minOccurs` indicates the minimum number of times an element can occur in a document (minimal value of the attribute is 0).

maxOccurs indicates the maximum number of times an element can appear in a document (if the element has the value of attribute maxOccurs=7, it means the element will appear a maximum 7 times). If there is no upper bound to the attribute maxOccurs, the value is unbounded.

These attributes have the following default values:

```
minOccurs=1
```

maxOccurs is equal to the value of minOccurs. If you do not declare maxOccurs (if you declare only minOccurs you set a default, but no possibility for a range of occurrences).

If minOccurs=0, as long as no maxOccurs is declared, the value is 0.

If you do not declare either minOccurs or maxOccurs, the default is 1.

With the following schema Example 11-3.

Example 11-3

```
<xsd:element name="product" type="productType" />
<xsd:complexType name="productType">
<xsd:sequence>
  <xsd:element name="productName" type="xsd:string" minOccurs="1"
maxOccurs="3" />
  <xsd:element name="price" type="xsd:float" />
  <xsd:element name="productionDate" type="string" minOccurs="0"
maxOccurs="1" />
</xsd:sequence>
</xsd:complexType>
```

<productName>occurs at least once, up to a maximum three times.

<price> appears once because the default minOccurs="1" and the default maxOccurs=minOccurs="1".

Using fixed attributes and defaults, you can define elements that must have some set values. For example, if you set in the schema

```
<xsd:name="price" type="xsd:integer" fixed="500.00" />
```

the value of element price must be 500.00.

If you use default attributes, the value of the elements is the same as the default if the user does not specify another value, as in

```
<xsd:name="price" type="xsd:integer" default="400" />
```

Attributes in XML schemas can be only of simple type and can appear only once. For example, if element price has the attribute currency, as in

```
<price currency="Euro">2,350</price>
```

The schema, Example 11-4, must be changed to

Example 11-4

```
<xsd:element name="product" type="productType" />
<xsd:complexType name="productType">
<xsd:sequence>
<xsd:element name="productName" type="xsd:string" />
<xsd:element name="price" type="xsd:float" />
<xsd:element name="productionDate" type="xsd:string" />
</xsd:sequence>
<xsd:attribute name="currency" type="xsd:string" use="required" />
</xsd:complexType>
</xsd:element>
```

And the attribute can have the following values:

`required` —there must be attribute with this name, it may have any value.
`fixed`—the value of the attribute is fixed.
In the following example, the fixed value is yen:

```
<xsd:attribute name="currency" type="xsd:string" use="fixed"
value="yen" />
```

`default`—if the value is not set, the attribute holds the default value. In the following example, the default value is `DEM`:

```
<xsd:attribute name="currency" type="xsd:string" use="default"
value="DEM" />
```

If, in the XML document, the value is set to some other value such as

```
<price currency="ATS">2,350</price>
```

the value of `currency` is `ATS`.
`optional`—the attribute is optional and may have any value.
`prohibited`—the attribute must not appear.

EXERCISE

11.3 Write a schema document to define the XML document with the following structure:

`<student>` complex type can occur, arbitrarily, many times and contains the following elements:

<firstName> type string must appear one time
<lastName> type string must appear one time
<socialSecurityNumber> Simple type that is created using pattern facet and must appear one time.
<address> complex type of addressType must appear at least one time and a maximum of four times.
<courses> type string can appear a maximum of 20 times
<website> type uriReference may appear 0 or a maximum of 5 times
<prize> type string may appear 0 or a maximum of 3 times

Complex type element address has the following elements:

<city> type string appears only once
<street> type string appears only once
<zip> type integer must appear one
<phone> type integer can appear once
<email> type string can appear a maximum of twice

Complex type for element student is used only once; complex type for element address is used several times.

11.5 SCHEMA SYNTAX

A schema consists of a preamble and zero or more definitions and declarations. The preamble is within the root element schema. It must consist of

1. a target NS, which is the namespace and uniform resource indicator (URI) of the schema you use.
2. the Version to specify the XML schema version.
3. XMLNS, which provides the namespace for the XML.

The following document, Example 11-5, helps to explain schemas:

Example 11-5

```
<?xml version="1.0"?>
<maintenanceOrder orderDate="2000-10-20">
  <maintainMachine>
    <name>welding robot</name>
    <shopFloor>washing machine</shopFloor>
    <company>Tuzla Mfg.</company>
    <city>Tuzla</city>
    <street>Partizanska 12</street>
    <phone>740-7490</phone>
```

```
  </maintainMachine>
  <delivery>
    <name>Tuzla Washing Machine Production</name>
    <street>Partizanska 12</street>
    <city>Tuzla</city>
    <contactPerson>Mirza Presley</contactPerson>
    <email>contact@tuzlawmp.com</email>
  </delivery>
  <comment>Order must be completed in five days.
  </comment>
  <machineToInspect>
    <machine partNumber="16-PUI">
      <partName>Processing unit</partName>
      <quantity>1</quantity>
      <documentation>Manual pages 12-23</documentation>
      <comment>First to test</comment>
  </machine>
    <machine partNum="14-ELE">
      <partName>electrode</partName>
      <quantity>4</quantity>
      <documentation>Manual pages 31-33</documentation>
      <availability>yes</availability>
    </machine>
    <machine partNum="12-PSU">
      <partName>power supply unit</partName>
      <quantity>1</quantity>
      <documentation>Manual pages 45-51</documentation>
      <availability>to be ordered</availability>
    </machine>
    </machineToInspect>
</maintenanceOrder>
```

This XML document has one root element, `maintenanceOrder`, with the following children:

```
maintainMachine, delivery, comment, machineToInspect
```

which must appear in that sequence (order). The element `maintenanceOrder` has an attribute, `orderDate`.

The element `maintainMachine` has five children, which must appear in the following sequence:

```
name, shopFloor, company, city, street
```

The element `delivery` has four children, which must appear in the following sequence:

```
name, city, street, contactPerson
```

The element comment has only one child, string "Order must be completed in five days."

The element machineToInspect can have several children named machine. The element machine has children, which must appear in the following order:

partName, quantity, documentation, availability (not obligatory), and comment

The element machine has an attribute, partNum

A schema for the document described above is

```
<xsd:schema xmlns:xsd="http://www.w3.org/2001 XMLSchema">
  <xsd:annotation>
    <xsd:documentation>
      Maintenance order schema.
    </xsd:documentation>
  </xsd:annotation>
    <xsd:element name="maintenanceOrder"
    type="maintenanceOrderType" />
    <xsd:element name="comment" type="xsd:string" />
  <xsd:complexType name="maintenanceOrderType">
  <xsd:sequence>
    <xsd:element name="maintainMachine"
    type="comAddress" />
    <xsd:element name="delivery"
    type="deliveryAddress" />
    <xsd:element ref="comment" minOccurs="0" />
    <xsd:element name="machineToInspect"
    type="machineType" />
  </xsd:sequence>
    <xsd:attribute name="orderDate" type="xsd:date" />
  </xsd:complexType>
  <xsd:complexType name="comAddress">
  <xsd:sequence>
    <xsd:element name="name"  type="xsd:string" />
    <xsd:element name="shopFloor"  type="xsd:string" />
    <xsd:element name="company"  type="xsd:string" />
    <xsd:element name="city"  type="xsd:string" />
    <xsd:element name="street"  type="xsd:string" />
    <xsd:element name="phone"  type="xsd:string" />
  </xsd:sequence>
  </xsd:complexType>
  <xsd:complexType name="deliveryAddress">
  <xsd:sequence>
    <xsd:element name="name"  type="xsd:string" />
    <xsd:element name="street"  type="xsd:string" />
    <xsd:element name="city"  type="xsd:string" />
```

```
    <xsd:element name="contactPerson"
    type="xsd:string" />
    <xsd:element name="email"  type="xsd:string" />
  </xsd:sequence>
  </xsd:complexType>
  <xsd:complexType name="machineType">
  <xsd:sequence>
    <xsd:element name="machine" minOccurs="0"
    maxOccurs="unbounded">
  <xsd:complexType>
  <xsd:sequence>
    <xsd:element name="partName"  type="xsd:string" />
    <xsd:element name="quantity">
  <xsd:simpleType>
  <xsd:restriction base="xsd:positiveInteger">
  <xsd:maxExclusive value="200" />
  </xsd:restriction>
  </xsd:simpleType>
  </xsd:element>
    <xsd:element name="documentation"
    type="xsd:string" />
    <xsd:element name="availability"  type="xsd:string"
    minOccurs="0" />
    <xsd:element ref="comment"  minOccurs="0" />
  </xsd:sequence>
    <xsd:attribute name="partNum" type="model" />
  </xsd:complexType>
  </xsd:element>
  </xsd:sequence>
  </xsd:complexType>
  <xsd:simpleType name="model">
  <xsd:restriction base="xsd:string">
  <xsd:pattern value="\d{2}-[A-Z]{3}" />
  </xsd:restriction>
  </xsd:simpleType>
</xsd:schema>
```

The schema document has a `schema` root element and children such as `element`, `complexType`, and `simpleType`, which determine the appearance of elements and their content in the instance document (XML document). Each element in the schema has a prefix `xsd:` (not mandatory, other prefixes can be used). This `xsd:` prefix is associated with the XML schema namespace through the declaration

```
<xsd:schema xmlns:xsd="http://www.w3.org/2001/XMLSchema">
```

<xsd:annotation> is the element for annotating a schema for the benefit of human readers and XML applications. The xsd:annotation element can have subelements documentation and appInfo, as in

```
<xsd:annotation>
  <xsd:documentation>
    Maintenance order schema.
  </xsd:documentation>
</xsd:annotation>
```

The root element maintenanceOrder is a complex type.

```
<xsd:element name="maintenanceOrder" type="maintenanceOrderType" />
```

defined in

```
<xsd:complexType name="maintenanceOrderType">
  <xsd:sequence>
    <xsd:element name="maintainMachine"
    type="comAddress " />
  <xsd:element name="delivery" type="deliveryAddress" />
  <xsd:element ref="comment" minOccurs="0" />
    <xsd:element name="machineToInspect"
    type="machineType" />
  </xsd:sequence>
  <xsd:attribute name="orderDate" type="xsd:date" />
  </xsd:complexType>
```

This means the root element must consist of four elements and one attribute. These elements must be called maintainMachine, delivery, comment, and item. They must appear in the same sequence in which they are declared. All of these elements, except comment (which may or may not appear because minOccurs is equal to zero), are a complex type, as in

```
<xsd:element name="comment" type="xsd:string" />
```

The element maintainMachine is a complex-type comAddress, defined with

```
<xsd:complexType name="comAddress">
  <xsd:sequence>
    <xsd:element name="name"  type="xsd:string" />
    <xsd:element name="shopFloor" type="xsd:string" />
    <xsd:element name="company" type="xsd:string" />
    <xsd:element name="city" type="xsd:string" />
    <xsd:element name="street" type="xsd:string" />
```

```
    <xsd:element name="phone"  type="xsd:string" />
  </xsd:sequence>
</xsd:complexType>
```

As defined in this schema, the elements must appear in the following sequence:

```
name, shopFloor, company, city, street, phone
```

All elements are strings.

The complex-type `deliveryAddress` is defined as

```
<xsd:complexType name="deliveryAddress">
  <xsd:sequence>
    <xsd:element name="name"  type="xsd:string" />
    <xsd:element name="street"  type="xsd:string" />
    <xsd:element name="city"  type="xsd:string" />
    <xsd:element name="contactPerson"
    type="xsd:string" />
    <xsd:element name="email"  type="xsd:string" />
  </xsd:sequence>
</xsd:complexType>
```

In the following example, the complex type `machineToInspect` has the complex element `machine`, which can not appear (`minOccurs="0"`) or appear several times (`maxOccurs="unbounded"`).

The complex element is defined as

```
<xsd:complexType>
<xsd:sequence>
  <xsd:element name="partName" type="xsd:string" />
  <xsd:element name="quantity" />
<xsd:simpleType>
<xsd:restriction base="xsd:positiveInteger">
<xsd:maxExclusive value="200" />
</xsd:restriction>
</xsd:simpleType>
</xsd:element>
  <xsd:element name="documentation"
  type="xsd:string" />
  <xsd:element name="availability"  type="xsd:string"
  minOccurs="0" />
  <xsd:element ref="comment"  minOccurs="0" />
</xsd:sequence>
  <xsd:attribute name="model" type="modelType" />
</xsd:complexType>
</xsd:element>
```

```
</xsd:sequence>
</xsd:complexType>
```

The element item consists of simple-type elements, which must appear in the following sequence:

```
partName, quantity, documentation,availability, comment
```

The element `productName` is a string declared by

```
<xsd:element name="partName" type="xsd:string" />
```

The element `quantity` is a positive integer that can not be greater than 200 as declared below.

```
<xsd:element name="quantity">
<xsd:simpleType>
<xsd:restriction base="xsd:positiveInteger">
  <xsd:maxExclusive value="200" />
</xsd:restriction>
</xsd:simpleType>
</xsd:element>
```

The element's availability and comment can appear (not mandatory because `minOccurs="0"`). The element `availability` is a simple type with string `content` and the element `comment` was defined earlier as a string.

```
<xsd:simpleType name="modelType">
<xsd:restriction base="xsd:string">
  <xsd:pattern value="\d{2}-[A-Z]{3}" />
</xsd:restriction>
</xsd:simpleType>
</xsd:schema>
```

EXERCISE

11.4 Write a schema for the following XML document:

```
<dns>
<domains>
  <domain_account>
  <domain_name>cool2code.com</domain_name>
  <create_date>1-31-01</create_date>
  <expire_date>1/31-03</expire_date>
  <price_per_year>15.00 USD</price_per_year>
  </domain_account>
```

```
</domains>
<hosting>
  <host_account>
  <hosted_domain>cool2code.com</hosted_domain>
  <hosting_service>none</hosting_service>
  <hosting_plan>none</hosting_plan>
  <price_per_month>none</price_per_month>
  </host_account>
</hosting>
<domains>
  <domain_account>
  <domain_name>mojpes.net</domain_name>
  <create_date>4-30-00</create_date>
  <expire_date>4-30-03</expire_date>
  <price_per_year>15.00 USD</price_per_year>
  </domain_account>
</domains>
<hosting>
  <host_account>
  <hosted_domain>mojpes.net</hosted_domain>
  <hosting_service>Hostway</hosting_service>
  <hosting_plan>Gold Plan</hosting_plan>
  <price_per_month>24.95 USD</price_per_month>
  </host_account>
</hosting>
<domains>
  <domain_account>
  <domain_name>dynamiclearning.org</domain_name>
  <create_date>2-4-00</create_date>
  <expire_date>2-4-03</expire_date>
  <price_per_year>35.00 USD</price_per_year>
  </domain_account>
</domains>
<hosting>
  <host_account>
  <hosted_domain>dynamiclearning.org</hosted_domain>
  <hosting_service>Hostway</hosting_service>
  <hosting_plan>Gold Plan</hosting_plan>
  <price_per_month>24.95 USD</price_per_month>
  </host_account>
</hosting>
</dns>
```

11.6 DTDS

DTDs, as defined earlier, are written in SGML rather than XML. They look significantly different at first but are repetitive and become understandable in a short time. Difficulty in writing DTDs is connected to modeling and determining how an XML document should be set up for best results with the document tree.

As an example of when a DTD is important to web development, read the following XML document:

```
<books>
   <book>
      <title>Megatrends 2000</title>
      <author>J. Naisbitt</author>
      <year>1991</year>
      <publisher>Avon Book</publisher>
      <isbn>0-380-70437</isbn>
      <price>6.99</price>
   </book>
   <book>
      <title>Third wave</title>
      <author>Alvin Toffler</author>
      <year>1980</year>
      <publisher>Pan books</publisher>
      <isbn>0-330-26337-4</isbn>
      <price>7.99</price>
   </book>
   <book>
      <title>Jobshift</title>
      <author>William Bridges</author>
      <year>1994</year>
      <publisher>Addison-Wesley</publisher>
      <isbn>0-201-48933-3</isbn>
      <price>13.00</price>
   </book>
   <book>
      <title>Zen in the Art of Archery</title>
      <author>Eugern Herrigel</author>
      <year>1989</year>
      <publisher>Vintage books</publisher>
      <isbn>0-679-72297</isbn>
      <price>10.00</price>
   </book>
   <book>
      <title>Lateral Thinking</title>
      <author>Edward de Bono</author>
      <year>1990</year>
      <publisher>Penguin Book</publisher>
      <isbn>0-14-013779-3</isbn>
      <price>12.99</price>
```

```
   </book>
</books>
```

This simple XML document is well formed and displaying it in Internet Explorer (IE) produces no warning message. What if when preparing this document, a few mistakes were made (easy to do with large-scale documents). Maybe you forgot `<author>Alvin Toffler</author>`, and instead of `<title>Jobshift</title>`, you keyed, `<Title>Jobshift</Title>`. If these mistakes seem like something you would not do, remember there will most likely be administrative staff maintaining your XML document. As a developer, it would be less typical for you to add products each week to the same XML document. The same document, with the mistakes included, looks like:

```
<books>
   <book>
      <title>Megatrends 2000</title>
      <author>J. Naisbitt</author>
      <year>1991</year>
      <publisher>Avon Book</publisher>
      <isbn>0-380-70437</isbn>
      <price>6.99</price>
   </book>
   <book>
      <title>Third wave</title>
            <year>1980</year>
      <publisher>Pan books</publisher>
      <isbn>0-330-26337-4</isbn>
      <price>7.99</price>
   </book>
   <book>
      <Title>Jobshift</Title>
      <author>William Bridges</author>
      <year>1994</year>
      <publisher>Addison-Wesley</publisher>
      <isbn>0-201-48933-3</isbn>
      <price>13.00</price>
   </book>
   <book>
      <title>Zen in the Art of Archery</title>
      <author>Eugern Herrigel</author>
      <year>1989</year>
      <publisher>Vintage books</publisher>
      <isbn>0-679-72297</isbn>
      <price>10.00</price>
   </book>
```

```
    <book>
       <title>Lateral Thinking</title>
       <author>Edward de Bono</author>
       <year>1990</year>
       <publisher>Penguin Book</publisher>
       <isbn>0-14-013779-3</isbn>
       <price>12.99</price>
    </book>
</books>
```

Note that this second document is still well formed, and IE will not detect any syntax error because all elements have start and end tags, element names are syntactically correct, and tags are properly (if maybe simply) nested. However, if you used DOM or XSLT to write an application, with which you wanted to sort for a book written by Alvin Toffler, you will return no hits. If you wanted to purchase a book titled *Jobshift*, it will show as not available. DTD is a mechanism to protect you from making this kind of mistake, or better to say, a DTD detects these kinds of mistakes or errors in the early stages of processing the document.

As another example, you have an XML document with an element `<person>`. The content of that element can only be `male` or `female` as in

```
<person>male</person>
```

Without a protecting mechanism, you might not detect miskeying.

```
<person gender="male">Danny Mainis</person>
<person gender="female">LeAnn Mainis</person>
```

The syntax of the above element is correct, and the parser will not warn you that something is wrong with the document. You need some protection to not allow you to put the wrong content in elements; in this case content must be male or female.

A third problem, not connected with mistakes or errors, that can be resolved with a DTD is as follows. If you write a large XML document with many elements, it would be difficult to set the document up correctly without some kind of structural definition. The DTD can define the structure of the document, to allow for better application development and faster application search results.

In the book example, on the previous pages, the XML document is simple, all records have the same structure, and it is easy to follow what the document describes. If the document was more complicated, you might add comments to reflect its organization to other developers. The problem with this, is that every developer would set comments up in her own way and still the document could not be used for locating errors in the document syntax, vocabulary, or with any specific values. A DTD allows you to determine structure and validate for these types of errors.

The future of XML seems more focused on schemas than DTDs; however, it is important that you can read, edit, and, in many cases, develop a DTD. A DTD can be an internal part of an XML document, or it can be external and saved as a .dtd file. The following DTD (Example 11-6) makes the XML document `catalog.xml`, from this chapter, valid.

Example 11-6

```
<?xml version="1.0"?>
<!DOCTYPE books [
<!ELEMENT books(book+)>
<!ELEMENT book(title,author,year,publisher,isbn,price)>
<!ELEMENT title(#PCDATA)>
<!ELEMENT author(#PCDATA)>
<!ELEMENT year(#PCDATA)>
<!ELEMENT publisher(#PCDATA)>
<!ELEMENT isbn(#PCDATA)>
<!ELEMENT price(#PCDATA)>
]>
<books>
   <book>
      <title>Megatrends 2000</title>
      <author>J. Naisbitt</author>
      <year>1991</year>
      <publisher>Avon Book</publisher>
      <isbn>0-380-70437</isbn>
      <price>6.99</price>
   </book>
//balance of document not keyed here to save space
  .........
   </books>
```

To understand the DTD more closely, begin with the following code:

```
<!DOCTYPE books [
<!ELEMENT books(book+)>
<!ELEMENT book(title,author,year,publisher,isbn,price)>
<!ELEMENT title(#PCDATA)>
<!ELEMENT author(#PCDATA)>
<!ELEMENT year(#PCDATA)>
<!ELEMENT publisher(#PCDATA)>
<!ELEMENT isbn(#PCDATA)>
<!ELEMENT price(#PCDATA)>
]>
```

The DTD begins with the DOCTYPE declaration, which connects the DTD declarations to an XML document. The DOCTYPE declaration must follow the XML declaration and precede any elements in the document. Comments and processing instructions may appear between the XML declaration and DOCTYPE declaration. The DOCTYPE declaration contains the keyword DOCTYPE followed by the name of the root element, `books` in this case, as in

```
<!DOCTYPE books [
```

The next line of code explains that the root element, `books`, has one or more (the sign + denotes or more) elements called `book`.

```
<!ELEMENT books(book+)>
```

The element `book` has the following children: `title`, `author`, `year`, `publisher`, `isbn`, `price`, as shown with

```
<!ELEMENT book(title,author,year,publisher,isbn,price)>
```

In this application, those same elements contain parsed character data and, as such, are represented as

```
<!ELEMENT title(#PCDATA)>
<!ELEMENT author(#PCDATA)>
<!ELEMENT year(#PCDATA)>
<!ELEMENT publisher(#PCDATA)>
<!ELEMENT isbn(#PCDATA)>
<!ELEMENT price(#PCDATA)>
```

The end of the DTD is indicated with

```
]>
```

Sometimes it is better to use external DTDs for added flexibility. With an external DTD, the DOCTYPE declaration consists of the root element followed by a keyword denoting the source and the location of the DTD. For this declaration of the source, use either the keyword `SYSTEM` or `PUBLIC`. Using `SYSTEM` means the parser should be able to find the DTD on the indicated uniform resource locator (URL). As an example,

```
<!DOCTYPE Catalog SYSTEM http://www.learningcentre.org/catalog.dtd>
```

In the above case, all declarations needed to validate the document containing the DOCTYPE declaration and are found in the file `catalog.dtd`.

If instead, you use the source `PUBLIC` and give an associated URI, applications will use an algorithm to locate the DTD. As an example,

```
<!DOCTYPE Catalog PUBLIC "Library/Book">
```

indicates Library/Book, well known to the application processing documents of this type.

DTDs allow four kinds of markup declarations with which the content of the XML document can be defined.

1. ELEMENT declarations of XML element types, as in

```
<!ELEMENT country(#PCDATA)
```

2. ATTLIST declarations of attributes that may be assigned to a specific element type, and the permissible value of those attributes, as in

```
<ATTLIST price currency PCDATA #REQUIRED
```

3. ENTITY declarations of resuable content (same content used in different part of the XML document) as in

```
<!ENTITY footnote "Institute for Symbolic Analysis and Development of
Information Technologies">
```

4. NOTATION format declarations for external content not meant to be parsed (binary data, as an example), and the external application that handles the content, as in

```
<!NOTATION jpg System "jpgviewer.exe">
```

11.7 ELEMENTS

The most important part of XML documents are elements declared in the DTD using the ELEMENT tag. There are four categories of element content:

1. empty
2. element
3. mixed
4. any

An empty element is denoted with the keyword EMPTY and has neither text nor child elements. Empty elements may have attributes, as in

```
<!ELEMENT Nodata EMPTY>
```

You can have empty elements with several attributes. For example, <product> can be described with the names, IDnumber, price, and so on. The code can be set up more than one way, as in

```
<product>
<name>valve</name>
```

```
<IDnumber>236</IDnumber>
<price>230</price>
<quantity>1234</quantity>
</product>
```

or by declaring the values in attributes, as in

```
<product name="valve" IDnumber="236" price="230"
quantity="1234"></product>
```

In this case, <product> is empty and has four attributes; as such, it needs to be defined in the DTD as

```
<!ELEMENT product EMPTY>
<!ATTLIST product
  name CDATA #REQUIRED
  IDnumber CDATA #REQUIRED
  price CDATA #IMPLIED
  quantity CDATA #IMPLIED>
```

If an element contains child elements but not text elements, you have element content, as in

```
<item>
 <partName>valve</partName>
 <partNumber>HV-152</partNumber>
 <partImage>valve.jpeg</partImage>
 <quantity>150</quantity>
</item>
```

In this example, <item> has four children that are declared in the DTD as:

```
<!ELEMENT item (partName, partNumber, partImage, quantity)>
```

If you mix elements and parsed character data (#PCDATA), you have mixed content, as in

```
<company>InovaIR
 <address>Velenje</address>
 <phone>386 3 5875475</phone>
</company>
```

In this case, <company> has text and child elements; it is mixed. The specification must start with #PCDATA, followed by alternate elements (using | pipe between elements), and must end with the "zero-or-more" asterisk symbol (*). As such, <company> is defined as

```
<!ELEMENT company (#PCDATA |address | phone)* >
```

#PCDATA must be before all children elements.

If you want to leave the content of an element open to any possible content, you declare the keyword ANY, as in

```
<!ELEMENT Anydata ANY>
```

The element structure is declared in content models. In principle, content models consist of a set of parentheses enclosing a combination of child element names, operators, and the #PCDATA keyword. The operator allows you to denote cardinality and indicate how many elements and character data may be combined. The two order operators are:

1. , (comma) strict sequence
2. | (pipe) choice

As such

```
<!ELEMENT movie (title, director, actor)>
```

indicates the elements `title`, `director`, and `actor` must appear in a specified order.

If they must appear in the specified order, then Example 11-7:

Example 11-7

```
<?xml version="1.0"?>
<!DOCTYPE movie [
<!ELEMENT movie (title,director,actor)>
<!ELEMENT title (#PCDATA)>
<!ELEMENT director (#PCDATA)>
<!ELEMENT actor (#PCDATA)>
]>
<movie>
<title> Aleksandar Nevski</title>
<director>S. Eisenstein</director>
<actor>N. Cherkasov</actor>
</movie>
```

is a valid document. If the order of elements appearing in the XML document is changed to Example 11-8

Example 11-8

```
<?xml version="1.0"?>
<!DOCTYPE movie [
<!ELEMENT movie (title,director,actor)>
<!ELEMENT title (#PCDATA)>
<!ELEMENT director (#PCDATA)>
```

```
<!ELEMENT actor (#PCDATA)>
]>
<movie>
<director>S. Eisenstein</director>
<actor>N. Cherkasov</actor>
<title> Aleksandar Nevski </title>
</movie>
```

or Example 11-9:

Example 11-9

```
<?xml version="1.0"?>
<!DOCTYPE movie [
<!ELEMENT movie (title,director,actor)>
<!ELEMENT title (#PCDATA)>
<!ELEMENT director (#PCDATA)>
<!ELEMENT actor (#PCDATA)>
]>
<movie>
<actor>N. Cherkasov</actor>
<director>S. Eisenstein</director>
<title> Aleksandar Nevski></title>
</movie>
```

validation of both documents returns an error because the element order has been changed. To return a valid document, in this case, you need to change the order of the elements or edit the DTD. In the first example of a non-valid document, the change

```
<!ELEMENT movie (title,director,actor)>
```

to

```
<!ELEMENT movie (director,actor,director)>
```

would result in validation. In the second example of a non-valid document, the change to

```
<!ELEMENT movie (actor,director,title)>
```

also results in validation.

EXERCISE

11.5 Write a DTD for the following XML document. Next, change the order of appearance of two elements in the source document. Validate the document and make changes in DTD so the document is valid.

```
<?xml version="1.0"?>
  <drugs>
    <drug>
      <name>aspirin</name>
      <content> 0.4 g. acetisalicil acid, 0.24 g.
      ascorbine acid </content>
      <therapy>analgetic </therapy>
      <available>yes</available>
      <analogon>andol</analogon>
      <contraindication>ulcer</contraindication>
  </drug>
</drugs>
```

11.8 CARDINALITY OPERATORS

If your code reads

```
<!ELEMENT travel (plane | train)>
```

the element `travel` can contain either `plane` or `train`.

In a more complex content model

```
<!ELEMENT travel (plane,(train | ship))>
```

element `plane` can be followed by either `train` or `ship`, but neither `train` nor `ship` is allowed before `plane`.

If you want to declare how many instances of an element are permitted, use **cardinality operators**, such as

1. ?, which means optional; may or may not appear
2. *, which means may appear zero or more times
3. +, which means must appear one or more times

The declaration of element type `travel`

```
<!ELEMENT travel (plane+,(train | ship)*)>
```

states that according to the content model group, the `travel` element contains one or more instances of the element `plane`, followed by zero or more instances of the choice between `train` and `ship`. As such, the XML document may be

```
<travel>
   <plane>Air France</plane>
   <plane>Adria</plane>
   <train>Blaue Enzian</train>
```

```
    <ship>Queen Elizabeth</ship>
    <ship>Normandie</ship>
</travel>
```

Using this content model and its potential multiple combinations, you can compose complex structures.

11.8.1 Examples

The following document returns an error, Example 11-10:

Example 11-10

```
<?xml version="1.0"?>
<!DOCTYPE travel [
<!ELEMENT travel (plane|train)>
<!ELEMENT plane (#PCDATA)>
<!ELEMENT train (#PCDATA)>
]>
<travel>
<plane>Boeing747</plane>
<train>Ravel</train>
</travel>
```

Why will the document not validate? Because, according to the DTD element, travel can have only children names plane or train. A valid document, in this case, would be Example 11-11

Example 11-11

```
<?xml version="1.0"?>
<!DOCTYPE travel [
<!ELEMENT travel (plane|train)>
<!ELEMENT plane (#PCDATA)>
<!ELEMENT train (#PCDATA)>
]>
<travel>
<train>Ravel</train>
</travel>
```

or Example 11-12.

Example 11-12

```
<?xml version="1.0"?>
<!DOCTYPE travel [
<!ELEMENT travel (plane|train)>
<!ELEMENT plane (#PCDATA)>
<!ELEMENT train (#PCDATA)>
```

```
]>
<travel>
<plane>Boeing747</plane>
</travel>
```

Two more examples of valid documents are Example 11-13

Example 11-13

```
<?xml version="1.0"?>
<!DOCTYPE travel [
<!ELEMENT travel (plane,(train|ship))>
<!ELEMENT plane (#PCDATA)>
<!ELEMENT train (#PCDATA)>
<!ELEMENT ship (#PCDATA)>
]>
<travel>
<plane>Boeing</plane>
<train>Ravel</train>
</travel>
```

and Example 11-14.

Example 11-14

```
<?xml version="1.0"?>
<!DOCTYPE travel [
<!ELEMENT travel (plane, (train|ship))>
<!ELEMENT plane (#PCDATA)>
<!ELEMENT train (#PCDATA)>
<!ELEMENT ship (#PCDATA)>
]>
<travel>
<plane>Boeing</plane>
<ship>Normandie</ship>
</travel>
```

Another set of documents would not be valid in accordance with the existing DTD, as in Example 11-15.

Example 11-15

```
<?xml version="1.0"?>
<!DOCTYPE travel [
<!ELEMENT travel (plane, (train|ship))>
<!ELEMENT plane (#PCDATA)>
<!ELEMENT train (#PCDATA)>
<!ELEMENT ship (#PCDATA)>
```

```
]>
<travel>
<ship>Normandie</ship>
</travel>
```

In the Example 11-15, there is a missing plane element that is mandatory. In the next example (Example 11-16), the order is incorrect, `plane` must be first.

Example 11-16

```
<?xml version="1.0"?>
<!DOCTYPE travel [
<!ELEMENT travel (plane, (train|ship))>
<!ELEMENT plane (#PCDATA)>
<!ELEMENT train (#PCDATA)>
<!ELEMENT ship (#PCDATA)>
]>
<travel>
<ship>Normandie</ship>
<plane>Boeing747</plane>
</travel>
```

In the following example (Example 11-17), either train or ship can occur, but not both in the same element.

Example 11-17

```
<?xml version="1.0"?>
<!DOCTYPE travel [
<!ELEMENT travel (plane,(train|ship))>
<!ELEMENT plane (#PCDATA)>
<!ELEMENT train (#PCDATA)>
<!ELEMENT ship (#PCDATA)>
]>
<travel>
<plane>Boeing747</plane>
<train>Ravel</train>
<ship>Normandie</ship>
</travel>
```

EXERCISES

11.6 Add the new element `<bus>Volvo</bus>` to to the DTD.

```
<?xml version="1.0"?>
<!DOCTYPE travel [
<!ELEMENT travel (ship, (plane|train|bus))>
```

```
<!ELEMENT plane (#PCDATA)>
<!ELEMENT train (#PCDATA)>
<!ELEMENT ship (#PCDATA)>
<!ELEMENT bus (#PCDATA)>
]>
<travel>
<ship>Normandie</ship>
<bus>Volvo</bus>
</travel>
```

Find all valid combinations (in accordance with the DTD) of elements in the XML document and a few combinations that are not valid. Explain why some work and others is not if the DTD is

```
<!DOCTYPE travel [
<!ELEMENT travel ((ship,bus), (plane|train)>
<!ELEMENT plane (#PCDATA)>
<!ELEMENT train (#PCDATA)>
<!ELEMENT ship (#PCDATA)>
<!ELEMENT bus (#PCDATA)>
]>
```

11.7 Write one valid XML document and one non-valid XML document. As an example,

```
<?xml version="1.0"?>
<!DOCTYPE travel [
<!ELEMENT travel (ship+, (plane|train|bus)*)>
<!ELEMENT plane (#PCDATA)>
<!ELEMENT train (#PCDATA)>
<!ELEMENT ship (#PCDATA)>
<!ELEMENT bus (#PCDATA)>
]>
<travel>
<ship>Normandie</ship>
<ship>Queen Elizabeth</ship>
<bus>Volvo</bus>
<bus>Mercedes</bus>
</travel>
```

is valid and

```
<?xml version="1.0"?>
<!DOCTYPE travel [
<!ELEMENT travel (ship+, (plane|train|bus)*)>
<!ELEMENT plane (#PCDATA)>
```

```
<!ELEMENT train (#PCDATA)>
<!ELEMENT ship (#PCDATA)>
<!ELEMENT bus (#PCDATA)>
]>
<travel>
<ship>Queen Elizabeth</ship>
<bus>Volvo</bus>
<bus>Mercedes</bus>
<ship>Normandie</ship>
</travel>
```

is not valid because <ship> must be before <bus>, <train>, or <plane>, according to the DTD

```
<!ELEMENT travel (ship+, (plane|train|bus)*)>
```

which reads that <ship> will appear at least once, in combination with <plane>, <train>, and <bus>, which may or may not appear several times.

11.8 Write a valid XML document for the following DTD:

```
<!DOCTYPE bill [
<!ELEMENT bill (customer, billNumber, amount, (address|condition))>
<!ELEMENT customer (#PCDATA)>
<!ELEMENT billNumber (#PCDATA)>
<!ELEMENT amount (#PCDATA)>
<!ELEMENT address (#PCDATA)>
<!ELEMENT condition (#PCDATA)>
]>
```

11.9 Write a DTD for the XML document, from Example 10-3 in Chapter 10 describing a portion of the employee records from a human resources department.

11.9 ATTRIBUTES

Each attribute consists of the name of the attribute, its type, and a default declaration. In the first example, you are declaring a single attribute, currency, that must occur (#REQUIRED is the default setting) in the start tag of element price. The value of the attribute is a parsed character string.

Allowed attribute defaults include

1. #REQUIRED—an attribute must appear on every instance of the element
2. #IMPLIED—an attribute may optionally appear on an instance of the element
3. #FIXED—plus a default value, as in

```
<ATTLIST price currency #FIXED "$">
```

4. Default value only. If the attribute does not appear, the default value is assumed by the parser. If the attribute appears, it may have another value, as in

```
<ATTLIST energy unit "Joule">
```

Examples of these attribute defaults include Example 11-18.

Example 11-18

```
<?xml version="1.0"?>
<!DOCTYPE catalog [
<!ELEMENT catalog (product+)>
<!ELEMENT product (#PCDATA)>
<!ATTLIST product
  price CDATA #REQUIRED>
  ]>
<catalog>
<product price ="2000">computer</product>
<product>printer</product>
<product price ="200">scanner</product>
</catalog>
```

In this example, since attribute `price` is `#REQUIRED`, the document is not valid because element `product` with text `printer` does not have an attribute `price`.

If you change the document to Example 11-19,

Example 11-19

```
<?xml version="1.0"?>
<!DOCTYPE catalog [
<!ELEMENT catalog (product+)>
<!ELEMENT product (#PCDATA)>
<!ATTLIST product
  price CDATA #IMPLIED>
  ]>
<catalog>
<product price ="2000">computer</product>
<product>printer</product>
<product price ="200">scanner</product>
</catalog>
```

the document is valid because `attribute` may appear optionally. If you change the DTD by adding attribute `#FIXED "2400"`, the document is not valid because all three attributes must have the value 2400. Instead, in the following code Example 11-20

Example 11-20

```
<?xml version="1.0"?>
<!DOCTYPE catalog [
<!ELEMENT catalog (product+)>
<!ELEMENT product (#PCDATA)>
<!ATTLIST product
  price CDATA #FIXED "2400">
  ]>
<catalog>
<product price ="2000">computer</product>
<product>printer</product>
<product price ="200">scanner</product>
</catalog>
```

if you change the DTD and place the attribute value to "2400", the document is valid because element product with text printer is not set with a specific value. CDATA, followed by the value of the attribute in quotes, results in that attribute to be set as the default value. Default value means you have no explicit attribute in that element, the value is default. If the value of attribute is explicit, as in computer and scanner, and if it is different from the default value, that declared value takes precedence over default.

```
<?xml version="1.0"?>
<!DOCTYPE catalog [
<!ELEMENT catalog (product+)>
<!ELEMENT product (#PCDATA)>
<!ATTLIST product
price CDATA #FIXED "2400">
]>
<catalog>
<product price ="2400">computer</product>
<product>printer</product>
<product price ="2400">scanner</product>
</catalog>
```

EXERCISES

11.10 You have the following XML document:

```
<?xml version="1.0"?>
<cars>
  <name price="30,000 USD" type ="300">Volvo</name>
  <name price="20,000 USD" color ="red"
  type ="350">BMW</name>
  <name color="green" >Ford</name>
```

```
  <name price="30,000 USD" color ="gray"
  inStock="no">Toyota</name>
</cars>
```

and the following DTD:

```
<!DOCTYPE cars [
<!ELEMENT cars (name+)
<!ELEMENT name (#PCDATA)
<!ATTLIST name
          price  CDATA #REQUIRED
          color  CDATA #IMPLIED
          type   CDATA "344"
          inStock #FIXED "yes">
]>
```

If you validate this document, a message returns that the document is not valid. Find the errors, run the document until valid, and explain the error(s).

11.11 Silicon Valley financial tables (from the *San Jose Mercury News*) include the following columns:

1. Name: (name of the public company)
2. Exchange: (the exchange on which the stock is traded NY: New York Stock Exchange; N: Nasdaq; A: American Stock Exchange)
3. Ticker Symbol: (the symbol used for trading the stock)
4. Last price: (the stock's closing price for the week)
5. 1-year return: (the percent change in price over the past 12 months assuming reinvestment of dividends during that time period)
6. 52-week high: (the stock's highest in the 52 week period, in dollars and cents)
7. 52-week low: (the stock's lowest points in the 52 week period, in dollars and cents)
8. Earnings per share: (the company's earning divided by the number of outstanding shares)
9. PE: (the company's price to earnings ratio derived by dividing the company's stock price per share by the profit per share for the previous quarter)
10. Market capitalization: (number of shares outstanding multiplied by the stock price, in hundred thousands)
11. Relative strength: (compares the weekly percent change in price with the average weekly percent change for the market as represented by the Media General Composite Index. The number shown represents the deviations from the average stock, using 100 as base. A stock with relative strength above 100 is outperforming the market, while a stock with a relative strength under 100 is under performing.)

Write DTDs for an XML document to represent this data as follows:

DTD #1, represent data without using attributes
DTD #2, use attributes as you determine
DTD #3, use attribute name for exchange and ticker symbol, and represent all other quantities as elements

11.9.1 Attribute Matching Values

Sometimes you will need an attribute to match one of the included values. In this case you can use the enumerated attribute type. For example, if you have element `product` and attribute `inStock` that gives data `yes` or `no` as in

```
<listOfProducts>
<product inStock ="yes">valve</product>
<product inStock ="no">pump</product>
<product inStock ="yes">power supply</product>
</listOfProducts>
```

The DTD for the document is

```
<!DOCTYPE listOfProducts [
<!ELEMENT listOfProducts (product+)
<!ELEMENT product (#PCDATA)
<!ATTLIST product onStock (yes|no)>
]>
```

The enumerated type was defined with

```
<!ATTLIST product onStock (yes|no) #REQUIRED>
```

If attribute `inStock` has any other value, other than `yes` or `no`, the document is valid and a warning message is displayed.

EXERCISE

11.12 The following DTD is not valid. Explain why. Fix the error(s) and validate.

```
<?xml version="1.0"?>
<!DOCTYPE listOfProducts [
<!ELEMENT listOfProducts (product+)
<!ELEMENT product (#PCDATA)
<!ATTLIST product inStock (yes|no)>
]>
<listOfProducts>
<product inStock ="yes">valve</product>
```

```
<product inStock ="n/a">pump</product>
<product inStock ="ok">power supply</product>
</listOfProducts>
```

Possible attribute types include

1. CDATA the value of the attribute may be any character data string of any length, although it may not contain markup. The DTD, as an example, might read

   ```
   <ATTLIST car color CDATA #IMPLIED>
   ```

   and the element

   ```
   <car color="red">Pontiac</car>
   ```

2. ID, IDREF, IDREFS explained on the companion web site
3. ENTITY, ENTITIES explained on the companion web site
4. NMTOKEN, NMTOKENS explained on the companion web site
5. NOTATION explained on the companion web site
6. ENUMERATIONS explained on the companion web site
7. CONDITIONAL SECTIONS explained on the companion web site

11.10 ATTRIBUTES AND DTD NOTES

When you are working with attributes and DTDs, remember

1. Attributes are not parsed, as such they are CDATA.
2. Elements can have only one attribute with a given name. If an attribute appears twice in the same document, the document will not be well formed.
3. Attributes are not ordered. You cannot define the sequence in which attributes must appear as you can with elements.

11.11 ENTITIES

If text, data, or a graphic are to be used in one or several places in a document, you can use an entity, which must be declared in a DTD. The entity will have a name and contents defined in the DTD. When you need to place that text, data, or graphic, declared in the DTD, into some part of your XML output, you need only write the name of the entity according to some basic syntax rules. As an example, you create a web site and print materials for a car dealer. In several places online and in print, the dealer wants to say

Vehicles subject to prior sale. Prices are plus tax, license and document preparations charge, smog fee and finance charges. Offers in effect 7 days from today.

You can create an entity named "fees", name it in the DTD, and every time you want to show the fees paragraph, you name the entity and the full text is returned. Other examples of entity use include logos, a block of text with the company name, address, phone number, email, etc. The main idea is if you have a short or a long piece of information you would like to standardize and call with a keyword, creating an entity is the way to do it. Legal contracts with long sections of repetitive legalese work well as entities as do short corporate statements such as

ART Software is an Equal Opportunity Employer. ART Software, ART Software Onsite, the ART Software logos, and all other ART Software product or service names are registered trademarks or trademarks of ART Software, Inc. All other trademarks or registered trademarks belong to their respective companies. ©2001 ART Software, Inc. All rights reserved.

An entity is declared in the DTD with the keyword ENTITY followed by the entity name and the text to be inserted in the XML document. As an example,

```
<!ENTITY trademark "Dynamic Learning is a registered trademark.">
```

When you want to include the text in an XML document, you write an ampersand (&) in front of the entity name and add a semicolon to the end of the entity, as in

```
&trademark;
```

which displays, `Dynamic Learning is a registered trademark.`

As another example, if your DTD reads

```
<?xml version="1.0"?>
<!DOCTYPE cars [
<!ELEMENT cars (name+)>
<!ELEMENT name (#PCDATA)>
<!ATTLIST name
          price CDATA #REQUIRED
          color CDATA #IMPLIED
          type CDATA "344"
          inStock CDATA #FIXED "yes">
]>
<cars>
  <name price ="30,000 USD" type ="300">Volvo</name>
  <name price ="20,000 USD" color ="red" type ="350">BMW
  </name>
  <name price ="25,000 USD" color ="green">Ford</name>
  <name price ="30,000 USD" color ="grey"
  inStock ="no">Toyota</name>
</cars>
```

and you want to add the text

1 at this price

and

All vehicles plus tax, license, doc. fees, smog + finance charges if any. Subject to prior sales + credit approval. Sale price excludes leases. SPECIAL APR IN LIEU OF REBATES. All new and unused vehicles over $25,000 come with 2 season passes for skiing at Heavenly Resort this season. This is non-transferable and may not be redeemed for cash. This offer can only be used by the registered owner together. 2 season passes together have a retail value of $2,600. Present the original certificate and a picture ID to pick up the season pass at Heavenly.

as an entity you name `message`, the revised files reads, Example 11-21.

Example 11-21

```
<?xml version="1.0"?>
<!DOCTYPE cars [
<!ELEMENT cars ((name+), text)>
<!ELEMENT name (#PCDATA)>
<!ELEMENT text (#PCDATA)
<!ENTITY message "1 at this price ">
```

`<!ENTITY feesSki` "All vehicles plus tax, license, doc. fees, smog + finance charges if any. Subject to prior sales + credit approval. Sale price excludes leases. SPECIAL APR IN LIEU OF REBATES. All new and unused vehicles over $25,000 come with 2 season passes for skiing at Heavenly Resort this season. This is non-transferable and may not be redeemed for cash. This offer can only be used by the registered owner together. 2 season passes together have a retail value of $2,600. Present the original certificate and a picture ID to pick up the season pass at Heavenly.">

```
<!ATTLIST name
          price CDATA #REQUIRED
          color CDATA #IMPLIED
          type CDATA "344"
          inStock CDATA  #FIXED "yes"> ]>
<cars>
  <name price ="30,000 USD" type ="300">&message;
   Volvo</name>
  <name price ="20,000 USD" color ="red" type ="350">
   &message; BMW</name>
  <name price ="25,000 USD" color ="green" >&message;
   Ford</name>
  <name price ="30,000 USD" color ="gray" inStock
   ="no">&message; Toyota</name>
  &feesSki;
</cars>
```

returns the result

```
<?xml version="1.0" ?>
  <!DOCTYPE cars (View Source for full doctype...)>
<cars>
  <name price="30,000 USD" type="300" inStock="yes">1 at this price
Volvo</name>
  <name price="20,000 USD" color="red" type="350" inStock="yes"> 1 at
this price BMW</name>
  <name price="25,000 USD" color="green" type="344" inStock="yes"> 1 at
this price Ford</name>
  <name price="30,000 USD" color="grey" inStock="no" type="344"
onStock="yes">1 at this price Toyota </name>
All vehicles plus tax, license, doc. fees, smog + finance charges if
any. Subject to prior sales + credit approval. Sale price excludes
leases. SPECIAL APR IN LIEU OF REBATES. All new and unused vehicles
over $25,000 come with 2 season passes for skiing at Heavenly Resort
this season. This is non-transferable and may not be redeemed for cash.
This offer can only be used by the registered owner together. 2 season
passes together have a retail value of $2,600. Present the original
certificate and a picture ID to pick up the season pass at Heavenly.
</cars>
```

Entities can be located in an external file and opened in a specific location of an XML document. In this case, an entity would be defined with

```
<!ENTITY report SYSTEM "http://www.learningcentre.org/reportA.txt">
```

EXERCISES

11.13 There are DTDs that have been developed and are commercially available for several purposes. You can buy a DTD and use it to develop your own document and edit it as you choose. Because there are more and more applications of XML, many new XML-based languages are in development. Each of these languages have their own DTD. The following code is a part of the DTD developed for Material Science. Try to develop an XML document using the Material Science DTD.

```
<!ELEMENT MatML_Materials_Doc (Material+)>
<!ELEMENT Material (MaterialDescription, Property+, Terms?, Graphs?)>
<!ELEMENT MaterialDescription (MaterialName, MaterialClass?,
MaterialSubclass*, MaterialSource?, MaterialForm?,
MaterialChemistry?, MaterialComments?)>
<!ATTLIST MaterialDescription xmlns CDATA #IMPLIED>
<!ELEMENT MaterialName (#PCDATA)>
<!ATTLIST MaterialName authority CDATA #IMPLIED>
<!ELEMENT MaterialClass (#PCDATA)>
<!ELEMENT MaterialSubclass (#PCDATA)>
```

```
<!ELEMENT MaterialSource (#PCDATA)>
<!ELEMENT MaterialForm (#PCDATA)>
<!ELEMENT MaterialChemistry (#CDATA)>
<!ELEMENT MaterialComments (#PCDATA)>
<!ELEMENT Property (PropertyDescription, PropertyValue,
PropertyValueQualifier?, Parameter*)>
<!ELEMENT PropertyDescription (PropertyName, PropertyUnits,
DataSource, DataType, MeasurementTechnique?,
PropertyComments?)>
<!ATTLIST PropertyDescription xmlns CDATA #IMPLIED>
<!ELEMENT PropertyName (#PCDATA)>
<!ATTLIST PropertyName authority #IMPLIED>
<!ELEMENT PropertyUnits (#PCDATA)>
<!ATTLIST PropertyUnits authority #IMPLIED>
<!ELEMENT DataSource (#PCDATA)>
<!ATTLIST DataSource xmlns CDATA #IMPLIED>
<!ELEMENT DataType (#PCDATA)>
<!ELEMENT MeasurementTechnique (TechniqueName,
TechniqueDescription?)>
<!ELEMENT TechniqueName (#PCDATA)>
<!ATTLIST TechniqueName authority #IMPLIED>
<!ELEMENT TechniqueDescription (#PCDATA)>
<!ELEMENT PropertyComments (#PCDATA)>
<!ELEMENT PropertyValue (#PCDATA)>
<!ELEMENT PropertyValueQualifier (#PCDATA)>
<!ATTLIST PropertyValueQualifier type (precision | type | uncertainty)
#REQUIRED>
<!ELEMENT Parameter (ParameterName, ParameterValue, ParameterUnits,
ParameterComments?)>
<!ELEMENT ParameterName (#PCDATA)>
<!ATTLIST ParameterName authority #IMPLIED>
<!ELEMENT ParameterValue (#PCDATA)>
<!ELEMENT ParameterUnits (#PCDATA)>
<!ATTLIST ParameterUnits authority #IMPLIED>
<!ELEMENT ParameterComments (#PCDATA)>
```

11.14 Write a DTD for the following XML document:

```
<?xml version ="1.0"?>
  <Spare_parts>
    <item>
      <Part_no>101524</Part_no>
      Type>FLP-PK-4</Type>
      <Article_designation>Sub-base </Article_designation>
      <Description>With barbed fitting PK-4, for valves </Description>
    </item>
```

```
    <item>
      <Part_no>10420</Part_no>
      <Type>VLHE-3-1/2</Type>
      <Article_designation>Single pilot pneumatic soft-start valve
</Article_ designation>
      <Description>Normally closed, slow start-up valve, for use
individually or in conjunction with S-series service units.
</Description>
    </item>
    <item>
      <Part_no>10421</Part_no>
      <Type>MFHE-3-1/2</Type>
      <Article_designation>Solenoid valve</Article_designation>
      <Description>Start-up valve for delayed pressure build-up, for
use individually or in conjunction with S-series service units, with
solenoid coil, manual override and socket.</Description>
    </item>
  </Spare_parts>
```

11.15 Create a DTD to describe the following XML document:

The root of the XML document is `moviecatalog`
Root has more children called `movie`
`movie` has the following chidren:

`title, director, actor, category, place, time, price`

The children must be organized in the following order:

`title, director, category, actor, place, price, time`

The elements `actor`, `place`, and `time` can appear several times.
The content of elements `title`, `director`, `place` are `#PCDATA`, all others are `CDATA`
The element `price` has attribute `currency` always has the default value `$`

11.12 DTD SHORTCOMINGS

DTD shortcomings include

1. DTDs have a different syntax than XML documents; they use a form of notation called EBNF and, as such, cannot be parsed with an XML parser.
2. DTDs are not extensible.
3. DTDs are short on possible data type notations.
4. There is no provision for inheritance from one DTD to another.
5. Good DTDs are not easy to write.

EXERCISES

11.16 Transform the DTD document below into a schema.

```
<!ELEMENT book(title,author,year,publisher,isbn,price)>
<!ELEMENT title(#PCDATA)>
<!ELEMENT author(#PCDATA)>
<!ELEMENT year(#PCDATA)>
<!ELEMENT publisher(#PCDATA)>
<!ELEMENT isbn(#PCDATA)>
<!ELEMENT price(#PCDATA)>
```

11.17 Write a schema for the following XML document. You originally keyed this document as Chapter 4 DOM Exercise 5-23 (this is half of that exercise)

```
<?xml version="1.0"?>
<?xml-stylesheet type="text/xsl" href="property.xsl"?>
<adNewHomes>
  <adDetail>
    <property>University Square</property>
    <area>San Mateo County</area>
    <developer>Summer Hill Homes</developer>
  <location>Exit University, off 101. Right on Donahoe</location>
    <price>from the high $500's</price>
    <adText>Ponderosa Series. 3 and 4 BR homes with Craftsman details
from 1,761 to 2,024 sq ft.</adText>
    <hours>11-5 Thurs-Sun</hours>
    <phone>650/466-8700M</phone>
  </adDetail>
  <adDetail>
    <property>Sonsara</property>
    <area>Contra Costa County</area>
    <developer>Taylor Woodrow Homes</developer>
    <location>Moraga. Camino Ricardo and Morago Way</location>
    <price>from the high $800's</price>
    <adText>3 to 5 BR homes with great views. Luxury Homes in a great
location.
    </adText>
    <hours>10-5 Daily</hours>
    <phone>925/431-2800</phone>
  </adDetail>
  <adDetail>
    <property>Vintners Green</property>
    <area>Alameda County</area>
    <developer>Greystone Homes</developer>
    <location>I-680 to 84. Rt on 84, go several mi. 84 turns into
```

```
Holmes. Left on Alden Lane.</location>
    <price>from the mid $600's</price>
    <adText>3, 4 & 5 bedroom single-family homes.</adText>
    <hours>11-5 Daily</hours>
    <phone>925/442-3200</phone>
  </adDetail>
  <adDetail>
    <property>Dublin Ranch</property>
    <area>Alameda County</area>
    <developer>Shore Homes</developer>
    <location>680 at Dublin Canyon</location>
    <price>from the $400-700's</price>
    <adText>Master planned community, 3-6 BR Shore Home.</adText>
    <hours>11-7 Tues-Sun</hours>
    <phone>925/779-9000</phone>
  </adDetail>
</adNewHomes>
```

CHAPTER SUMMARY

1. The need for valid XML documents, with a defined structure is growing because of e-commerce, B2B, and the development of the global networked economy.
2. The main advantages of schemas are that they are XML documents, they support data types, and they support namespace.
3. The order of appearance of elements in the document is defined by `<xsd:sequence>`. Elements in the document must be in the same order as their declarations appear in the schema document.
4. The elements of schemas are of complex type (with subelements and attributes) and simple type (with no subelements).
5. The schema is developed as an XML document. To define the structure, determine which elements are of complex type and which are of simple type. Next, declare complex-type elements in the terms of other complex element attributes and simple-type elements.
6. There are built in schema specifications for simple types such as `string`, `integer`, `float`, and `boolean`.
7. Users can create simple-type elements using facets.
8. It is possible to define the sequence of appearance with `xsd:sequence` and number of appearances of elements in document using `minOccurs` and `maxOccurs` attributes.
9. Attributes are described `xsd:attribute` elements in schemas. It is possible to define default, required, fixed, optional, and prohibited with the different values of attribute use.

10. A schema consists of a preamble and zero or more definitions and declarations. The preamble is within the root element schema. It must consist of

    (a) a targets NS, which is the namespace and URI of the schema you use, (b) the version to specify the XML schema version, and (c) xmlns, which provides the namespace for the XML.
11. The schema document has a `schema` root element and children such as `element`, `complexType`, and `simpleType`, which determine the appearance of elements and their content in the instance document (XML document).
12. DTD are older than schemas but have disadvantages because they are not developed with XML, do not support data types, and are more difficult to learn.
13. DTDs, as defined earlier, are written in SGML rather than XML. The DTD can define the structure of the document to allow for better application development and faster application search results.
14. The DTD begins with the DOCTYPE declaration, which connects the DTD declarations to an XML document. The DOCTYPE declaration must follow the XML declaration and precede any elements in the document. Comments and processing instructions may appear between the XML declaration and DOCTYPE declaration.
15. Sometimes it is better to use external DTDs for added flexibility. With an external DTD, the DOCTYPE declaration consists of the root element followed by a keyword denoting the source and the location of the DTD. For this declaration of the source, use either the keyword SYSTEM or PUBLIC. Using SYSTEM means the parser should be able to find the DTD on the indicated URL.
16. The most important part of XML documents are elements declared in the DTD, using the ELEMENT tag. There are four categories of element content: empty, element, mixed, and any.
17. The element structure is declared in content models. In principle, content models consist of a set of parentheses enclosing a combination of child element names, operators, and the #PCDATA keyword. The operator allows you to denote cardinality and indicate how many elements and character data may be combined.
18. If you want to declare how many instances of an element are permitted, use cardinality operators, such as ?, which means optional (i.e., may or may not appear); *, which means may appear zero or more times; and +, which means must appear one or more times.
19. Each attribute consists of the name of the attribute, its type, and a default declaration.
20. If text, data, or a graphic are to be used in one or several places in a document, you can use an entity, which must be declared in a DTD. The entity has a name

and contents defined in the DTD. When you need to place that text, data, or graphic, declared in the DTD, into some part of your XML output, you need only write the name of the entity according to some basic syntax rules.

SELF-ASSESSMENT

1. Demonstrate an understanding of schemas and DTDs and why are they important.
2. Demonstrate an understanding of the difference between well-formed and valid documents.
3. Demonstrate an understanding of the difference between and be able to write simple- and complex-type elements.
4. Read and write the main simple-type elements declared in the schema specification.
5. Read and write simple-type elements using facets and built-in simple-type elements.
6. Read and write complex-type elements using simple type (both built-in schema and self-created).
7. Read and write a sequence of appearance elements in an XML document, and define the number of occurrences of elements in the document.
8. Read and code a schema for a complex XML document.
9. Read and write internal and external DTDs.
10. Read and write `DOCTYPE` and `ELEMENT` declarations.
11. Recognize and write empty, mixed, and any elements.
12. Define the order of elements and how many times an element occurs in the document.
13. Read and write `ATTLIST` and understand how attributes are declared in DTDs.
14. Read and write ENTITY declarations and understand why and how entities are used in XML documents.
15. Read, edit, and write complex DTDs for XML documents, and create XML documents in accordance with earlier defined DTDs.
16. Demonstrate an understanding of the difference between DTDs and schemas, and determine whether a project should use schemas or DTDs.

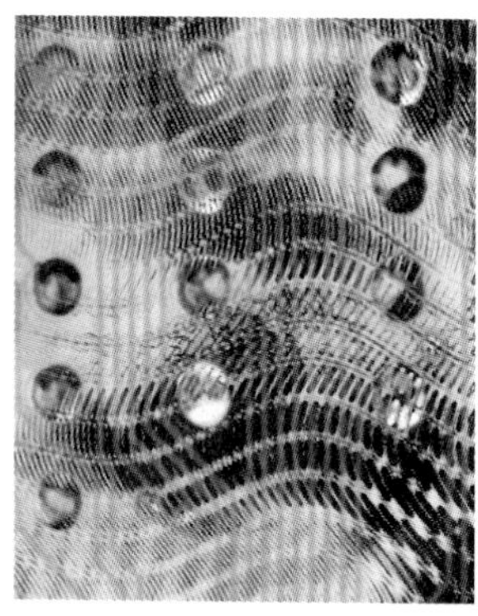

12 Wireless Markup Language

CHAPTER OBJECTIVES

By reading the information and practicing the code in this chapter, you will understand and be able to

1. Differentiate between wireless and web development, and work with wireless markup language (WML) structure and syntax to create WML applications.
2. Develop server-side applications using wireless application protocol (WAP) and active server page (ASP).
3. Determine appropriate tools for development and testing.
4. Select and develop with WAP tools from the companion web site.

12.1 DESIGNING FOR WIRELESS DEVICES

The audience for wireless applications is broader than for the Internet. Additionally, children, teenagers, and older citizens will have different expectations from their wireless applications than will business people or students. There is much to take in account when designing Internet applications to be accessed on a wireless device. For example,

1. With small displays it is impossible to output large amounts of text.
2. Typically only four lines of text are available, with 15 to 18 characters each.
3. Graphics capabilities are minimal.
4. Text entry is difficult. Phone keypads, as an example, are not user friendly.
5. Limited bandwidth makes for slow access.
6. Batteries limit the power of electronic circuits, resulting in low processing power.

The **wireless application protocol (WAP)** is currently the primary way of accessing the Internet via a cellular phone. The **WAP forum** (wap.org) has defined specifications that include complementary application, session, transaction, security, and transport protocol layers. In the same time period, the **wireless markup language (WML)** was developed by the World Wide Web Consortium (W3C), as a subset of XML. Current typical applications over WAP include trading, banking, shopping, and email interfaces. Additional sites offer news, radio, and entertainment listings.

The intention of WAP is to utilize the underlying web structure to render communication between content providers and cellular phones more efficient than if the current web protocols were used. The significant difference between WAP and the existing web is the **WAP gateway** for translating between hypertext transfer protocol (HTTP) and WAP. The WAP gateway sits (logically) between the **WAP device** and the origin server, acting as interpreter between the two, enabling them to communicate. You can use an operator network as WAP gateway, or install your own. The WAP device is the physical device you use to access WAP applications, mobile phones, PDAs, or handheld computers, as an example. Software running on the WAP device that interprets content coming from the Internet and determines how to display that content on the WAP device, is the WAP browser. **WAP browsers** are available for all WAP devices and can be referred to as microbrowsers.

The requirement for a WAP device to be WAP compliant, is that it must implement a wireless application environment user agent (**WAE User Agent**) to render the content for display. WAP compliance also requires a wireless telephony applications user agent (**WTA User Agent**) to receive compiled WTA files from a WAP server and execute them. The WTA user agent includes access to the interface to the phone and functionality such as number dialing, call answering, phone book organization, message management, and location indication services. The **WAP Stack** implementation allows the phone to connect to the WAP gateway, using the WAP protocols.

WAP servers function in much the same way as a web server and can coexist on the same WAP device. The difference between WAP and web servers is in the content they store and send to the client. Web servers support files such as hypertext markup language (HTML), JavaScript, extensible HTML (XHTML), XML, and images. WAP servers support files such as WML, WMLScript, wireless bitmap image files (WBMP). WAP servers are typically WAP application servers with gateway functionality, providing services web origin servers provide and acting as a WAP gateway.

12.2 WIRELESS MARKUP LANGUAGE

WML displays, for the most part, text-based pages. WML shares elements of HTML 4 and handheld device markup language (HDML) 2, and is defined as an XML document type. Every WML document is called a single deck, made up of one or more than one card. As users access a WAP enabled site, the deck is sent to the WAP device of which the user sees the first card, reads the content, and may enter information or proceed to a second card. The way the cards are displayed is dependent on the browser, through such interfaces as user prompts.

Every WML deck begins the XML header

```
<?xml version="1.0"?>
<!DOCTYPE wml PUBLIC "-//WAPFORUM//DTD WML 1.1//EN"
"http://www.wapforum.org/DTD/wml_1.1.xml">
```

The first line is your usual XML prolog. The second line selects the document type definition (DTD) and gives its uniform resource locator (URL). Many WML toolkits automatically generate the WML header.

The main WML code of a deck is enclosed in the element pair

```
<wml></wml>
```

which act as the body of the document. Cards are defined within the deck within the element pair.

```
<card></card>
```

`<card>` may have different attributes. In this chapter you will work with attributes `id` and `title`. The `id` attributes gives the card an identifier to be used as reference by other parts of the WML. The `title` attribute gives the name of the card to be presented by the user. Not all WML browsers support `title`, card design should not rely on `title` unless tested. Use of `card` and `title` is shown in Example 12-1.

Example 12-1

```
<wml>
<card id="MainCard" title="This is a first card">
<p align="center">
 Welcome to WML
</p>
</card>
</wml>
```

In this example, <p> has the same meaning as in HTML but must be closed, as in XHTML and XML. Space limits the numbers of <p> used. Adding a small paragraph can be accomplished, as in Example 12-2.

Example 12-2

```
<?xml version="1.0"?>
<!DOCTYPE wml PUBLIC "-//WAPFORUM//DTD WML 1.1//EN"
"http://www.wapforum.org/DTD/wml_1.1.xml">
```

```
<wml>
 <card id="MainCard" title="This is a first card">
    <p align="center">
    Welcome to WML
    </p>
    <p>This is first wml example</p>
  </card>
```

Although the number of supported elements is smaller than the full specification of HTML or XHTML, several options are available. The WAP browser may allow presentation of text in bold, underlined, italics, with line breaks and tables, checkboxes, and radio buttons, depending on the capabilities of the WAP device. Black and white images, compliant with WBMP standards, are supported on some WAP browsers.

EXERCISE

12.1 Key the code given in WML Example 12-2. Change the <p> text to Welcome to YourName's!

In the nested <p>, add a comment for your friends, something like "Come on in for Pizza." Save the file as `example1.wml`. Open the code of Opera or with a WML editor, which previews the code similarly to how it will display on a WAP device.

12.3 WML STYLE

WML supports the following text style tags:

<b>..</b> bold, text will display as bold
<i<>..</i> italic, text will display in italic
<u>..</u> underlined, text will display underlined
<e>..</e> emphasis, text will display emphasized
<strong>..</strong> strong, text will display stronger
<big>..</big> big, text will display larger
<small>..</small> small, text will display smaller

To see how style is implemented, key the following code (Example 12-3):

Example 12-3

```
<?xml version="1.0"?>
<!-- created by YourName -->
<!DOCTYPE wml PUBLIC "-//WAPFORUM//DTD WML 1.1//EN"
"http://www.wapforum.org/DTD/wml_1.1.xml">
<wml>
 <card id="MainCard" title="This is a style example">
    <p align="center">
```

```
    <b>bold</b><br/>
    <i>italic</i><br/>
    <u>underline</u><br/>
    <em>emphasis</em><br/>
    <big>big</big><br/>
    <small>small</small><br/>
    <strong>strong</strong><br/>
    </p>
  </card>
```

EXERCISES

12.2 Key the following application and test your result:

```
<?xml version="1.0"?>
<!-- created by YourName -->
<!DOCTYPE wml PUBLIC "-//WAPFORUM//DTD WML 1.1//EN"
"http://www.wapforum.org/DTD/wml_1.1.xml">
<wml>
 <card id="MainCard" title="This is a first card">
    <p align="center">
    Name please
    <input type="text" name="searchkey" value="" />
    a href="search.asp">Submit data</a>
    </p>
 </card>
</wml>
```

12.3 Key the following site, adding style elements to the code and additional teams to the application:

```
<?xml version="1.0"?>
<!-- created by YourName -->
<!DOCTYPE wml PUBLIC "-//WAPFORUM//DTD WML 1.1//EN"
"http://www.wapforum.org/DTD/wml_1.1.xml">
<wml>
 <card id="MainCard" title="This is a first card">
    <p align="center">
    Select a Sport
    </p>
    <p align="left"><a href="#b">Basketball</a></p>
    <p align="left"><a href="#f">Football</a></p>
    <p align="left"><a href="#h">Hockey</a></p>
 </card>
 <card id="b" title="basketball">
    <p align="left">Choose a team</p>
    <p align="left"><a href="#Lakers">LA Lakers</a></p>
```

```
        <p align="left"><a href="#ChBulls">Chicago Bulls
        </a></p>
        <p align="left"><a href="#Harlem">Harlem
        Globetrotters</a></p>
    </card>
    <card id="f" title="football">
        <p align="left">Choose a team</p>
    </card>
    <card id="h" title="hockey">
        <p align="left">Choose a team</p>
    </card>
</wml>
```

12.4 ESCAPE CHARACTERS

Rather than the characters <, >, "" , use the following escape characters:

```
>     &gt;
<     &lt;
"     &quot;
```

As an example, the expression `10>20 ="false"` is written as

```
10 &gt; 20 =&qout;false&quot
```

EXERCISE

12.4 Key the following example, then change the math symbols and write a new set of escape characters:

```
<?xml version="1.0"?>
<!-- created by YourName -->
<!DOCTYPE wml PUBLIC "-//WAPFORUM//DTD WML 1.1//EN"
"http://www.wapforum.org/DTD/wml_1.1.xml">
<wml>
  <card id="MainCard" title="MathSymbolExam">
      <p align="center">
      10 &gt; 20 =&quot;False&quot;<br/>
      10 &lt; 20 =&quot;True&quot;<br/>
      </p>
  </card>
</wml>
```

12.5 GRAPHICS

WML supports graphics, although minimally because of screen size. Images have the extension .wbmp. Some companies offer tools to transform images from jpeg or gif to the .WBMP format [see companion web site for links to these resources (www.prenhall.com/carey)]. There are also tools that can be used to create drawings. A simple example of how to insert images into your WML application is Example 12-4.

Example 12-4

```
<?xml version="1.0"?>
<!DOCTYPE wml PUBLIC "-//WAPFORUM//DTD WML 1.1//EN"
"http://www.wapforum.org/DTD/wml_1.1.xml">
<wml>
 <card title="Image">
  <p>
    This is an example of an image in a paragraph.
  <img src="rabbit.wbmp" alt="The logo rabbit can not be displayed" />
  </p>
 </card>
</wml>
```

To insert the image into the card, use `<img/>`. As you see in Example 12-4, `img` has two attributes, `src` and `alt`. The `src` attribute defines the location of image to be inserted. The `alt` attribute displays text (the value of the attribute) if the user's device is not able to display images.

EXERCISES

12.5 Create a WML card, using style, for the following news item:

7.0 Earthquake-5 am (use `<big>`)
Rocks CA's Bay Area (use `<b>`)
Epicenter, Santa Cruz (use `<em>`)
Aftershocks 5@ 6.0 (use `<strong>`)

12.6 Create a WML card, using style you determine, for the following meeting change:

Emergency Staff Meeting
Today 3 pm—All Hands
Main Conference Room
RE: Noon System Failure

12.7 Key the following table:

```
<?xml version="1.0"?>
<!-- created by YourName -->
```

```
<!DOCTYPE wml PUBLIC "-//WAPFORUM//DTD WML 1.1//EN"
"http://www.wapforum.org/DTD/wml_1.1.xml">
<wml>
  <card id="MainCard" title="Tables">
    <p align="center">
      This is an example of table
      <table columns="2">
        <tr><td>Company</td><td>phone</td></tr>
        <tr><td>Ipak</td><td>891-9040</td></tr>
        <tr><td>Inova</td><td>587-5476</td></tr>
      </table>
    </p>
  </card>
</wml>
```

12.8 Create a table displaying the following information. Note that `$` is reserved for variables; to get `$`, you need to key `$$`.

The client offers two-hour delivery on common office supplies customers seem to run out of and need in a hurry. Design a way for customers to select, price, and purchase the following:

Toner, HP, Black, \$29.00
Toner, HP, Color, \$40.00
Toner, Oki, Black, \$28.00
Toner, Oki, Color, \$39.00
Zip disks, 10-pk, \$99.00
3.5 Floppy disks, 50-pk, \$9.99
CD-R, 10-pk, \$8.99
Copy Paper, 500 sh, \$4.99
Copy Paper, case, \$39.99

12.6 WML NAVIGATION

The WAP device loads the deck of cards and displays cards one at a time. Each card contains both content and navigational control, since a WAP device has the capability to hold many different cards. Navigation is important because by accessing or returning several cards at once, trips to the WAP browser are reduced, allowing additional content to be stored locally.

Linking from one resource to another is accomplished with an anchor link, the WML form of which is

```
<anchor>go href="location"</anchor>
```

It is possible to substitute `<anchor></anchor>` for `<a></a>`. `location` can be a URL such as

```
href="http://www.learningcentre.org/index.wml"
```

or a file, in the same directory, such as

```
href="style.wml"
```

or a new card selected with

```
href="#nextCard"
```

specified with the symbol # before the card ID.

Example 12-5 shows the above different styles of linking.

Example 12-5

```
<?xml version="1.0"?>
<!-- created by YourName -->
<!DOCTYPE wml PUBLIC "-//WAPFORUM//DTD WML 1.1//EN"
"http://www.wapforum.org/DTD/wml_1.1.xml">
<wml>
<card id="MainCard" title="Example of links">
<p align="center">
An example of linking to a URL<br/>
</p>
<p align="center">
<a href="http://www.learningcentre.org/index">to the URL</a>
</p>
<p align="center">
 <a href="Sol_12-8.wml">An example of linking to another WML document
</a>
 </p>
 <p align="center"> Link example <br/></p>
<p align="center"><a href="#nextCard">An example of linking to another
card in the same document</a>
 </p>
</card>
<card id="nextCard" title="new link">
<p align="left">Hello!</p>
</card>
</wml>
```

12.7 OPTIMIZATION

WML is designed to adapt to the high-latency and narrow-band characteristics of wireless networks. According to the WAP specifications, connections with the origin server should be avoided unless absolutely necessary. This can be accomplished by introducing variables that last longer than a single deck and by grouping cards in decks, along with client-side user input validation with WMLScript.

In the wireless networks where WAP is implemented, a WAP gateway is installed and connected to the wireless network Local Area Network (LAN). A new phone number is defined and assigned to an access server. When a browsing session is initiated, a call is placed to that number. The access server only authenticates the subscriber attempting to contact the gateway. Authentication takes place via a database storing valid subscribers and their number. Once validation is complete, the call is connected to the internal LAN and is allowed to communicate directly with the WAP gateway.

Once the gateway connection is established, the browser in the phone automatically sends subscriber details to the gateway along with a user name and password. The gateway checks against a database, much like a dialup connection to the Internet is checked and validated with a PC. The WAP browser has an associated homepage deck, set up by the service provider, which loads into the microbrowser after the user has been authenticated. The deck is a WAP portal, allowing links and services from that gateway. The challenge for the developer is to create cards with which the user can, with the limitations of a phone keypad, accomplish their goals and tasks.

12.8 DO ELEMENTS

The do elements in WML documents define an event to be triggered as in

```
<do type "typelist"
   actionlist
</do>
```

The possible values of the type attributes are

`accept`—acceptance on mobile phone it is usually the left softkey
`prev`—previous is the back bottom, usually the right softkey
`help`—button pressed to request help
`reset`—the reset button for the device
`options`—the button request asking for more operations
`delete`—the button pressed to remove an item
`unknown`—can be mapped to any key on the device

as in Example 12-6.

Example 12-6

```
<?xml version="1.0"?>
<!DOCTYPE wml PUBLIC "-//WAPFORUM//DTD WML 1.1//EN"
"http://www.wapforum.org/DTD/wml_1.1.xml">
<wml>
 <card id="card1" title="doExample">
```

```
 <do type="accept" label="Go to the next card">
  <go href="#nextcard" />
 </do>
   <p>
   Example of using do, press accept<br/>
   to go to next card
   </p>
 </card>
<card id="nextcard" title="display">
   <p>
Hello, you are on the next card
   </p>
</card>
</wml>
```

When you want to select between different options you can use the `select` element. If the value of attribute multiple is true, the user can make multiple choices as in Example 12-7.

Example 12-7

```
<?xml version="1.0"?>
<!DOCTYPE wml PUBLIC "-//WAPFORUM//DTD WML 1.1//EN"
"http://www.wapforum.org/DTD/wml_1.1.xml">
<wml>
 <card id="products" title="Select product">
  <p>
   <select name="name" multiple="true">
    <option value="gift">Gifts</option>
    <option value="wine">Wines</option>
    <option value="toys">Toys</option>
   </select>
  </p>
 </card>
</wml>
```

12.9 USER INPUT

Cards can contain input elements. The browser decodes input tags then determines the best way to prompt the user for the input requested. WML specifies tags for allowing users to submit text entries, choose among a list of options, or begin a navigation or history managment task such as going to the previous card or jumping to a specified link. Example 12-8 shows a simple approach to user input.

Example 12-8

```
<?xml version="1.0"?>
<!DOCTYPE wml PUBLIC "-//WAPFORUM//DTD WML 1.1//EN"
"http://www.wapforum.org/DTD/wml_1.1.xml">
```

```
<wml>
  <card id="MainCard" title="examplePizza">
    <p align="center">
    Welcome to pizza online
    </p>
    <p align="center">
      <do type="accept" label="Choose a pizza">
      <go href="pizza.wml"/>
      </do>
    </p>
  </card>
</wml>
```

The code for `pizza.wml` is

```
<?xml version="1.0"?>
<!DOCTYPE wml PUBLIC "-//WAPFORUM//DTD WML 1.1//EN"
"http://www.wapforum.org/DTD/wml_1.1.xml">
<wml>
<card id="MainCard" title="This is a first card">
<p align="left">
<do type="accept" label="Combination">
<go href="#combination"/>
</do>
</p>
<p align="left">
<do type="help" label="Four Cheese">
<go href="#fcheese"/>
</do>
</p><p align="left">
<do type="previous" label="Pepperoni">
<go href="#pepperoni"/>
</do>
</p>
</card>
<card id="combination" title="Your choice">
<do type="prev">
<go href="#MainCard"/>
</do>
<p>Combination</p>
<p>Price $$ 13</p>
</card>
<card id="fcheese" title="Your choice">
<do type="prev">
<go href="#MainCard"/>
```

```
</do>
<p>Four Cheese</p>
<p>Price $$ 10</p>
</card>
<card id="pepperoni" title="Your choice">
<do type="prev">
<go href="#MainCard"/>
</do>
<p>Pepperoni</p>
<p>Price $$ 9</p>
</card>
</wml>
```

EXERCISE

12.9 Using Example 12-8 as guide, change the available items to a taxi, carpool van, or limousine. Add style and add input for the user to key in the pick up point.

12.10 NAVIGATION AND HISTORY TRACKING

WML includes common navigation and history functionalities. User input determines how previous and next cards are accessed. Example 12-9 allows access to the previous card.

Example 12-9

```
<?xml version="1.0"?>
<!DOCTYPE wml PUBLIC "-//WAPFORUM//DTD WML 1.1//EN"
"http://www.wapforum.org/DTD/wml_1.1.xml">
<wml>
 <card>
  <p>
   <anchor>
    Previous Page
    <prev/>
   </anchor>
  </p>
 </card>
</wml>
```

The next example (Example 12-10) refreshes the current card.

Example 12-10

```
<?xml version="1.0"?>
<!DOCTYPE wml PUBLIC "-//WAPFORUM//DTD WML 1.1//EN"
"http://www.wapforum.org/DTD/wml_1.1.xml">
<wml>
```

```
 <card>
  <p>
   <anchor>
    Refresh This Page
    <refresh/>
   </anchor>
  </p>
 </card>
</wml>
```

12.11 VARIABLES

Variables in WML are simple and are used to store data to be used in different cards. Variables can be specified with the `setvar` (set variable) command or an `input` element. Both are case sensitive and must be referenced with the sign `$` in front of name as in, `$(name)`. Example 12-11 is an example of specifying variables with input element.

Example 12-11

```
<?xml version="1.0"?>
<!DOCTYPE wml PUBLIC "-//WAPFORUM//DTD WML 1.1//EN"
"http://www.wapforum.org/DTD/wml_1.1.xml">
<wml>
 <card id="card1" title="city">
 <do type="accept" label="Choice">
 <go href="#outputCard"/>
 </do>
   <p>
   <select name="nameCity">
    <option value="Roma">Roma</option>
    <option value="Paris">Paris</option>
    <option value="London">London</option>
   </select>
  </p>
</card>
<card id="outputCard" title="choice">
<p>
Your destination is: $nameCity
</p>
</card>
</wml>
```

When the user selects the name of a city, control is transferred to card `outputCard` by the `go` command and the choice is displayed. Similarly, you can use variables specified with `setvar` command inside of `<go>`, `<previous>`, and `<refresh>` .

Example 12-12

```
<?xml version="1.0"?>
<!DOCTYPE wml PUBLIC "-//WAPFORUM//DTD WML 1.1//EN"
"http://www.wapforum.org/DTD/wml_1.1.xml">
<wml>
  <card id="card1" title="Example variables">
      <do type="accept" label="setvar">
      <go href="#outputCard">
      <setvar name="test" value="Example of setvar"/>
      </go>
      </do>
  </card>
  <card id="outputCard" title="result">
    <p>
    The value of the variable is: $test
    </p>
  </card>
</wml>
```

12.12 ADDITIONAL INPUT

When users interact with links, the option list and select list give limited possibilities because users can only make choices determined in the application. In many applications there is a need for a more active user role, such as key in of numbers (credit card) or strings (name, password). In WAP for this kind of activity you can use `<input>`. The data keyed in the input field are captured and assigned to a variable. The `name` attribute of `<input>` is used to specify the name of variable, as in

```
<input name="movieName" />
```

An example of `<input> is` Example 12-13.

Example 12-13

```
<?xml version="1.0"?>
<!-- created by YourName -->
<!DOCTYPE wml PUBLIC "-//WAPFORUM//DTD WML 1.1//EN"
"http://www.wapforum.org/DTD/wml_1.1.xml">
<wml>
  <card id="Movies" title="Searching Movies">
    <p align="center">
    Key in movie name
    <input name="movieName"/><br/>
    <a href="#cardS">To the next card</a>
    </p>
```

```
    </card>
    <card id="cardS" title="Selection">
      <p>
      Would you like to see $(movieName)
      </p>
    </card>
  </wml>
```

After the data is obtained, it is sent to a server. This can be done with the `get` or `post` method. Example 12-14 uses `post` for sending a customer name and password to a server.

Example 12-14

```
  <?xml version="1.0"?>
  <!DOCTYPE wml PUBLIC "-//WAPFORUM//DTD WML 1.1//EN"
  "http://www.wapforum.org/DTD/wml_1.1.xml">
  <wml>
  <card id="Login" title="Cool2Code">
     <p>
        Welcome to Cool2Code
      <br />
       Key name  <input name="memberName" type="text" maxlength="6"/>
      Key password <input name="Password" type="password" maxlength="6"/>
        <do type="accept" label="Login">
        <go href="LoginCool2Code.asp" method="post">
    <postfield name="memberName" value="$(memberName)"/>
    <postfield name="Password" value="$(Password)"/>
        </go>
        </do>
      </p>
    </card>
  </wml>
```

EXERCISE

12.10 Write code to generate two variables; one using the `setvar` command and another using input. The variables will be transfered to the next card and displayed.

12.13 TIMERS

In WAP applications you can use timers to open an application for a defined period of time. This feature can be used for displaying logos, advertising, or for updating information at regular intervals.

An example of using timers is Example 12-15.

Example 12-15

```
<?xml version="1.0"?>
<!DOCTYPE wml PUBLIC "-//WAPFORUM//DTD WML 1.1//EN"
"http://www.wapforum.org/DTD/wml_1.1.xml">
<wml>
 <card ontimer="demo.wml">
  <timer value="100"/>
  <p>This message will show for 10 seconds</p>
 </card>
</wml>
```

When document opens the message, "This message will show for 10 seconds" appears on screen and remains for 10 seconds. The amount of time can be set with `<timer value="" />`. The value is an integer, the unit is 1/10 of the second so, `value="100"` is the equivalent of 10 seconds.

EXERCISE

12.11 Adjust the sports team example you keyed in earlier in the chapter to show scores for five sporting events, each timed to change in 5-second intervals.

12.14 WML HYBRID TECHNOLOGIES

You can use XSLT to transform XML documents to WML documents. This technique is especially useful on the server side when you want to create documents for different output devices. As an example, if you want to expand the pizzeria web site you wrote earlier because the customer wants to use the standard Internet and WAP, you can use the same source XML document for creating different output documents to be sent to the users. One document is opened by the standard browser (Internet Explorer 5 [IE5], Netscape, Opera) and the other with a microbrowser. Because the devices on which the documents will be displayed have different features, you will need to develop different layouts, taking into account all limitations of the devices.
If your XML document has the form,

```
<?xml version="1.0"?>
<?xml-stylesheet type="text/xsl" href="PizWML.xsl"?>
<pizzaList>
<item>
<name>Four Seasons</name>
<price>6</price>
</item>
  <item>
<name>Margharita</name>
```

```
<price>5</price>
</item>
 <item>
<name>Four cheese</name>
<price>5.5</price>
</item>
</pizzaList>
```

then using the following XSLT document, you can transform the source document to WML to open on WAP devices using a microbrowser:

```
<?xml version="1.0"?>
<xsl:stylesheet version="1.0" xmlns:xsl="http://www.w3.org/1999/XSL/
Transform">
<xsl:output doctype-public="-//WAPFORUM//DTD WML 1.1//EN"
doctype-system="http://www.wapforum.org/DTD/wml_1.1.xml"/>
<xsl:template match="/pizzaList">
<wml>
  <card>
  <xsl:for-each select="item">
    <p> name is
  <xsl:value-of select="name"/></p>
    <p> price is
  <xsl:value-of select="price"/>
    </p>
  </xsl:for-each>
  </card>
</wml>
</xsl:template>
</xsl:stylesheet>
```

As you can see, the difference between creating a standard HTML output and the WML document is <xsl:output> with the form

```
<xsl:output doctype-public="-//WAPFORUM//DTD WML 1.1//EN"
doctype-system="http://www.wapforum.org/DTD/wml_1.1.xml"/>
```

And it defines the DTD for WML in addition to defining its URL.

Using Saxon you can generate a WML document with the following command line:

```
c:>saxon pizza.xml pizza.xsl>pizza.wml
```

where `pizza.xml` is the name of the source XML document, `pizza.xsl` is the name of XSLT document, which is performing the transformation, and `pizza.wml` is the resulting WML document.

The WML document has the form of Example 12-16.

Example 12-16

```
<?xml version="1.0" encoding="utf-8"?>
<!DOCTYPE wml
  PUBLIC "-//WAPFORUM//DTD WML 1.1//EN" "http://www.wapforum.org/DTD/
wml_1.1.xml">
<wml>
  <card>
    <p align="center"> The name is Four Seasons</p>
    <p>The price is $$6</p>
    <p>The name is Margharita</p>
    <p>The price is $$5</p>
    <p>The name is Four Cheese</p>
    <p>The price is $$5.50</p>
  </card>
</wml>
```

12.15 SERVER-SIDE WML

Because the processing power of WAP devices is limited (because of short battery life) the main processing needs to be done on the server side. As such, it is important to use server side technologies such as ASP or JSP for processing documents. A weather report can be used as an example.

You want to develop a weather report application for WAP users. The weather data are saved in an XML document on a server. The user can send the search keyword city to the server and get a response, which displays the name of the city, the temperature, and the weather conditions. The XML document will be searched on server side and the results of searching are sent to the user. The XML document has the form of Example 12-17.

Example 12-17

```
<?xml version="1.0"?>
  <weatherRep>
    <city>San Jose
      <temperature>68</temperature>
      <conditions>sunny</conditions>
    </city>
    <city>San Francisco
      <temperature>65</temperature>
      <conditions>cloudy, windy</conditions>
    </city>
```

```
    <city>Santa Cruz
      <temperature>70</temperature>
      <conditions>fog, late sun</conditions>
    </city>
</weatherRep>
```

The ASP document has the form

```
<% Response.ContentType = "text/vnd.wap.wml" %>
<?xml version="1.0"?>
<!DOCTYPE wml PUBLIC "-//WAPFORUM//DTD WML 1.1//EN"
"http://www.wapforum.org/DTD/wml_1.1.xml">
<wml>
<card id="Weather" title="WeatherReport">
   <p>
      Weather Report Search
      <br/>
      Key in city name. <input name="city" type="text" maxlength="12"/>
           <do type="accept" label="Search">
           <go href="searchWeather.asp" method="post">
               <postfield name="city" value="$(city)"/>
             </go>
      </do>
   </p>
</card>
</wml>
The line:
<% Response.ContentType = "text/vnd.wap.wml" %>
```

which sets a new MIME type (multipurpose internet mail extension is a specification for the format of data that can be sent over Internet). All other lines are WML. The input value is transferred to an ASP document using the `post` method. The application on the server side is in an ASP document; `searchWeather.asp` is

```
<%@Language ="JavaScript"%>
<% Response.ContentType = "text/vnd.wap.wml" %>
<?xml version='1.0'?>
<!DOCTYPE wml PUBLIC "-//WAPFORUM//DTD WML 1.1//EN"
"http://www.wapforum.org/DTD/wml_1.1.xml">
<wml>
<card id="card1">
<p>
<%
Response.Write("Welcome")
%>
</p>
```

```
<%
  WeatherXml=Server.CreateObject("Microsoft.XMLDOM")
  WeatherXml.async=false
  WeatherXml.load(Server.MapPath("weather.xml"))
var searchKey=Request.Form("city")
 root=WeatherXml.documentElement
 CityList= root.getElementsByTagName("city")
 len=CityList.length
k=0
 for(i=0;i<len;i++)
   {
    a=CityList.item(i).firstChild.nodeValue
    if(a==searchKey)
    {
     k++
     tem=CityList.item(i).firstChild.nextSibling.firstChild.nodeValue
     con=CityList.item(i).lastChild.firstChild.nodeValue
%>
<p>
<%
     Response.Write("City - "+a+"<br />")
     Response.Write("Temperature - "+tem+"<br/>")
     Response.Write("Condition - "+con+"<br/>")
%>
</p>
<%
    }
   }
if(k==0)
  {
   %>
  <p>
  <%
    Response.Write("Sorry no data")
  %>
</p>
<%
 }
%>
</card>
</wml>
```

Use ASP technology to develop a server side-application. In the ASP document, DOM is used to get weather data from the weather.xml document with the `getElementsByTagName` method. If the searched location is found, the data are sent to the user. If there is no hit (the variable did not change from its initial value 0) the message "Sorry no data" is sent to the user.

Because phone manufacturers have slightly different implementations of the WML language, it could happen that your application will not run correctly on different browsers. There are several tools to test your application that you can load down from the manufacturer's site (see the companion web site for links to tools) and to see how your application is working. Real applications are more complex; some of them are described in the commercial projects on the companion web site.

EXERCISE

12.12 Write an application that will inform WAP users about traffic conditions on the highways in your area. Change the XML document section letters to actual roads or locations near you where traffic is congested. Adjust the XML document as you see fit for more accurate and accessible traffic reporting information.

The original data are saved in the XML document

```
<?xml version="1.0"?>
<trafficReport>
  <highway>17
    <section>A
      <conditions>Heavy Traffic</conditions>
    </section>
    <section>B
      <conditions>Fatal Accident</conditions>
    </section>
    <section>C
      <conditions>Fender Bender</conditions>
    </section>
    <section>D
      <conditions>Debris</conditions>
    </section>
    <section>E
      <conditions>Spill</conditions>
    </section>
  </highway>
  <highway>680
    <section>A
      <conditions>Stall</conditions>
    </section>
    <section>B
      <conditions>Spill</conditions>
    </section>
```

```
    <section>C
      <conditions>Fender Bender</conditions>
    </section>
    <section>D
      <conditions>Heavy Traffic</conditions>
    </section>
    <section>E
      <conditions>Spill</conditions>
    </section>
  </highway>
  <highway>17
    <section>A
      <conditions>Spill</conditions>
    </section>
    <section>B
      <conditions>Fatal Accident</conditions>
    </section>
    <section>C
      <conditions>Fender Bender</conditions>
    </section>
    <section>D
      <conditions>Stall</conditions>
    </section>
    <section>E
      <conditions>Heavy Traffic</conditions>
    </section>
  </highway>
</trafficReport>
```

12.13 Develop an application to inform a WAP user about movie theater availability. Include

title
movie theatre
time
price
if seats are available

The information about the movies should be saved in the XML document on server side. The search should be done using DOM in the ASP environment.

CHAPTER SUMMARY

1. The audience for wireless devices is broader than for the Internet. You need to define the user's needs carefully before starting to develop wireless applications.
2. There are several limitations because most of wireless devices have small displays, poor graphical capabilities, slow data transfer rates, limited input possibilities, and low processing power.
3. The wireless application protocol (WAP) is the primary way of accessing the Internet via a cellular phone. Wireless markup language (WML), a subset of XML is used for application development for WAP devices.
4. The significant difference between WAP and the existing web is the WAP gateway for translating between HTTP and WAP. The WAP gateway sits (logically) between the WAP device and the origin server, acting as interpreter between the two, enabling them to communicate.
5. Browsers for WAP devices are called microbrowsers.
6. The requirement for a WAP device to be WAP compliant, is that it must implement a wireless application environment user agent (WAE user agent) to render the content for display. WAP compliance also requires a wireless telephony applications user agent (WTA user agent) to receive compiled WTA files from a WAP server and execute them.
7. The WAP Stack implementation allows the phone to connect to the WAP gateway using the WAP protocols.
8. WAP servers function in much the same way as a web server and can coexist on the same WAP device. The difference between WAP and web servers is in the content they store and send to the client. Web servers support files such as HTML, JavaScript, XHTML, XML, and images. WAP servers support files such as WML, WMLScript, and WBMP (wireless bitmap image files).
9. WML displays, for the most part, text-based pages. WML shares elements of HTML 4 and HDML 2 (handheld device markup language), and is defined as an XML document type.
10. Every WML document is called a single deck, made up of one or more than one card. As users access a WAP enabled site, the deck is sent to the WAP device of which the user sees the first card, reads the content, and may enter information or proceed to a second card. The way the cards are displayed is dependent on the browser, through such interfaces as user prompts.
11. Although the number of supported elements is smaller than the full specification of HTML or XHTML, several options are available. The WAP browser may allow presentation of text in bold, underlined, italics, with line breaks and tables, checkboxes, and radio buttons depending on the capabilities of the WAP device. Black and white images, compliant with WBMP standards, are supported on some WAP browsers.

12. Every WML document start with the header

```
<?xml version="1.0"?>
<!DOCTYPE wml PUBLIC "-//WAPFORUM//DTD WML 1.1//EN"
"http://www.wapforum.org/DTD/wml_1.1.xml">.
```

    and has to be well formed and valid as with other XML documents.
13. Every WML document is a single deck made from one or more cards. The deck is enclosed in the element pair `<wml>..</wml>` and cards are within `<card>..</card>`.
14. WML offers styling, navigation, and input.
15. WML supports graphics, although minimally because of screen size. Images have the extension .wbmp.
16. The WAP device loads the deck of cards, and displays cards one at a time. Each card contains both content and navigational control, since a WAP device has the capability to hold many different cards. Navigation is important because by accessing or returning several cards at once; trips to the WAP browser are reduced, allowing additional content to be stored locally.
17. In WAP applications you can use timers to open an application for a defined period of time. This feature can be used for displaying logos, advertising, or for updating information at regular intervals.
18. Transforming from an XML to a WML document is done most efficiently using XSLT. This is important because you can use the same XML source document for creation of output for different media.
19. Because of the limited processing power of WAP devices, for the most part application processing is done on the server-side using server-side programming technologies such ASP and JSP.
20. In the future there will be more users accessing information, trade, and email using wireless devices.

SELF-ASSESSMENT

1. Demonstrate an understanding of what WAP is, who the users are, and what the difference between WAP and web is.
2. Plan and create a WML document using multiple cards.
3. Plan and create a WML document using basic WML elements `wml`, `p`, `br`, `card`, organizing the WML document in different sets of cards.
4. Create small WML applications using different style, inserting images, creating links, and optional and select lists.
5. Write WML applications using variables and input elements.
6. Send data to a server using `get` and `post` methods.

7. Plan and write small WML applications running on the server side using DOM and XSLT for processing data and using ASP technology.

13 Commercial Projects

CHAPTER OBJECTIVES

By reading the information and practicing the code in this chapter, you will understand and be able to

1. Model extensible markup language (XML) applications by following documentation specifications.
2. Determine XML technologies and tools suitable for client-based development.
3. Consider users needs in code development.
4. Test and debug applications based on outside requirements.
5. Combine experience and understanding toward beginning commercial development.

13.1 CLIENT-BASED PROJECTS

Transitioning from simple exercises to code in the workplace is complex. On the one hand, understanding current technologies is an advantage; yet, on the other, pseudocode does not prepare developers or students for the problematic nature of commercial development. This chapter, Commercial Projects, and the web site (www.prenhall.com/carey) portion of the chapter, pose problems that require critical thinking and problem solving and raises some of the development issues you will encounter in the working world. The web site portion of the chapter offers the assets you will need and five additional commercial-type problems.

The materials for the commercial projects are presented as Requirements Specifications. In this case, modification of Suzanne and James Robertson's Volere Requirements (www.atlsysguild.com) from their book, *Mastering the Requirements Process*, serves to introduce most of the information you will need to find potential solutions to the client-based problems.

User analysis and requirements specifications are key in commercial web site development. If you would like to learn or review the topic, please see the web site for how user analysis and documentation can significantly improve the quality of your interface and reduce your build time. As you review each problem, remember to check the web site for additional information, updates, and any materials you need.

13.2 PROJECT 1—FREQUENTLY ASKED QUESTIONS

13.2.1 The Purpose of the Product

13.2.1.1 The User Problem or Background to the Project Effort. The client has released a new product that requires qualification to determine if the product is a good fit for the client's customer. The product is for large-scale customers and requires a heavy up-front investment. For those customers who qualify, the product will result in significant cost savings for their organization. The word qualify implies there needs to be a high level of transaction volume, executive management commitment, and a significant investment in information technology (IT) human resources within an organization to implement and test the new product.

The client can demonstrate that this level of investment will still result in significant savings for the right customer. The client has additional levels of products for small customers and wants to ensure that if a customer "disqualifies" himself from this one particular product, he can look toward the additional levels, rather than decide to go elsewhere.

A significant number of the client's customers research potential partnerships and product purchases on the web. As such, the client has developed a large frequently asked question (FAQ) list to clearly communicate the levels of products available in addition to answering a large number of technical questions. This set of questions and answers has now reached the point where it is doubtful customers will read and scroll through the entire set.

13.2.1.2 Goals of the Product. The product is a searchable FAQ to allow customers to enter a keyword, the result of which produces a window with a set of questions and answers that best target the keyword. The client is not looking for a typical search engine scenario with linked returns and percentage matches noted. Rather, this search will sort through the data bank of questions and answers, identifying those that match the search request, and returning a presentation of the matching questions and answers the customer may scroll and read through. There may be 20 questions and answers in their return result; this will still be a more targeted selection than the current complete listing of FAQ and their responses.

13.2.2 Client, Customer, and Other Stakeholders

13.2.2.1 The Client. The client for the product is Mr. Steve Contreras, Program Manager of Internet Commerce for Commerce Technologies and the Project Managers supporting Mr. Contreras.

13.2.2.2 Other Stakeholders. Stakeholders outside of Commerce Technologies Internet Commerce Division include in-house IT, marketing, and customer service. With all three internal division stakeholders, the priority is on content of the FAQ more than the search module itself.

13.2.3 Users of the Product

13.2.3.1 Users. Potential customers for the product include large-scale, international telecommunications firms. From those organizations, users of the FAQ typically include initial decision-makers such as directors purchasing. Executive management often follows up with the site as well.

13.2.3.2 User Priorities. Ease of initiating search, ease of reading questions and answers returned. No need for graphics; clear priority is accessing desired content.

13.2.4 Requirements Constraints

13.2.4.1 Solution Constraints. The client requests the solution be XML based. The product in question utilizes XML messaging and the client wants to show support for XML technologies on the information site as well.

Additional design constraints include the company policy regarding web pages, white background, sans-serif font, and corporate graphics for identification purposes rather than for artistic creativity.

13.2.4.2 Implementation Environment. The search must work in Netscape 4 and above in addition to Internet Explorer 4.0 (IE 4) and Opera 3.5 and above. Commerce Technologies' default browser is Netscape. U.S. customers often use IE and international customers, Opera.

13.2.4.3 How Long Do the Developers Have to Build the Product? Content including a set of sample questions and answers is currently available. The product should be approved within one week and uploaded after a one-week modification period. Go-live will be within two weeks.

13.2.5 Naming Conventions and Definitions

FAQ—Frequently Asked Questions.

13.2.6 The Scope of the Product

Access to targeted questions and answers regarding the client's product must be simple and clear. User focus will be on the meaning of content. The page and interface should only support the interaction between the user and the content. Simple questions and answers describing and defining a complex product will allow the customer to experience an informed interaction of content, rather than a complex interaction to a complicated set of data.

The user links to the search module from the project home page. Keyword(s) are entered by the user. The user clicks a button to initiate the search. A second page opens with the targeted questions and answers displayed. The user has the option to scroll through the questions and answers. There are two buttons on the bottom right of the FAQ page; one reads "New Search", the other "Return to Project Page".

13.2.7 Functional and Data Requirements

13.2.7.1 Functional Requirements. The product will return a targeted set of questions and answer as a result of a keyword search.

13.2.8 Look and Feel Requirements

Must match project home page, to include white background, sans-serif font, and corporate logo.

13.2.9 Usability Requirements

13.2.9.1 Ease of Use. The first search page links from the corporate project home page. Clear indication of a search mechanism and enough space to key a series of 50 characters is needed. The return page, with FAQ result should be easily scrolled, with an obvious, simple option to return to the search menu or to return to the project home page.

13.2.10 Performance Requirements

13.2.10.1 Speed Requirements. Initial search page should be 15K or smaller. Window with questions and answers should be 35K or smaller.

13.2.10.2 Reliability and Availability Requirements. Multiple search attempt capabilities.

13.2.11 Operational Requirements

13.2.11.1 Expected Physical Environment . Desktop computers with browsers. No mobile capabilities are needed at this time.

13.2.11.2 Expected Technological Environment. Netscape 4+, IE4+, Opera 3.5+.

13.2.12 Maintainability and Portability Requirements

13.2.12.1 How Easy Must It Be To Maintain the Product? Administrative staff will add questions and answers as they come in from customer service, IT, marketing, and Internet Commerce. Content maintenance needs to take place without XML skills other than opening a file, copying and pasting elements, and adding data.

13.2.13 Security Requirements

The product is not confidential.

13.3 PROJECT 2—CONSTRUCTION SCHEDULE

13.3.1 The Purpose of the Product

13.3.1.1 The User Problem or Background to the Project Effort. The client is a construction developer specializing in demolishing old homes and rebuilding 1 to 4 homes on the building site. Typical construction includes small townhouse projects from 10 to 20 units each, small semi-custom home projects with 1 to 5 houses, and single-family homes. The company is large enough that is has a construction superintendent and several subcontractors but not large enough to have an office support staff. Keeping subcontractors up to date on their job status per site is an important factor in maintaining a building schedule. The construction sites are within a 15 to 20 mile radius, but there are enough projects going at one time that a day or a half-day can easily be lost in miscommunication.

13.3.1.2 Goals of the Product. The client wants to develop a web site (to be password protected) in which subcontractors can check where they are expected to report in the morning. Typically, subcontractors arrive on the job early in the morning and check their expected jobs each night. The product should be consistent from site to site for easy understanding and readability.

13.3.2 Client, Customer, and Other Stakeholders

13.3.2.1 The Client. The client is Jay Graham, superintendent of construction, Sunway Development.

13.3.2.2 The Customer. The customer is the 30+ subcontractors under contract with Sunway Development.

13.3.2.3 Other Stakeholders. The owner of Sunway Development, Mr. Bill Lei (contact will be the client).

13.3.2.4 Users of the Product. Subcontracts for all trades contracting with Sunway Development.

13.3.2.5 User Priorities. Simple to read, simple to use, runs on low-end computers with 28.8 baud modems.

13.3.3 Requirements Constraints

13.3.3.1 Solution Constraints. Needs to run on Netscape, IE, or America Online (AOL).

13.3.3.2 Anticipated Workplace Environment. Typically, subcontractors access information at home in the evening. Some have offices with Internet connections. If so, a typical area is a shop building or office. The amount of dust expected, in those cases, is similar to a warehouse environment. Electricity is not a problem.

13.3.3.3 Partner Applications. The product will run online; the only partner applications are the browsers. Some customers have expressed an interest in downloading the information to an Excel worksheet. This is not necessary in the first phase of development.

13.3.3.4 How Long Do the Developers Have to Build the Product? 60 days.

13.3.4 Naming Conventions and Definitions

Definitions of the construction terms can be found on the companion web site.

13.3.5 Relevant Facts

The site will be updated by the client daily, there needs to be a simple interface so the files can be accessed, saved, and uploaded in a low-end computing environment. The client has intermediate user skills but no programming experience.

13.3.6 Assumptions

Customization to the layout will not be made by the client. Updates to dates will be made, although the template structure of the worksheet will remain the same. Names and dates will change. Trade, day #, and job days will not change.

13.3.7 The Scope of the Product

13.3.7.1 The Context of the Work. The project will eventually act as an XML database. The first phase may include creation of a site and an easily modified table on the site. Because later database and data manipulation capabilities are important, the source document should contain no style elements.

13.3.7.2 Work Partitioning. Ideally, the information per job could be updated without an enormous amount of keying. The use of a search engine for subcontractor information, forms for entering data, extensible style sheet language transformation (XSLT) for transforming to hypertext markup language (HTML) may be included in the project depending on if there is time and/or a group of developers available.

13.3.8 Functional and Data Requirements

13.3.8.1 Functional Requirements. The information must be accessible for low-level users, it must be printable, and it would be a plus to be able to search by subcontractor, so each subcontractor could pull their own expected schedule from multiple job files.

13.3.8.2 Data Requirements. The standard data template is Table 13-1.

Table 13-1

Construction Schedule—Basic; Sunway Construction	Single Story; Raised Floor/Stucco		Two Story; Raised Floor/Stucco	
Trade	**Day #**	**Job Days**	**Day #**	**Job Days**
Lot Grading	1	1	1	1
Trench Foundation	3	1	3	1
Form and Place Steel	4–5	2	14–51	2
Inspection—Foundation	6	1	6	1
Pour Concrete	7	1	7	1
Under Floor Plumbing	8–9	2	8–9	2
Under Floor HVAC	10	1	10	1
Inspection—Under Floor	11	1	11	1

Table 13-1 (continued)

Construction Schedule—Basic; Sunway Construction	Single Story; Raised Floor/Stucco		Two Story; Raised Floor/Stucco	
Trade	Day #	Job Days	Day #	Job Days
Under Floor Insulation	12	1	12	1
Inspection—Insulation	13	1	13	1
Framing	14–30	17	14–33	20
Inspection—Roof and Exterior Sheer	31	1	34	1
Rough Plumbing	32–34	3	35–37	3
Sheetmetal and HVAC	35–38	4	37–40	4
Windows	37	1	38	1
Exterior Doors	38	1	39	1
Rough Electrical	39–41	3	41–43	3
Inspection—Framing	42	1	44	1
Lath	43–44	2	45–47	2
Lath Nailing	45	1	48	1
Stucco	46–55	10	49–60	12
Insulation	43	1	45	1
Inspection—Insulation	44	1	46	1
Sheetrock	45–48	4	47–50	4
Inspection—Sheetrock Nail	49	1	51	1
Tape, Top, Texture Sheetrock	50–58	9	52–61	10
Finish Grade	56	1	61	1
Flatwork—Drive, Block, Stoops	57–58	2	62–63	2
Exterior Overhead Door	58	1	63	1
Interior Trim	59–64	6	62–67	6
Handrail	0	0	68	1
Exterior Paint Touch-Up	65	1	68	1
Paint	65–68	4	69–73	5
Landscaping	67–69	3	70–72	3
Set Cabinets	69–70	2	74	1
Ceramic Tile	71–74	3	75–78	4
Electrical—Trim	75	1	79	1
Sheetmetal—Trim	76	1	80	1
Cult Marble and Tub Surround	77	1	81	1

Table 13-1 (continued)

Construction Schedule—Basic; Sunway Construction	Single Story; Raised Floor/Stucco		Two Story; Raised Floor/Stucco	
Trade	Day #	Job Days	Day #	Job Days
Plumbing—Finish	78	1	82	1
Floor Coverings	79	1	83	1
Inspection—Final	80	1	84	1
Detail & Cleanup	80–85	6	85–90	6
Homeowner Walk—Thru	86	1	96	1

Additional information to be made available is an area for the Name of the subcontractor under contract for each phase of the job, and the Name of the job site (typically, there are six active job sites at any given time).

13.3.9 Look and Feel Requirements

The client is looking for something simple and clean. There are no specific color, space, or graphic considerations.

13.3.10 Usability Requirements

13.3.10.1 Ease of Use. Users will need to be prompted for action. The client needs a simple interface due to time constraints but has intermediate computing skills (although no coding experience).

13.3.10.2 Ease of Learning. Learning curve must be 30 minutes for customers; client is willing to spend time to learn.

13.3.11 Performance Requirements

13.3.11.1 Speed Requirements. 20 second downloads per page.

13.3.11.2 Reliability and Availability Requirements. Simple availability within browser, no downloads.

13.3.11.3 Capacity Requirements.

13.3.12 Operational Requirements

13.3.12.1 Expected Physical Environment. Office/workshop. Dust, no power issues.

13.3.12.2 Expected Technological Environment. Medium level technology, desktop computers, 28.8 baud modems.

13.3.12.3 Partner Applications. Browsers, possibly AOL.

13.3.13 Maintainability and Portability Requirements

13.3.13.1 How Easy Must It Be To Maintain the Product? The client plans to spend 1 hour per day maintaining data.

13.3.14 Security Requirements

Simple password access, not confidential, but client wants to keep out curious outsiders.

13.3.15 Cultural and Political Requirements

Consider code for future translation to Cantonese and Spanish.

13.4 PROJECT 3—DIGITALNET

13.4.1 The Purpose of the Product

DigitalNet manufacturers and sells Internet infrastructure products such as multiplex processors, routers, switches, and hundreds of other network hardware products. The company is small, but there are some creative engineers who have developed a couple of products that have an increasingly large market share. For the past few years, the company web site has consisted of a simple HTML intro page, made with frames, and links 1,300 product specifications, portable document format (PDF) files, and a hundred or so .html files on topics such as press releases and employment opportunities. At some point, DigitalNet plans to redesign all of the site's navigation structure, but for now, because of the vast number of PDF files and product specifications, they would like to update the main page without frames.

13.4.2 Client, Customer, and Other Stakeholders

Shawn McDowell, Director of Marketing at DigitalNet oversees the planning of the site. Maggie Chin, Marketing Specialist maintains the current web site and will act as the primary contact.

DigitalNet's primary clients are value-added resellers (VARs), typically network installation organizations with around 10 employees who install wide area networks in small, mid-, and large-sized companies. Because of the suite of hardware products mentioned earlier, gaining large market-share, DigitalNet has several large, international clients with the need for large-scale Internet infrastructures. These large customers typically purchase large quantities of a limited number of products. VARs purchase lower volume but a wider range of products.

Julia Rogers, the Director of IT, maintains the site server. Gita Hazemi, the Director of Sales, is available for feedback on user preferences.

13.4.3 Users of the Product

Product users are typically purchasing agents. A second users group includes VAR employees reading support documentation for training purposes. Both groups agree their top priority is a fast site, simple to navigate, where technical content is key.

13.4.4 Requirements Constraints

The client views this project as an interim fix. There is not a large budget available. The implementation environment is Netscape 4.5 and higher and IE 5.0 and higher. Resolution should be 640 × 480; client systems are typically simple. A few VAR clients use IE 4.0 or Netscape 4.0. The product needs to be changed over within 30 days. The financial budget for the project is 3,000 USD.

13.4.5 Assumptions

The home page transition appears simpler than it is because of the large number of links involved. See the companion web site for the needed links, graphics, and a sample of supporting files.

13.4.6 The Scope of the Product

Reworking of the main home page, by alleviating frames. Using CSS for style and positioning. Maintaining the underlying link structure. Developing a main page under 40K.

13.4.7 Functional and Data Requirements

The HTML for the existing page is available on the companion web site.

13.4.8 Look and Feel Requirements

DigitalNet understands transitioning from frames to cascading style sheets (CSS) positioning will result in a modified layout. The priority is ease of navigation for the user. Modifications to the screen design are acceptable.

13.4.9 Usability Requirements

Ease of use and ease of locating documentation is the user priority.

13.4.10 Performance Requirements

No page should download in more than 20 seconds on a 28.8K baud modem.

13.4.11 Maintainability and Portability Requirements

Information such as product specifications currently in the main frame will be updated weekly by Maggie Chin. Adding links from that information, changing positioning, changing font information should not require complex recoding, but can require an intermediate level of HTML skills. Maggie does not know XML but is comfortable with changing text in an existing shell.

13.4.12 Security Requirements

There are no security requirements.

13.4.13 Cultural and Political Requirements

There is pressure from some stakeholders that the site should be innovative and include a large flash intro. The contact states and the user analysis supports user requests for low graphics. Flash may become a part of the new site, but simplicity and fast download time remain the priority for the interim fix.

13.4.14 Off-the-Shelf Solutions

Maggie Chin will be maintaining the site and is comfortable with some code (HTML, no DOM) and has good skills using Dreamweaver. Ready-made applications are available for developing without frames. The client asks that the code be extensible hypertext markup language (XHTML) or XML with CSS.

13.5 PROJECT 4—HOUSEHOLD MANUFACTURER

13.5.1 The Purpose of the Product

13.5.1.1 The User Problem or Background to the Project Effort. A large household company has decided to use their Intranet for the organization of their in-house maintenance service. The Intranet has been running in the company for two years, although maintenance service does not use it. Currently, maintenance service has their computer network; all necessary documents are generated on computer and distributed in hard copy form. After repairs are made, the maintenance serviceperson fills out forms by hand, which are then input into a computer. Maintenance workers cannot search the warehouse for parts using the Intranet. Over the years, a large base of information about mechanical and other failures has accumulated, although it is not regularly used. One problem is in the updating of the maintenance database due to the amount of generated paperwork for service orders.

After a preliminary analysis of the maintenance service, management of the company decided to reorganize the division and update procedures, supporting a transition to using the Intranet as an information source and for daily processes. The product needs to improve the maintenance service, making it more efficient and more transparent.

Return of investment (ROI) must be within two years. The system needs to be developed, tested, and implemented within nine months.

13.5.1.2 Goals of the Product. The product is an Intranet-based maintenance service information system, a subset of the company information system. The system needs to perform the following functions:

Preparation of work-orders
Database of machine and assembly lines
Automatic updating of that database
Scheduling of maintenance
Searching and ordering of spare parts online
Database of former failures and repair procedures
Online ordering of maintenance service
Online report of repair action

13.5.2 Client, Customer, and Other Stakeholders

13.5.2.1 The Client. Clients of the product are maintenance service employees of the company.

13.5.2.2 Other Stakeholders. The information Service Department, Commerce Division, four manufacturing units (refrigerator, oven, washing machine, and preparation of material) are included. General Management and Research and Development Department of the company are interested in access to some segments of the system.

13.5.3 Users of the Product

13.5.3.1 Users. There are several types of users.

Management of maintenance service
Shop-floor maintenance worker
The responsible worker in manufacturing units
Worker in commerce division responsible for ordering spare parts
Financial service for analysis of maintenance costs

Research and development (R&D) for improvement of technology machines and assembly lines
Employees in warehouses
Information Service Department for maintenance; further development and incorporation of maintenance subsystem in the integrated information system of company
General management for monitoring maintenance service

13.5.3.2 User Priorities. All users have different priorities.

Maintenance service management, which will have access to all components of the system, is interested in efficient monitoring of maintenance activities, scheduling, tracing costs, improving repair procedures, and controlling employees time at work.
On the shop-floor, maintenance worker priorities are access to the database of spare-parts and a technological procedures database.
Users responsible for the manufacturing process place as priority efficient ordering of maintenance, scheduling, and monitoring of the repair process.
The Information Service Department sets as priority good, reliable connectivity to other parts of the information system.
R&D people want access to the technological procedures database.
Commerce and Financial division members place priority on transparent monitoring of orders and costs of maintenance service.
General management is highly interested in monitoring maintenance service, especially scheduling during peaks of maintenance work on holidays in summer.
All users are interested in ease of use in searching and retrieval of information.

13.5.4 Requirements Constraints

13.5.4.1 Solution Constraints. The client requests the solution be XML based. The technological procedure and work order database need to be in XML because of variant record and graphical materials (image of spare parts, instructions on how to repair). The messaging over the Intranet with other databases (Oracle products) needs to be done with XML messaging. Additional design constraints include company policy regarding web pages, white background, sans-serif font, and corporate graphics for identification purposes rather than artistic creativity.

13.5.4.2 Implementation Environment. The system must run on IE, the default browser in the company.

13.5.4.3 How Long Do the Developers Have to Build the Product? Components of the system exist that are not XML based. The Intranet has been working for two years, standard business information system is running well, database of previous maintenance activity was developed in Microsoft Access. The client requires developing, test, and implementing within nine months.

13.5.5 The Scope of the Product

An Information System for maintenance service, based on XML, needs to be developed. The system needs to integrate as a subsystem. You will need to determine the scope of work based on user information gathered (in this document and on the web site).

13.5.6 Functional and Data Requirements

Because there are several different levels of access, users will identify themselves by password and gain access to different parts of the system. Maintenance managers have access to all components. They can create work orders, schedule, confirm final repair reports, monitor costs and spare parts, and prepare other reports. Maintenance service workers pick up work orders online, have access to warehouse database, technological procedures database, can make repair reports online, and order smaller spare parts (depending on cost). The responsible person in the manufacturing unit can order service online, has access to the scheduling of maintenance in their unit, and can monitor progress of maintenance activities in the unit online.

13.5.6.1 Functional Requirements. The product will generate necessary documents, send results to earlier defined sites, search databases, generating reports, and execute XML messaging.

13.5.7 Look and Feel Requirements

Must match project home page to include white background, sans-serif font, and corporate logo.

13.5.8 Usability Requirements

13.5.8.1 Ease of Use. Most users do not have strong IT skills and experience; user interface needs to be simple. Access to different topics must be easy and simple.

13.5.9 Performance Requirements

13.5.9.1 Speed Requirements. Initial search page should be 15K or smaller. Window with images and maintenance procedures needs to be loaded fast and print quickly.

13.5.9.2 Reliability and Availability Requirements. Multiple search attempt capabilities.

13.5.10 Operational Requirements

13.5.10.1 Expected Physical Environment. Desktop computers with browsers. Industrial PC in shop-floor level, mobile for informing workers in emergency cases (option).

13.5.10.2 Expected Technological Environment. IE

13.5.11 Maintainability and Portability Requirements

13.5.11.1 How Easy Must It Be to Maintain the Product? The product will be maintained by the Information Service Department, which, technically, operates on a high professional level. However, employees in the department have no operational knowledge or experience with XML. The training of personal and good technical user manual needs to be developed.

13.5.12 Security Requirements

The product is confidential. The exact level of access for all users will be defined and implemented.

13.6 PROJECT 5—SMARTHOME

The following problem is not laid out as a specification. Sift through the application, create a specification (the full outline is available in PDF form at www.atlsysguild.com), plan, and build all or part of the application.

13.6.1 SmartHome

InovaLabs, a small software company decided to develop a system for data acquisition and remote control of household appliances, heating systems, and security systems at home. Their idea is to use the Internet as a medium for transferring data from home to the server of the local Internet provider. Users can then get access from the server side and send control commands to the control system at home.

A home system collects data about

household appliances (refrigerator, oven, washing machine, TV set)
heating system (temperature in different rooms, external temperature)
light system
security system
fire signal

Data are scanned and sent to servers that process the data and send an emergency signal to the owner or/and security service, Fireworks. The home system, which is PC controlled with an interface to a small control and collecting system, processes input data forming an XML file that is sent to the server.

At the server, data are transformed, saved in a database, and, on request, can be sent to the owner. In an emergency, an emergency signal is triggered and sent to the owner of the home.

Data from that database are extracted in the form of an XML document that is then processed with the XSLT processor and sent on the request to the owner. There can be two output files, one HTML file and one WML file, which can be sent to the user via wireless.

The request from the user is processed on the server side and a corresponding response is produced. Users can use the product for communication, ordinary Internet, or wireless devices. If an action must be triggered at the home system, the necessary data are sent as XML files from the server side.

To simplify the problem, the process part of the system is not the focus of this project. Focus is on data exchange between the home server and the user, the security and reliability of the system. Data exchange must be done using XML, the server technology is Active Server Pages. Define user data needs, how often data will be transferred, and what possible feedback will take place with changes that occurred at the system.

Discuss the time you need to develop the system after a user analysis has been done and the application requirements are defined.

13.7 AUTHORS' NOTE

Sample materials such as graphics and text are available on the companion web site, as are five additional commercial projects.

Students and faculty are often frustrated by emerging technologies. Tools do not work, materials are not available, and browsers never seem to keep up with user expectations and developer needs. Creating projects related to industry, education, and business allows you to approach code considering the user perspective as you plan, write, troubleshoot, and rewrite your way through application development.

In any event, keep exploring, keep coding, and remember you won't have it all memorized or perfected. However, you will have a great time creating innovative applications accessible around the world, across distance, language, platform, and proprietary boundaries.

Index

U

V

W

X